FINANCE OF INTERNATIONAL TRA[illegible]

D. P. [illegible]ING
MTech, BSc(Econ), ACIB

FIFTH EDITION

PITMAN
150
YEARS

PITMAN PUBLISHING
128 Long Acre London WC2E 9AN

Fifth edition published in Great Britain 1987

British Library Cataloguing in Publication Data
Whiting, D.P.
Finance of international trade.- — 5th ed.
1. Foreign exchange 2. Commerce
3. Finance
I. title
332.4'5 HG3851

ISBN 0-273-02734-4

Printed and bound in Great Britain at the Bath Press, Avon

CONTENTS

PREFACE

This streamlined fifth edition, of what has become a standard work on international trade finance, has been prepared with the banking student very much in mind. It fully covers the syllabus of Finance of International Trade in the Banking Diploma examination and is also more than adequate for the student taking International Trade and Payments in the Institute of Export examinations and for those studying Finance of International Trade for the Institute of Freight Forwarders examinations.

Not only does it meet the requirements of students, but it will also be of interest and help to anyone who is involved in the mechanism of importing and exporting, such as an export manager. The general reader may also wish to read all of this book and learn more about a subject that is vital to all of us in Britain.

Since the fourth edition was published five years ago, a new revision of *Uniform Customs and Practice for Documentary Credits* has taken place and the English text of the new version is reproduced in full in Appendix 1, and the text of the Uniform Rules for collection appears in Appendix 2. Quite apart from that revision, I have made some major changes in the structure of the book. I have removed those chapters which had become irrelevant to the Institute of Bankers' syllabus and brought in Examination Guidelines at the end of each chapter that include many examples of examination questions and the answers to them. Those for which answers are given are all Institute of Bankers' questions but the solutions are my own and I accept full responsibility for them. I hope this 'study manual' approach will be helpful to the student reader as he prepares for his examinations. The examination paper has become much more of a practical banker's paper, dealing with the everyday problems which face the banker rather than one asking the traditional type of question that can be answered straight from the textbook. These guidelines will help the student to discover how to pick out the facts that apply to a particular problem.

Foreign exchange terminology is always very difficult for the non-expert to understand and so too is exchange arithmetic, but these are concisely explained and the solutions to a number of exchange arithmetic problems are given to illustrate the terminology used.

Detailed chapters cover the banking services available to facilitate importing and exporting goods, the role of Export Credits Guarantee Department, and the use of exchange and documentary credits.

I make no apology for the fact that much of the material contained in this volume can be found in my book *Finance of Foreign Trade* in the M. & E. Handbook Series. This volume deals with those facts in more detail than the Handbook and in more expansive style.

Chipstead, Surrey
July 1986

D. P. Whiting

ACKNOWLEDGEMENTS

Copyright for *Uniform Customs and Practice for Documentary Credits* (Publication No. 400) and *Uniform Rules for Collections* (Publication No. 322) is held by the International Chamber of Commerce, Paris, and I am most grateful to the ICC for permission to reproduce the English versions of the publications in Appendix I and Appendix II of this book.

ICC publications are available from the International Chamber of Commerce, 38 Cours Albert 1er, 75008 Paris, from the British National Committee of the ICC, Centre Point, 103 New Oxford Street, London WC1A 1QB, and from National Committees throughout the world.

The following ICC publications will be of particular interest to students of banking and the export trade and are available from the above addresses:

- 283 The Problem of Clean Bills of Lading
- 298 Uniform Rules for a Combined Transport Document
- 322 Uniform Rules for Collections
- 325 Uniform Rules for Contract Guarantees
- 350 INCOTERMS (1980 edition)
- 354 Guide to INCOTERMS (includes the INCOTERMS)
- 400 Uniform Customs and Practice for Documentary Credits
- 411 Documentary Credits: 1974 Rules and 1983 Rules. Compared and Explained
- 415 Guide to Documentary Credit Operations
- 417 Key Words in International Trade
- 422 Managing Exchange Rate Risks

My thanks must go to the Institute of Bankers, the Institute of Export and the Institute of Freight Fowarders who have kindly allowed me to reproduce questions from their past examination papers. My thanks are due also to Sleepeezee Ltd for allowing me to reproduce their set of documents relating to an imaginary shipment of divans, and to the other parties involved for agreeing to this. I also wish to thank British Airways for allowing me to reproduce one of their air waybills.

1

THE FOREIGN EXCHANGE MARKET

PRINCIPLES OF FOREIGN EXCHANGE TRANSACTIONS

FINANCIAL transactions between two countries, whether they are in respect of the sale and purchase of goods or services, or relate to capital transactions, do not involve a physical movement of currency from one country to another. Such transactions are carried out through the banking systems of the two countries concerned, and this is made possible by the fact that banks keep accounts in foreign currencies with other banks throughout the world.

A customer of a London bank who wishes to pay $1000 to someone in New York can do so quite easily by arranging with his bank for the dollars to be remitted to the beneficiary. The London bank will, in effect, sell some of its deposit with a New York bank, doing so at the current market rate of exchange between the pound and the dollar. The New York bank will be instructed to pay $1000 to the beneficiary from the London bank's account. This assumes that the person buying the dollars in London instructs his bank to cable the instructions to New York, in other words to make a cable transfer. There are other ways of carrying out the transaction, such as allowing the beneficiary to draw a bill of exchange, with or without a documentary credit, sending a banker's draft, sending a cheque or a mail transfer. These will be dealt with fully in Chapters 6–9, whilst Chapter 6 deals in greater detail with the actual book-keeping entries the banks have to make in order to carry out the payments abroad on behalf of their customers.

Such commercial transactions as these between banker and customer are partially, but only partially, responsible for the activities of the banks in the foreign exchange market. A running down of a bank's balances overseas in terms of a particular currency will cause it to buy additional supplies of the currency through the market, whereas if balances build up then some of them can be sold in the market. Furthermore, if a bank agrees to sell some of a currency to a customer at some future date (i.e. enters into a forward exchange contract) it might resort to the foreign exchange market in order to cover itself by buying the currency forward. In practice, transactions in the market are for large amounts (£100 000 or its equivalent would probably be regarded as a minimum by a London Clearing Bank), and a bank's activities in the market would be determined by aggregating all the transactions with individual customers. It is not the practice of central banks to operate directly in the foreign exchange market. Instead, they operate through a commercial bank or merchant bank.

Some of the foreign currency balance kept by a British bank with a bank overseas may consist of currency held on behalf of a customer. The balance is used by the bank as if the currency were its own in the same way that it makes use of the ordinary sterling deposits of its customers. If the bank receives interest on the deposit in the foreign centre it may pass some of it on to the customer, but it is under no obligation to do so. If the customer wishes to make use of his deposit he must request the bank to make a transfer to some other person or firm, or to issue a draft. As far as the bank abroad is concerned, it is unable to distinguish the deposit from the bank's own balances.

THE LONDON FOREIGN EXCHANGE MARKET

In Britain there is no such place as a foreign exchange market, unlike some of the continental countries, where foreign exchange dealers meet together in one building and carry out transactions with one another. Instead, there are in London two to three hundred dealers (consisting mainly of the clearing and merchant banks and the London offices of foreign banks), and a handful of foreign exchange brokers. Between them there are good communications which, in the case of the larger dealers, involve most sophisticated electronic systems, through which an exchange dealer sitting at his desk is able to watch developments on a visual display unit and make immediate contact with brokers. In this way, transactions can be carried out very speedily and brokers and dealers are able to keep in immediate touch with developments in the market. There is almost a perfect market in the sense that the economist uses this expression. Homogeneous 'commodities' such as sterling, dollars and francs are dealt in and because the buyers and sellers in the market are able to watch closely the prices of these commodities through their excellent system of communications, there tends to be only one price for a currency in terms of another at any one time. The telecommunications system extends not only between dealers and brokers in London, but also between banks in the city and banks in foreign centres. Telephones and the telex and computerized systems are used and contact with foreign centres is very speedy.

The foreign exchange markets now work a five-day week, all of them being closed on Saturday mornings. In London the brokers and dealers are represented by two associations, the Foreign Exchange Brokers' Association and the London Foreign Exchange Banker's Committee. In order to meet for social and educational purposes, brokers and dealers in the main financial centres have formed Forex Clubs and these are linked together through the international Forex Club.

In a London Clearing Bank the Foreign Exchange Department forms but a small section of the Overseas Branch. It consists of a small staff of dealers and clerical assistants. Information is fed to them by other departments of the Overseas Branch about the bank's dealings with its customers and with its overseas correspondent banks, so that it is possible for the dealers to know the up-to-the-minute position of the bank's holdings of foreign currencies. The department also functions with a background of information about the economic and political situations in all foreign countries, fed to it by the personnel within the Overseas Branch whose task it is to visit foreign centres, and by the economic intelligence department of the bank. It will be appreciated by the reader that an exchange dealer who is able to foresee economic or political events that will cause the exchange value of a country's currency to alter is forearmed in his dealings on the market. He will be in a better position to avoid loss to the bank and even to make profit by taking up a position in the currency.

There is only one foreign exchange market in Britain. The large banks have foreign exchange departments but, apart from relatively small transactions direct with their customers, all their dealings are passed through Head Office and are accounted for in the day-to-day activities in the market of the main foreign exchange department.

In the late 1950s the foreign exchange markets took on an additional role. They have always exchanged currencies one for another (this is why the markets came into existence) but to this function was added that of borrowing and lending foreign currency deposits such as Euro-dollars and Euro-sterling. The banks are no longer entirely dependent upon sterling deposits received over the counter at branches, (retail deposits), and are very much involved with wholesale deposits in both sterling and foreign currencies, and in relending these deposits and swapping from one to another. Foreign exchange departments are involved with other money market dealers in carrying out the bank's day-to-day transactions in sterling and foreign currencies.

TERMINOLOGY OF THE MARKET

The foreign exchange brokers and dealers have a language of their own and some of the terms used may cause confusion to the layman. They must, therefore, be considered here in some detail.

In transactions, speed is essential and therefore the briefest amount of detail is usually given. For instance, the usual practice now as far as most currencies are concerned is to express rates of exchange to four decimals, so that sterling would be quoted at say $2.4075–2.4080; but this quotation would be abbreviated to 75–80 between dealers. They would know full well what is meant, for it is inconceivable that the first two decimals would have changed without their becoming aware of the drastic movement in the rate.

Spot rates

The majority of transactions in the market are '*spot*' transactions. This means that the currencies are bought and sold for immediate delivery. In actual fact, such transactions are completed two days after the agreement to buy and sell, to allow time for cable instructions to be sent to the foreign bank holding the currency concerned to pay it over to the bank nominated by the purchaser. If, for example, Barclays Bank sells $250 000 to the Midland Bank, and this represents part of Barclays Bank's deposit with a bank in New York, then the bank in New York must be notified that it is to credit the $250 000 to a bank Midland nominate, and to debit Barclays' account. The date for completion (i.e. two days later in the case of spot transactions) is known as the *value date.* Where a bank buys foreign currency direct from a customer, the value date is the same day, there being no need for cable transactions, and the rate used will be the spot rate currently quoted in the market.

Spot rates are also TT rates, i.e. telegraphic transfer rates (see Chapter 6), for, as has been shown, spot transactions involving the movement of foreign balances necessitate the use of cables to send out the instructions. All other rates quoted in the foreign exchange market are based on the TT rate. For instance, the rate of exchange at which a bill of exchange will be bought by a bank will be the TT rate, with an adjustment reflecting an allowance for interest to the date of maturity, based on the rates of interest in the centre in which it is sold.

Quotation of rates

There are two ways in which a rate of exchange can be quoted. It may be quoted as so many units per one unit of the home currency—this is known as a *currency rate*. The other type of quotation is a *pence rate*, in which a unit of a foreign currency is expressed to be worth so many units of the home currency. Reference to Table 1.1 will reveal that all the quotations in the London Foreign Exchange Market are now in the form of currency rates.

It will be noticed that rates are also quoted in a 'double-barrelled' fashion, e.g. $1.5405 – $1.5415. These are in fact two prices; one is the dealer's buying price and the other the dealer's selling price. The dealer's maxim will be 'buy high, sell low', because when buying he will want as many units as possible of foreign currency for each unit of the home currency, and when selling he will want to hand over as few units of foreign currency as possible for each unit of the home currency. In this example, therefore, the dealer will sell at $1.5405 = £1 and buy at $1.5415 = £1. It is essential that the student should clearly understand that the rates quoted in the market are those the bank will use as a dealer and that if a customer sells the bank buys, and vice versa. If the student is given the quotation of $1.3570 – $1.3590 in an examination question, and is told that a bank's customer is selling dollars, then he must use the rate $1.3590 because the bank will *buy* at that rate from the customer.

The information contained in Table 1.1 has been extracted from the *Financial Times* for 12 May 1986. The first part of the table gives the spot rates for the US and Canadian dollars, followed by the main European currencies and the Japanese yen. Note that in the *Financial Times* the rates (other than those for the US and Canadian dollars) are given in alphabetical order of the financial centres involved, starting off with the Netherlands (Amsterdam) and ending up with Switzerland (Zurich).

The second part gives some of the Commonwealth rates of exchange, and a number of other quotations. Traditionally many of the Commonwealth currencies had exchange values fixed in terms of sterling, and some countries, e.g. Australia, New Zealand and South Africa called their main currency units the pound. In these three examples the main units were renamed the dollar, the dollar and the rand respectively when the currencies were decimalized in the 1960s. The relationship with the pound sterling became less direct as each Commonwealth country declared to the IMF a parity with the US dollar. Once sterling and these other currencies were allowed to float

Table 1.1. Spot rates of exchange

	Market rates	
	Day's spread	*Close*
United States	1.5325 – 1.5410	1.5405 – 1.5415
Canada	2.1182 – 2.1281	2.1235 – 2.1245
Netherlands	3.7625 – 3.7879	3.7725 – 3.7825
Belgium	68.26 – 68.65	68.45 68.55
Denmark	12.385 – 12.439	12.407 – 12.417
Ireland	1.0965 – 1.1025	1.1000 – 1.1010
West Germany	3.34 – 3.36$\frac{1}{4}$	3.35$\frac{1}{4}$ – 3.36$\frac{1}{4}$
Portugal	214.97 – 226.38	222.24 – 225.46
Spain	213.13 – 213.90	213.47 – 213.77
Italy	2293$\frac{3}{4}$ – 2310$\frac{3}{4}$	2299$\frac{1}{2}$ – 2300$\frac{1}{2}$
Norway	10.64$\frac{1}{4}$ – 10.69	10.68 – 10.69
France	10.63$\frac{3}{4}$ – 10.70$\frac{3}{4}$	10.68$\frac{1}{2}$ – 10.69$\frac{1}{2}$
Sweden	10.77$\frac{1}{4}$ – 10.81$\frac{3}{4}$	10.79$\frac{1}{4}$ – 10.80$\frac{1}{4}$
Japan	249 – 250$\frac{3}{4}$	249$\frac{1}{2}$ – 250$\frac{1}{2}$
Austria	23.57 – 23.66	23.60 – 23.64
Switzerland	2.77$\frac{3}{4}$ – 2.79$\frac{3}{4}$	2.78$\frac{1}{4}$ – 2.79$\frac{1}{4}$

Other market rates

	£
Argentina peso	1.2915 – 1.2943
Australia dollar	2.0645 – 2.0680
Brazil cruzeiro	21.17 – 21.35
Finland markka	7.5939 – 7.6142
Greek drachma	210.39 – 212.07
Hong Kong dollar	11.9752 – 11.9861
Iran rial	120.40*
Kuwait dinar (KD)	0.28660 – 0.28700
Luxembourg franc	68.45 – 68.55
Malaysia dollar	3.9605 – 3.9708
New Zealand dollar	2.6095 – 2.6170
Saudi Arabia riyal	5.6170 – 5.6225
Singapore dollar	3.3805 – 3.3858
South African rand (Commercial)	3.2274 – 3.2341
(Financial)	4.9661 – 5.1316
UAE dirham	5.6515 – 5.6575

*Selling rate.

even this indirect fixed relationship with the pound was lost of course. The destruction of the very close ties between our own currency and those of the Commonwealth countries is not surprising in view of the virtual abolition of the Sterling Area and the ending of Commonwealth preference when we joined the EEC and the removal of exchange control in 1979.

There are two sets of quotations for the main currencies giving the market rates for the 'day's spread' and the 'Close'. The first of these indicates the highest and lowest quotation during the previous day, whereas the second gives the buying and selling rates at the close of business on that day. The divergence between the higher and the lower quotation in the close column would of course normally be very much narrower than the range between the quotations for the day's spread.

The rates of exchange at which the UK banks carry out transactions with customers are based on the market quotations. For most transactions, branches of the banks receive a list each morning of rates to be used during the day. These allow a fairly wide spread between buying and selling rates to allow for any modest variation in the market rates during the day, and are usually less favourable to the customer than the rates used between foreign exchange dealers (those quoted in the daily press). The list also quotes rates to be used when buying and selling banknotes and these are slightly less favourable than the rates for other transactions. For large transactions, branches must obtain a rate from Head Office. In calculating this rate, Head Office must assume that when they cover themselves for the transaction in the market (e.g. buy the currency being sold to the customer) they will do so at the least favourable of current quotations in the market. If the bank managed to cover itself at a rate more favourable to itself than the one quoted to the customer, it would, of course, make a profit, and if it succeeded in 'marrying' a transaction of one customer with that of another, its profit would be equal to the gap between the price at which it bought the currency on the one hand and the price at which it sold it on the other. In practice the banks do not usually 'marry' individual transactions in this way, but they do in effect, in that they aggregate their sales and purchases and cover themselves only for the difference between the two totals.

A bank is not obliged to cover itself by the sale or purchase of similar instruments. It may, for instance, cover the purchase of ninety-day bills by selling spot. Much will depend upon the relative interest rates in London and in the foreign centre concerned and upon the bank's holdings of the currency.

Other foreign exchange quotations to be found in the daily press include those for forward rates, for Euro-currencies and for exchange cross-rates. In addition, tables listing the value of the pound in terms of local currencies throughout the world are published in the *Financial Times* at intervals.

The quotations for forward rates are illustrated in Table 1.2

Table 1.2. Forward rates of exchange

	One month	*% p.a.*	*Three months*	*% p.a.*
United States	0.51–0.48 c pm	3.85	1.41–1.37 pm	3.60
Canada	0.37–0.27 c pm	1.80	0.94–0.80 pm	1.63
Netherlands	1⅝–1⅜ c pm	4.76	4½–4¼ pm	4.57
Belgium	18–12 c pm	2.62	48–39 pm	2.54
Denmark	3⅝–2⅝ øre pm	−3.02	9⅜–8⅝ pm	2.86
Iceland	par–0.10 dis	−0.54	0.20–par dis	−0.36
West Germany	1⅞–1⅝ pf pm	6.25	5–4¾ pm	5.74
Portugal	105–360 c dis	−12.49	320–1020 d	−12.00
Spain	20–60 c dis	−2.24	60–180 dis	−2.24
Italy	1–5 lire dis	−1.56	6–12 dis	−1.56
Norway	17–18⅞øre dis	−19.93	22–23⅞ dis	−8.54
France	3¼–2⅝ c pm	3.17	8⅜–7⅝ pm	2.99
Sweden	⅜–⅞ öre dis	−1.77	1⅛–1¾ dis	−0.54
Japan	1½–1¼ y pm	6.60	3¾–3½ pm	5.80
Austria	13–11 gro pm	6.09	34–28½ pm	5.16
Switzerland	1¾–1½ c pm	6.99	4½–4¼ pm	6.27

These give the rates for one month forward and for three months forward and each quotation is 'double-barrelled', i.e. gives the buying rate and the selling rate. A premium is indicated by pm and a discount by dis. The former means that the forward currency is dearer, i.e. lower, than the spot rate. Par means that the forward rate is at a parity (equal to) the spot rate. The % p.a. columns show the premium or discount as an annual rate of interest based on the spot rate. The uses of this table will be more fully explained in Chapter 3, which deals with forward rates.

Euro-currency quotations are illustrated in Table 1.3. The lower of the two rates of interest are the rates that are paid for deposits of the currency concerned, whilst the higher quotation in each case is the rate charged for the loan of the currency for the period stated. These Euro-currencies and the rates of interest that apply to them will be more fully discussed in Chapter 3.

Table 1.3. *Euro-currency interest rates*

9 May	*Short term*	*7 days notice*	*One Month*	*Three Months*	*Six Months*	*One Year*
Sterling	$10\frac{3}{8}-10\frac{1}{2}$	$10\frac{7}{16}-10\frac{1}{2}$	$10\frac{9}{16}-10\frac{11}{16}$	$10\frac{3}{8}-10\frac{1}{2}$	$10-10\frac{1}{16}$	$9\frac{5}{8}-9\frac{3}{4}$
US dollar	$6\frac{3}{4}-6\frac{7}{8}$	$6\frac{13}{16}-6\frac{15}{16}$	$6\frac{13}{16}-6\frac{15}{16}$	$6\frac{3}{4}-6\frac{7}{8}$	$6\frac{3}{4}-6\frac{7}{8}$	$6\frac{13}{16}-6\frac{15}{16}$
Canadian dollar	$8-8\frac{1}{2}$	$8\frac{1}{8}-8\frac{5}{8}$	$8\frac{3}{8}-8\frac{5}{8}$	$8\frac{3}{8}-8\frac{5}{8}$	$8\frac{7}{16}-8\frac{11}{16}$	$8\frac{9}{16}-8\frac{13}{16}$
Dutch guilder	$6\frac{1}{2}-6\frac{3}{4}$	$6\frac{1}{4}-6\frac{1}{2}$	$6\frac{1}{8}-6\frac{1}{4}$	$5\frac{3}{4}-5\frac{7}{8}$	$5\frac{9}{16}-5\frac{11}{16}$	$5\frac{9}{16}-5\frac{11}{16}$
Swiss franc	$1\frac{5}{8}-1\frac{7}{8}$	$1\frac{3}{4}-2$	$4\frac{1}{16}-4\frac{3}{16}$	$4\frac{1}{16}-4\frac{3}{16}$	$4-4\frac{1}{8}$	$3\frac{15}{16}-4\frac{1}{16}$
Deutschemark	$4\frac{3}{8}-4\frac{1}{2}$	$4\frac{7}{16}-4\frac{9}{16}$	$4\frac{1}{2}-4\frac{5}{8}$	$4\frac{1}{2}-4\frac{5}{8}$	$4\frac{7}{16}-4\frac{9}{16}$	$4\frac{7}{16}-4\frac{9}{16}$
French franc	$7\frac{1}{2}-7\frac{5}{8}$	$7\frac{1}{8}-7\frac{5}{8}$	$7\frac{1}{2}-7\frac{5}{8}$	$7\frac{3}{8}-7\frac{1}{2}$	$7\frac{5}{16}-7\frac{7}{16}$	$7\frac{3}{8}-7\frac{1}{2}$
Italian lire	$10-12$	$11\frac{3}{8}-12\frac{3}{8}$	$11\frac{1}{2}-12\frac{1}{2}$	$11\frac{3}{4}-12\frac{1}{4}$	$11\frac{3}{4}-12\frac{1}{4}$	$12-12\frac{1}{2}$
Belgian franc (fin)	$7\frac{1}{4}-7\frac{3}{4}$	$7\frac{1}{2}-8$	$8-8\frac{1}{4}$	$7\frac{7}{8}-8\frac{1}{8}$	$7\frac{1}{2}-7\frac{3}{4}$	$7\frac{1}{4}-7\frac{1}{2}$
Belgian franc (com)	$6\frac{1}{2}-7\frac{1}{2}$	$7\frac{3}{8}-8\frac{3}{8}$	$7\frac{3}{4}-8\frac{1}{4}$	$7\frac{1}{2}-8$	$7\frac{1}{4}-7\frac{3}{4}$	$7-7\frac{1}{2}$
Yen	$4\frac{1}{4}-4\frac{3}{8}$	$4\frac{3}{8}-4\frac{7}{16}$	$4\frac{5}{8}-4\frac{11}{16}$	$4\frac{9}{16}-4\frac{5}{8}$	$4\frac{1}{2}-4\frac{9}{16}$	$4\frac{9}{16}-4\frac{5}{8}$
Danish krone	$7\frac{1}{4}-7\frac{3}{4}$	$7\frac{1}{4}-7\frac{3}{4}$	$7\frac{1}{2}-8$	$7\frac{1}{4}-7\frac{3}{4}$	$7\frac{1}{4}-7\frac{3}{4}$	$7-7\frac{1}{2}$
Asian dollar (Sing.)	$6\frac{7}{8}-7$	$6\frac{7}{8}-7$	$6\frac{13}{16}-6\frac{15}{16}$	$6\frac{11}{16}-6\frac{13}{16}$	$6\frac{11}{16}-6\frac{13}{16}$	$6\frac{3}{4}-6\frac{7}{8}$

Note: Long-term Euro-dollars: two years $7\frac{3}{8}-7\frac{5}{8}$ per cent; three years $7\frac{5}{8}-7\frac{7}{8}$ per cent; four years $7\frac{7}{8}-8\frac{1}{8}$ per cent; five years $8\frac{1}{8}-8\frac{3}{8}$ per cent nominal. Short-term rates are call for US dollars and Japanese yen; others, two days' notice.

Table 1.4. Exchange Cross-rates

	Pound sterling	*US dollar*	*Deutsche-mark*	*Japanese yen*	*French franc*	*Swiss franc*	*Dutch guilder*	*Italian lira*	*Canada dollar*	*Belgian franc*
Pound sterling	1.000	1.541	3.358	250.0	10.69	2.788	3.778	2300.	2134	68.50
US dollar	0.649	1.000	2.179	162.2	6.937	1.809	2.451	1493.	1.385	44.85
Deutschemark	0.298	0.459	1.000	74.46	3.184	0.830	1.125	685.0	0.636	20.40
Japanese yen 1000	4.000	6.164	13.43	1000.	42.76	11.15	15.11	9200.	8.536	274.0
French franc 10	0.935	1.442	3.141	233.9	10.000	2.608	3.534	2152.	1.996	64.08
Swiss franc	0.359	0.553	1.204	89.69	3.835	1.000	1.355	825.1	0.766	24.57
Dutch guilder	0.265	0.408	0.889	66.18	2.830	0.738	1.000	608.9	0.565	18.13
Italian lira 1,000	0.435	0.670	1.460	108.7	4.648	1.212	1.642	1000.	0.928	29.78
Canadian dollar	0.469	0.722	1.573	117.2	5.009	1.306	1.770	1078.	1.000	32.10
Belgian franc 100	1.460	2.250	4.901	365.0	15.61	4.069	5.515	3358.	3.115	100.00

Note: Yen per 1000: French franc per 10: lire per 1000: Belgian franc per 100.

If the rate of exchange in one financial centre falls out of line with the rate in another centre, then it is possible for an exchange dealer to make a profit out of arbitrage transactions. In other words, he carries out a series of swaps of currencies. For instance, if the rates of exchange for Deutschemarks, sterling and US dollars, are as follows:

£1=DM 12
£1=$3
$1=DM 4

and the dollar/Deutschemark rate in New York moves to $1=DM 3, it will be worth the dealer's while to buy, say, DM 1 200 000 in London for £100 000, and sell the Deutschemarks in New York at $1=DM 3 for $400 000. The US dollars could then be sold at £1=$3 for £133 333. The dealer would then have made a handsome 33.3 per cent profit on his arbitrage transactions. His transactions would help to push the rate of exchange back to $1=DM 4 through creating an additional supply of Deutschemarks in New York. In reality, discrepancies which do occur in cross-rates of exchange, as they are called, are unlikely to be very appreciable, but foreign exchange dealers keep a careful watch on these rates in order to take advantage of an opportunity to make a profit. As far as the currencies of the EEC are concerned, the cross-rates of exchange are now of particular importance since the introduction of the European Monetary System (EMS) in which most of the EEC countries participate, which is referred to in detail on p. 13. Quotations for currencies in each of the main financial centres are published and a typical table is given in Table 1.4.

Rates of exchange are often referred to as being favourable or unfavourable, but this is misleading. If a currency rate of exchange increases, then the new rate can quite correctly be called more favourable from a national point of view. For example, if the US dollar/sterling rate increases from $1.40=£1 to $1.42=£1, the rate is more favourable to Britain because as a nation we can obtain more dollars for every pound. Likewise, for the importer who has to pay dollars for goods he has purchased, this is a favourable move in the rate because the dollars will cost him less in terms of pounds and pence. But what of the exporter who will be receiving dollars? To him the new rate is less favourable because he will have to hand over more dollars and cents for every pound when it comes to exchanging his dollars for sterling. The same applies to any person who is owed dollars, but to anyone who has incurred a debt in dollars, the movement in the rate is a favourable one.

Favourable and unfavourable movements in rates of exchange can be denoted by a number of other terms. These can be tabulated as follows:

Rate rises from say, \$1.40 to \$1.42=£1.	A favourable movement from national point of view.
Favourable to those who owe dollars.	Unfavourable to those who are to receive dollars.
Pound harder.	Dollar weaker.
Pound firmer.	Dollar softer.
Pound dearer.	Dollar cheaper.
Pound appreciated in terms of dollars.	Dollar easier.
Rate falls from, say, \$1.42 to \$1.40=£1.	An unfavourable movement from national point of view.
Unfavourable to those who owe dollars.	Favourable to those who are owed dollars.
Pound softer.	Dollar firmer.
Pound weaker.	Dollar harder.
Pound cheaper.	Dollar dearer.
Pound has depreciated in terms of dollars.	Dollar stronger.

EXAMINATION GUIDELINES

The structure of the foreign exchange market and the ways in which exchange rates are quoted are not in themselves topics for examination questions, but clearly the student must be fully conversant with the facts contained in this chapter in order properly to use them in answering questions on other topics.

2

THE DETERMINATION OF EXCHANGE RATES

INTRODUCTION

FOREIGN exchange rates are determined by supply and demand in the same way that prices of ordinary commodities are determined by supply and demand. It is perhaps easier to understand how exchange rates are determined if the individual currencies are regarded as separate commodities. If the dollar/sterling exchange rate is \$4=£1, then the price of the commodity called the pound is \$4 and the price of the commodity called the dollar is £$\frac{1}{4}$=25p. If there is an increased demand for dollars (perhaps because more American goods are being imported into Britain), then this will tend to increase the value of the dollar, e.g. it may rise to, say, 33p. To buy the extra dollars, more sterling will have to be put on the market and this will cause its value to fall from, say, \$4 to \$3.

Although exchange rates fluctuate with supply and demand in this way, the extent to which they are allowed to fluctuate without government intervention can be rather limited. Until 1972 Britain adhered to the system of fixed exchange rates, established when the International Monetary Fund (IMF) was formed in 1946. Fixed parity rates were laid down between each individual currency and the US dollar, and, because there was a fixed price of gold in terms of dollars, exchange rates were indirectly linked to gold. Day-to-day fluctuations around the parity rates were permitted up to a modest extent. The IMF system of fixed exchange rates has now been abandoned and countries allow the exchange value of their currencies to be determined by market forces but with some intervention by their Exchange Equalization Accounts as and when considered necessary. Within the EEC, however, exchange rates are fixed within certain margins through the European Monetary System (EMS), but at present the UK is not a member of the EMS.

The valuation of each of the national currencies within the EMS is expressed in relation to the ECU (European Currency Unit) and the value of the ECU itself is based on the value of a given amount of each constituent currency. The day-to-day values of the EMS currencies are allowed to fluctuate within a margin of $2\frac{1}{4}$ per cent round their central rates and a table giving the daily fluctuations is published in the *Financial Times*.

Member countries of the EMS have deposited some of their foreign currency reserves and gold holdings with the European Monetary Co-operation Fund (EMCF) and received ECUs in exchange that they have been able to put into their reserves to be used to settle transactions between member countries. There are unlimited swap facilities between the member countries and member countries are able to purchase ECUs from the Fund up to certain limits.

THE IMF SYSTEM

The IMF was formed as a result of the international monetary conference at Bretton Woods, USA, in 1944. The forty-four nations participating sought to establish an international monetary system that would have the benefits of the pre-1931 gold standard, but not its disadvantages. In short, stability of exchange rates would be achieved by linking individual currencies to gold, without tying countries down to monetary policies dictated by the flow of gold. Each member country would be free to adopt the monetary policy best suited to the state of its economy at any particular time—to reflate when the economy could be expanded without inflation and to carry out a policy of disinflation if there was inflation. In this way it was more likely that full employment would be achieved.

In addition, the IMF was designed to provide a pool of gold and foreign currencies from which member countries could borrow when they were in deficit on their balance of payments.

Another intention in setting up the Fund was to encourage international co-operation. In this, the Fund has been quite successful. Since the Second World War the degree of co-operation between countries on international monetary affairs has been very high and the reasonable stability of exchange rates up to the 1970s was attributable not only to the existence of the Fund but to the determination of the member countries to make the system work. When countries have run into balance of payments trouble, help has been forthcoming not only from the Fund but also from the individual member countries. Even though there were major crises causing the realignment of currencies during the time of fixed exchange rates, the system was sufficiently strong and flexible for the problems to be overcome until 1972 when Britain and other member countries opted for floating exchange rates.

By way of contrast, under the pre-1931 gold standard the automatic regulating device, the flow of gold, was considered enough to keep international trade on an even keel, in that no country should for long have an adverse balance of payments.

Countries related the value of their currencies to gold and freely converted their currencies into gold and vice versa. When a country had an adverse balance of payments, its currency would depreciate on the foreign exchange market. It became worthwhile to convert the home currency into gold, ship the gold to the other financial centre, convert it into the currency of that centre and make a profit on the transactions. When gold was exported, the proceeds in foreign currency would be sold, reducing the value of that currency back to the mint parity of exchange. If gold was imported, then foreign currency had to be bought to pay for the gold, and this caused the value of that currency to appreciate back to the mint par of exchange. International co-operation was not necessary if this device worked. In the event, the device did not work when the gold standard was restored in 1925 and there was little co-operation; countries jealously watched their own trading positions, imposing high tariff barriers, where necessary, to prevent foreign goods from being imported that were cheaper than home-produced goods. In the post-war period, trade barriers have been whittled down through mutual agreement, mostly since 1947 when the General Agreement on Tariffs and Trade (GATT) was signed.

On joining the Fund, member countries had to declare a value for their currencies in terms of the US dollar. For sterling, for instance, the agreed parity in 1946 was \$4.03=£1. This was reduced in 1949 to \$2.80=£1 and to \$2.40=£1 in November 1967. In December 1971 a new middle rate for sterling of \$2.6057 was agreed but in June 1972 it was announced that the pound would be allowed to float. By declaring parities with the dollar in this way a system of fixed exchange rates between all member countries of the IMF was established. If the agreed values of the French franc and the pound were \$0.5=1 franc and \$5=£1 respectively, then the value of the pound in terms of francs would be 10 francs=£1.

The currencies of member countries on fixed exchange rates were kept stable in terms of dollars and this is all that was required to be done officially under the IMF rules. In practice, countries maintained the values of their currencies in terms of other currencies as well, as indeed they had to or arbitrage transactions occurred that forced exchange rates back to their cross-parities (see p. 11).

As far as the dollar was concerned, currencies were not allowed to fluctuate from day to day to more than $2\frac{1}{4}$ per cent either side of the fixed parity, though at one time the margin was only 1 per cent. When the UK was last on a fixed parity (up to June 1972), the pound, in terms of US dollars, was allowed to fluctuate either side of \$2.6057=£1 to a maximum of \$2.6643 and a minimum of \$2.5471. These margins applied to spot rates. As far as foward rates were concerned member countries of the IMF were under no obligation to keep them within any particular margin either side of the dollar parity.

Switzerland is not a member of the Fund but nevertheless the Swiss have played an active part in international monetary negotiations. The Communist bloc countries (apart from Yugoslavia) are not members either. Their rates of exchange are kept stable by rigid enforcement of exchange controls.

Now that currencies are allowed to float, the former links with the dollar and with gold no longer exist, and there is no longer an official price for gold. There are advantages in having floating exchange rates and these will be considered later in this chapter (see p. 23).

THE EXCHANGE EQUALIZATION ACCOUNT

To prevent their currencies from fluctuating beyond these set limits when the system of fixed exchange rates existed, central banks intervened in the market by either buying or selling dollars. When for instance Britain was on a fixed parity of \$2.6057, the Bank of England stood ready to sell an unlimited amount of dollars when the rate fell to \$2.5741 and to buy an unlimited amount of dollars when the rate reached \$2.6643. For this purpose the Bank of England used the Exchange Equalization Account, which was set up in 1932, soon after the gold standard broke down. It was credited with the UK's reserves of foreign currencies, with which to operate on the foreign exchange market. In 1939, the Bank of England's holding of gold (about £300 million), which up to that time was held as partial backing for the note issue, was transferred to the Account.

In practice, the bank did not wait until the two extreme limits were reached before intervening. The 'authorities' were always anxious to build up the reserves by buying dollars with sterling, so whenever sterling was firmly in demand, even if the market rate was relatively low, the opportunity might be taken to buy dollars if it was thought that in doing so the market rate would not be depressed. When sterling was weak, the bank had to sell dollars for sterling to force up the value of the pound in terms of dollars and again, the bank did not wait until rock bottom was reached before intervening.

Even though the pound is allowed to float at the present time, the Bank of England intervenes in the market to prevent sterling from depreciating too violently and also to buy foreign currencies for the reserves when the pound is relatively strong. There has been a tendency to let the market find its own level and not to intervene until the fall or rise in the exchange rate is considered excessive.

The effects of the Exchange Equalization Account's intervention in the foreign exchange market can best be understood by regarding dollars and sterling as commodities in the way suggested in the opening paragraph of this chapter. When the supply of sterling is increased, its value in terms of dollars will fall. When the supply of sterling is reduced its value will rise. The same applies to dollars—their value in terms of pounds will rise or fall with changes in supply. Consider the following, in which we have assumed a desirable parity with the US dollar of \$1.50=£1, which shows two extreme situations in which the Bank of England might decide to intervene.

\$2.00=£1 (\$1=50p)	Exchange Equalization Account *sells* sterling for dollars to prevent rate from rising above \$2.00. Supply of sterling increased and its value falls back in direction of \$1.50. Supply of dollars reduced and their value increases from \$1=50p towards \$1=66.7p.
Desired parity \$1.50	=£1 (\$1=66.7p)
\$1.00=£1	Exchange Equalization Account *buys* sterling with dollars. Supply of sterling reduced and its value rises towards \$1.50=£1. Supply of dollars increased and their value falls towards \$1=66.7p.

FACTORS AFFECTING SUPPLY AND DEMAND

Fluctuations in exchange rates are determined by the demand for, and supply of, currencies. It is a mistake to imagine that the demand and supply situation is affected only by commercial transactions. On the contrary, there are a variety of factors that affect supply and demand and these must now be considered.

Commercial transactions are concerned with exports and imports of both goods and services which give rise to the balance of trade and balance of payments. If there is an adverse balance of payments on current account because we have imported more goods and services than we have exported, foreign exchange rates will have been affected in two ways. Firstly, the increase in imports will have created extra demand for foreign currencies and, secondly, in order to buy these currencies additional sterling will have been placed on the market. The extra demand for foreign currencies will cause their values to appreciate and the increased supply of sterling will reduce its value in terms of foreign currencies. A favourable movement in the balance of payments would, of course, have the opposite effects upon exchange rates.

The balance of trade and payments affects our gold and convertible currency reserves. The increased demand for foreign currencies by British importers that occurs when the balance of trade is adverse causes our reserves of currencies to fall. The same applies when foreign holders of sterling exchange their sterling for other currencies in order to pay for goods. It is perhaps unfortunate that published figures for our gold and convertible currency reserves are so closely watched and commented upon. A fall in the reserves can have strong 'psychological' effects and cause sterling to be marked down, whilst an improvement in the reserves can have the opposite effect upon opinion and confidence and bring about an appreciation in the value of the pound. Once started, a weakening of sterling following a fall in the reserves can have a snowball effect. The Exchange Equalization Account may have to be used to intervene in the market to support sterling and thus cause another drain upon the reserves. When the resulting drop in the reserves is made known it may trigger off a further weakening of the pound, and so on.

The size of the reserves is not the only economic indicator closely watched by foreign holders of sterling. Other symptoms include rising prices and wage increases in excess of the increase in production, and the level of unemployment. These, together with the excess of imports over exports (which has brought about the fall in reserves) are indicative of a state of inflation that might ultimately result in a further depreciation of the pound. To restore confidence, the Government would have to adopt measures that would clearly show the foreign holder of sterling that the inflation was going to be combated and the value of the pound maintained.

Leads and lags occur when a currency weakens in the foreign exchange market and it is in danger of depreciating further. A *lead* occurs where importers obtain the foreign currency they require earlier than they would otherwise do. If it is thought that sterling is going to depreciate, i.e. that a new rate of \$1.00=£1 will be established instead of, say, \$1.50=1, then obviously more currency will be obtained for each pound before depreciation than after the depreciation. Sterling is thus made weaker by an accelerated demand for foreign currencies. A *lag* also makes matters worse rather than better. Exporters who are to receive payments in foreign currencies delay exchanging them for sterling until after the depreciation because, when it has occurred, less units of foreign currency will have to be handed over for every pound. Withholding foreign currencies in this way keeps up their value and hence prevents any appreciation of sterling that might have occurred. When confidence in the home currency is restored, the leads and lags are 'undone,' which is beneficial to the country's currency. The demand for foreign currencies is reduced temporarily, whilst the normal time-lag in paying for imports is restored. The proceeds in foreign currencies are accelerated whilst the normal narrower time-lag for the payment in respect of exports is restored.

Exchange rates themselves can affect the supply and demand position. If a rate of exchange is out of line with 'purchasing power parity' then, in theory at least, the demand for and supply of a currency will change to force the exchange rate back to parity. According to the *Purchasing Power Parity Theory*, the rate of exchange between two currencies will reflect their relative purchasing powers. For example, if a sample of goods in Britain costs £1 million and the same parcel of goods costs 10 million francs in France, the rate of exchange should be 10 francs = £1. If the rate moves up to 12 francs = £1, then British goods will become dearer to the French because they will have to pay more francs for every pound. The demand for British goods and for sterling will fall and the supply of francs will do likewise. Consequently, the exchange rate will tend to move back to 10 francs = £1. If the rate falls to 8 francs = £1, British goods will become cheaper and the demand for sterling will rise. The supply of francs will also increase and the value of sterling will tend to appreciate to 10 francs = £1.

There is obviously a lot of truth in the theory and it may well apply to some extent in the long run, but it must be appreciated that exchange rates are influenced by far more than just commercial transactions alone. Furthermore, it is very difficult to measure and compare the relative purchasing powers of currencies and to decide on the correct purchasing power parity. In reality, purchasing powers tend to adjust themselves to the rates of exchange, because a movement in exchange rates may cause the industrialist to alter his prices. There is clearly a connection between the external value of a currency and its internal value and, therefore, a government must endeavour to resist inflation and the consequent fall in the value of its currency if it wants to avoid a fall in its external value. Costs and prices must not increase more rapidly than in other countries or a fall in exchange rates will be the inevitable result.

Another factor affecting the values of currencies is investment. When a British company constructs or acquires assets overseas (i.e. carries out direct investment) or a British firm or resident acquires foreign stocks or shares (this is called indirect or portfolio investment), a demand for foreign currency is created. This export of capital therefore has a similar effect upon the value of sterling as an import of merchandise, for in both cases, unless payment is to be made in sterling, foreign currencies have to be acquired through the market, and even if payment is made in sterling the effect is the same because the increased supply of sterling in the foreign exchange market will cause its value to fall. Where foreigners invest in Britain, the opposite will apply, in other words the effect upon the market value of sterling will be the same as that of an export of goods. Foreigners will be demanding sterling and its value will tend to rise.

These are long-term investments, as distinct from the movement of short-term capital, quite frequently referred to as 'hot money'. This capital is 'hot' in the sense that it will be very quickly withdrawn from a financial centre once there is any lack of confidence in that country's currency. If, for instance, US dollars are attracted to London because of the relatively high rates of interest being paid on UK Treasury bills and local government loans, the flow of dollars will very quickly be reversed should the pound become worthless or interest rates in other centres become more advantageous.

Usually, when a currency is sent to a financial centre for short-term investment, the sale of the currency concerned is covered by a forward purchase in the forward exchange market. For instance, when an American buys sterling with dollars and invests the sterling in Treasury bills, he knows that after ninety-one days the bills will mature and he will receive the sterling proceeds for repatriation or reinvestment. To ensure that, when he sells the sterling and repatriates his dollars, he does not receive fewer dollars than were originally remitted, he can buy the dollars three months forward at the time of the investment. This might cost a premium, as will be explained in Chapter 3, but provided this is less than the extra interest received from investing in UK rather than US Treasury bills, the investment will still be worthwhile. If sterling was likely to depreciate in value, the demand for forward dollars would increase because it would be unwise not to cover the exchange risk. Consequently, the premium on forward dollars would increase and reduce the advantage of investing in London rather than New York.

Movements of short-term capital affect the spot rates for currencies in the same way as movements of long-term capital. But an inflow or outflow of short-term capital affects the forward values as well. Furthermore, the fact that the capital is invested on only a short-term basis means that its existence has a far more disturbing effect upon exchange rates than long-term capital.

Stock exchange dealers can operate internationally and carry out the practice of *stock arbitrage*. In other words, exchange dealers buy shares in the market in which the stock exchange price, coupled with the exchange rate, is the most favourable to them, and sell securities through the stock exchange in which the local quotation and exchange rate will produce the best return. This means, then, that share prices are an influencing factor in the determination of exchange rates. If share prices in a particular centre are low, then the demand for that country's currency may rise as the result of stock arbitrage transactions by stock dealers who take advantage of the opportunity to buy cheap securities.

Government loans and grants, and transactions with international institutions, also affect the demand for, and the supply of, currencies. To the extent that a government lends its currency or makes gifts of it to other countries, the supply of the currency is increased and therefore its market value will tend to fall. If a country subscribes its currency to an international institution such as the IMF, or to the International Bank for Reconstruction and Development, and the currency is used by the institution to make a loan to another country, then the supply of that currency on the market is increased, with a weakening effect upon its value.

TECHNICAL FACTORS

The factors already considered rather imply that supply and demand are affected by them in determinable amounts and that the exchange rates are affected by them in a rather mechanical way. This is an over-simplification, for the foreign exchange market is a highly sensitive one and exchange rates are affected by personal whims and fancies as well as hard and fast consideration of trade and commerce, and these personal attitudes depend very greatly on the degree of confidence in a currency. These less concrete factors are those that cause foreign exchange dealers to carry out transactions on their own account. To some extent they must buy and sell currencies to cover the transactions with their customers and they will endeavour to choose the right moment to cover. If they have sold currencies to customers, then they will buy in the market, endeavouring to do so at rates as favourable as or, if possible, more favourable than, those used in dealing with the customers. If they have bought currencies, then they will cover themselves by selling them in the market.

For technical or speculative reasons, however, exchange dealers will carry out transactions with one another quite apart from those necessary to cover their dealings with their customers. Their motives are very much related to the degree of confidence in each particular currency, to the rate of interest they receive on their deposits with foreign banks, to the mood of the market and to individual insight or foresight on the part of exchange dealers. The reactions of exchange dealers to developments in the market must depend a great deal upon the extent to which their banks will allow them to maintain an uncovered position and upon their particular commitments at the time. These will include domestic commitments as well as currency purchases, for the ways of employing funds have become so varied and complex, especially since the introduction of the Euro-currencies, sterling certificates of deposit and inter-bank lending, that the financial benefits of each must be assessed before a decision is made to increase the bank's holding of a currency.

Technical influences on exchange rates that occur at weekends and at the end of the month and end of the year must also be considered. Some banks, especially those abroad, carry out transactions for window-dressing purposes at particular times. In other words, when returns or balance sheets have to be prepared, they will buy or sell currencies in order to show a satisfactory position. At week-ends several days elapse between a spot transaction and its completion. As all foreign exchange markets are now closed on Saturdays, spot transactions on Thursdays are completed on the following Monday (i.e. the value date is two working days later than the date of the transaction) and the value date for Friday's transactions is the following Tuesday. Because in the past adjustments to exchange rates mostly occurred over week-ends, there was reluctance to hold over the week-end balances in a currency that was in danger of being devalued. Similarly, there was reluctance to 'go short' in a currency that might be revalued, i.e. to borrow a currency because more has been sold than is held. Even though exchange rates are no longer pegged, and hence subject to devaluation and revaluation, events can occur over a week-end that would bring about a depreciation or an appreciation in the value of a currency when the market re-opens on the following Monday.

Another technical factor affecting the London market is the way it is used as an intermediary between the Continent and the US market.

London is the major market for dollars, and banks in Europe, in buying and selling dollars through London banks, will use sterling for the purpose and thus bring about an appreciation or depreciation of sterling.

Speculation on the foreign exchange market by individuals is permitted in the UK and the man in the street and corporate bodies are at liberty to dabble in the foreign exchange market in the hope of buying a currency at one price (in terms of the home currency) and selling it at a higher price. The banks can also speculate and are in fact doing so when they 'take up a position' in a currency, i.e. when they deliberately hold more of a currency than they normally require, or, alternatively, hold less than they need and borrow some of the currency, if necessary, to meet their day-to-day requirements. By building up their holdings of a currency that is likely to appreciate, the banks are, in effect, speculating in the hope that the currency will become worth more in terms of their own currency, but they must beware that the loss of interest through holding such balances does not exceed the gain. When a currency is likely to depreciate the banks will speculate by borrowing the currency on a day-to-day basis in preference to buying their requirements. In this way they can ultimately meet their commitments more cheaply, by buying the currency after the depreciation, when it is less expensive in terms of the home currency. The cost of borrowing in anticipation of the depreciation might, however, exceed the gain from the depreciation if the latter does not occur as quickly as expected.

The degree of confidence in a currency on the part of both exchange dealers and foreign traders and investors is obviously a vital factor in the determination of its value. This confidence is easily influenced by economic and political events in the country whose currency it is.

FIXED v. FLOATING EXCHANGE RATES

There are many economists who consider that a system of floating exchange rates is preferable to a system of fixed parities and who are against the idea that we should join the EMS, thus fixing the value of sterling in terms of other EEC currencies. In their view, the advantage of being free to carry out our own independent monetary policy, without too much attention to the balance of payments, far outweighs the disadvantages. If exchange rates are left free to establish their own level, then the balance of payments is brought into equilibrium. An adverse balance causes the exchange value of a currency to fall so that exports of the country concerned become cheaper, bringing the balance of payments back into equilibrium. This stabilizing effect of free exchange rates reduces the reliance upon exchange reserves—the exchange rates take the strain of an adverse balance of payments and not the reserves. This, together with the uncertainty about the most desirable exchange rates for the pound, was a prime reason for letting sterling float in 1972. All the periods of credit restrictions since the Second World War have been necessitated by balance of payments considerations. If we had had a system of variable exchange rates much earlier in the post-war era, it is claimed, the restraints upon the economy would not have been so necessary. There would have been less 'stop-go' and longer periods of reasonably steady economic growth.

These arguments in favour of flexible exchange rates seem very plausible, but it is not as simple as has been suggested. There are many factors affecting exchange rates, as we have seen, so that the automatic adjustment of the balance of payments through fluctuations in exchange rates may not occur. Furthermore, there is a very important factor that has been overlooked. This is that stable rates of exchange foster growth in international trade. Without the system of fixed exchange rates through the IMF it is unlikely that the post-war rise in trade would have been so rapid.

When exchange rates are allowed to fluctuate, incurring debts overseas becomes a risky business. When goods are bought for \$50 000 and the rate of exchange is \$5=£1, the cost is £10 000. If, when the time comes to pay, the rate is \$4=£1, the cost in sterling is £12 500. Similarly, goods sold to the US for \$50 000 will produce £10 000 at \$5=£1, but if the rate appreciates to \$6=£1 the proceeds will be only £8333. The same risks apply to capital investment: high yields from overseas investment might be very attractive, but they could easily be taken away by exchange losses. Admittedly, the risks of exchange loss can be covered in the forward exchange market, but there are limits to the period that can be covered by forward contracts and, in any case, by no means all commercial transactions are covered for loss in exchange in this way. The system of forward cover may be there, but having to protect oneself in this way may well be a disincentive to the manufacturer who is contemplating entering the export market.

On the other hand, fixed exchange rates have the advantage of avoiding the competitive depreciation of exchange rates that might occur with floating exchange rates. When a currency depreciates in terms of other currencies, that country's goods are cheaper overseas and, therefore, exports are stimulated. Other countries, seeing this happen, might then allow their currencies to depreciate in order to stimulate exports, with the result that in the end no country would benefit and rates of exchange would be very unstable. However, where a system of fixed rates is employed, it is very difficult to arrive at true purchasing power parities when deciding on the rates of exchange to use. An alternative policy is to broaden the margins either side of the fixed parities up to which day-to-day fluctuations in exchange rates may occur without formal devaluations or revaluations. This was in fact done in 1971, when the IMF's previous maximum margin of 1 per cent either side of parity was increased to $2\frac{1}{4}$ per cent, but this was not enough to stop member countries from switching to floating exchange rates.

EXAMINATION GUIDELINES

As far as the Institute of Bankers' examination is concerned, the topics covered in this chapter are not likely to make up a question in themselves but, once again, a knowledge of them is essential as they may well occur as part of another question, and in any case, it is vital to be able to draw upon this information if the occasion arises.

Straightforward questions about these topics do appear in the Institute of Export examination as illustrated by the following two questions:

1. Why is it considered desirable to keep the fluctuation of exchange rates to a minimum?
What are the main factors which influence the movement of exchange rates?
(*Inst. of Export*)

2. Write brief notes on four of the following:

(*a*) IMF
(*b*) Euro-dollars
(*c*) Floating exchange rates
(*d*) Non-tariff barriers
(*e*) Free trade
(*f*) Exchange Equalisation Account

(*Inst. of Export*)

3
AVOIDING THE EXCHANGE RISK

QUOTING IN FOREIGN CURRENCY TERMS

THERE are obvious advantages to an exporter in making his goods attractive to the foreign buyer by ensuring that the design, colour and packaging appeal to consumers in the particular market, and by writing the instructions that go with them and the labels on them in the language of the country concerned. Similarly, the catalogues and brochures, correspondence and invoices will be more readily understood in that language, and sales might be more forthcoming.

Potential buyers are also more likely to be influenced in the exporter's favour if the price is quoted in their currency, as they can judge more readily the competitiveness of the product, or the effect upon the prices of their own finished goods of using the raw material, semi-manufactured goods or capital item concerned. There may also be some advantage in quoting in a third currency (e.g. US dollars when selling to oil-producing countries), because the buyer's country is used to carrying out transactions in that currency and can compare quotations easily. It may well be that the country concerned holds large reserves of the third currency built up from its sales overseas, and the oil-producing countries are again a good example of this.

If goods are invoiced in the buyer's home currency, he is absolved from the exchange risk and of the inconvenience, slight though it may be, of obtaining foreign currency to make his payments. Both factors may be an extra inducement to him to buy the exporter's goods, but, as we shall see later in this chapter, the exchange risk can be covered and there may well be a bonus in store for the buyer if he accepts the exchange risk. For example, if he buys in sterling and the value of sterling falls between the time he places his order and the time he has to pay, he will have to hand over fewer units of his own currency when buying the sterling from his bank.

The exporter need not be fearful of taking the exchange risk as it is possible to cover this in the forward exchange market once the contract has been placed, and he knows within reason when the payment in foreign currency is going to be received.

It is true that the risk of loss through the depreciation of a currency really starts from the time the buyer receives the seller's price lists, unless these contain a rider to the effect that the prices are subject to confirmation at the time the orders are placed. But the risk of loss applies whatever currency is used, and even for domestic sales there is always the likelihood that the sale proceeds will be worth less in real terms by the time they are received. At a time of high inflation, when a currency is falling in value, there is a lot to be said for quoting in more stable currency which, when it is converted into sterling, is going to produce a larger reward to the exporter. With floating exchange rates the danger of having profits reduced through fluctuating rates is of course greater than under fixed exchange rates as there are no set limits to which the home currency may depreciate or appreciate.

Exchange risks can be avoided by covering in the forward exchange market. Through this market, an exporter who is to receive payment for his goods in a foreign currency at some future date can fix immediately the rate of exchange at which he is to sell the currency when he receives it. If the value of the currency concerned depreciates before the settlement of the transaction, then a loss will be avoided. If the currency appreciates in value during the lapse of time between shipping the goods and receiving payment, the exporter would receive less for his currency under the forward contract than he would do in the spot market, but he cannot have the best of both worlds. If he wishes to protect himself against the risk of loss through fluctuations in exchange rates, then he cannot expect to receive the benefits that would have accrued to him had he not protected himself. The vital point is that he has been able to determine how much he is to receive in his own currency and is assured that his profit on the transaction remains intact.

Similarly, a forward exchange contract is invaluable to an importer. He knows in advance how much he is to pay out in foreign currency in the near future and will want to know how much this will be in terms of his own currency. If he can determine this in advance, he is better able to fix his prices for the resale of the goods at a level that will provide a satisfactory profit margin. This margin might well be lost (if he did not cover himself) through an appreciation of the foreign currency in the spot market.

Forward exchange deals between bank and customer are entered into by way of formal contract. This is to protect the bank, for it may lose by fluctuations in exchange rates through having bought or sold currency in order to meet the customer's requirements which is subsequently not taken up by the customer. Even with a formal contract, there is always the risk that the customer may not be able to carry it through and, therefore, the bank may insist on a cash margin. This is kept on a special account on which interest is paid, with an understanding that the balance be maintained at a fixed percentage (usually between 10 per cent and 25 per cent) of the current sterling value of the currency to be purchased or supplied by the bank. The process of closing out a contract or extending it is described later in this chapter (see p. 37).

CALCULATING THE RATE

Forward rates, frequently referred to as swap rates, are quoted as a premium or discount on spot. A *premium* means *dearer*, so that for a currency rate it will be *deducted from spot*. A *discount* means *cheaper*, so that it will be *added to spot* in the case of a currency rate. For pence rates a premium would be added and a discount deducted. Where a forward rate is quoted as *par*, it means that it is the same as spot rate. In exchange tables premium is usually abbreviated to pm, pr or prem and discount to dis or disc. To work out the actual rate to be used for a forward deal it is necessary then to refer to two tables in the daily press, that for spot rates and that for forward margins. Let us assume that the spot rate for the dollar was quoted at \$2.0210 – \$2.0220 and that the premium on forward dollars was 1.10 – 1.00 cents for one month and 2.80 – 2.70 cents for three months. Of the two rates for spot dollars, the higher quotation will be the dealer's (the bank's) buying rate and the lower quotation the dealer's selling rate, as the dealer will buy high and sell low. Because of this maxim, the bank will deduct the higher premium from the spot selling rate and the lower premium from the buying rate, and it will be noted that the premiums are in fact quoted with the higher figure to the left and the lower figure to the right, so that if the spot quotations and premiums are written one under the other the premiums are ready for subtraction as follows:

	Selling rate	*Buying rate*
Spot	\$1.5210	\$1.5220
1 month premium	110	100
1 month forward rate	\$1.5100	\$1.5120
	Selling rate	*Buying rate*
Spot	\$1.5210	\$1.5220
3 months premium	280	270
3 months forward rate	\$1.4930	\$1.4950

Where a discount is involved, the same principle applies, but, of course, the discount must be added and not subtracted. The dealer is again buying high and selling low and will want to add the bigger discount when buying and the lower discount when selling. The discount is conveniently expressed with the larger amount on the right, so again the forward rates can be calculated by setting out the spot rates and discounts in the order they appear in the tables. Let us take some imaginary spot rates and forward margins and work out the actual forward rates. If the spot rates were 222.24 – 225.46 escudo = £1 the one month forward margin 105 – 360 cents discount and the three months forward margin 320 cents – 1020 cents discount the forward rates would be as follows.

	Selling rate (escudo)	*Buying rate* (escudo)
Spot	222.24	225.46
1 month discount	1.05 dis	3.60 dis
1 month forward rate	223.29	229.06
	Selling rate (escudo)	*Buying rate* (escudo)
Spot	222.24	225.46
3 months discount or premium	3.20 dis	10.20 dis
3 months forward rate	225.44	235.66

The quotations given in the daily press are for one month and three months forward, but it is possible to obtain a quotation in the market for up to twelve months forward and even longer. Transactions twelve months forward are by no means unusual and there have been contracts for as far ahead as seven years. For such long periods as this, however, it might be more advantageous to borrow through the Euro-currency markets and sell the proceeds spot, in order to determine the rate of exchange. This procedure is explained more fully in Chapter 3. It is possible to cover forward for an odd period such as forty-seven days, but the rate for such a transaction would have to be negotiated with a dealer. The rate would not be determined on a *pro rata* basis and would almost certainly be less favourable to the customer than a quotation for a standard period because the transaction is more difficult to cover in the market.

The premium, or discount, on a forward currency does not widen in exact proportion to the length of time to maturity, though there is a tendency in this direction. This is because there is a separate demand and supply situation for each length of maturity. For instance, the premium or discount on three months forward would be considerably influenced by transactions to cover the reconversion of funds invested in ninety-one-day Treasury bills. Furthermore, interest rates vary for different maturity dates. Money lent for a longer period usually attracts a higher rate of interest per annum than funds invested for a shorter period.

THE FORWARD MARKET

The forward exchange market is of use not only to traders who are to pay or receive a foreign currency, but also to other people who have debts to pay, or who are to receive payments. This applies to those persons, or firms, or institutions, who have purchased foreign investments and to those who have realized some of their overseas assets. Of particular importance, as far as forward exchange business is concerned, is the flow of short-term capital attracted to a country by relatively higher interest rates, or by the wide range of short-term investment opportunities, or possibly distrust of the investor's own currency. This capital, frequently known as 'hot money', is invested in such securities as Treasury bills, local government loans and hire-purchase companies. It is essentially short-term and usually the investor will buy his own currency back again through the forward exchange market to avoid loss. This is known as a *swap*. The premium (if there is one) on the forward contract is an expense that must be taken into account in deciding whether or not the higher yield being received on the investment is sufficiently high to make the movement of funds from financial centre to another worth while. Supposing, for instance, that the Treasury bill rate in London was $6\frac{1}{2}$ per cent whilst for US Treasury bills it was $5\frac{1}{2}$ per cent. The American could obtain an extra 1 per cent on his money by selling his dollars for sterling and investing the proceeds in UK Treasury bills. If the premium on three months forward dollars was equivalent to $\frac{19}{32}$ per cent, then the net differential (i.e. the 1 per cent extra interest less the premium on forward cover) in favour of the American would be $\frac{13}{32}$ per cent per annum. Movements in interest rates and in the premium on forward dollars have a powerful influence upon the flow of short-term capital to and from the UK. On occasions the differential has been in favour of investment in the US but the most usual situation has been for interest rates to be higher in the UK than in the US and for there to be a premium on the forward dollar amounting to less than the margin between the two rates of interest.

The pull of high interest rates applies not only to private investors but also to banks and other financial institutions. Banks receive interest on their foreign currency balances with other banks and the rate of interest varies with fluctuations in the general level of interest rates in the financial centre concerned. An increase in the British interest rates would therefore encourage foreign banks to build up their holdings of sterling with the London banks. A bank may enter into what is known as a *swap and deposit* arrangement with another bank. Supposing, for instance, a French bank required sterling for a certain period. It would obtain it by selling francs spot to a London bank and entering into a forward exchange contract to buy back the francs for sterling after the period has elapsed. This is a swap. At the same time as the swap, the French bank may agree to accept the francs on deposit from the London bank and to pay interest thereon at the rate appropriate to such a deposit in Paris at the time. This is a swap and deposit. It would only be worth the London bank's while depositing the francs in Paris if it could not earn as high a rate of interest in London by selling the francs for sterling and investing the proceeds, covering itself in the forward market to ensure that the francs were available when the time came to meet the contract with the French bank to sell back the francs.

The transactions in forward currencies between the banks and their customers are either married up with one another or are covered in the market. Where a bank agrees to buy a currency from a customer three months forward, it will either match it with a contract with another customer to sell three months forward or will sell three months forward in the market. As with spot transactions, the bank will normally use the market rates in transactions with customers and endeavour to cover as favourably as possible. The bank may succeed in obtaining a rate in the market well within the extremes in price quoted. In bargaining in the market to cover a forward deal, the bank may persuade a dealer to give way a little from the quoted rate, so that, if the bank has quoted the extreme market rates to its customer, it may make a small additional profit. It does not have to cover immediately and may, in fact, wait some time before doing so. When a bank contracts to sell, say dollars, forward to a customer, and interest rates in New York are high, it may decide to cover the sale immediately by buying dollars spot. The dollars will then yield interest as a deposit with an American bank, or could be used in the US market for day-to-day loans, or, possibly, invested in US Treasury bills.

Transactions in the market are for large amounts, e.g. £100 000, so that small transactions with customers will be aggregated in order to calculate the extent to which the bank needs to cover in the market. Of major importance are the transactions between dealers on their own account; transactions reflecting their particular views on future movements in exchange rates, based, as with spot rates, on their own foresight or purely on hunches. Dealings in the market also depend upon technical factors such as the approach of the week-end or return day, on confidence in the currency and upon the amount of activity on behalf of the Exchange Equalization Account. Forward quotations are then determined by very similar forces to those that determine spot rates, but in addition they are influenced by spot rates themselves. Spot and forward rates move in sympathy with one another, a change in the spot parity being accompanied by a movement in the forward rate in the same direction, but this is not necessarily to the same extent.

There is not a separate forward exchange market—its brokers and dealers are the same as those who carry out spot transactions. Furthermore, although the forward market has its own supply and demand situation and its own quotations, it is very closely related to the spot market and both markets are very dependent upon one another, in that many transactions in the foreign exchange market involve both spot and forward deals. Forward quotations are expressed as a premium or discount on the spot rate (as mentioned above on p. 28). However, under normal circumstances, the premium or discount on the spot rate is a modest one and only when confidence in a currency is low will the foward rate move very far from parity.

The margin, i.e. the premium or discount, tends to equal the differential in the rates of interest in the two centres concerned. If this was not so, arbitrage transactions would almost certainly take place that would tend to put right the discrepancy. When interest rates change, the movement is reflected in forward premiums and discounts, but it is not possible to state categorically what the margin should be at a particular time. This is because there are many types of investment, each with its own level of interest rates, and there are a number of factors other than interest rates affecting forward margins, as we have seen. When the level of interest rates in London rises, the change may cause an opposite movement in forward rates to that in the spot market. Spot rates tend to appreciate when interest rates in London rise, because of the increased attractiveness of London as a centre for investment. More spot pounds are demanded, but at the same time the forward discount on the pound (premium on the dollar) tends to increase, because more forward dollars are in demand to ensure that the foreign funds can be repatriated, if need be, at a rate only a little less favourable than the spot rate.

Much depends upon the degree of confidence. If depreciation seems imminent, there will obviously be more covering, and consequently bigger margins, than if it is not, and once the depreciation in the value of the currency has occurred, when there is little likelihood of any drastic depreciation or appreciation of the currency, there will be less covering.

Another important factor affecting the supply and demand situation for forward rates is the extent of the funds the banks have available for transactions in forward currencies. This, in turn, depends upon the liquidity position of the banks and upon the rewards to be obtained by making alternative uses of their funds.

Central banks intervene in the forward market as well as the spot market.

This intervention has the advantages that, firstly, it sometimes avoids a drain upon the reserves, and, secondly, it may avoid a 'lead' on import payments. We have seen (p. 18) that leads and lags intensify a sterling crisis, and if their effects can be avoided by forward intervention, it is to the Bank of England's advantage. A British importer will want to buy foreign currency forward (i.e. sell sterling forward in exchange for the currency concerned), to protect himself from a possible depreciation of sterling. Alternatively, he could buy the currency spot and invest it abroad until it is required, and this he will be tempted to do if the discount on forward sterling is too high. If, by its intervention in the forward market, the Bank of England can reduce the discount, then it will encourage importers to buy currencies forward rather than spot and delay the drain upon the reserves. Likewise, the foreign exporter will sell sterling forward to avoid loss through depreciation, and may be discouraged from doing so by the wide discount on sterling. Instead, he may choose to borrow sterling and sell it spot, which would be an immediate drain upon the reserves. This drain might also be delayed until the immediate crisis is over, by official intervention in the forward market to reduce the discount on forward sterling.

Forward intervention, then, can relieve the spot rate when it is most in need of support. By deferring sales of sterling (i.e. purchases of other currencies), it helps to maintain the spot rate and reduces the immediate drain upon reserves.

FORWARD OPTIONS

Considerable use is made of forward option contracts whereby an importer or exporter can fix the rate of exchange at which an amount of foreign currency is to be bought or sold at a rather indefinite future date. The need for such a contract arises from the fact that the shipment dates cannot always be known for certain in advance, and neither can the date on which payment is to be made or received. An exporter may be fairly certain that he will receive payment for his goods within three months and certainly not before two months have elapsed. He could protect himself from the exchange risk under such circumstances by entering into a contract with his bank to sell them the currency proceeds three months forward with an option over the third month. Under this contract, he has pledged himself to sell the currency at the agreed rate of exchange and he has no option as to whether he does so or not. The option is concerned with the date of completion of the contract. He must sell the currency to the bank during the third month but can choose the actual day in that third month to suit his own convenience. Similarly, if he might possibly receive payment during either the second or the third month, he could enter into a three months forward contract with option over the second and third months. If he might receive payment at any time during the three months, he could sell at three months forward with option over the three months.

Forward option contracts are also advantageous to importers who have payments to make in foreign currency but who are not absolutely certain as to precise date of payment. They can enter into a forward option contract to buy the currency at, for example, three months forward, option over the second and third months.

In fixing the rate for a forward option contract the bank must bear in mind that the customer might buy (or sell) the currency on the first day of the option period or the last day (or some day in between, of course). Therefore, the rates of exchange appropriate to the beginning and the end of the option period must be compared and the rate less favourable to the customer will be used. Table 3.1 shows the various forward option rates that would apply if the following were the market quotations for spot and fixed forward currencies.*

	US $	*Portuguese escudo*
Spot	1.3960 – 1.3970	223.15–225.25
1 month forward	0.25 – 0.10 c pm	105 – 360 c dis
2 months forward	0.35 – 0.25 c pm	210 – 745 c dis
3 months forward	0.50 – 0.35 c pm	320 – 1020 c dis

* These are imaginary rates and are not meant to be representative of rates of exchange for the dollar or the escudo at any particular point of time.

Table 3.1. Forward option rates

Currency	Dealer's selling price	Dealer's buying price
US dollars (premium)		
Spot	1.3960	1.3970
1 month forward fixed	1.3935	1.3960
1 month forward option	1.3935	1.3970
2 months forward fixed	1.3925	1.3945
2 months forward, option over 2 months	1.3925	1.3970
2 months forward, option over 2nd month	1.3925	1.3960
3 months forward fixed	1.3910	1.3935
3 months forward, option over 3 months	1.3910	1.3970
3 months forward, option over 2nd and 3rd months	1.3910	1.3960
3 months forward, option over 3rd month	1.3910	1.3945
Portuguese escudos (discount)		
Spot	223.15	225.25
1 month forward fixed	223.15	225.30
1 month forward option	223.15	225.30
2 months forward fixed	223.20	225.35
2 months forward, option over 2 months	223.15	225.35
2 months forward, option over 2nd month	223.15	225.35
3 months forward fixed	223.25	225.40
3 months forward, option over 3 months	223.15	225.40
3 months forward, option over 2nd and 3rd months	223.15	225.40
3 months forward, option over 3rd month	223.20	225.40

It has been assumed that one currency (the dollar) is at a premium and the other (the Portuguese escudo) is at a discount. Tables 3.2 and 3.3 show the basis on which the option rates have been calculated. Students preparing for examinations would be well advised to study these tables carefully and to work out the rates independently, several times if necessary, until the technique has been mastered. It will be noticed that where the currency is at a premium (Table 3.2) the bank will sell at the rate applicable to the end of the option period and buy at the rate applicable to the beginning of the option period. Where the currency is at a discount (Table 3.3) the bank will sell at the rate for the

Table 3.2. Option forward rates: basis of calculation (currency at premium (US Dollars))

	Rate of beginning of option period		*Rate at end of option period*		*Rate less favourable to customer*
Selling rates					
1 month forward option	Spot	1.3960	1 month forward	1.3935	1.3935
2 months forward, option over 2 months	Spot	1.3960	2 months forward	1.3925	1.3925
2 months forward, option over 2nd month	1 month forward	1.3935	2 months forward	1.3925	1.3925
3 months forward, option over 3 months	Spot	1.3960	3 months forward	1.3910	1.3910
3 months forward, option over 2nd and 3rd months	1 month forward	1.3935	3 months forward	1.3910	1.3910
3 months forward, option over 3rd month	2 months forward	1.3925	3 months forward	1.3910	1.3910
Buying rates					
1 month forward option	Spot	1.3970	1 month forward	1.3960	1.3970
2 months forward, option over 2 months	Spot	1.3970	2 months forward	1.3945	1.3970
2 months forward, option over 2nd month	1 month forward	1.3960	2 months forward	1.3945	1.3960
3 months forward, option over 3 months	Spot	1.3970	3 months forward	1.3935	1.3970
3 months forward, option over 2nd and 3rd months	1 month forward	1.3960	3 months forward	1.3935	1.3960
3 months forward, option over 3rd month	2 months forward	1.3945	3 months forward	1.3935	1.3945

beginning of the period and buy at the rate applicable to the end of the option period.

Where forward rates change from a premium to a discount or vice versa over a period of time great care must be taken in selecting the rate to apply to a particular forward option contract. For example, if in the above quotations for the Portuguese escudos the one month forward rate margin was 95–90 cents pm and the quotations for two months and three months unchanged at 210–745 cents dis and 320–1020 cents dis at what rate would a bank enter into a three months forward option contract to sell escudos? The option period is from spot (223.15) to three months forward (226.35) and of these two rates the bank would opt to sell low at 223.15. However, it has another choice in this instance, that of 222.20, which is the new rate for one month forward (223.15 *less* 95 cents premium) and it would in fact quote this rate.

CLOSE-OUTS AND EXTENSIONS

For a number of reasons an exporter or an importer may not be able to complete his forward contract to sell currency to or buy currency from his bank. Such reasons would include shipping delays, faults in the goods supplied, and disputes about the quality of the goods, or simply the failure of the buyer to pay for the goods. The bank's customer has no option but to complete his contract, and therefore if he has undertaken to sell foreign currency to the bank on a particular date (e.g. one month forward) or by the end of an option period, he must buy that amount of currency in order to complete the contract if it is not forthcoming from his overseas buyer. Similarly an importer who has undertaken by forward contract to purchase foreign currency from his bank on or by a certain date must do so and then dispose of it if it is no longer required. The banks will in the first case sell the customer the currency he requires at the spot rate on the date of maturity of the contract in order to complete the contract, and in the second case of the importer, buy the foreign currency back from him at the spot rate. In reality, the bank will *close out* the contract by simply charging the customer the difference (or crediting him with the difference) between the spot rate and the forward rate. For instance, if an exporter has undertaken to sell DM50 000 to his bank at a forward rate of DM4.50 =£1 and on the day on which (or by which) the contract is due to be completed the spot rate is DM4.60=£1 his account will be credited with £241.54 (ignoring exchange commission). This is arrived at as follows:

Table 3.3. Option forward rates: basis of calculation (currency at discount (escudos))

	Rate of beginning of option period		*Rate at end of option period*		*Rate less favourable to customer*
Selling rates					
1 month forward option	Spot	223.15	1 month forward	224.20	223.15
2 months forward, option over 2 months	Spot	223.15	2 months forward	225.25	223.15
2 months forward, option over 2nd month	1 month forward	224.20	2 months forward	225.25	224.20
3 months forward, option over 3 months	Spot	223.15	3 months forward	226.35	223.15
3 months forward, option over 2nd and 3rd months	1 month forward	224.20	3 months forward	226.35	224.20
3 months forward, option over 3rd month	2 months forward	225.25	3 months forward	226.35	225.25
Buying rates					
1 month forward option	Spot	225.25	1 month forward	228.85	228.85
2 months forward, option over 2 months	Spot	225.25	2 months forward	232.70	232.70
2 months forward, option over 2nd month	1 month forward	228.85	2 months forward	232.70	232.70
3 months forward, option over 3 months	Spot	225.25	3 months forward	235.45	235.45
3 months forward, option over 2nd and 3rd months	1 month forward	228.85	3 months forward	235.45	235.45
3 months forward, option over 3rd month	2 months forward	232.70	3 months forward	235.45	235.45

Proceeds of contract DM50 000 @ 4.50 =	£11 111.11
Cost of spot DM	10 869.57
	241.54

The spot rate is more favourable to the exporter than the forward rate and hence he gained £241.54.

Where a forward contract has been closed out it may be *extended* forward to the new date on which or by which the bank customer expects to receive or require the foreign currency concerned. This is usually done by simply entering into a new forward contract in the normal way with an adjustment for the close-out. Examples of close-outs and extensions are given on pp. 69 and 78 and the reader should refer to those examples in order to understand more fully the principles involved. When a bank extends a contract it is usually generous to its customer and deducts the forward *buying* premium from the spot *selling* rate or the forward *selling* premium from the spot *buying* rate when determining the rate for the extended contract. This is called the *diagonal rule* and is employed only by the British banks.

EURO-CURRENCY MARKET

For an exporter, another way of avoiding the exchange risk is to borrow the currency that is ultimately to be received from the overseas buyer and to sell it on the spot market for sterling. The currency loan can then be repaid with the payment from the buyer when it is received. This process not only fixes the exchange rate immediately but also provides the exporter with immediate finance. The Euro-currency market provides an ideal channel through which to borrow the required currency, but it must be stressed that this is by no means the only use to which the market can be put.

The term Euro-currency is used to describe deposits of currency held outside the country whose currency it is, and which are re-deposited with a bank in Europe. Thus, a bank in London receiving a deposit in US dollars from someone in France, for instance, would come into the possession of Euro-dollars. Euro-dollars are, in fact, the principal type of Euro-currency. The next largest in quantity is Euro-sterling, and others include Swiss francs, Canadian dollars, Deutschemarks and Dutch guilders. Euro-currency markets exist in London (the main centre for Euro-dollars), Paris (the biggest market for Euro-sterling), Frankfurt, Milan, Brussels, Amsterdam and Stockholm, and at financial centres in Canada, Switzerland and the Middle East.

Holders of foreign currency balances often find it more convenient or more profitable to deposit them at a bank outside the country of origin. This applied especially to holders of dollars in Eastern European countries who, principally for political reasons, chose not to place their dollars with banks in the US. Instead, they kept their balances with banks in Western Europe, and it was this in fact that was largely responsible for the development of the Euro-dollar market.

Strictly speaking, deposits of Euro-currencies are not deposits but loans. Holders of deposits, banks and customers of banks, lend these deposits to banks and these banks in turn re-lend them, making a modest profit equal to the difference between the rate of interest they pay on the deposits and the rate of interest they receive on the loan of them. The margins are very narrow and therefore dealers make their profits from the large turnover in them rather than from wide margins.

The dealers and brokers in Euro-currencies are the same ones who make up the normal foreign exchange market and the London banks play a very active part. Although brokers are used for many transactions, they are not used to the same extent as for ordinary foreign exchange transactions. In London the large commercial banks have a supply line for Euro-currencies through their foreign subsidiary banks.

Transactions in Euro-currencies are carried out in a rather similar way to other transactions in the foreign exchange market. Deals are of large amounts, such as $100 000, or multiples thereof. The majority of transactions are spot or for seven days. Delivery for spot transactions normally takes place on the third working day after the transaction is agreed. Confirmation of deals is sent by banks 'accepting' deposits, giving instruction for delivery and, because Euro-currency transactions are tantamount to unsecured loans, it is usual for brokers to disclose the borrower's identity.

Dealers are able to marry up some loans and deposits, and if they can borrow short-term and lend long-term, they gain the advantage of paying relatively low rates of interest and receiving relatively high rates, for as is usual in a money market, short-term rates are lower than long-term rates of interest. Currency deposits are for standard periods, depending upon the currency concerned, as can be seen from Table 3.3 on p. 38. The lower quotation is the rate paid on deposits and the higher quotation is the rate at which the dealers are prepared to lend. It will be realised that quotations for Euro-currencies are the rates of interest at which they will be borrowed or lent, not bought or sold, and therefore rates of exchange are not involved.

When deciding whether to cover himself by borrowing Euro-currency or by entering into a forward exchange contract, the exporter must compare the rate of interest he has to pay to borrow the currency with the margin on the forward exchange deal. If the forward contract is at a discount, he has to hand over more units of the foreign currency proceeds for every pound than if he were selling spot and therefore the discount is an expense to him. If the forward currency is at a premium, however, this is a bonus to him and he would be wise to take if rather than borrow Euro-currency, unless the advantage of having the sterling proceeds now, rather than at the maturity of a forward contract, outweighs the expense of borrowing and the loss of the forward premium.

Any discrepancy between the two rates of interest provides an opportunity for an exchange dealer to profit from arbitrage transactions, and as Euro-currency rates are subject to world-wide influences and tend to fluctuate, there are plenty of these opportunities. The exchange speculator has found additional ways of making a profit since Euro-currencies have become a large and growing part of the activities of the foreign exchange market. A foreign exchange dealer may find it worth while to borrow a Euro-currency and to sell the currency in the spot market for sterling. The sterling could then be used in order to invest short-term at a relatively high rate of interest.

FOREIGN CURRENCY ACCOUNTS

Where the trader is both buying and selling in a particular foreign currency, he may find it worthwhile covering the exchange risk by opening a foreign currency account. He will be able to use this account to pay in proceeds from exports and to make payments for goods he is buying. If necessary, he may be able to negotiate an overdraft limit in the foreign currency to cover periods when the outgoings exceed receipts. The chances are, of course, that he will accrue surplus balances on the account from time to time representing his profits on transactions, and he would be wise to cover by forward exchange contracts for the sale of these expected balances.

EXAMINATION GUIDELINES

The material contained in this chapter covers a wide range of possible examination questions and is therefore worthy of thorough study. Invariably the compulsory exchange arithmetic question in the Institute of Bankers' paper involves the student in determining what a number of forward exchange rates will be and therefrom the sterling cost of the transactions and/or the customer's profit in sterling. Many examples of this type of question, and suggested solutions, will be found at the end of Chapter 5, but one which is purely concerned with avoiding the exchange risk is included below (see Question 3).

Quite apart from exchange arithmetic questions other questions do appear from time to time that are exclusively concerned with forward exchange, requiring definitions of terms such as premium and discount and explanations of the advantages to importers and exporters of forward exchange contracts. Let us start off by looking at two such straightforward questions and their solutions, which may help to crystallize in the reader's mind what forward contracts involve, and then look at the exchange arithmetic question referred to above.

Question 1

Explain what is meant by a forward exchange contract and explain why a British importer might enter into a forward option contract (*Inst. of Bankers*).

SOLUTION

Where an importer must make a payment in foreign currency at some date in the future, he will want to know how much the goods are going to cost him in terms of his own currency. Calculating at the current rate of exchange he may know that the goods will cost him £x, and therefore if he sells them at £$x+y$ he will make a profit of £y. If in the meantime, however, the rate of exchange deteriorates, he will receive fewer units of foreign currency for each unit of the home currency, and therefore the goods may cost him £$x+y$ and his profit will disappear. A rather similar situation applies to the exporter who is to receive a certain amount of foreign currency in the future. He has based his price in the foreign currency on the current rate of exchange, but if in the meantime the value of the home currency appreciates, he will receive fewer units of the home currency for each unit of foreign currency, and thus make a loss on his export.

Both the importer and the exporter can avoid the risk of loss by entering into a forward exchange contract. The importer can contract to buy the currency from his bank in, say, two months' time at a rate of exchange to be fixed immediately, while the exporter can enter into a contract to sell the currency at a future date at a rate to be fixed now. The bank, having bought currency forward, will sell it forward on the foreign exchange market; and if it has sold forward then it will buy the necessary currency forward through the market. It may be possible in effect for the bank to offset a forward purchase from one customer against a forward sale to another, and thus not require to cover itself through the foreign exchange market. In reality it will add together all its forward purchases and forward sales and buy or sell in the foreign exchange market only to the extent that it is necessary to make up the difference.

It is quite possible, of course, that the importer will find that the rate of exchange appreciates instead of depreciates, so that he would have been better off if he had bought the currency spot when it was actually required. Likewise, the exporter might find that the home currency depreciates instead of appreciates, but they cannot have it both ways. If there is any danger of loss, then it is wise to avoid it if possible.

A forward option contract is one which gives the bank customer an option as to *when* he completes the transaction. It is not an option as to *whether* he completes the contract. When a trader is to make a payment in foreign currency or is to receive foreign currency in the near future and knows only approximately when, he can enter into an option contract that will give him a set period in which to complete the transaction. For instance, a three months forward contract with option over the second and third months would be suitable when it is known that the currency will be required or paid at any time after a month but within three months.

An importer might enter into a forward option contract, therefore, when he knows that he has to pay for some goods in foreign currency in the near future, but is not sure of the exact date on which the currency will be required. He may, for instance, have contracted to pay for the goods one month after notification of shipment and be awaiting that notification. He knows that he will not have to pay for at least a month, but will for certain have to pay within the second month. He would therefore require a two months forward contract with option over the second month.

Question 2

Explain briefly what is meant by forward exchange and how the rates are quoted, and show the principal factors which influence them (*Inst. of Bankers*).

SOLUTION

A forward exchange contract is a contract between an importer or an exporter and his bank to buy from, or sell foreign currency to, the bank at a time in the future at a rate of exchange agreed immediately. In this way the importer can fix the rate he will have to pay for the foreign currency he will require to pay for the goods he is buying, and the exporter is able to determine the rate at which he will sell his foreign currency proceeds, and thus they are able to calculate the sterling cost and sterling proceeds respectively. The essential purpose of the forward exchange contract is to avoid any possible loss caused by a fluctuation in the exchange rate by the time the foreign currency is required or is to be received. However the customer cannot have it both ways; if the spot rate of exchange in three months' time (or whenever the forward contract is to be completed) turns out to be more favourable than the forward rate at which he agreed to complete the contract, he cannot opt to apply that spot rate rather than the forward rate. In other words he must fulfil his contract with the bank.

Forward contracts are quoted at either a premium or a discount over the spot rate. A premium means that the forward currency is dearer than spot and hence the purchaser of it gets fewer units for each pound than he would do if he were buying on the spot market, i.e. the forward premium is deducted from the spot rate. Discount means cheaper and therefore the buyer receives more units of the foreign currency for every pound sterling, i.e. the discount is added to the spot rate. In the same way that two spot rates are quoted, one for selling and the other buying, the premium or discount is quoted in a double-barrelled fashion. Thus if the spot rate is \$1.4945 – \$1.4965 the bank will sell at \$1.4945 and buy at \$1.4965. If the forward premium is quoted at 0.75 – 0.65 cents the bank's selling premium is 0.75 cents and its buying premium is 0.65 cents. Where there is a premium the higher figure is quoted on the left and the lower on the right, whereas with a discount the lower figure is on the left and the higher figure is on the right. To arrive at the actual buying and selling forward rates the premiums are simply written down below the spot rates and deducted, namely

\$1.4945	\$1.4965
75	65
\$1.4870	\$1.4900

and thus in this example the bank will sell forward at \$1.4870 and buy forward at \$1.4900. Similarly forward discounts are written below the spot rates and added to arrive at the forward rates.

If the importer is uncertain as to exactly when he will require the foreign currency, he may enter into a forward option contract. This gives him an option as to the date of completion of the contract—there is no option as to whether or not the contract will be completed. As an example, if he is certain that he will not require the currency for at least two months, but will certainly require it during the third month, he can enter into a three months forward, option over third month, contract. He must then complete the contract between the first and the last day of the third month after the date of the contract. To arrive at the rate for the contract the bank will work out the rate for a two months forward fixed contract and that for a three months forward fixed and use whichever of these two rates is less favourable to the customer.

Forward exchange rates are influenced by a number of factors of which the most predominant is rates of interest. Amongst other things a higher rate of interest in one country than in another will tend to cause a flow of short-term capital to the country with the higher rate of interest, and as investors of such capital usually cover themselves forward against fluctuations in the exchange rate, this causes a demand in the forward market for that currency and sends it to a premium, i.e. the forward currency becomes dearer than spot. Interest rates also reflect a number of other factors that in themselves influence forward exchange rates, such as the degree of confidence in a currency, political factors, intervention by the Exchange Equalization Account, and also what is happening to spot rates.

Question 3

Buzzer Ltd is a high technology company selling ideas, preparing specifications, drawings and computer programs for the chemical process industry. It has been particularly successful in selling to the US and has recently received an order from Germany that has meant sending a number of staff to work there. It is a sterling-based company that wishes to ensure its profit margins by avoiding exchange risks.

The company accountant has just called to see you to discuss covering Buzzer's foreign exchange commitments. He would like the bank to purchase the company's expected receipts of US dollars and also to sell Deutschemarks to the company to settle the salaries and living expenses of those employees based in Germany. He tells you that, during the next three months or so, Buzzer expects its total receipts and payments to be as follows:

Receipts	*Payments*
US \$200 000	DM100 000

Please now assume that the following developments take place:

(*a*) On 7 October 1985 you are asked to cover these commitments forward in respect of both transactions. The sterling rates on that day are:

	US \$	*DM*
Spot	1.2160 – 1.2270	3.6810 – 3.7025
1 month	0.10 – 0.05 c pm	1.50 – 1.25 pf pm
2 months	0.11 – 0.06 c pm	2.65 – 2.30 pf pm
3 months	0.12 – 0.07 c pm	3.60 – 3.35 pf pm

(*b*) On 7 January 1986 you are informed that \$50 000 of the expected US \$ receipts will not now be received until the middle of that month. You are asked to extend that part of the dollar forward contract on behalf of your customer.

(*c*) On the same day (7 January), you are told that a productivity bonus is due to the German-based employees. You are asked to remit a total of DM10 000 in addition to the salaries you have already arranged to pay under the forward contract arrangements. The foreign exchange rates on 7 January 1986 are as follows:

	US \$	*DM*
Spot	1.2290 – 1.2300	3.75 – 3.80
1 month	0.10 – 0.5 c pm	3.50 – 3.0 pf pm

REQUIRED

(*a*) Calculations showing the sterling sums to be passed to the company on

7 January and, finally, on 21 January when all of these transactions have been completed.

NOTE: *Assume that all the receipts and payments in respect of the contracts established take place on 7 January, apart from the final transaction on 21 January.*

(*b*) Any suggestions you would make to Buzzer Ltd on foreign exchange matters when the directors advise that they expect the German business to increase and that they believe they will need to arrange for a number of their employees to stay in Germany for some considerable time.

SOLUTION

(*a*) *7 October*

Bank *buys* \$200 000 at three months forward option and *sells* DM100 000 on the same basis.

Rates are	\$1.2270	Beginning of the option period	DM3.6810
Premium	07		360
	\$1.2263	At end of option period	DM3.6450

Therefore bank chooses to trade at \$1.2270 and DM3.6450 respectively.

Calculations \$200 000 @ 1.2270 = £162 999.19
DM100 000 @ 3.6450 = £27 434.84

7 January

Dollars: Bank sells customers \$50 000 to close-out the contract @ spot rate of \$1.2290

Calculation \$50 000 @ 1.2290 = \$40 683.48.

Bank extends this contract one month forward option. Therefore the rate at the beginning of the option period is \$1.2290 (the close-out rate). The bank is using the *diagonal rule* in using the spot selling rate, rather than the spot buying rate, as a gesture to the customer, and will take the forward *buying* premium from this to arrive at the rate for the end of the option period, thus 1.2290 less 0.05 = 1.2285.

As the bank is in fact buying it will choose the higher rate of 1.2290 for this contract.

Calculation \$50 000 @ 1.2290 = £40 683.48.

Deutschemarks: Bank sells customer extra DM10 000 at the spot selling rate of 3.75

Calculation DM10 000 at 3.75 = £2 666.67.

Therefore the transactions on the customer's account of 7 January are:

Dollars	£162 999.19	
less	40 683.48	
	£122 315.71	Account credited
Deutschemarks	£27 434.84	
plus	2 666.67	
	£30 101.51	Account debited

On 21 January the customer's account is credited with £40 683.48.

(*b*) As far as the second part of the question is concerned, the customer would be well advised to ask for payment in Deutschemarks instead of dollars for their services to German buyers. This would enable them to avoid the exchange risk by opening a Deutschemark account and offsetting the payments to their staff based in Germany against the Deutschemark receipts. Any surplus that accrues on this account could be transferred to an interest-bearing Deutschemark account or, if the funds could be used more profitably in the UK, they could be switched into sterling by forward contracts at appropriate intervals.

If the business with the US is likely to expand, the customer ought to consider opening a US dollar account as well, on the assumption that they will also incur expenses in US dollars that could be met from this account. If this development is not likely to take place then, as now, the dollar receipts could be covered by forward contracts, the dollars being switched either into sterling or into Deutschemarks.

Other questions

The following is a sample of other examination questions concerning the avoidance of the exchange risk that have been set by the various examining bodies. No model answers are given but the student reader would be wise to work through them on his own and check his answers with the text.

1. Explain what is meant by a 'forward exchange contract' and distinguish between a 'fixed forward' and a 'forward option'.

On the basis of the rates shown below, give the rates quoted by a bank:

(*a*) to buy Belgian francs and Norwegian kroner from a customer at one month forward fixed; and

(*b*) to sell Belgian francs and Norwegian kroner, at customer's option, three months forward.

	Belgian francs	*Norwegian kroner*
Spot	120.05 – 120.15	17.01 – 17.01½
1 month forward	100 – 200 c dis	10 øre pm – par
3 months forward	150 – 250 c dis	26 – 16 øre pm

(*Inst. of Bankers*)

2. Explain what is meant by a 'forward exchange' contract, and explain why a British importer might enter into a 'forward option' contract.

(Inst. of Bankers)

3. (*a*) Explain the following terms used when forward rates are quoted:

(*i*) par;
(*ii*) discount;
(*iii*) premium.

(*b*) On the basis of the rates given below, quote rates to a customer who wishes to:

(*i*) sell Austrian schillings three months forward fixed;
(*ii*) buy Danish kroner three months forward option;
(*iii*) sell Dutch florins three months forward fixed;
(*iv*) buy Italian lire three months forward option.

	Spot	*3 months forward*
Austria	62.17 – 62.22	40 groschen pm – par
Denmark	18.01 – 18.01½	4½ – 6½ øre dis
Holland	8.73½ – 8.74	3¼ – 2⅞ cents pm
Italy	1512½ – 1513	2 lire pm – 1 lira dis

(Inst. of Bankers)

4. What is meant by:

(*a*) a forward exchange contract;
(*b*) the statement that 'forward marks were quoted at a premium against sterling';
(*c*) a 'close-out' of a forward exchange contract?

(Inst. of Bankers)

5. Using the rates quoted below, determine what a bank would quote for the following transactions:

(*a*) An importer who must deliver US dollars some time in the next three months.
(*b*) An exporter will be receiving Swiss francs in two months' time.
(*c*) The beneficiary of a sight documentary credit payable in US dollars.
(*d*) The drawee of an accepted term bill in Swiss francs maturing in one month.
(*e*) For delivery of US dollars to a customer in one month's time.

Spot	US $1.8090 – 1.8110	Spot	Swiss francs 4.00 – 4.01
1 month	0.25 – 0.35 c	dis	1½ – ½ c pm
2 months	0.40 – 0.50 c	dis	2½ – 1¾ c pm
3 months	0.72 – 0.82 c	dis	4 – 3 c pm

(Inst. of Export)

6. You have despatched goods to Germany on 1 January, invoice value DM20 000. Payment is expected during the following month of March and you have asked your bank to cover this amount forward.

(*a*) Using the rates quoted below, calculate the rate which the bank will quote:

Spot	3.96–3.97
1 month	4–3 pfg premium
2 months	7–6 pfg premium
3 months	11–10 pfg premium

(*b*) What would you do about the forward contract if the payment was delayed until April.

(*c*) If at the end of the period you have not completed nor given any instructions to the bank, what action would the bank take?

(*Inst. of Export*)

7. Describe the procedure and guidelines for the calculation of fixed and option forward rates of exchange.

Using the rates quoted below, what rates would the bank quote for the following transactions:

(*a*) An importer trading with France on a two month credit basis.

(*b*) An exporter wanting an option over three months for Italian lire.

(*c*) A customer wishing to sell Deutschemarks with option over the third month only.

(*d*) A customer buying US dollars with an option over first and second months only.

	US $	*DM*
Spot	1.9045–1.9055	$3.89\frac{1}{4}$–$3.90\frac{3}{4}$
1 month	0.05 pm–0.05 dis	$1\frac{1}{2}$–1 pfg pm
2 months	0.10 pm–par	$2\frac{1}{2}$–2 pfg pm
3 months	0.15 pm–0.05 pm	$4\frac{3}{4}$–$4\frac{1}{4}$ pfg pm
	F. francs	*Italian lire*
Spot	8.58–8.62	1655–1660
1 month	$4\frac{1}{4}$–$3\frac{1}{4}$ c pm	4–7 dis
2 months	$7\frac{3}{4}$–$6\frac{3}{4}$ c pm	9–12 dis
3 months	$9\frac{1}{4}$–$8\frac{1}{2}$ c pm	14–17 dis

(*Inst. of Export*)

8. Determine from the rates below, what a bank would quote now for the following transactions:

(*a*) An importer who must deliver US dollars some time in the next three months.
(*b*) An exporter will be receiving Swiss francs for delivery in two months' time.
(*c*) The beneficiary of a Sight Documentary Credit payable in US dollars.
(*d*) The drawee of an accepted term bill in Swiss francs maturing in one month.
(*e*) For delivery of US dollars to a customer in one months' time.

Spot	US $2.1090 – 2.1110	Spot	Sw.fr.3.48 – 3.49
1 month	0.25 – 0.35 c dis	1 month	$1\frac{1}{2}$ – $\frac{1}{2}$ c pm
2 months	0.40 – 0.50 c dis	2 months	$2\frac{1}{2}$ – $1\frac{3}{4}$ c pm
3 months	0.72 – 0.82 c dis	3 months	4 – 3 c pm

(*Inst. of Freight Forwarders*)

9. You have sold goods invoice value DM10 000 to a German buyer—payment to be made in sixty days. As you wish to protect yourself against exchange fluctuations you have asked your bank to cover this in the forward market. The bank's quotations are as follows:

Spot DM5.60 – 5.65
1 month forward premium 7 – 6 pfg
2 months forward premium $7\frac{1}{2}$ – $6\frac{1}{2}$ pfg
3 months forward premium 8 – 7 pfg

What rate will the bank quote? Could the exchange risk have been covered in any other way? (*Inst. of Freight Forwarders*)

Exercise on selection of rates

From the table of exchange rates given below, answer the following questions. Remember that a bank is a foreign exchange dealer and therefore carries out transactions at the market rates, and that when a bank's customer *sells* the bank *buys*; when a customer *buys* the banks *sells.* Furthermore, remember the dictum that for currency rates a dealer *buys high and sells low.*

(*a*) At what rate will a bank buy spot dollars?
(*b*) At what rate will a customer buy escudos three months forward?
(*c*) At what rate will a customer sell dollars one month forward?
(*d*) At what rate will a bank sell escudos three months forward, option over three months?
(*e*) At what rate will a bank sell spot escudos?
(*f*) At what rate will a customer buy guilders spot?

(*g*) At what rate will a bank buy escudos three months forward, option over third month?
(*h*) At what rate will a customer sell guilders two months forward, option over second month?
(*i*) At what rate will a customer sell guilders three months forward, option over second and third month?
(*j*) At what rate will a bank buy escudos two months forward?
(*k*) At what rate will a customer buy dollars two months forward?
(*l*) At what rate will a customer buy dollars two months forward, option over second month?
(*m*) At what rate will a bank sell dollars two months forward?
(*n*) At what rate will a bank buy guilders three months forward?
(*o*) At what rate will a customer sell escudos one month forward?
(*p*) At what rate will a bank buy dollars three months forward?

	$	*Guilders*	*Escudos*
Spot	1.3915 – 1.3925	3.70 – 3.70$\frac{1}{4}$	263.15 – 263.25
	Premium	*Premium*	
1 month forward	1 – 0.90 c	4$\frac{1}{2}$ – 4$\frac{1}{4}$	15 c pm – 10 c dis
2 months forward	1.60 – 1.50 c	8$\frac{1}{2}$ – 8$\frac{1}{4}$ c	17 c pm – 8 c dis
3 months forward	2.10 – 2.00 c	10$\frac{1}{2}$ – 10$\frac{1}{4}$ c	19 c pm – 6 c dis

Answers

(*a*) 1.3925
(*b*) 262.96
(*c*) 1.3835 (1.3925 – .90)
(*d*) 262.96 (263.15 – 19)
(*e*) 263.15
(*f*) 3.70
(*g*) 263.33 (263.25 + 8)
(*h*) 3.66 (3.70$\frac{1}{4}$ – 4$\frac{1}{4}$)
(*i*) 3.66 (3.70$\frac{1}{4}$ – 4$\frac{1}{4}$)
(*j*) 263.33 (263.25 + 8)
(*k*) 1.3755 (1.3915 – 1.60)
(*l*) 1.3755 (1.3915 – 1.60)
(*m*) 1.3755 (1.3915 – 1.60)
(*n*) 3.60 (3.70$\frac{1}{4}$ – 10$\frac{1}{4}$)
(*o*) 263.35 (263.25 + 10)
(*p*) 1.3725 (1.3925 – 2.00)

4
EXPORT AND IMPORT PRICES

TERMS OF DELIVERY

THE price quoted by an exporter to an overseas buyer will naturally depend upon who is to pay the various expenses involved in getting the goods from the factory or warehouse in the UK to the buyer's premises abroad. The terms of delivery may range from 'Ex works' at the one extreme to 'franco domicile' at the other and the price will range similarly. Another factor that the exporter must take into account in deciding on his price will be whether or not it is to be expressed in the importer's currency. If it is, then he must make sure that his price to the buyer in terms of the foreign currency is sufficient, when converted into sterling through his bank, and after paying the bank's charges, to give him the profit margin that he expects to receive.

Let us consider each of the possible terms of delivery in turn, starting with an ex works quotation and working towards franco domicile. In this way we will see how the retail price of the goods in the buyer's country is built up.

Ex works

If the contract between the exporter and the overseas buyer stipulates an ex works price this means that the buyer will pay the basic price of the goods, i.e. the price the exporter needs to charge in order to cover this cost of production and give him his normal profit margin. To this will be added some charge for packing, the extent of which will depend upon how the goods are to be transported. If the buyer wants them to be crated up ready for shipment the cost of packing will naturally be higher than if he wants the goods to be only lightly packed so that he may, for instance, pack them into containers. If the buyer requires the exporter to provide particular documents, such as certificates of origin and consular invoices, the cost of them will also be included. The title to the goods and the risk pass to the buyer when the goods leave the works.

Free on rail (for)

The price here will be the basic price plus packaging and the cost of getting the goods to the railhead, where the title to the goods is to change hands and the risks of loss or damage then become the buyer's responsibility. The seller must provide the buyer with rail documents.

Free alongside ship (fas)

In addition to the basic price, the exporter will include packaging and transport to the docks and, possibly, some of the dock charges, if he is to deliver the goods at the quayside or on a lighter at the ship's side. If a lighter is used the exporter will include the lighterage in his price, as he will have to pay it, but not the cost of loading the goods from the lighter to on board ship.

Free on board (fob)

This involves an undertaking by the exporter to get the goods over the ship's rail, where delivery and change of title take place. This, in the case of a UK exporter, may be simply an undertaking to get the goods on board ship at a British port or, if the importer requires it, at a specific port, e.g. fob Liverpool. He may agree to load the goods on a specific ship at that particular port.

To arrive at the fob price the exporter will add to the basic price packing and transport to the docks, plus the UK dock charges, which will include both the port dues and the loading charges. Usually freight is payable at destination and the importer is informed when shipment is arranged so that he may take out insurance cover.

Free carrier... (Named point)

This term is used where goods are carried in containers and/or where roll-on/roll-off transportation by lorries and trailers is involved. It is somewhat similar to fob, but instead of discharging his responsibilities when he gets the goods over the ship's rail, the exporter does so when he hands them over to the carrier at the named point. A carrier is a person who has contracted to carry the goods by road, rail, sea or air or a combination of these.

Cost and freight (c & f)

To arrive at this price the freight to the port of destination must be added to the fob price. Usually the port of destination is indicated, e.g. c & f Bombay.

Freight (or carriage) paid to...

This term is similar to c & f but again takes into account modern forms of transportation. In other words it applies to multi-modal transport and containers, and ownership and risks are passed on when the goods are handed over to the carrier and carriage is paid to a named point of destination.

Cost, insurance and freight (cif)

This is a similar quotation to c & f but also includes the cost of insurance, which becomes the responsibility of the exporter. A variation of this is CIF Liner Terms. The responsibilities are similar to those under a CIF contract but the goods are to be transported by regular scheduled liner which works to a published timetable picking up consignments at ports en route. Freight charges tend to be cheaper than on chartered vessels.

Freight (or carriage) and insurance paid to...

Again this is a term used to cover the goods the title for which does not pass at the ship's rail but when the goods are handed to the carrier and carriage and insurance is paid. It equates with cif which applies to carriage by ship under a traditional arrangement whereby the exporter is responsible for getting the goods to the ship.

Franco

The price includes all charges and is usually quoted as franco domicile, i.e. free to the importer's premises.

The build-up from the exporter's basic price to that actually quoted to the buyer can thus be demonstrated as shown below, but this is only an example using "traditional" quotations. The reader will be able to work out for himself how the price will be built up if containers and multi-modal forms of transport are used.

basic price + packaging = *ex works*
ex works + transport to railhead = *for*
ex works + transport to docks, some dock charges and lighterage = *fas*
fas + loading charges = *fob*
fob + freight to port of destination = *c & f*
c & f + insurance = *cif*
cif + transport from docks to importer's premises = *franco* or *franco domicile*

We have dealt only with the main forms of quotation and of these fob and cif have been the most common up till now though the terms quoted for transportation by lorry are becoming increasingly common in view of the rapid expansion of our trade with Europe. There are many others such as 'ex warehouse' and 'free on truck' (fot), but the reader will be able to understand these from the terms of sale that have already been covered. The International Chamber of Commerce has produced a set of definitions called Incoterms which define the terms and the rights and obligations of the parties involved, and the exporter would be wise to refer to these Incoterms in giving his quotation so that there can be no misunderstanding about the terms used. The exporter will include all the costs involved, taking into account such things as bank charges and documentation, and where special charges are incurred by the exporter, for instance where additional documentation has to be obtained from and approved by the importer's embassy in Britain, these of course will be passed on in the price quoted. Where the buyer is to be allowed a period of credit, e.g. ninety days sight bill D/A (see Chapter 9), the exporter may want to raise his price to allow for the cost (notional or real) of financing this.

THE PRICE TO THE ULTIMATE BUYER

If the importer is buying for his own use, then we have arrived at the price at which the exporter's goods are being sold in the country concerned. However, if the goods are to be resold by the importer, then, when quoting to his customer, he is going to add costs and his profit margin to the price he paid. There may indeed be more than one intermediary between the exporter and the final buyer, e.g. importer, then wholesaler, and finally retailer, and the price quoted at the final stage could be considerably above that the exporter receives. This is obviously of considerable importance to the exporter because his ability to compete with other supplies in the market must depend on how successful he is in keeping down the final price.

The exporter may wish to ensure that the ultimate buyer of his goods can get a period of credit and this would apply particularly to durable goods such as cars, caravans, motor cycles, etc. His sales in the market concerned are likely to be enhanced if instalment credit is easily obtained and to this end he may be able to negotiate with the importer the terms on which his product is to be resold, and this is more likely if he gives generous credit terms to the importer. Through a credit union (see Chapter 12) it is possible not only to arrange for a bank or a finance house overseas to grant credit to the importer, but also for hire-purchase arrangements to be made for ultimate buyers. We will return to the question of credit in a later chapter, but it is obviously important to consider it at this stage as a possible cost that must be taken into account in the determination of price, and it is a factor that will affect the degree of competitiveness in overseas markets.

EXAMINATION GUIDELINES

Questions concerning shipping terms are usually quite straightforward and can be answered easily provided that the student knows what the main shipping terms mean, e.g. fob and cif, and therefore who is responsible for freight and insurance. It is also necessary to know at what point technical delivery takes place, and this again should cause no difficulty.

No doubt because of the straightforward nature of the subject the examiner tends to bring in other topics into the question, which is certainly the case with most of the following questions. In order to concern ourselves only with the subject of this chapter the second part of Question 1 has not been answered, nor have the terms of payment been discussed in Question 2.

Question 1

Bright Sparks Ltd are buyers and sellers of electrical goods and components. They have successfully competed for a contract to sell goods to an American electronics company based in Atlanta. Many of the goods will be manufactured in the UK but, because of the complexity of the contract, a number of components will have to be imported from Germany and Norway for processing in the UK.

As the company have not imported goods before, they need to know the meaning of the following terms quoted to them:

Germany	Terms cif UK airport. Payment in Deutschemarks by SWIFT to a nominated bank in Dusseldorf ten days after the shipment of goods from Germany to the UK.
Norway	Terms fob Oslo airport. Payment in sterling by TT to a named bank in Oslo within five days of the shipment of goods from Oslo airport to the UK.

REQUIRED

A brief explanation of

(*a*) the terms of shipment mentioned above and the respective responsibilities of buyer and seller;
(*b*) the terms 'SWIFT' and 'TT' and how these methods of payment operate.

SOLUTION

The term *cif UK airport* means that the price which Bright Sparks have to pay, as stated in the invoice, includes not only the basic cost of the goods but insurance and freight as well. The supplier is responsible for all the packing charges, transporting the goods to the German airport, handing them over to the airline against an air waybill and paying the cost of transport to the UK airport. Technical delivery takes place as the goods are handed over to the airline. The exporter must also pay for insurance of the goods up to the point at which they are handed over to Bright Sparks or their agent at the UK airport.

The term *fob Oslo airport* means that the price does not include the cost of freight nor the cost of insurance, both of which are payable by Bright Sparks. The seller's responsibility is to pack the goods and pay for carriage as far as Oslo airport. Once they are handed over at the airport to an airline technical delivery takes place and Bright Sparks are responsible for them from that point. If the sellers do pay for the air freight and/or insurance they do so as agent for Bright Sparks who must pay the costs involved in addition to the invoice amount.

Question 2

Held & Sons are steel stockholders in London whose account is operated on an overdraft basis. Hitherto they have obtained their stocks in the UK, but they are now forced to look elsewhere for supplies of a specialised steel, for which they have received the following quotations:

	Country	*Price per ton*	*Terms for payment*
(*a*)	Belgium	B.fr. 11 030 fob Antwerp	Open account—settlement 1 month after shipment
(*b*)	Spain	S.pts. 26 500 c & f London	Draft drawn payable 2 months after shipment D/A (Collection charges for buyer)
(*c*)	France	F.fr. 1697 cif London	Irrevocable documentary credit payment 3 months after shipment
(*d*)	Germany	DM 740 franco buyer's premises	Payment with order

Explain briefly the four methods of delivery and terms of payment in order to show the relative responsibilities of the possible contracting parties.

(*Inst. of Bankers*)

SOLUTION

(*a*) *Fob Antwerp.* The Belgian supplier is responsible for getting the steel to the docks at Antwerp and on board the vessel, and must pay all the charges up to that point. Technical delivery takes place as the steel is hoisted over the ship's rail and Held & Sons are responsible for it after that point. The price quoted does not include freight and insurance, which must be paid for by Held & Sons. If the supplier pays for either or both of these he does so as agent for Held & Sons and will add the cost of the invoice amount.

(*b*) *C & f London.* The Spanish exporter is responsible for getting the steel onto a ship at a Spanish port and for paying the freight charges to London. Insurance is not included in the price and must be paid for by Held & Sons, who are also responsible for getting the steel from the London docks. Technical delivery takes place as the steel is hoisted over the ship's rail at the Spanish port.

(*c*) *Cif London.* The invoice price quoted by the French exporter includes insurance and freight. The exporter is responsible for getting the steel onto a vessel at a French port and paying the carriage to London, as well as paying for insurance of course. Technical delivery takes place as the steel is hoisted over the ship's rail at the French port. The buyers are responsible for the cost of getting the steel from the docks in London.

(*d*) *Franco buyers' premises.* The price quoted by the German suppliers includes all expenses right through to Held & Sons' premises at which point technical and physical delivery takes place.

Other questions

1. Identify four different methods of quoting prices in foreign trade and show exactly what costs are included in each price.

(*Inst. of Export*)

2(*a*) Express the following terms in full:

(*i*) fas
(*ii*) fob
(*iii*) c & f
(*iv*) cif

Which party (seller or buyer), is responsible in the case of each of the four types of contract referred to above:

(*i*) for arranging insurance;
(*ii*) for cost of carriage?

(*b*) Apart from the normal requirements, what particular details would you look for to ensure that the conditions as regards shipment had been met, if a bill of lading were presented under the following contract terms:

(*i*) fas UK Port;
(*ii*) fob Southampton;
(*iii*) c & f New York;
(*iv*) cif Hamburg?

(*c*) Explain briefly the difference between a liner bill of lading and a charter party bill of lading.

(*Inst. of Bankers*)

3. Your customers, Home Fires Ltd, have been successful in selling a wide range of consumer products in the UK for a number of years, but they are now seeking markets overseas. They have been asked by a potential overseas buyer to quote prices based upon the following terms:

(*a*) fob
(*b*) c & f
(*c*) cif
(*d*) cif liner terms

Give an explanation of these terms for your customers, indicating the precise meaning and the contractual relationship that will exist between buyer and seller arising out of those terms.

(*Inst. of Bankers*)

5
EXCHANGE ARITHMETIC

IMPORTANCE OF ACCURACY

ALMOST inevitably, anyone who has any dealings whatever in foreign currency will have to do some exchange arithmetic from time to time. To some the rather long calculations often involved seem a nightmare, but this should not be so once the methods to be employed have been fully understood. All that is involved really is an ability to add, subtract, divide and multiply. But this must be done carefully and precisely, for a small margin of error can become very large when multiplied. An error of 2 per cent on a small amount may be insignificant, but when it is multiplied by a large number it becomes 2 per cent of a large amount and is significant. In an examination an electronic calculator can now be used so that the student does not have to do it the hard way. Nevertheless the principles involved must be clearly understood.

The student preparing to take the Institute of Bankers Finance of International Trade examination will find that an exchange arithmetic question will occur in the paper and that it will be a compulsory one. The wise student will therefore study and practice exchange arithmetic until he is able to answer such questions with confidence that he will arrive at the right answer.

The student is well advised to check his calculations as he proceeds, for a moment spent in going over a calculation before starting the next might save a great deal of time in the end. He should prepare a rough estimate of the answer at the outset and get into the habit of doing this automatically. If the final answer does not agree with the estimate, then it will prompt the student to re-check his work and locate the error. A rough estimate is particularly useful where decimals are involved, for it is easy to put the decimal point in the wrong place, and this is especially so when a calculator is used.

THE USE OF DECIMALS

Decimals save time and effort in exchange calculations, but they must be taken to sufficient decimal places to ensure accuracy. This is especially important where multiplication is involved. If an amount of currency is to be multiplied by a large number, a good rule of thumb is to take it to five decimal places before it is multiplied, unless of course it works out exactly to a smaller number of places, e.g. $\$103\frac{1}{8} = \$103.125$. In converting an amount of foreign currency into sterling by division (e.g. dividing \$100 000 by \$1.37925) it is necessary to take the answer to only three decimal places.

When calculating the cost in sterling of some foreign currency, or the proceeds of the sale of currency, the answer should never be given in fractions or decimals of a penny. The best policy is to take it to the nearest penny, i.e. the penny above if the fraction or decimal is more than a half-penny and to the penny below if it is less. Although in the foreign exchange market, most rates of exchange are expressed in decimals, a few are still expressed in the form of fractions of the subsidiary currency unit. In examination answers, it may therefore be necessary still to convert fractions to decimals and vice versa. To facilitate this, the following four decimal equivalents must be known, but always express your answer in fractions if the question shows fractions or decimals if the rate is quoted in decimals.

$\frac{1}{2} = 0.5$
$\frac{1}{4} = 0.25$
$\frac{1}{8} = 0.125$
$\frac{1}{16} = 0.0625$

From these it is possible to work out the decimal equivalent of any fraction that is likely to be used, e.g. $\frac{3}{16} = \frac{1}{8} + \frac{1}{16} = 0.125 + 0.0625 = 0.1875$.

CALCULATION OF INTEREST

The formula for calculating interest where the answer is to be in units of currency is:

$$I = \frac{P \times N \times R}{100 \times 365}$$

Where I=interest;
P=principal;
N=number of days;
R=rate per annum.

(The American practice in calculating interest is to work on the basis of a 360-day year, which greatly simplifies the calculation, e.g. a sixty-day period is $\frac{1}{6}$ of a year and a ninety-day period $\frac{1}{4}$. In some examination questions, the student is told to work on this basis, but if he is not he must calculate on a 365-day year in the normal way.)

The following examples will help to make the formula understood:

EXAMPLES

1. Find the interest on £581 for 7 days at 6 per cent per annum.

Rough estimate $\dfrac{600 \times 7 \times 6}{100 \times 360} = \dfrac{7}{10} = £0.70.$

Method $\dfrac{581 \times 7 \times 6}{100 \times 365} = \dfrac{24\,402}{365} = £0.67.$

NOTE: *In calculating the denominator the 100 can be ignored, i.e. it can be taken as 365, because the rough estimate tells us where to put the decimal point.*

2. Find the interest on £30 881 for 12 days at 7 per cent.

Rough estimate $\dfrac{30\,000 \times 12 \times 7}{100 \times 360} = £70.$

Method $\dfrac{30\,881 \times 12 \times 7}{100 \times 365} = \dfrac{2\,594\,004}{365} = £71.07.$

The banking student is often required in an examination to calculate a forward discount or premium as an annual percentage rate. The forward rate tables in the *Financial Times* (see Table 1.2) show both the actual premiums and discounts as a percentage but this is of little comfort to the examination candidate of course who must be able to work such percentages out for himself. The process is actually quite simple if a calculator is at hand, but do be careful with the decimal point. It is usual practice now to express the premium or discount as a percentage of the *forward rate* though sometimes an examination question will specifically instruct you to use the required spot rate. Quite often you are asked for, or clearly require, only an approximate answer which simplifies matters.

The formula is as follows:

$$\frac{\text{Premium (or discount) for the period} \times \text{number required to raise the period to 12 months} \times 100}{\text{Forward rate}}$$

A three months discount of 1.20 cents on a forward rate of \$2.40 will therefore be

$$\frac{1.20\ \text{c} \times 4 \times 100}{\$2.40} = \frac{1.20 \times 4 \times 100}{240} = 2 \text{ per cent.}$$

The period of three months needs to be multiplied by 4 to make it an annual premium. If it was the one month forward premium it would of course have to be multiplied by 12.

EXAMINATION GUIDELINES

Examination questions on exchange arithmetic are usually designed to test the candidate's ability to apply principles to practice. They contain much detail, so the student must decide what is required. He is normally required to select the appropriate rates of exchange from the table of rates and, having done so, calculate the cost or proceeds in sterling. This may involve making allowances for interest, insurance, freight, and working out the appropriate exchange commission. To give the student practice in selecting the right rate of exchange, an exercise is included at the end of Chapter 3 and is followed by the correct answers. He should test himself and repeat the exercise until he has thoroughly mastered the technique.

The student must not let himself be discouraged by the amount of detail involved. He should ask himself the question, 'what amounts of foreign currency are to be paid or received, and when?' Some simple calculations may be involved here, such as multiplying the price per ton by the number of tons being bought, so that the total cost in foreign currency can be ascertained. These must be done accurately, of course, or the sum will be wrong from the outset.

The student must work logically through the answer, commenting on the steps he is taking and why so that the examiner is able to follow the reasoning and give marks for the right approach, even if the correct answer is not arrived at. This is particularly important when a calculator is used because, without the workings that would be shown if the calculations were done manually, it is difficult to see how figures have been arrived at.

A rough estimate at the beginning of the answer is essential in answering exchange arithmetic problems, of course, and the wise student will be neat and methodical. He will work steadily, carefully, and not too hastily, through the answer. In this way errors that would cause the loss of valuable marks will be avoided.

Banks charge exchange commission on foreign exchange transactions, but the rate charged varies from bank to bank: e.g. 1‰, minimum £10; 1½‰, minimum £15 (1‰ means one per mille, i.e. £1 per £1000). In examination questions the student is given guidance in this matter, however, and the examinee must be careful to follow the instructions carefully. There are two things to watch out for: firstly, that exchange commission must be *deducted* from the proceeds from the sale to a bank of foreign currency and *added* to the charge for currency purchased from a bank, and, secondly, that the maximum quoted must be observed. This means that the exchange commission on £50 000 of proceeds will be £10 and not £50 if a maximum of £10 is stated.

The following questions and their solutions should be studied carefully. Students should try to work them out independently, and do so several times, if necessary, until the technique is mastered. The questions are all taken from past Institute of Bankers' examination papers. Some of these questions involve the opening of a documentary credit and, therefore Chapters 7 and 8 should be studied before trying to work through these particular questions. (Various commercial abbreviations used are also explained in these two later chapters.) The suggested solutions to these problems have been made somewhat fuller and more detailed than is necessary in an examination to assist the student reader to understand the steps involved. He will, I am sure, be able to determine what is necessary to include and what can be cut out. The essential thing is to explain each stage in your reasoning to the examiner in as concise a way as possible.

Question 1

A UK manufacturing company contracts to sell machinery to a buyer in Germany for DM177 350. 30 per cent to be paid upon shipment, which is due during July, and the balance in equal instalments one month and two months after shipment. On 1st July, the UK company asks its bank to provide forward cover for these transactions.

During the early part of September one machine develops a minor fault that is soon rectified by engineers sent out to Germany. However, compensation for loss of production time is agreed and the final payment is subsequently reduced by DM4000. The balance of the forward contract is cancelled on 17 September.

On the basis of the rates quoted below and exchange commission of 1 per mille, maximum £10 (not to be charged when cancelling the balance of the forward contract), calculate the total sterling amount received by the manufacturers.

		DM
1 July	Spot	8.86¼–8.86¾
	1 month	1–¾ pfg pm
	2 months	1½–1¼ pfg pm
	3 months	2–1¾ pfg pm
17 September	Spot	8.85–8.85½

SOLUTION

The UK manufacturing company is to secure 30 per cent of DM177 350 during July (i.e. upon shipment) and 35 per cent during August and 35 per cent during September (one and two months after shipment)). The company will therefore enter into forward exchange contracts to sell Deutschemarks to the bank as follows:

DM53 205 at 1 month forward option ∴ rate is 8.86¾

DM62 072.50 at 2 months forward, option over 2nd month ∴ rate is 8.86

(Deutschemarks will definitely not be received during July, but may be received at any time during August. Therefore, the bank will take the rate at the beginning or the end of the option period less favourable to the customer: 1 August=8.86, 1 September=8.85½ ∴ the bank will buy at 8.86.)

DM62 072.50 at 3 months forward, option over third month ∴ rate is 8.85½ (option period is September and rate at the beginning, i.e. 1 September, is less favourable to customer).

When the forward contract is due for completion by the sale of the third instalment of Deutschemarks to the bank, the company is DM4000 short because of the compensation payment. It must therefore buy DM4000 from the bank at the spot rate on the date of completion (17 September), i.e. at 8.85.

The sterling amount received from the sale of the machinery is therefore as follows:

DM53 205 at 8.86 $\frac{3}{4}$

Rough estimate of proceeds $= \dfrac{54\,000}{9} = £6\,000.$

$\dfrac{53\,205}{8.8675} = £6\,000.00$

less exchange commission 6.00

£5 994.00

DM62 072 at 8.86

Rough estimate of proceeds $= \dfrac{63\,000}{9} = £7\,000.$

$\dfrac{62\,072.50}{8.86} = £7\,005.92$

less exchange commission 7.01

£6 998.91

DM62 072.50 at 8.85 $\frac{1}{2}$

Rough estimate of proceeds $= \dfrac{63\,000}{9} = £7\,000.$

$\dfrac{62\,072.5}{8.855} = £7\,009.88$

less exchange commission 7.01

£7 002.87

Close-out
DM 4 000 at 8.85

Rough estimate of cost $= \dfrac{4\,000}{8} = £500.$

$\dfrac{4\,000}{8.85} = £451.98$

∴ *Total proceeds*

£5 994.00
£6 998.91
£7 002.87

19 995.78
451.98

less close-out

£19 543.80

Question 2

Your customers, Gem Merchants Ltd, contracted to buy industrial gems from West Germany for US $100 000, payment to be made by telegraphic transfer on 10 September in exchange for the goods.

Gem Merchants Ltd keep an account in US dollars with you and it is your customer's practice to sell the goods for US dollars, crediting the funds received to their US dollar account. Each half-year they convert the credit balance on the account into sterling. They overdraw the account from time to time. On 9 September the credit balance was $60 000, and the payment out of $100 000 on 10 September overdraw the account by $40 000.

On 30 September Gem Merchants Ltd calculated from their sales figures that sums totalling in all $140 000 would be credited to their dollar account by 30 December and that there would be no debits during those three months. They therefore sold to you on 30 September, forward fixed for delivery on 30 December, the estimated credit balance on their dollar account on the latter date. On 30 December the credit balance was $120 000 and Gem Merchants instructed you to apply the appropriate amount to the forward contract and convert the surplus into sterling at the spot rate, crediting the whole, less expenses, to their sterling account with you. Using the rates below as appropriate, and allowing for Exchange Commission at 1 per mille, maximum £10, calculate the net sterling credit on 30 December:

	Spot	*3 months forward*
10 September	US $2.6055 – 2.6065	0.35 c – 0.25 c pm
30 September	US $2.6060 – 2.6070	0.35 c – 0.25 c pm
30 December	US $2.6040 – 2.6050	0.35 c – 0.25 c pm

SOLUTION

The customers' estimated credit balance on 30 December was $100 000 (i.e. $140 000 being credited by then, *less* the $40 000 overdraft created by the payment on 10 September). This estimated balance was sold to the bank as a three months forward fixed contract on 30 September (i.e. for delivery on 30 December) at the rate at that date (spot $2.6070, *less* forward premium 0.25 cents = $2.6045).

On 30 December the customer had an extra $20 000 to sell to the bank beyond the $100 000 estimated credit balance. This they sold at the spot rate on that day, i.e. $2.6050.

They were therefore credited with sterling on 30 December as follows:

$100 000 at $2.6045

$$\text{Rough estimate of proceeds} = \frac{100\,000}{2.5} = £40\,000.$$

$$\frac{100\,000}{2.6045} = £38\,395.09$$

= *less* exchange commission (maximum)	10.00
	£38 385.09

$20 000 at 2.6050

$$\text{Rough estimate of cost} = \frac{20\,000}{2.5} = £8\,000.$$

$$\frac{20\,000}{2.6050} = £7\,677.54$$

less exchange commission	7.68
	£7 669.86

∴ *Total proceeds*	£38 385.09
	7 669.86
	£46 054.95

Question 3

A British importer contracts to purchase from a French manufacturer 50 dozen pairs of ladies' fashion boots at a cost of Fr. 1195.20 per dozen. Despatch is to be by air freight in two separate consignments of 25 dozen pairs (one in January, and one in February), and payment is to be made immediately upon receipt of telex advice of despatch. On 1 January, the importer requests his bank to cover him forward for these transactions.

Whilst the first consignment arrives safely and is paid for on 25 January, the second is delayed by industrial action, with the result that delivery cannot take place until some time in March. The importer arranges for his bank to extend the contract, and the goods are eventually despatched on 20 March.

On the basis of the rates quoted below and exchange commission of 1 per mille, maximum £10 (but charging only $\frac{1}{2}$ per mille, maximum £10, on the extension), calculate the total sterling amount paid by the importer.

	1 January	1 March
Spot	13.34½–13.35	13.35½–13.36
1 month	4½–3¾ c pm	5–4¼ c pm
2 months	6½–5¾ c pm	7–6¼ c pm
3 months	8½–7¾ c pm	9–8¼ c pm

SOLUTION

The importer will have to pay Fr.1195.20 × 25 = 29 880 during January, i.e. one month forward option and a similar amount in February, i.e. two month forward, option over second month. He will enter into a contract with the bank to buy these at Fr.13.30 and Fr.13.28 = £1 respectively. The basis used in calculating these rates is as follows.

The first payment will have to be made at any time during January, and therefore the bank will assume that it will occur at the least favourable time of the month from the customer's point of view. This will be on the last day (one month forward from 1st January). The bank will wish to supply as few francs for each £1 as possible, so therefore will pay 13.34½ less 4½ premium. Likewise for the second contract it will pay out as few francs as possible and will use the rate for two months forward, i.e. 13.34½ less 6½ premium, rather than the rate at the beginning of the option period.

To complete the contract on 1 March (the end of the second option period), the customer sells the temporarily unwanted francs back on the spot rate of 13.36. He extends for one month his option to purchase francs and will be quoted the close-out rate 13.36 less the selling margin for one month (5 cents) = 13.31.

NOTE: *Students should note that diagonal rule has been used when extending the forward contract in accordance with the practice of British banks. Hence the bank's selling margin of 5 cents has been deducted from the close-out rate (which was the bank's buying rate).*

The calculations involved are as follows:

Fr.29 880 at 13.30

Rough estimate of cost $= \dfrac{30\,000}{13}$ = £2300 approx.

$\dfrac{29\,880}{1330} =$ 2246.62

add exchange commission 2.25

£2248.87

Fr 29 880 at 13.28	= £2 300 approx.	
	$\frac{29\,880}{1328}$ =	2250.00
add exchange commission		2.25
		£2252.25

Fr. 29 880 at 13.36	= £2300 approx.	
	$\frac{29\,880}{1336}$ =	£2236.53
∴ Customer debited with		£2252.25
	less	2236.53
	=	£ 15.72

Extension

Fr. 29 880 at 13.31	= £2300 approx.	
	$\frac{29\,880}{1331}$ =	£2 244.93
add exchange commission at ½ per mille		1.12
		£2246.05
∴ Importer will have to pay		£2248.87
		15.72
		2246.05
		£4510.64

Question 4

In early May you are asked to confirm an irrevocable letter of credit on bahalf of a Japanese correspondent bank. The terms are briefly as follows:

In favour of: Associated Noxious Distributors, London
For account of: Nippon Oriental Traders, Yokohama
Expiring: 15 November 19xx in London
Amount: About Japanese yen 43 000 000 (forty-three million)
Covering: About 1000 metric tons of chemicals to be shipped in two approximately equal instalments, one during the first half of July and one during the first half of August.

Price: Yen 43 000 per metric ton cif Yokohama, shipment from UK port.
Drawings will be made as follows:

(*a*) 95 per cent of the value of a provisional invoice upon presentation of documents strictly in order.
(*b*) The remaining 5 per cent will be available against final invoice accompanied by an independent weight and analysis certificate showing the final weight and chemical analysis.

On 25 May the beneficiary asks you to cover the forward receivables in the foreign exchange market, as follows:

(*a*) Arrange forward contracts immediately in respect of the value of each 500 metric ton shipment.
(*b*) Upon presentation of documents close out any differences between the forward contract amounts and the actual values claimed.
(*c*) Ignore forward cover for the balance to be claimed in October.

The documents were presented in order on the following dates:

15 July —Documents showing a shipment of exactly 490 metric tons.
10 August —Documents showing a shipment of exactly 526.316 metric tons.
31 October —Final invoice claiming an agreed figure of Japanese yen 43 550.

REQUIRED

Using the following rates of exchange calculate the sterling sums your customers will receive on the appropriate presentation dates.

25 May	Spot	430.50	434.50
	1 month forward	2.50 pm	2.00 pm
	2 months forward	3.90 pm	3.10 pm
	3 months forward	6.75 pm	6.25 pm
	6 months forward	12.40 pm	11.65 pm
15 July	Spot	429.00	433.50
10 August	Spot	433.50	438.00
31 October	Spot	432.00	434.40

NOTES:

1. *For the purpose of this question, the bank and the beneficiary assume that shipment and presentation of documents will be made on the same day.*
2. *Ignore letter of credit charges as these are for the buyer's account.*
3. *Ignore any close out figures of less than 100 yen.*

SOLUTION

As chemicals are a bulk commodity the precise amount of each shipment cannot be determined precisely in advance and *Uniform Customs and Practice for*

Documentary Credits states that the word *about* means that the exporter can ship up to 10 per cent more or less than stated in the credit. In view of the doubt as to the actual amount that will therefore be claimed (e.g. 95 per cent of 550 metric tonnes) it is best to arrange the forward contracts for the full value of 500 metric tonnes. Each contract will therefore be for 500 × 43 000 yen = 21 500,000 yen.

For the first shipment a two months forward, option over second month, contract would be appropriate as this would enable the exporter to sell the currency to the bank between 25 June and 25 July. For the second shipment a three months forward, option over third month, contract would enable the exporter to complete between 25 July and 25 August.

The bank's forward buying rates are as follow:

Spot	434.50		434.50		434.50
	2.00		3.10		6.25
1 month	432.50	2 months	431.40	3 months	428.25

For the first contract the beginning of the option period is one month forward and the end of the option period is two months forward. Of the two rates, 432.50 and 431.40, the bank will choose the former as it is buying high. Similarly the bank will choose the rate at the beginning of the option period as far as the second contract is concerned, i.e. two months forward, i.e. 431.40.

The two forward contracts will therefore be as follows:

1. 21 500 000 yen @ 432.50 = £49 710.98
2. 21 500 000 yen @ 431.40 = £49 837.74

The actual financial transactions on 15 July and 10 August respectively are as follows:

15 July

$$490 \text{ tonnes @ } 43\,000 \text{ yen} \times 95 \text{ per cent} = \frac{21\,070\,000 \times 95}{100}$$

= 20 016 500 @ 432.50 =		£46 280.92
This is 1 483 500 short of what has been provided by the forward contract and this is sold spot @ 429.00 to produce	£3458.04	
less balance of forward contract @ 432.50 =	£3430.06	
gives customer credit of	27.98	27.98
Proceeds of first shipment		£46 252.94

10 August

$$526.316 \text{ tonnes @ } 43\,000 \text{ yen} = \frac{22\,631\,588 \times 95}{100}$$

$$= 21\,500\,008 \text{ @ } 431.40 \qquad £49\,837.76$$

On 21 October

The balance of 43 550 yen is received and sold to bank at spot rate of 434.40	=	100.25
Total sterling proceeds of shipments	=	£96 190.95

Question 5

Your customers, Ancient Mariners Ltd, are sterling-based and are negotiating with a major UK contracting company to transport building equipment and materials to a remote island in the Indian ocean. Payment is secure and will be made in US dollars, the contract being worth US $900 000. To complete the deal successfully they will need to charter the following vessels:

(*a*) one roll-on/roll-off vessel from the USA;
(*b*) one tug and landing barge, complete with derrick, from Holland;
(*c*) one general cargo vessel, of about 5000 tons cargo weight, from Singapore.

You know your customers will require bank finance and the directors call to see you to discuss the matter. Your enquiries reveal that Ancient Mariners Ltd will obtain the contract subject to their agreeing to the following financial arrangements:

(*a*) Payment in respect of (*a*) above is to be $100 000 in all and is to be payable *to the US owners* upon the sailing of the vessel from the USA. (The charter will be for one month from the date of the contract and sailing will take place immediately upon signing of the contract.)
(*b*) Payment in respect of (*b*) above is for a total of DM300 000 payable *to the Dutch owners* in two equal lots. The first is to be made upon the sailing of the vessel, which will take place immediately the contract is signed, and the balance is to be paid three months later. (The total charter time will be exactly six months).
(*c*) Payment in respect of (*c*) above is for a total price of US 500 000, payable *to the Singapore owners* in two equal lots. The first payment is to be made one month after the signing of the contract and the second exactly six months after signing the contract.

(*d*) Payment *from the main contractor* will be in three instalments as follows:

US $200 000 immediately upon signing the contract;
US $500 000 three months after signing the contract;
US $200 000 six months after signing the contract.

Additional information:

(*a*) Assume that the contract is awarded and signed on 1 June and the bank is willing to support the customers.
(*b*) Ignore commercial risks, such as chartering risks, weather and penalty clauses that might be included in the commercial contract.
(*c*) Ignore any charges or interest payable in connection with any overdrawings.
(*d*) Assume that the vessels sail on the same day as the contract is awarded, i.e. 1 June.

The rates applying on 1 June are as follows:

	£/US $	US $/DM
Spot	1.6100 – 1.6180	2.4096 – 2.4145
1 month	0.21 – 0.16 c pm	8.33 – 8.30 pf pm
2 months	0.38 – 0.33 c pm	8.55 – 8.25 pf pm
3 months	0.51 – 0.46 c pm	9.00 – 8.83 pf pm
6 months	0.66 – 0.61 c pm	13.03 – 12.95 pf pm

REQUIRED

Your advice to the company covering the following points:

(*a*) The risks that the company will have to face in accepting and arranging the contract described above;
(*b*) how the bank can help to *minimize* those risks, indicating quite clearly the technical description of the risks;
(*c*) a statement of the currency account and a calculation of the total sterling receipts the company will have at the end of the contract period, assuming that they will sell forward any surplus dollars to the bank.

SOLUTION

(*a*) This part of the question is concerned with the exchange risk and not the commercial risk (as the question states that payment is secure). The customers are trading in US dollars and Deutschemarks and should the exchange rates for these two currencies move against them they could end up with considerably less profit than what might have been expected from the spot rates at the outset on 1 June.
(*b*) These exchange risks can be minimized by opening a dollar currency account into which the customers pay in their dollar receipts and from which they make their dollar payments. As they will be making a

substantial profit from their transactions, they would be wise to sell forward to the bank the expected surplus of dollars at the end of the project. In these two ways they will obviate any loss through fluctuations in the value of the dollar. As far as the second Deutschemark transaction is concerned (not the first as this is an immediate transaction), they should enter into a forward exchange contract to buy the Deutschemarks and thus cover the exchange risk. The Deutschemarks could be bought for US dollars and the cost debited to the dollar currency account.

(*c*) Two forward exchange contracts are involved:

(*i*) To sell to the customers DM150 000 for US dollars three months forward. The rate for this transaction on 1 June is DM2.3196 per $1 (spot 2.4096 less 9.00 pfennigs premium). The cost is therefore DM150 000 @ 2.3196=$64 666.32.

(*ii*) The bank will buy the expected dollar balance on the account as 1 December by a six months forward contract for which the rate will be $1.6119 (spot 1.6180 less 0.61 cents premium). The actual amount of dollars to be sold must be worked out by preparing the dollar currency account up to 1 December on the basis of the information given in the question as follows:

		Debit	*Credit*	*Balance*
1 June	From main contractor		200 000	200 000 cr
	Payment to US owners	100 000		100 000 cr
	Payment to Dutch owners	62 251		37 749 cr
1 July	Payment to Singapore	250 000		212 251 dr
1 Sept.	From main contractors		500 000	287 749 cr
	Payment to Dutch owners	64 666.32		223 082.68 cr
1 Dec.	From main contractors		200 000	423 082.68 cr
	Payment to Singapore	250 000		173 082.68 cr

The spot transaction in respect of DM150 000 payable to the Dutch owners on 1 June was at the rate of DM2.4096=$1 which works out at $62 250.996 and hence the precise figure of $62 251.

The forward exchange contract (*ii*) above, would, as we can now see, have to be in respect of the outstanding balance of $173 082.68, which at $1.6119 works out at £107,378.05.

If Ancient Mariners had chosen in advance to receive the sterling earlier on 1 September, they could have entered into a three months forward contract to sell $173 082.68, leaving $50 000 on the account for the net outgoings on 1 December. The rate would be 1.6134 (1.6180 – 0.0046) and the sum credited would be £107 278.21.

Question 6

Your customers Blacksheep Ltd, call to see you on 15 January to discuss a new contract they have signed with a French meat importer, Agneau-Mouton SA, Paris. The terms of the contract are as follows:

Quantity: About 200 metric tons of chilled carcases, to be shipped in two equal lots, the first during the second half of January and the balance during the second half of March.
Price: Fr.fr.1600 per metric ton.
Terms: Free delivery Paris by refrigerated road truck from the UK.
Payment: To be effected in French francs through a documentary collection —one for each consignment—whereby the documents will be forwarded to the bankers of Agneau-Mouton SA through your office. The collection will be subject to *Uniform Rules for Collections* (ICC Publication 322).

Your customers are satisfied with the credit rating of the buyers and expect that payment will be made within a few days of presentation of the documents through your correspondent in Paris. Blacksheep Ltd require forward exchange cover to be taken out to protect their sterling profit margin. You therefore arrange two forward exchange contracts to cover the two deliveries.

The rates of exchange for French francs on 15 January are as follows:

Spot	12.0966 – 12.1336
1 month	0.0275 – 0.0375 c disc
2 months	0.0575 – 0.0775 c disc
3 months	0.1050 – 0.1250 c disc
4 months	0.2350 – 0.2650 c disc

Shipments are effected in accordance with the contract, the first of 100 metric tons on 20 January and the second, also of 100 metric tons, on 18 March. However, on 20 March your customers call to see you again and inform you that, owing to industrial trouble in France, the March shipment has been delayed and they are unlikely to be paid on time since the carcases will now be subject to rigorous health inspections. The proceeds are unlikely, therefore, to be received until the third week in April. They ask you to cancel the March forward contract, which falls due towards the middle of April, and to arrange a new one for the value of 80 metric tons only since a fifth of the consignment has 'disappeared' and will be subject to a separate insurance claim.

The rates for French francs on 20 March are as follows:

Spot	12.1350 – 12.1645
1 Month	0.0245 – 0.0355 c disc

REQUIRED

(*a*) A statement of the meaning and purpose of the phrase 'subject to *Uniform Rules for Collections* (ICC Publication No. 322)'.
(*b*) Details of the forward contracts your customer would take out on

15 January to protect their sterling receipts and calculations of the sterling proceeds of each contract.

(*c*) Calculation of the sterling entries that will be passed to your customers' account on 20 March in respect of the March close-out.

(*d*) Details of the extended forward contract you arrange for your customers to cover the shipment of 80 metric tons, and a calculation of the expected sterling proceeds of the contract.

SOLUTION

(*a*) This calls for a short, straightforward statement of the meaning and purpose of the *Uniform Rules for Collections* and the reader should refer to Chapter 9 for this.

(*b*) Blacksheep Ltd will require two forward option contracts each for 100 metric tons Fr.1600=160 000. The first contract will be a one month forward option giving the customer up to 15 February to receive and sell the proceeds to the bank. The second will be a three months forward, option over third month, contract, giving the customer the period 15 March to 15 April in which to receive the proceeds.

The rates and sterling amounts are as follows:

Contract 1

Rate at beginning of the option period	12.1336
1 month's forward discount	0.0375
Rate at end of option period	12.1711

As the bank is buying it will buy high at 12.1711 and the sterling proceeds would therefore be £13 145.90.

Contract 2

Rate at beginning of option period 12.1336+0.0775	=12.2111
Rate at end of option period 12.1336+0.1250	=12.2586

The bank will again choose the higher rate of 12.2586 and the sterling proceeds will therefore be £13 052.06.

(*c*) Because of the delay and short shipment the second forward contract has to be closed-out on 20 March.

It is necessary for Blacksheep to buy the whole of the Fr.160 000 at the spot rate of 12.1350 on 20 March in order to be able to sell them back to the bank at 12.2586 as agreed under the contract.

They will therefore be credited and debited as follows on that day:

160,000 @ 12.2586=£13 052.06 credited
160,000 @ 12.1350=£13 185.00 debited
N.B. This would most likely be posted to the account as a net debit of £132.94

(*d*) A new contract, as an extension of the old one, will be established on 20 March for 80 metric tons @ Fr.1600 per ton = 128 000. This will be a one month forward option and, as before, the bank will use the rate at the end of the option period, i.e. one month forward.

In determining the rate to use the bank will adopt the *diagonal rule* and add to the close-out rate (its selling rate) at one month's *buying* margin, thus:

	Selling	*Buying*
Spot	12.1350	12.1645
1 month discount	0.0245	0.0355

The bank will therefore add 0.0355 to its selling rate of 12.1350 to arrive at the rate of 12.1705 for the transaction.

The total expected proceeds are therefore £10 517.23.

Other questions

(The following are sample questions and no worked answers are provided.)

1. A British importer contracts to purchase 250 dozen pairs of shoes from Italy at a price of 45,000 lire per dozen, cif London airport.

Payment is to be made upon cable advice of dispatch by air freight, and consignments are to be made as follows:

100 dozen during April;
100 dozen during April/May;
50 dozen during May/June.

On 1 April, the importer asks his bank to cover him forward for these transactions.

The first and second consignments are made on 20 April and 10 May respectively. As the shoes are selling well, the importer arranges for the third consignment to be increased by 50 dozen and requests his bank to sell him the necessary extra amount of currency when the cable advice arrives on 5 June.

On the basis of the rates quoted below and exchange commission at 1 per mille, maximum £10 (to be charged on each transaction), calculate the total sterling cost to the importer.

		Lire
1 April	Spot	1504–1505
	1 month forward	4–1 premium
	2 months forward	9–6 premium
	3 months forward	14–11 premium
5 June	Spot	1505–1506

(*Inst. of Bankers*)

2. On 1 March, a London merchant contracts to buy 1200 tons of cattle-

cake from the Argentine at a price of \$65.70 per ton, of which 200 tons is to be shipped during March and the balance of 1000 tons not later than 30 April, payment in each case being by cable transfer immediately on shipment.

He at once resells the goods to a German buyer, at a price of DM275 per ton, on terms of payment one month after shipment.

The London merchant asks you to arrange the necessary forward exchange for him, the rates on 1 March being as below:

	\$	*DM*
Spot	2.8012 – 2.8037	11.18 – 11.18½
1 month forward	0.375 – 0.34 c pm	1¼ – 1 pfg pm
2 months forward	0.625 – 0.59 c pm	2½ – 2¼ pfg pm
3 months forward	0.875 – 0.83 c pm	3¾ – 3½ pfg pm

Exchange commission is 1 per mille, maximum £10.

How much gross profit does the London merchant make on the transaction?

(*Inst. of Bankers*)

3. Your customer ABC Ltd places an order in New York on 10 September for forty-eight machines at a cost of \$6000 each. Shipment is to be not later than 10 December, in lots of not less than sixteen each. The payment terms are 33⅓ per cent on placing the order, the balance to be remitted to New York on receipt of cable advice that each consignment of machines is on the quayside in New York awaiting shipment.

You are instructed to make the immediate payment on 14 September of \$96 000 by mail payment order and to cover the balance forward.

Cables are received by the the customer on 9 October, 14 November and 3 December advising that in each case sixteen machines are ready for shipment. The customer instructs you to make the remittances by cable on 11 October, 15 November and 7 December. The rates of exchange on 14 September are:

Spot	2.4612 – 2.4625
1 month forward	0.34 – 0.46 c dis
2 months forward	0.46 – 0.59 c dis
3 months forward	0.62 – 0.75 c dis

Show the total debits to the customer's account on the dates concerned. You should allow for:

(*a*) exchange commission at 1 per mille, minimum 25p, maximum £10, on the spot deal and the total forward deal;
(*b*) cable expenses of £1.50 per cable;
(*c*) mail payment order postages of 5p. (*Inst. of Bankers*)

4. On 15 March a British merchant orders two machines from a West German factory at cif UK port prices of DM105 000 and DM104 466 respectively, for shipment within one month, on '30 days (from bill of lading date) open account' terms (i.e. shipping documents are sent to the British merchant, for him to remit thirty days after bill of lading date).

The British merchant at once covers the exchange forward.

The machine costing DM105 000 is shipped on a bill of lading dated 12 April, but the UK merchant is advised that because of a fire at the West German factory, shipment of the second machine will be between two weeks and a month later than arranged. On the maturity date of the forward exchange contract the UK merchant therefore arranges the appropriate extension of the unused balance, at the rates then ruling.

The second machine is eventually shipped on a bill of lading dated 16 May.

On the basis of the exchange rates below, and exchange commission of 1 per mille, maximum £10 per item (*not* to be charged on the extension of the original forward exchange contract), calculate the total cost of the machines.

Rates	*15 March*	*15 May*
Spot	11.12½ – 11.13	11.13 – 11.13½
1 month forward (premium)	¾ – ½ pfg	½ – ¼ pfg
2 months forward (premium)	1½ – 1¼ pfg	1 – ¾ pfg
3 months forward (premium)	3 – 2¾ pfg	2¼ – 2 pfg

(*Inst. of Bankers*)

5. Your customer, Home Appliances Ltd, has signed a contract with a German company to purchase 1200 washing machines at a price of DM1000 each, cif London. Delivery is to be phased over a period of six months and payment is to be made by means of an irrevocable letter of credit valid for six months from 1 March. You establish the credit on 1 March, for the full value of all the machines and, at the same time, sell the total amount of Deutschemarks forward to your customer, option six months, to meet payments under the credit.

Documents are presented under the credit as follows:

15 April for 400 machines;
24 May for 200 machines;
16 July for 300 machines;
3 August for 300 machines.

(*a*) Using the rates below show the total value of the forward contract and the rate applicable.

(*b*) What were the amounts debited to the customer's account on the various dates concerned including exchange commission at 1 per mille, maximum £10, on the total forward exchange contract, but ignoring any commission on the letter of credit?

	Spot	*Forward 1 month*	*Forward 3 months*	*Forward 6 months*
1 March	7.10 – 7.13	9¼ – 8¼ pfg pm	21¼ – 19¼ pfg pm	30¼ – 28¼ pfg pm

(*Inst. of Bankers*)

6. From the rates below determine the total sterling due to a trader who buys goods value DM19 510 cif Frankfurt paying for them at once and sells them on three months credit terms against his invoice for DM21 422.50 cif Frankfurt.

Spot DM3.9020 – 3.9050
1 month 0.30 – 0.20 pfg pm
2 months 0.50 – 0.40 pfg pm
3 months 1.10 – 1.00 pfg pm

Exchange commission of 1 per mille, maximum £10, is charged on each transaction. *(Inst. of Freight Forwarders)*

7. On 1 May a UK importer contracted to buy goods from a Pittsburgh manufacturer for US $113 600, payment terms involving remittances to be made as follows:

US $14 320 by cable at once.
US $59 640 on 1 June.
US $39 640 between 1 June and 1 July.

All the above payments were made on time and on the 1 July the importer paid another invoice of US $3924 in respect of further goods ordered. Determine from the rates below the total sterling amount paid. Ignore exchange commission.

1 May spot 2.0000 – 2.0030
1 month forward 1.20 c – 0.90 c pm
2 months forward 1.80 c – 1.50 c pm
1 July spot 1.9620 – 1.9640 *(Inst. of Freight Forwarders)*

8. Held & Sons are steel stockholders in London whose account is operated on an overdraft basis. Hitherto they have obtained their stocks in the UK, but they are now forced to look elsewhere for supplies of a specialized steel, for which they have received the following quotations:

Country	*Price per ton*	*Terms for payment*
(*a*) Belgium	B.fr.11 030 fob Antwerp	Open account—settlement 1 month after shipment
(*b*) Spain	S.pts.26 500 c & f London	Draft drawn payable 2 months after shipment D/A (collection charges for buyer)
(*c*) France	F.fr.1697 cif London	Irrevocable documentary credit payment 3 months after shipment
(*d*) Germany	DM740 franco Buyer's premises	Payment with order

Using the additional information set out below show by calculating the cost of 100 tons of steel which of quotations (*a*), (*b*) and (*c*) would be cheapest for your customers:

Freight charges from any Western European port	£5 per ton
Insurance (to be effected on 110 per cent of c & f value or equivalent)	1 per cent payable in sterling
Collection charges (total for both banks)	$\frac{1}{4}$ per cent
Documentary credit charges (including acceptance commission)	$\frac{3}{4}$ per cent
Overdraft interest (one month may be considered as one twelfth of a year)	15 per cent p.a.

Ignore all other possible charges

It is to be assumed that your customers would have covered any exchange risk on day of shipment, in accordance with rates quoted below, and that all payments and charges relative to any particular quotation are debited on the same day.

		1 month	*2 months*	*3 months*
Belgium	64.00–64.10	15–5 c pm	26–16 pm	38–28 pm
Spain	145.45–145.55	100–150 c dis	220–290 dis	335–435 dis
France	9.32–9.33	2–1 c pm	3–2 pm	4–3 pm

(*Inst. of Bankers*)

9. John Brown & Co. have, until now, purchased spare parts in the UK, but have recently agreed with a German supplier to purchase direct and to make payment in DM. Their normal requirement is 500 items per calendar month. The arrangement is that the supplies will reach this level in the third month after the commencement of production, on the basis of progressively doubling the previous month's output and delivery. The price of each item is DM247.50. Payment for each consignment is due six days after despatch from the factory.

(*a*) Define and explain briefly the purpose of a forward contract in such circumstances.

(*b*) A contract was signed and production began immediately at the beginning of January. The despatch of the goods took place on 20 January, 16 February and 23 March. On the basis of the following rates, calculate the difference in the cost to John Brown & Co. that would have resulted if they had entered into forward contracts at the commencement of the transaction.

	Spot	*1 month*	*2 months*	*3 months*
2 January	$3.73\frac{1}{2}$–$3.74\frac{1}{2}$	$3\frac{3}{8}$–$2\frac{3}{8}$ pfg pm	$6\frac{1}{8}$–$5\frac{1}{8}$ pfg pm	9–8 pfg pm
26 January	$3.72\frac{3}{4}$–$3.73\frac{3}{4}$	$3\frac{1}{8}$–$2\frac{1}{8}$ pfg pm	$6\frac{1}{4}$–$5\frac{1}{4}$ pfg pm	$9\frac{1}{4}$–$8\frac{1}{4}$ pfg pm
22 February	$3.70\frac{3}{4}$–$3.71\frac{3}{4}$	$3\frac{1}{4}$–$2\frac{1}{4}$ pfg pm	$6\frac{1}{2}$–$5\frac{1}{2}$ pfg pm	$9\frac{5}{8}$–$8\frac{5}{8}$ pfg pm
29 March	3.69–3.70	$3\frac{1}{2}$–$2\frac{1}{2}$ pfg pm	$6\frac{3}{8}$–$5\frac{3}{8}$ pfg pm	$9\frac{1}{8}$–$8\frac{1}{8}$ pfg pm

(*Inst. of Bankers*)

10. Your customers, Autobuy Ltd, signed a contract to supply a total of 120 vehicles to a buyer in the US. The terms are as follows:

Price: US $24.725 per vehicle cif New York.
Delivery: Three equal monthly shipments January/February/March.
Special conditions: Penalties for short shipments in the first two months relating solely to the shipment due that particular month:

(*a*) first month US $750 per vehicle not shipped;
(*b*) second month US $500 per vehicle not shipped;
(*c*) any such shortages to be made up by increased shipment in third month.

Payment:
(*a*) 20 per cent of total contract value (i.e. of 120 vehicles) on first shipment.
(*b*) 30 per cent of total contract value one month after first shipment.
(*c*) 50 per cent of total contract value three months after first shipment.

(All adjustments regarding penalty clause to be made from final 50 per cent.)

Your customers, on making a first shipment of only thirty-six vehicles on 4 January, decide to cover their then estimated exchange risk by entering into forward contracts, on the basis that they will be in a position to meet the further shipments fully. They are able to ship only thirty vehicles in the second month, but complete the contract by shipping fifty-four vehicles in the final period.

From the following quoted rates, ignoring all commission, calculate the total proceeds they would receive in sterling:

	4 January	*4 April*
Spot	US $1.9295 – 1.9365	US $1.9400 – 1.9410
1 month forward	0.72 – 0.62 c pm	0.63 – 0.53 c pm
3 months forward	1.47 – 1.37 c pm	1.22 – 1.12 c pm

(*Inst. of Bankers*)

11. Tiger Moth Ltd, customers of your bank, are a sterling-based aircraft charter company operating mainly in the UK, Western Europe and the Caribbean. They have been awarded a contract to provide freight and passenger services for a number of remote islands in the mid-Atlantic and the Caribbean.

The contract, which is guaranteed by the governments of the various territories, is to be signed on 1 June. The value of the contract to the customer is US $1.5 million, and it will be necessary for Tiger Moth Ltd to charter three aircraft at a total cost of US $900 000. Payment and receipt terms are as follows:

Payments by Tiger Moth
(*a*) One-third upon signing the contract.
(*b*) One-third six months after signing the contract.
(*c*) One-third twelve months after signing the contract.

Receipts by Tiger Moth
(*a*) One-third ($500 000) three months after signing the contract (guaranteed).

(*b*) One-third ($500 000) six months after signing the contract (guaranteed).
(*c*) A third payment of up to $500 000 (one-third of the contract value) twelve months after signing the contract. (According to the contract the payment may be reduced if Tiger Moth generate extra business on their own account).

Your customers ask you to make the best possible financial arrangements to obviate any risks to them.

US dollar rates on 1 June 19x5 are as follows:

Spot	1.3195 – 1.3210
3 months	0.16 – 0.21 c dis
6 months	0.44 – 0.72 c dis
12 months	0.85 – 1.05 c dis
Spot 1 June	1.4610 – 1.4670

You should take note of the following additional information and assumptions:

(*a*) The *full* expected *net* receipts are sold forward on 1 June 19x5 for delivery on 1 June 19x6
(*b*) For the purpose of this question, ignore the possibility of any other forward contracts that might be arranged.
(*c*) The contract is performed in its entirety except that, when the third payment falls due on 1 June 19x6, it is calculated that Tiger Moth Ltd have generated extra business on their own account that requires a reduction in the contract payment from US $500 000 to US $250 000. (The 'extra earnings' should be ignored for the purpose of the calculations required in (*c*) below).
(*d*) All commercial risks, such as chartering risks, credit risks, etc., that may be included in the commercial contract may be ignored.
(*e*) Any charges or interest payable in connection with any overdraft or transfers may be ignored

What advice would you give to the company covering the following:

(*a*) The risk that the company has to face in accepting the contract awarded to them.
(*b*) The method you would recommend to Tiger Moth Ltd in order to minimize the risk mentioned in (*a*).
(*c*) A statement of the currency account you would operate on behalf of the customers, including a calculation at the end of the period showing the total sterling proceeds that would be credited to the customers' sterling account. (*Inst. of Bankers*)

12. Your customers, Scrap Metals Ltd are scrap metal dealers exploiting the flourishing merchanting trade between the US and the Far East. They buy scrap

metal from the US and sell it to buyers in the Republic of Korea, Republic of China (Taiwan) and Japan.

The American suppliers generally require secure methods of payment, and your customers have been able to arrange for the buyers in the Far East to establish in their favour (i.e. the first beneficiary—your customers) an irrevocable letter of credit, transferable in whole or in part, some of the terms of which are as follows:

Amount: *about* US$1 000 000
Expiry: 10 July in London (i.e. at your counters).
Covering: A shipment of non-ferrous metal scrap to be effected in one lot between 1 May and 30 June inclusive.
Shipment: From San Francisco to Kaohsiung.

On 1 April, you, as the advising bank, are asked to transfer 75 per cent of the value of the letter of credit in favour of a second beneficiary—the US Scrap Co. Inc., San Francisco. On the same day your customers ask you to cover their potential earnings of US $250 000 forward, based upon the following rates:

1 April	Spot $1.7755 – $1.7775
1 month forward	0.36 – 0.41 c dis
2 months forward	1.18 – 1.23 c dis
3 months forward	2.40 – 2.45 c dis
15 May	Spot $1.7950 – 1.8000

The documents are presented in order at your counters on 15 May. The documents cover a shipment valued at US $760 000 exactly. On that day your customers substitute their invoices to allow claims for the full value of the scrap metal shipped. In effect, they are increasing the value of their invoices by one-third of the value of the invoices presented by the second beneficiary. This claim brings it into line with the amount available under the letter of credit.

NOTE: *For the purposes of this question, assume that the entries will be passed on the day that the documents are presented, namely, 15 May. Ignore the proceeds which will be made available to the second beneficiary in the US and any commissions that might be claimed in connection with documents presented under the credit.*

You are asked to supply the following:

(*a*) Your calculations showing the rates that would be applied, and a final figure of the sterling proceeds that will be credited to your customer's account.
(*b*) Brief notes indicating any specific international rules that apply to this particular transaction. (*Inst. of Bankers*)

6
PAYMENTS ABROAD

TRADING ON OPEN ACCOUNT

TO the exporter of goods, the most satisfactory arrangement as far as payment is concerned is to receive it in advance. Whilst this is practicable for small consignments, such as postal packages sent to a large number of individual customers who have ordered goods in response to a mail-order advertisement, it is unlikely that many large orders would be paid for in this way.

At the other extreme, because he has developed a sound relationship with the foreign buyer of his goods, an exporter may decide to trade with him on an *open account* basis. The seller dispatches the goods, debits the purchaser's account and sends his invoice. At some agreed period of time, say once a month or every three months or after an agreed time following the dispatch of each consignment, the buyer sends a remittance to the seller to settle the outstanding balance on the account. The supplier sends the documents relating to freight and insurance etc. to the buyer so that he may take possession of the goods when they arrive.

Whichever of these two extremes is decided upon, payment in advance or trading on open account, the same methods of payment are available to the importer: these are *telegraphic transfers* (TT) or SWIFT, *mail transfers* (MT), and *cheques* or *drafts.*

A *telegraphic transfer* is an instruction from the importer's bank to the exporter's bank to transfer some of the balance on its account to the person named in the transfer. The importer pays his bank the local currency equivalent of the sum in foreign currency that the correspondent bank hands over to the exporter. The bank's charges for the transfer will be either paid by the importer or deducted from the currency paid to the exporter. The banks' own telecommunications system, called SWIFT, has in recent years taken over much of the work of the TT system. SWIFT stands for Society for Worldwide Interbank Financial Telecommunications which is an organization based in Brussels and owned by 1200 member banks throughout the world. It is designed to cope with a million messages a day, and because these transfers are telegraphic, they, like TTs, are the speediest form of payment; urgent messages take as little as twenty minutes and those that are not urgent take only about two hours. Facilities exist for retrieving data up to four months old and for monitoring and controlling the priorities given to messages.

Mail transfers are similar to TTs, but are less immediate because the advice to the correspondent bank is sent by mail and not by telegraph. The normal practice now is to send all mail transfers by airmail.

The importer could, if he wished, send his own *cheque* to the exporter, but before doing so he would have to make sure that the exporter was in agreement (it should be written into the contract between the importer and exporter). When an exporter receives such a cheque, he sends it to his bank for collection. It may take some weeks for the cheque to be presented to the bank on which it is drawn and for the notification that it has been paid to be received, and the expenses of collection are likely to be quite considerable. Thus, to the exporter, it is far less satisfactory to receive a cheque drawn by the importing firm than to receive a cheque drawn by a foreign bank which would be readily purchased for cash by the exporter's bank.

A cheque drawn by the importer's bank in this way is known as a *banker's draft.* This may be a draft drawn in terms of foreign currency by a bank on its account with a bank overseas, i.e. it is an instruction to the correspondent bank overseas to debit the account of the bank drawing the draft and pay over the amount of it to the exporter. Alternatively it may be a draft drawn by the bank upon itself in which case it will be in sterling and the overseas collecting bank will have its account with the British bank credited with the proceeds.

BILLS AND CREDITS

By far the greater part of international merchandise transactions is settled by *bill of exchange*, either a *clean* bill, i.e. without documents relating to the goods concerned attached to it, or a *documentary* bill, in which case the documents are attached. If documents are attached then the bill may be drawn under a documentary credit, which gives the exporter the satisfaction of knowing that if the documents are in order he will receive payment either immediately or at an agreed future date. The documentary credit is thus a very satisfactory method of payment as far as he is concerned, and this device will be considered in detail in Chapters 7 and 8. Bills of exchange must also be thoroughly understood and these are the subject of Chapter 9. The rest of the present chapter will be concerned with the ways in which the banks actually conduct their transactions with one another, not only to make payments on behalf of importers and to receive payments from exporters, but also to provide financial services for the customer travelling abroad.

PAYMENTS BETWEEN BANKS

When a bank's customer instructs it to make a payment abroad on his behalf it will do so by using whatever form of transfer it is called upon to use from those listed in the first part of this chapter (see pp. 86–7). As we saw in Chapter 1 (p. 1) the bank must, in making this transfer, bring about appropriate book-keeping entries in the books of the banks involved and it is these entries we must now concern ourselves with. The banking student in particular must be fully conversant with this book-keeping aspect.

Banks keep two types of international account, vostro and nostro accounts. 'Vostro' means *your* and is the term used when communicating with a bank overseas to inform it that its account has been credited, e.g. 'We have credited your vostro account with £10 000 in respect of the bill of exchange sent to us for collection.' The term 'nostro' means *our* and this is used when communicating with a bank overseas to instruct them to debit a foreign currency account, e.g. 'Pay 10 000 francs to XYZ and debit our nostro account with that amount.' A London bank's accounts in sterling in its own books maintained on behalf of correspondent banks abroad are its vostro accounts whilst those belonging to itself held with banks abroad in foreign currencies are its nostro accounts. In order to make a payment to a bank abroad either of the two activities mentioned above will take place, but not both, i.e. *either* that bank's vostro account will be credited in the books of the London bank *or* the London bank's account abroad will be debited. The reader will realize that if both things are done the transaction will be paid for twice. It is, however, necessary for a bank to keep a record of its nostro account in just the same way that a customer of a bank will keep a record of his account, albeit only on the cheque stubs, in order to be able to verify the bank statement when it is received. The bank's record account is merely a mirror account, reflecting the transactions that have taken place in the nostro account, but it is usually incorporated into its book-keeping system.

The balances on its nostro accounts represent a bank's holding of foreign currencies (apart from those relatively small amounts held in the form of notes and coins), and it is these holdings that are used by the bank's dealers in the foreign exchange market. The bank will sell surplus balances of a currency and buy in additional balances if they are required. Transactions by foreign exchange dealers are followed through behind the scenes. For instance, if Barclays agrees to sell Midland \$100 000, an instruction will be sent to a bank in, possibly, New York, with which Barclays holds a nostro dollar account, instructing that bank to debit that account with \$100 000 and credit the nostro account of Midland Bank either with that bank or with another bank in New York.

The transactions in a mirror account are the opposite to those on a nostro account so that, in carrying out the transactions above, Barclays will credit its mirror account with the \$100 000 that has been debited to its nostro account. At any one time the credit balance on its nostro account in the US will be reflected by a debit balance on the mirror account. In order fully to appreciate the book-keeping aspects of transactions between banks, it would be helpful to the reader if we looked at a few typical transactions. If a customer of Barclays Bank wants to make a payment of DM5000 by telegraphic transfer to someone in Germany, Barclays will take written instructions on its standard TT form. These instructions will include the name and address of the beneficiary and an indication as to whether the customer is to pay the charges or whether they are to be deducted from the remittance. Barclays Bank will then debit its customer with the sterling equivalent of the DM5000 at the spot rate of exchange and instruct a bank in Germany by SWIFT or cable to debit its nostro account with DM5000 after paying the sum over to the beneficiary. Barclays will credit its mirror account with the DM5000. If the customer of Barclays asked for a banker's draft for DM5000 the mechanics involved would be somewhat different but the net result would be the same, i.e. the nostro account would be debited. Barclays would draw its draft on the bank in West Germany and notify that bank the draft had been drawn. Barclays would hand the draft to its customer and debit his account with the sterling equivalent. When the draft is received by the beneficiary in West Germany he would pay it into his account with a German bank. If his bank was not the bank on which the draft was drawn, it would be sent through the bankers' clearing in Germany. The drawee bank would debit Barclays' nostro account when the draft was received and Barclays would credit its mirror account.

For payments in sterling the usual method of settlement is by way of crediting the foreign bank's vostro account with the sterling amount. A TT or SWIFT for £10 000 to a beneficiary in West Germany would therefore involve Barclays in sending TT instructions to a bank in Germany to pay over the equivalent of £10 000 in sterling to the beneficiary and at the same time informing the bank that £10 000 had been credited to its vostro account. If payment was to be made by way of banker's draft, Barclays would draw a draft upon itself and hand it to its customer who would send it to the beneficiary abroad. The beneficiary would then ask his bank to negotiate the draft or collect the proceeds for him. In either case the German bank would send the draft to Barclays and ask for the £10 000 to be credited to its vostro account. If it negotiated the draft it would pay the Deutschemark equivalent less discount to the beneficiary's account immediately, or if it collected the draft would wait until notification from Barclays that its vostro account had been credited before crediting the customer with the Deutschemark equivalent, less the charges for the collection. In both of these examples concerning a payment in sterling, if the beneficiary in West Germany had a sterling account with his bank, he would be credited in sterling with sterling face value of the transfer or draft less any charges involved.

Where a payment is to be made in the currency of a third country, Barclays will use a nostro account in that country in order to complete the transactions. For instance, if the payment to the German beneficiary was to be by TT or SWIFT in French francs, Barclays would send a message to a bank in France instructing it to make the payment (say 20 000 francs) and to debit Barclays' nostro account with that sum. If the German beneficiary had a French franc account with the French bank it would be credited with that amount, or if required by the beneficiary, the French bank could instruct a German bank by mail or TT to pay the beneficiary the Deutschemark equivalent, and the French bank would then credit the German bank's French franc nostro account. If Barclays bank were asked to make the payment by banker's draft they would draw it on a French bank and debit their customer with the sterling equivalent. The customer would then send the draft to the beneficiary in Germany who would pay it into his French franc account, if he had one, or ask his bank to negotiate or collect the draft and credit his Deutschemark account with the proceeds. The German bank would then send the draft to the French bank on which it was drawn asking for its nostro account to be credited. Barclays' nostro account with the French bank would be debited.

The reader will appreciate that the terms nostro and vostro will be looked at in completely opposite ways by the two banks involved. To Barclays Bank its Deutschemark accounts in West Germany are its nostro accounts, 'our' accounts, whilst the West German bank's accounts in sterling with Barclays are regarded by Barclays as vostro, 'your', accounts. To the German banks the Deutschemark accounts are vostro accounts and the sterling accounts are nostro accounts! The student reader must therefore be very careful in an examination to make it clear whose nostro and vostro accounts he is writing about.

TRAVEL TRANSACTIONS

Travellers abroad make use of the banking system to finance their journeys and their requirements are met in a number of ways.

Firstly, the traveller may take his own country's banknotes abroad and as there is no exchange control in the UK there is no restriction on the amount that may be taken. However, he would be unwise to take more of these notes than he required for the actual journey to and from Britain, taking into account whether or not he was travelling on a British vessel or aircraft. Beyond that need he would run into difficulties in exchanging his sterling notes for local currency in the countries he visited, especially outside banking hours, and would not, in any case, get as favourable a rate of exchange as he would if he used other methods of financing himself. There is also the danger of theft of course.

Apart from a small amount of Bank of England notes, the traveller would be wise to obtain some foreign currency notes from a British bank before leaving on his journey. He can rely on getting these at a reasonable rate of exchange from a British bank and would be sure of coping with his immediate spending needs in the countries he visits without having to wait for the banks to open or relying on the willingness of his hotel, for instance, to provide him with local currency in exchange maybe for a traveller's cheque.

In addition to local currency notes it would be prudent to take some traveller's cheques and/or some Euro-currency cheques. As far as traveller's cheques are concerned, these could be either in sterling or in foreign currency. Traveller's cheques are convenient and safe. The traveller signs the cheques once in front of the cashier in the issuing bank and then again in front of the cashier in the bank abroad where he is encashing them, or at his hotel, if they are prepared to encash them or take them in settlement of his account. Usually, a refund can be claimed from the British bank if traveller's cheques are lost. If the cheques are in sterling the traveller must bear the exchange loss for he will have little choice but to accept the rate of exchange offered by the banks abroad. This risk can be avoided, however, by purchasing traveller's cheques in the UK that are denominated in foreign currency and this is possible as far as the main currencies are concerned. The rate of exchange is then determined by the bank in Britain and this may well be more favourable than the rates offered by banks abroad for sterling traveller's cheques, especially at a time when the value of the pound is depreciating. Traveller's cheques are issued in convenient denominations to suit the traveller's requirements

The alternative to traveller's cheques, Eurocheques, necessitates obtaining a special cheque guarantee card (a Eurocheque card) from the bank before travelling and most banks now supply the traveller with a number of special cheque forms which have to be used abroad instead of the customer's normal cheque. Eurocheques are usually written in the currency of the country in which the traveller is staying and are a convenient method of payment in shops and hotels, as well as a method of drawing local currency at a bank. Each cheque is guaranteed for approximately £100 and is eventually debited to the customer's current account at the rate of exchange that applies on the day on which the debiting takes place. Some banks have also made arrangements whereby their Eurocheque cards may be used to obtain currency from cash dispensers at banks in Europe. A small annual charge is made for the issue of a Eurocheque card and a small commission is added to the sterling amount when a cheque is debited to the customer's account.

A method of satisfying a traveller's foreign currency requirements that has become much less popular in recent years is the *letter of credit*, either in sterling or in foreign currency. There is always the danger of forgery, and in consequence some British banks have discontinued issuing traveller's letters of credit and persuade their customers to use other means of meeting their requirements. A personal letter of credit is in the form of a request to a bank abroad (if it is a fixed credit), or a number of banks abroad (if it is a circular letter of credit) to cash drafts drawn on the issuing bank for the customer up to a prescribed limit. The bank issues its customer with a separate document, called a *letter of indication*, that he signs in front of the cashier at the issuing bank. The document also bears the authorized signatures of the bank's officers, as does the letter of credit itself, and these signatures can be verified by the bank(s) abroad, who will hold copies of the issuing bank's authorized signatures. The traveller can draw drafts at the bank(s) abroad and his signature is then compared with that on the letter of indication and the letter of credit is marked with the amount that has been drawn. If the draft is in sterling, the traveller will be paid the foreign currency equivalent at the encashing bank's rate of exchange for such drafts at the time. If it is in local currency he will be paid in that currency and the amount will be debited to the issuing bank's nostro account. A draft in sterling would be sent for collection by the encashing bank with a request that its value be credited to its nostro account with the London bank (which would be a vostro account in the eyes of the London bank!).

A traveller may, if he wishes, have a remittance sent out by TT or SWIFT, or MT to a bank(s) abroad in anticipation of his arrival (and, in an emergency after he has arrived, when he may need funds in addition to those he has taken with him, this is certainly the method that would be adopted). In this way he is assured that his local currency requirements will be there when he arrives abroad, but he will be restricted to one or more points at which he can draw the currency and he will have to wait until the bank(s) is open. If he has a payment sent in the foreign currency required he will not run any exchange risk because his bank in the UK will have debited his account with the sterling equivalent at the outset. If the remittance is in sterling, on the other hand, the bank abroad will pay him in local currency at the rate of exchange appertaining at the time of payment.

Another possibility is for the traveller to take a banker's draft with him payable at a named correspondent bank. Here again he is restricted to one encashment point and he can only cash the draft during banking hours. If it is in sterling he runs the exchange risk but if it is in local currency this is not so.

Barclaycards and Access cards may be used abroad to buy goods and services at all establishments that are recognized outlets for these two systems. Barclaycards may be used to draw cash at banks that are part of the VISA system and Access cards can be used in this way through Mastercard. Transactions abroad against credit cards are converted into sterling by the credit organizations and debited to the users' accounts.

The financial requirements of business executives travelling abroad are provided by the banks according to the particular needs of the individuals concerned. Short, and maybe sudden, visits by a firm's employees can be catered for by foreign currency notes (if available in time), traveller's cheques and the use of cheque cards and credit cards, whilst for longer visits, in addition to these facilities, TTs can be made in advance of departure or on receipt of an urgent request from the firm once the traveller has arrived abroad. Where expatriate employees will need to be able to draw sums of money each month to cover expenses, a credit could be established with a bank in the country concerned to meet these drawings up to a revolving limit. The firm would have to nominate a person or persons who could be made responsible for administrating the facility.

To meet the financial needs of a firm's subsidiary company overseas engaged on a project over a short period of years, it is possible for a bank to arrange for an overdraft facility to be available at a correspondent bank in the country concerned, if the parent company does not wish to provide the funds.

EXAMINATION GUIDELINES

Examination questions related to the subject matter in this chapter come under two categories: firstly, those concerned with methods by which payments are made abroad and the book-keeping entries involved, and secondly, questions concerned with travel facilities and the remittance of funds for expatriates working abroad. Sometimes a question cuts across these two areas as is the case with Question 1 below.

Question 1

Oaken Casks Ltd markets oak barrels used in the wine and brewing industries. Sales have expanded and their sales director, A. Carpenter, calls to see you to discuss a business trip he is making to Australia to buy supplies of used oak barrels surplus to the requirements of an Australian wine producer.

REQUIRED

(*a*) Tabulate the various methods by which funds may be remitted to Australia in settlement of the company's debts.

(*b*) Describe the two fastest methods mentioned in (*a*) and the accounting procedures that will be involved in respect of a sterling and an Australian dollar transfer.

(*c*) Details of the travel facilities *appropriate to his needs* you would recommend to A. Carpenter in connection with his forthcoming trip.

SOLUTION

(*a*) (*i*) Telegraphic transfer (TT) by cable or telex.
(*ii*) SWIFT transfer (ordinary or urgent).
(*iii*) Mail transfer (MT).
(*iv*) Bankers' draft.

(*b*) The two fastest methods would be (*i*) and (*ii*), i.e. TT and SWIFT. Whether the transfer is made by TT or SWIFT, the accounting procedures will be the same. The only difference is in the method of notification, TT involving the use of Post Office cables or telex whilst the SWIFT system is a closed system not open to the public whereby messages are sent by a computerized method owned and controlled by the banks.

If the payment is to be made *in sterling*, the customers' account will be debited with the sterling amount plus charges (if they are to pay them). An Australian correspondent bank will be sent the message requesting it to notify and pay the beneficiary the sum, or to credit his account if it is known that he has an account with that bank. The beneficiary will most likely want the Australian dollar equivalent of the sterling and therefore the Australian bank will buy the sterling at the buying rate at the time. If the charges are to be paid by the beneficiary, they will be deducted from the proceeds, and the UK bank will deduct its charges from the amount remitted.

Settlement between the two banks will be achieved through the UK bank's vostro account in sterling held in the name of the correspondent bank. This account will be credited by the UK bank with the appropriate amount in sterling. The Australian bank will debit its nostro memorandum account with this amount as it is a record of the account (vostro to the UK bank and nostro to the Australian bank) held with the UK bank.

If the remittance is to be in Australian dollars, the customer of the UK bank will be debited with the sterling equivalent plus charges, if they are payable by the remitter. The instructions to the Australian bank will be the same as they would be for a sterling remittance, but the Australian bank will be authorized to debit the UK bank's nostro account with the amount concerned (this is a vostro account in the eyes of the Australian bank). The UK bank will credit its nostro memorandum account with the dollar sum. The Australian bank will pay over the dollars to the beneficiary or credit his account with them if there is one.

(*c*) For his particular purposes, the customer should be advised to take a small quantity of Australian dollars with him, plus some Australian dollar traveller's cheques. He should also be advised to take a credit card with him, such as an Access card or Barclaycard. If he is likely to be in Australia for any length of time and his itinerary is fairly certain, open credit facilities could be opened at named banks in particular towns so as to enable him to cash his ordinary cheques up to specific limits at these banks.

Question 2

Your customer, James Jones, has been sent by his company, an international corporation, to work in Stavanger for six months on a special assignment. His salary will continue to be paid in the UK in sterling and he asks for advice as to the best way of drawing money in Stavanger to meet his living expenses in Norway.

REQUIRED

(*a*) A list of suggestions *appropriate to his needs.*

(*b*) Brief notes on the advantages and disadvantages of each method.

SOLUTION

(*a*) (*i*) Arrangements should be made with a correspondent bank in Stavanger for a bank account to be opened for Mr Jones and monthly remittances sent on a standing order basis for the credit of that account. These should preferably be sent by TT or SWIFT and could be remitted in sterling or in kroner.

(*ii*) A Eurocheque card and some special cheques (if it is the bank's policy to issue special cheques for use under the Eurocheque scheme).

(*iii*) Open credit facility with a nominated bank to enable the customer to encash cheques drawn on the UK bank.

(*b*) (*i*) The customer will have the advantage of being able to draw cheques on the local bank, which should be more readily acceptable for transactions in Norway. It is possible, though doubtful, that the Norwegian bank would allow him a cheque card facility and the facility of being able to draw cash at automated teller machines. There is always the possibility of delay in receipt of remittances, especially if they are sent by MT, but the use of the SWIFT system should reduce this risk.

If remittances are in Norwegian kroner the rate of exchange will be determined by the UK bank, whereas if they are in sterling Mr Jones will have to accept the rate of exchange determined by the Norwegian bank.

(*ii*) Eurocheques are acceptable at only those banks and shops that participate in the Eurocheque scheme. There is a limit up to which each cheque is guaranteed (usually the equivalent of £100), but this limit is fairly generous.

(*iii*) The open credit facility will only be available at a particular nominated bank(s) and the customer will need to carry his UK cheque-book with him. Also, the cheques will be drawn in sterling and the exchange rate determined by the Norwegian bank.

Question 3

Runway Renovators Ltd, customers of yours, have recently been awarded a contract to repair and rebuild runways at Hong Kong International Airport. This is the first international contract they have been awarded and you are advised that payment is to be made to them in sterling. Although local subcontractors will be employed, your customers will have to send out a team of qualified people to supervise and control the operation, which is likely to take some eighteen months to complete.

You are approached by the company to discuss all the financial aspects of the contract. Arising out of the discussions, the company ask you the various methods by which they could pay, in local currency, part of the salaries of the expatriate staff in Hong Kong during their stay in the colony. In addition to the salary arrangements, the company will have to make available, to its senior representatives in Hong Kong, funds to cover company expenses.

REQUIRED

Your recommendations regarding:

(*a*) the provision of appropriate travel facilities for the company representatives at the start of the project;

(*b*) the payment in local currency of part of salaries of expatriate staff during their stay in Hong Kong;

(*c*) the provision of day-to-day funds for the company's senior representatives for expenses/disbursements during the eighteen months, indicating any disadvantages that there may be to the company in your suggestion.

SOLUTION

(*a*) (*i*) Each representative should have a small supply of Hong Kong dollar notes.

(*ii*) Traveller's cheques should be supplied (these could be in sterling, Hong Kong dollars or US dollars).

(*iii*) It should be recommended that each person takes a credit card with him or a banker's charge card, such as American Express. A company credit card could be made available to some or all of the representatives if the company are willing to accept the risk of misuse.

(*b*) Arrange with a bank in Hong Kong to open an account for each of the representatives and for them to be issued with cheque-books to be used locally. Take instructions to remit part of each representative's salary each month in sterling or in Hong Kong dollars. If the remittance(s) is to be in dollars the exchange rate will be determined by the UK bank, but if it is in sterling the exchange risk will have to be borne by the representatives, as the rate will be determined by the bank in Hong Kong when the remittance(s) is converted into local currency. It may be advisable for the company to arrange a series of forward contracts for the purchase of Hong Kong dollars.

(*c*) Arrange either a drawing facility for senior representatives with the Hong Kong bank, or alternatively arrange for that bank to open a local account in Hong Kong dollars to which remittances can be sent, in order that senior representatives may draw sums as required. The drawing facility, if that is the method used, could be either for cheques to be drawn in sterling or in Hong Kong dollars, and for an agreed amount each week or month so as to control the amount that may be drawn.

If the Hong Kong bank is out of funds whilst it is awaiting reimbursement, it will charge interest at the local rate and this will have to be passed on to the company.

Question 4

Two very good customers of yours, Mr and Mrs Jones, call to see you as a matter of urgency. They ask what suppport, advice and action you can provide in the circumstances described below.

(*a*) Their son, who is abroad on holiday in Portugal, requires funds immediately.

(*b*) Within the next few weeks, Mr and Mrs Jones plan to fly to the Spanish island of Minorca on holiday and, whilst they are there, to look for a suitable second home. They wish to know:

(*i*) the travel facilities you can arrange to cover their expenses whilst in Minorca;

(*ii*) what help and advice you can give in connection with finding and purchasing a suitable property.

REQUIRED

Set out in brief note form the action you would recommend in both cases and include the office procedures and accounting entries involved under (*a*).

SOLUTION

(*a*) (*i*) The funds are required immediately and therefore they should be remitted by TT or SWIFT to a correspondent bank near to where the son is staying. Authority should be taken from the parents to debit their account with the sterling equivalent of the escudos to be remitted plus charges, and on the application form for the transfer they should give as much information as possible to help the son identify himself when he calls to collect the currency. The son's passport number, if known, would be very helpful in this connection. If the son has suggested a bank through which the funds could be remitted, this would be helpful.

(*ii*) The Portuguese bank will be instructed in the TT or SWIFT message to debit the UK bank's nostro account with the escudos and to make the payment against positive identification.

(*iii*) When the parents' account is debited, the UK bank will at the same time credit its nostro memorandum account.

(*b*) (*i*) Supply customers with small amount of Spanish peseta notes and sufficient Spanish peseta traveller's cheques and/or sterling traveller's cheques for their estimated needs. If peseta traveller's cheques, the rate of exchange is fixed immediately and not left to the Spanish bank.

(*ii*) Instead of, or in addition to, the traveller's cheques, the customers could take a Eurocheque card and Eurocheques which will be guaranteed up to the equivalent of £100 each cheque. These can be used to obtain local currency at participating banks and to buy goods from shops that are prepared to accept them.

(*iii*) Advise the customers to take an Access or Barclaycard credit card or similar.

(*iv*) If the customers' stay in Minorca is likely to be a protracted, arrangements could be made to remit funds out to a named correspondent bank to be paid over to them against identification.

(*c*) (*i*) Arrange a letter of introduction to a bank asking that they arrange appointments for Mr and Mrs Jones with appropriate people, such as estate agents and a lawyer.

(*ii*) There is no exchange control in the UK and therefore it will be possible to remit funds if and when required to pay for a property. The customers must be advised to check whilst in Spain that this remittance will meet with the approval of the Spanish authorities, however.

(*iii*) If they do buy a property the Jones's might find it helpful to have a local bank account and this could be arranged through the correspondent bank to whom the letter of introduction is sent.

Other Questions

1\. (*a*) Define:

(*i*) a TT; (*ii*) a SWIFT payment; (*iii*) a banker's draft.

(*b*) Describe the procedure followed when a UK bank transfers by mail payment order on behalf of a UK resident a given sum of money to a beneficiary in Paris in French francs. (*Inst. of Freight Forwarders*)

2\. (*a*) List the various methods by which UK banks are involved in the remitting of funds abroad on behalf of their resident customers.

(*b*) Give the procedures to be adopted in respect of these methods, where an account relationship exists between the UK and overseas bank, and remittances are in one or other of their two currencies. State in your answer which of these procedures are common to the two currencies, and which relate only to sterling or to the other currency involved. Include an explanation of nostro and vostro accounts, and the way they are used in such transactions. (*Inst. of Bankers*)

3\. Your customers, Overseas Contractors Ltd, are engaged in large export contracts overseas, and they seek your advice as to the best ways in which funds can be provided in the following situations:

(*a*) very brief visits abroad from time to time by their managing director to a variety of countries;
(*b*) longer visits sometimes of uncertain duration by their marketing and sales directors;
(*c*) monthly expenses of up to a total of £10 000 incurred by their expatriate on-site engineers;
(*d*) working capital for a small overseas subsidiary over a period of about two years, during which time it is likely to become self-financing. (The parent company does not itself wish to provide the funds.)

(*Inst. of Bankers [adapted]*)

4. You call to see I.M.A. Bowler, a keen cricket fan and an esteemed personal customer. He is going to the West Indies for a two month tour to watch the forthcoming Test series and wishes to know what facilities you can arrange for him so that he will have ready access to funds, appropriate to his needs, for his expenses in the West Indies. Give brief notes setting out your recommendations. (*Inst. of Bankers*)

5. Every year Arthur Rose, a gardener of some standing, organizes party visits to many gardens throughout the world. This year he is organizing a number of visits to gardens in the US and, as in the past, each member of the party will pay for his hotel and travelling costs through Mr Rose's company, Hybrid Tea Ltd. Mr Rose now approaches you to make a series of payments in US dollars to various beneficiaries in the US. In addition, Mr Rose wishes to discuss the provision of suitable funds during the forthcoming visit.

Give a brief description of the following:

(*a*) The system by which you would arrange to remit the funds to the US.
(*b*) The appropriate accounting procedures employed.

Giving reasons, tabulate the travel facilities you would recommend that Mr Rose take with him on this tour to cover his expenses, limiting your answer to the facilities *appropriate to his needs*. (*Inst. of Bankers*)

7
DOCUMENTARY CREDITS: I

TYPES OF CREDITS

AN international code of practice for documentary credits is contained in the *Uniform Customs and Practice for Documentary Credits* (1983 *Revision*) drawn up by the International Chamber of Commerce (ICC) in conjunction with a committee of international bankers, an English version of which is given in full in Appendix I (see p. 215).

The *Uniform Customs and Practice* protects the banks involved in dealing with documentary credits provided they fulfil the requirements laid down. It is therefore important that the banker should be fully conversant with these requirements and this fact is reflected in the frequency with which examination questions are set on the subject. The provisions of the code of practice are considered in detail in this chapter and the next and the student reader would be wise to ensure that he is fully conversant with them.

A documentary credit is defined in Article 2 of *Uniform Customs and Practice:*

> Any arrangement however named or described, whereby a bank (the issuing bank), acting at the request and in accordance with the instructions of a customer (the applicant for the credit),
>
> (*i*) is to make payment to or to the order of a third party (the beneficiary), or is to pay, or accept bills of exchange (drafts) drawn by the beneficiary, or
>
> (*ii*) authorises another bank to make such payment or to pay, accept or negotiate such bills of exchange (drafts), against stipulated documents, provided that the terms and conditions of the credit are complied with.

The 'applicant for the credit' is the importer who asks his bank, 'the issuing bank', to arrange for a payment to be made to, or to the order of, 'the beneficiary', i.e. the exporter, or for the exporter's bills of exchange ('drafts') to be accepted or negotiated. Normally, the issuing bank will instruct a correspondent bank in the exporter's country (which need not be the exporter's own bank) to make the payment or to pay, accept or negotiate the bill of exchange, provided the stipulated documents have been received by that bank and the terms and conditions stipulated in the credit have been complied with.

From the exporter's point of view, payment by documentary credit is very satisfactory. He has the satisfaction of knowing that the importer's bank is willing to stand in the shoes of the importer and make the payment either immediately or at an agreed future time. All he has to do is to ship the goods on time and produce the commercial documents called for in the credit. But he must be sure that there is nothing technically wrong with these documents.

The letter of credit is addressed to the beneficiary and may or may not be *confirmed* by the correspondent bank. If the issuing bank simply asks the advising bank to pass on the credit to the beneficiary, in other words, act as a post office, then the credit is not confirmed, the bank concerned is simply the advising bank; but if the issuing bank authorizes or requests that bank to add its confirmation before passing the credit to the beneficiary, then it becomes a confirmed credit. Article 10 of the *Uniform Customs* stipulates that 'such confirmation constitutes a definite undertaking of the confirming bank in addition to that of the issuing bank, provided that the stipulated documents are presented and that the terms and conditions of the credit are complied with'.

The exporter is thus likely to be more satisfied with a confirmed credit than one not confirmed, for he would prefer to have an undertaking from a bank he knows rather than from an overseas bank about which he knows nothing, but what is more important is that he will find it much more convenient to obtain payment of the draft or to obtain acceptance of it, and if the credit is available by negotiation of drafts, these will be negotiated *without recourse.* Another important factor is that there is no currency exchange risk. Whereas a foreign bank may be precluded by government exchange control regulations from making a payment to a British exporter, a British confirming bank would not be restricted from making the payment. Furthermore, as far as credits opened in favour of a British exporter are concerned, the undertaking of a British bank to accept bills drawn by him would enable him to draw bills which would be readily discountable in the London money market. Bills drawn upon and accepted by offices of foreign banks outside the UK, i.e. foreign domicile bills, are not saleable on the London market, and are not eligible for re-discount at the Bank of England.

A credit is either revocable or irrevocable. A *revocable credit* 'may be amended or cancelled by the issuing bank at any moment without prior notice to the beneficiary' (Article 9). An importer may choose to open a revocable credit rather than an irrevocable one because it will give him greater control over the activities of the exporter. If the importer is not satisfied with the goods he receives or with delivery dates, or is in any other way annoyed with the way the exporter is handling his side of the contract, he can modify or cancel the documentary credit, or threaten to do so. As far as a bank is concerned, it has the right to be reimbursed for any payment, acceptance or negotiation made by it prior to receipt of notice of the modification or cancellation of a revocable credit.

An *irrevocable credit* is a 'definite undertaking of the issuing bank, provided that the stipulated documents are presented and the terms and conditions of the credit are complied with' (Article 10). The undertaking cannot be amended nor cancelled without the agreement of the issuing bank, the confirming bank (if any), and the beneficiary.

A documentary credit may be a *sight credit* or a *term* or *acceptance credit*,* or negotiation credit. A sight credit usually requires the exporter to draw a sight or demand draft and this is paid on presentation to the correspondent bank, provided that all the terms of the credit have been fulfilled. The modern tendency is for payment to be made upon presentation of the documents without the formality of drawing and presenting a sight draft. A term or acceptance credit requires the exporter to draw a draft of a particular usance, such as thirty, sixty or ninety days, or possibly longer. The credit will specify that the draft must be drawn upon the issuing bank or the confirming bank. The confirming bank may have been instructed to negotiate the bill for the exporter (*a negotiation credit*) or, if it is drawn upon itself, it will accept the bill and the exporter will then have a bank bill he can hold until maturity or discount at a fine rate of interest.

A credit may also be a *standby* letter of credit. As the name suggests, this is a credit that the beneficiary can fall back on if the need arises. Payment under the credit can be called upon if payment is not forthcoming under whatever other arrangement for payment has been made. A credit may also provide for a *deferred payment*, in which case payment will be made on a date determinable in accordance with the stipulations in the credit.

There is no standard form of documentary credit; in fact they vary considerably depending upon the precise functions they are intended to

* This type of documentary acceptance credit must be distinguished from an acceptance credit issued by a merchant bank to an importer to enable him to pay a foreign exporter when the goods are shipped, or to a British exporter as a means of obtaining immediate finance against term bills drawn on the importer. The acceptance credit of a merchant bank is discussed in Chapters 10 and 13.

fulfil. They are designed to meet the circumstances of each particular case. However, the ICC has endeavoured to encourage the banks to introduce a suggested form of standardized credit that is uniform in both size and layout but so far without much success.

OPENING A CREDIT

If a documentary credit is to be opened, it is usually stipulated in the contract between the importer and the exporter. It is up to these two parties to fulfil the contract and the banker is in no way obliged to see that the terms of the contract are adhered to. Article 3 of *Uniform Customs* states that credits, by their nature, are separate transactions from the sales or other contracts on which they may be based and banks are in no way concerned with or bound by such contracts. If, for instance, an importer asks to defer payment because the goods were shipped earlier than arranged in the contract (as in Question 6 on p. 142) such a request must be declined if the exporter has nevertheless fulfilled the terms of the documentary credit. It is up to the importer to ensure that such matters as the earliest and latest dates for shipment are clearly stipulated in the credit. The banker's mandate is in the instructions to open the credit and he must ensure that these instructions are clear and precise so that no dispute can arise concerning their fulfilment. The credit, too, must be clear and must pass on to the exporter the provisions laid down in the instructions to the bank. These points are covered by Article 5 of *Uniform Customs and Practice*, which stipulates that 'Instructions for the issuance of credits, the credits themselves, instructions for any amendments thereto and the amendments themselves must be complete and precise. In order to guard against confusion and misunderstanding, issuing banks should discourage any attempt to include excessive detail in the credit or any amendment thereto'.

The point about 'excessive detail' applies especially to the description of the goods, for the banker is not a merchant and cannot be expected to know much about the technical terminology used in particular trades. He is much happier when his instructions refer to commodities in general terms so that when he is presented with an invoice referring in considerable detail to the goods concerned, he needs to satisfy himself only to the extent that these are, for instance, 100 bales of wool.

Figs. 7.1 and 7.2 give a typical request form used in opening a documentary credit and also the general instructions to the customer on the completion of the form. It will be seen from the latter that the customer is advised that it should be clearly understood that the bank is not directly concerned with the proper fulfilment of the contract between the seller and the buyer. If conditions are brought into the credit not strictly within the agreement between seller and buyer, difficulties are likely to arise between bank and beneficiary. To assist the customer in providing the correct information and instructions, the form sets out the main items, requiring the importer to cross out that which is not applicable and to fill in the blank spaces.

As a natural corollary to the implementation of the *Uniform Customs and Practice for Documentary Credits*, the ICC has now drawn up a set of standard forms applicable to most documentary credit transactions as well as the standard documentary credits referred to on p. 108. These forms are based on the terminology of the *Uniform Customs* and include various headings that should make it possible to give clear, accurate and complete instructions so as to eliminate the difficulties that arise in practice when the terms used are incorrect or confusing. However, these have not as yet been commonly adopted by the British banks.

The specimen application form in Fig. 7.1 and the specimen documentary credit given in Fig. 7.3 should be compared, and it will be seen how the instructions given by the importer are passed on in the letter of credit to the exporter. It will be noticed that on both the application form and the credit itself the following clause is contained: 'Except so far as otherwise expressly stated, this Credit is subject to the *Uniform Customs and Practice for Documentary Credits* (1983 Revision), International Chamber of Commerce Brochure No. 400).' In effect, all the terms and conditions of this code of practice are thus written into the contract between the bank and the customer to open a documentary credit, and the bank is thus likely to gain the protection of a court of law should there be a dispute concerning a documentary credit provided that it fulfils these terms and conditions. There can be clauses in the credit that are contrary to the uniform code, but these must be *expressly stated.*

The applicant for the credit is required to stipulate the date by which the documents must be presented under the credit, for payment, acceptance or negotiation (*Uniform Customs*, Article 46). The words 'to', 'until', 'till', and words of similar import applying to this expiry date or to any other term date in the credit include the date mentioned (Article 51), and where the expiry date occurs on a day when the banks are normally closed, the period of validity is extended to the first following business day. Where the expiry date is extended in this way, a bank must certify on the documents

Metropolitan Bank Limited

Request to open Documentary Credit

Branch DOWNTOWN Date 2nd January

Please open for my/our account a Documentary Credit, in accordance with the undermentioned particulars.
I/We agree that, except so far as otherwise expressly stated, this Credit will be subject to the Uniform Customs and Practice for Documentary Credits (1983 Revision), International Chamber of Commerce Publication No. 400.
I/We undertake to execute (if not already executed) the Bank's usual Form of Indemnity.

Signed Downtown Import Co.Ltd.

Entries must not be made in this margin	When completing this form please follow carefully the general instructions overleaf. **Delete as appropriate*
Type of credit	**Irrevocable** i.e. cannot be cancelled without beneficiaries' agreement ~~**Revocable** i.e. subject to cancellation~~
Method of advice	*airmail/~~*cable~~ ~~*full rate~~ ~~cheapest rate~~ *full advice ~~brief details~~
Advising Bank	*As far as possible this should be left to Metropolitan Bank Limited*
Name and Address of beneficiary	Fabbrica Speciale,S/A,Milan
Amount	£100,000 say One Hundred Thousand Pounds
Availability	Valid until 31st March (*Enter date*) in Milan (*Enter place*) for *negotiation/acceptance/payment This credit is available by drafts drawn at 90 days sight accompanied by the required documents
Documents required	Invoice *Full set shipped Bills of Lading to order and blank endorsed, marked *Freight paid/ ~~freight payable at destination~~ or ~~*Air Consignment Note~~ or ~~*Combined Transport Document Issued by~~ ______ } ~~evidencing goods address to~~ ______ ~~marked *Freight paid/freight payable at destination~~
†	*Insurance *Policy/~~Certificate~~ for invoice amount plus 10 % covering Marine and War Risks and including other conditions and risks as follows: "theft,pilferage and non-delivery W.P.A." ~~*Insurance effected by~~ ______ ~~where no insurance is called for~~ **Other Documents** Certificate of Italian origin
Quantity & description of goods	200,000 SPARKING PLUGS
Price per unit *if any*	£ 0.50p
Terms & relative port or place	*C.I.F., ~~C. & F., F.O.B., F.A.S., F.O.R.~~, etc. *This information is required in all cases*
Despatch/Shipment	From Genoa to London Part Shipments *allowed/~~not allowed~~ Transhipment * allowed/~~not allowed~~
Documents to be presented	For *negotiation/~~acceptance/payment~~ within 90 days of the date of issue of the Bills of Lading or other shipping documents but in any event within the credit validity
Special instructions *if any*	No Special Instructions

Fig. 7.1. Request form for opening a documentary credit

General instructions for opening Documentary Credit

Responsibility at Bank

It should be clearly understood that the Bank is not directly concerned with the proper fulfilment of the contract between the seller and the buyer. Its duty is simply to receive documents on behalf of the customer which purport to comply with the conditions stated when opening the credit.

The Bank has the right to realise the goods or to take any steps, at its discretion, with a view to safe-guarding its position.

Type of Credit

Irrevocable or Revocable: It is essential that definite instructions on this point are given on all occasions. An Irrevocable Credit becomes an engagement of the Bank itself, incapable of cancellation or of modification except by consent of the beneficiary. A Revocable Credit may be cancelled without the beneficiary's consent by the customer at any time, subject, however, to the customer remaining liable in respect of any negotiation, acceptance, or payment made by the Bank through which the Credit is advised, prior to receipt of notice of cancellation by the Bank.

Availability

Expiry Date: This must always be given. The expiry date can, of course, be extended on instructions from the customer. When credits are to be opened/advised through a bank abroad, expiry dates are understood to apply to the date of negotiation, or acceptance, or payment (as the case may be) in the place abroad at which the negotiation, or acceptance, or payment is to take place, and not to the date of arrival of documents or advices in London. Credits with a London expiry date can be opened in favour of beneficiaries abroad but it is not customary to advise such credits through a foreign bank.

"Negotiated": This instruction should be used where drafts drawn by the beneficiary on Metropolitan Bank Limited either in sterling or in the currency of a country other than that of the beneficiary are to be honoured if negotiated at the place and within the period of validity of the credit.

"Accepted"/"Paid": These instructions are appropriate where the currency of the credit is that of the country of the beneficiary who is to draw drafts for acceptance on a bank abroad or claim payment from them. They are also appropriate where credits are to be opened in sterling with a London expiry date in favour of beneficiaries abroad or in favour of beneficiaries in the United Kingdom.

Documents Required

It is not sufficient to state "usual documents". The documents should be mentioned in detail. "On Board" (i.e. "shipped") Bills of Lading are normally required but if "Received for Shipment" Bills of lading are acceptable, this should be indicated.

Short Form Bills of Lading and Bills of Lading evidencing shipment in containers will be accepted unless the credit specifically prohibits either or both of them.

If the credit terms provide for carriage by more than one method of transport or combined transport documents are called for without stating either the form of the documents and/or the party to issue them, the documents will be accepted as tendered, without regard to the content or to the name of the issuer.

General

Unless the credit provides otherwise, shipping documents bearing reference to extra charges in addition to the freight charges will be accepted. These charges include, for example, "Free **In/Out**" and other costs and charges incurred in container transport. Should additional charges not be acceptable the specific charges prohibited must be stated.

Unless instructions are given to the contrary, banks will take up documents presented to them up to 21 days from the date of the Bills of Lading or other shipping document, even for a short sea voyage. It is essential, therefore, for customers to calculate the maximum period they would wish to accept for presentation of documents to our correspondents abroad bearing in mind the normal airmail time required for the documents to reach us, and to stipulate the maximum number of days permitted between date of issue of Bills of Lading or other Shipping Document and the date of presentation, even if a latest shipment date is stipulated.

Fig. 7.2 Reverse side of request form for opening a documentary credit

Metropolitan Bank Limited **Overseas Branch**
PO Box XA27 606 Lothbury London EC2Z 2LM

7

Copy for advising bank

Date 3rd January

IRREVOCABLE DOCUMENTARY CREDIT	Credit number — of issuing bank: 935790 — of advising bank:
Advising bank:	Applicant: The Downtown Import Co.Ltd., Downtown
Beneficiary: Fabrica Speciale S/A Milan	Amount: £100,000
	Expiry — Date: 31st March — in Milan for negotiation

Except so far as otherwise expressly stated, this documentary credit is subject to the "Uniform Customs and Practice for Documentary Credits" (1983 Revision) International Chamber of Commerce (Publication No. 400).
This Document conforms with the standard Form No. 1 of the I.C.C.

Dear Sir(s)

We hereby issue in your favour this documentary credit which is available by negotiation of your draft at 90 days' sight
drawn on Metropolitan Bank Ltd. Overseas Branch, PO Box XA27, 606 Lothbury London EC2Z 2LM bearing the clause. "Drawn under documentary credit No. 935790 of Metropolitan Bank Ltd." accompanied by the following documents.

INVOICE
SHIPPED BILLS OF LADING in complete set to order and blank endorsed marked freight paid

INSURANCE POLICY covering marine and war risk, theft, pilferage and non-delivery, WPA for invoice amount plus 10%

CERTIFICATE OF ITALIAN ORIGIN

Covering

Shipment of 200,000 SPARKING PLUGS @ 50p each C.I.F. London

Despatch/Shipment from Genoa to London	Partial shipments Allowed	Transhipments Allowed

Special conditions

We hereby engage with drawers and/or bona fide holders that drafts drawn and negotiated in conformity with the terms of this credit will be duly honoured on presentation and that drafts accepted within the terms of this credit will be duly honoured at maturity.

The amount of each draft must be endorsed on the reverse of this credit by the negotiating bank.

THE ADVISING BANK IS REQUESTED TO NOTIFY THE BENEFICIARY ADDING / WITHOUT ADDING THEIR CONFIRMATION.

Yours faithfully,
Metropolitan Bank Limited Overseas Branch
PO Box XA27 606 Lothbury London EC2Z 2LM

Countersigned

Advising bank's notification

Place, date, name and signature of the advising bank

Fig. 7.3 A documentary credit

that this has been done within the time limits extended in accordance with Article 48 of Uniform Customs. Banks are under no obligation to accept presentation of documents outside the banking hours (Article 49).

Transport documents must be presented within a reasonable time after issuance and credits should specify such a period of time but if no such period is stipulated banks will refuse documents presented to them later than twenty-one days after the date of issuance of the transport document (Article 47). The terms 'first half', 'second half', are construed to mean the 1st to the 15th and the 16th to the last day of the month inclusive, and 'beginning', 'middle', or 'end', of the month are construed respectively as from the 1st to the 10th, the 11th to the 20th, and the 21st to the last day of the month, inclusive (Articles 52 and 53).

It will be noticed that on the application form the importer is required to stipulate whether or not partial shipments are to be allowed. This is because partial shipments will be allowed unless the credit specifically states otherwise. Shipments made on the same ship and for the same voyage, even if the transport documents evidencing shipment 'on board' bear different dates, are not regarded as partial shipments (Article 44). If shipment by instalments within given periods is stipulated in the credit, and any instalment is not shipped within the period allowed for that instalment, the credit ceases to be available for that or any subsequent instalment, unless otherwise specified in the credit (Article 45).

For some commodities, such as oilseeds and feeding-stuffs, the exact quantity cannot always be ascertained in advance and a certain amount of flexibility is required for both the value of the credit and the quantity of goods. The *Uniform Customs* (Article 43) is quite specific as to these allowances. The words 'about', '*circa*', or similar expressions, are construed as allowing a difference not to exceed 10 per cent more or less, applicable to the amount of the credit, or to the quantity or unit price of the goods. Where a precise quantity is specified, and the credit does not provide that the amount must not be exceeded or reduced, a tolerance of 5 per cent more or less is permissible, provided that the amount of the drawings does not exceed the amount of the credit. This tolerance does not apply when the credit specifies quantity in terms of packing units or individual items. Bigger tolerances can be specifically provided for in the credit, of course, and this is common practice for some commodities delivered in bulk. The contract between importer and exporter often provides for 95 per cent of the value to be payable by drawings under a documentary credit and for the other 5 per cent to be settled direct later, when the shipment has been delivered and the final weight has been agreed. Furthermore, because it is not always possible for the exact quantity to be delivered to the ship, these contracts usually provide for a leeway in quantity, not exceeding 10 per cent more or less. Letters of credit in such transactions are, therefore, opened to pay for 95 per cent of the basic contract amount, but with the proviso against both the value of the credit and the quantity of goods '10 per cent more or less', so that automatically if the basic contract quantity is exceeded by up to 10 per cent the amount of the credit is correspondingly increased, and vice versa if less than the basic quantity is shipped.

Both the 1974 and the 1983 revisions of *Uniform Customs* take into account the growth of containerization and stipulate that shipment by container is permissible. To overcome the problems that may arise from the difficulties of checking the contents of containers, Article 32 provides that transport documents which bear a clause on the face thereof such as 'shipper's load and count' or 'said by shipper to contain' or words of similar effect, will be accepted unless otherwise specified in the credit.

The latest version of *Uniform Customs* also takes into account the growing use of reprographic and computerized systems. Article 22 states that unless otherwise stipulated in the credit, banks will accept as originals, documents produced, or appearing to have been produced, by reprographic systems, by automated or computerized systems or as carbon copies, *if they are marked as originals and appear to have been authenticated.*

RED CLAUSE CREDITS

A *red clause* credit, often referred to as a *packing* or *anticipatory* credit, has a clause printed in it in red that permits the correspondent bank in the exporter's country to grant advances to the beneficiary. The issuing bank accepts responsibility for such advances, which are intended to enable the exporter to obtain his raw materials, or finance the movement of commodities such as wool, from the interior of the country to the ports. The majority of red clause credits are in respect of wool and they apply to trade with Australia and South Africa in particular. The shipper buys wool from sheep farmers inland and, when he negotiates his bills drawn under the credit, the correspondent bank deducts any advances made from the proceeds of the bills.

Students are advised to be cautious in their references to red clause credits as a means of payment. In answer to a question which states that payment is to be made 'directly the wool is shipped', do not suggest that such a credit would be suitable, because the purpose of a red clause credit is in effect to make an advance payment to the exporter *before* shipment. Furthermore, remember that red clause credits are used to some extent in respect of trade in other commodities, such as timber.

BACK-TO-BACK AND TRANSFERABLE CREDITS

Where a customer of a bank has had a documentary credit opened in his favour by a foreign importer of his goods, he may be able to persuade his bank to open a credit for the benefit of the original supplier of the goods on the strength of the existing credit. These two credits are *back-to-back credits,* the one being issued on the security of the other. This enables a merchant who has resold the goods he has imported to finance the purchase by way of a documentary credit when, in normal circumstances, his credit standing would not have been such as to justify the granting of documentary credit facilities. This does not mean to say that back-to-back credits are of use only to middlemen with slender capital resources. All traders may become fully extended as far as credit facilities are concerned. Once they have reached the limit to which credit is readily available, they may well take advantage of the back-to-back credits to avoid seeking additional credit facilities. An alternative way of financing the two transactions would be for the merchant to insist that the credit opened in his favour by the ultimate buyer should be a *transferable credit* so that he can transfer some of it to the supplier of the goods.

Generally speaking the big clearing banks do not like back-to-back credits and would prefer to be in a position where they can open the second credit to stand on its own. This means of course that the merchant must be sufficiently creditworthy for the bank to be willing to open a credit for him without the backing of the credit that has been opened in his favour. There are no special provisions in *Uniform Customs* for back-to-back credits and therefore, as far as this code of practice is concerned, they are regarded as two quite separate credits. There is, however, ample provision for transferable credits and they are therefore much preferred by the banks.

Back-to-back credits

When a back-to-back credit is opened, the bank concerned will almost certainly require a margin between the amount of the first credit and the amount of the second, i.e. the second credit must be for a smaller sum than the first. This is likely to be the case anyway, because the merchant must sell his goods for a larger amount than he paid for them if he is to make a profit. The extent of the margin the bank will require must depend upon the creditworthiness of the customer. The reason for the bank's cautiousness is that there may be a time-lag between making payment under the second credit and receiving payment under the first. The merchant must have his invoices ready so that he is prepared to substitute them for the invoices of the original supplier when the documents arrive, and he must obtain 'increased value cover' if the insurance cover under the second credit is insufficient for the purposes of the first credit. He can then present the documents and request payments under the first letter of credit (which has most likely been advised through another bank) without delay and may be able to settle both transactions on the same day. The bank opening the second credit (the back-to-back credit) must be careful to ensure that the expiry date of the first credit allows a margin of time for the documents to arrive, for the invoices to be changed, and the documents presented to the negotiating bank before the expiry date. Furthermore, it must be particularly careful in checking the documents, for if they are irregular they may be refused under the first credit.

A bank will open a back-to-back credit only on the strength of an irrevocable credit; the reason for this is obvious. It will hold this credit as quasi-security for the second credit. As two credits are involved, banker's commission is payable twice, but the merchant may be able to insist that the ultimate buyer pays the commission on the credit he opens in favour of the merchant.

It will be appreciated that *the same goods* are involved with both credits; a back-to-back credit in respect of an import of canned fish will not be issued on the strength of a credit in respect of a consignment of tinned rhubarb.

Students should not suggest that there is a greater danger of poor quality goods being received by the buyer where a back-to-back credit is involved. There is no reason why this is so, for the buyer takes exactly the same safeguards, when specifying the documents as he would do in normal circumstances. He is, in fact, unaware of the existence of the second credit.

The diagram in Fig. 7.4 below will help the reader to understand what back-to-back credits involve. There are two credits, one drawn by the ultimate buyer C in favour of B, the merchant, and the second is drawn by B in favour of A, the original supplier. There is a flow of benefit under the credits from right to left at the bottom of the diagram. At the top of the diagram there is a flow of documents from left to right, halting temporarily with B in the middle whilst invoices and, possibly, insurance documents are switched.

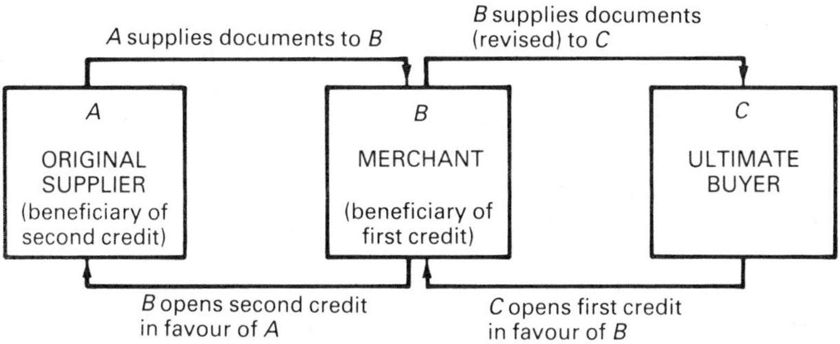

Fig. 7.4. Back-to-back credits

Transferable credits

The main difference between a transferable credit and a back-to-back credit is that a transferable credit involves just one credit whereas a back-to-back credit is issued on the strength of another credit. Furthermore, the middleman's bank, through which the credit is advised, is the only bank involved other than the issuing bank and is therefore fully in control of the situation. Article 54 of the *Uniform Customs* deals with transferable credits in detail and describes such a credit as one 'under which the beneficiary has the right to request the bank called upon to effect payment or acceptance or any bank entitled to effect negotiation to make the credit available, in whole or in part to one or more other parties (second beneficiaries)'.

A credit is transferable only if it is designated as such by the issuing bank. The words 'divisible', 'fractionable', 'assignable' and 'transmissible' must not be used instead of, nor additionally to, the word 'transferable'. The transfer of a credit can occur once only, but fractions of a credit can be transferred separately provided that partial shipments are not prohibited. This means that the second beneficiary(ies) has no right to insist that part or all of the benefit to which he is entitled should be passed on to a third beneficiary(ies).

A credit is transferred only on the terms and conditions specified in the original credit, with the exception of the amount of the credit, of any unit price stated therein, and of the period of validity or period of shipment, any or all of which may be reduced or curtailed. The name of the first beneficiary can be substituted for that of the applicant for the credit, but if the name of the applicant for the credit is specifically required by the original credit to appear in any document other than the invoice, such requirement must be fulfilled.

The *Uniform Customs and Practice* is very careful to protect the paying, accepting or negotiating bank in its dealings with invoices. Naturally, the merchant will not want the original supplier's invoices passed on to the buyer of the goods, firstly because he will want to substitute his own invoices for a larger amount and, secondly, because he will not want the ultimate buyer to know the source of the goods, otherwise the buyer might decide to deal direct with the supplier and cut out the middleman. The first beneficiary (the merchant or middleman) has this right to substitute his own invoices and his own unit prices when transferring the benefit (or some of the benefit) to the original supplier, and he can himself draw under the credit for the difference, if any, between the two sets of invoices, i.e. his profit. But if he fails to supply his own invoices in exchange for the second beneficiary's on demand, *the paying, accepting or negotiating bank has the right to deliver to the issuing bank the documents received under the credit, including the second beneficiary's invoices and drafts, without further responsibility to the first beneficiary.*

The first beneficiary of a transferable credit can transfer the credit to a second beneficiary in the same country or in another country unless the credit specifically states otherwise.

The bank charges in respect of the transfer are payable by the first beneficiary unless otherwise specified, and the bank instructed to effect the transfer, whether it has confirmed the credit or not, is under no obligation to make the transfer, except to the extent and in the manner expressly consented to by the bank, and until the bank's charges for the transfer are paid.

These provisions of Article 54 will probably be understood more easily if they are read in conjunction with the following definitions:

Original supplier	The second beneficiary, i.e. the person to whom some of the benefit of the original credit is transferred. His invoices are taken by the merchant and replaced by new ones for larger amount.

Merchant or middleman	The first beneficiary. Instructs the paying, accepting or negotiating bank to transfer part of the benefit to the original supplier, and draws the difference.
Ultimate buyer	The applicant for the credit. Opens it for benefit of the merchant but agrees that it shall be transferable. Receives the merchant's invoices.

These parties and their roles in the mechanism involved with a transferable credit are indicated in Fig. 7.5. As with a back-to-back credit there is a flow of benefit from right to left and a flow of documents from left to right.

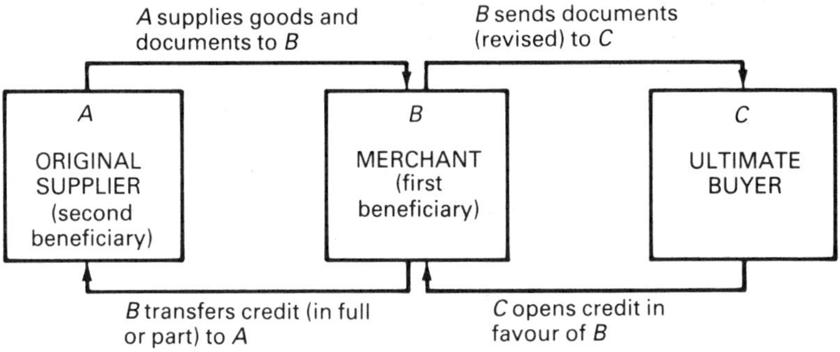

Fig. 7.5. Transferable credits

DOCUMENTARY CREDITS DEPARTMENTS

The Documentary Credits Department of the overseas branch of a large London bank is usually divided into three sections, Import Credits, Export Credits, and Transit Credits.

The *Import Credits Section* deals with the opening of credits for its importer customers. When the customer contracts to buy goods from overseas, he instructs the bank to open a documentary credit in favour of the foreign exporter. A correspondent bank overseas will receive the documents called for in the credit and they will be sent on to the British bank which will examine them and make sure that they comply with the credit. As the correspondent bank will have checked them before paying, accepting or negotiating the draft drawn under the credit or simply making a payment, the documents are usually in order; but discrepancies do occur and it may be necessary to contact the importer and ask whether or not he is prepared to overlook them.

Export credits are those opened by importers overseas in favour of British exporters. The London bank's Export Credits Section will receive an advice from a bank overseas, possibly by letter or by cable, and not necessarily in English, to the effect that a credit is opened in favour of the exporter. The British bank may be asked simply to advise the exporter of the fact that the foreign bank has opened the credit or to add its confirmation.

On receipt of the advice the exporter must consider whether or not he is able to get all the documents required by the buyer in the time that is allowed in the credit, and whether he is prepared to pay any expenses involved in getting them. This applies especially to the supplementary documents, such as a *certificate of quality* or *consular invoice*, which do take some time to obtain and may be quite expensive; for instance, a consular invoice from the consulate of one of the South American states may cost as much as 2 per cent of the invoice value of the goods. If the exporter knows in advance that this expense will be incurred he can allow for it in his price, but if this has not been done he must consider whether or not to seek an amendment to the amount of the documentary credit so as to include this fee.

Other points that the exporter needs to check when examining a documentary credit are listed below.

(*a*) Is his name and that of the buyer correctly spelt?
(*b*) Is the credit irrevocable or revocable?
(*c*) Is it confirmed?
(*d*) Is the description of the goods correct?
(*e*) Is the amount of the credit sufficient to cover the price and the costs? Is the right quotation given, e.g. cif or fob?
(*f*) Do last date of shipment and date of expiry allow enough time?
(*g*) Is the quantity of the goods correct and are there sufficient tolerances (for bulk commodities)?
(*h*) What insurance risks have to be covered?

In the case of transportation by sea:

(*i*) Are partial shipments and transhipments allowed?
(*j*) Is shipment permitted only from a named British port?
(*k*) Is port of destination correct?
(*l*) Is shipment on deck permitted (if required) and are there any acceptable clauses on the bill of lading?

(*m*) Is it acceptable for bill of lading to be issued by forwarding agent or under charter-party (if required)?

The exporter will present his commercial documents to the bank in Britain, which must be completely satisfied that they are in compliance with the credit before passing them on to the issuing bank overseas. The British bank must be particularly careful if it is to make a payment against the documents or it may find itself in the position of having paid the beneficiary and yet not being able to obtain reimbursement from the foreign bank because of some discrepancy in the documents. As far as some discrepancies are concerned, such as a foul bill of lading (*see* p. 128), the bank may be prepared to overlook the discrepancy when forwarding the documents to the issuing bank, if the exporter is prepared to sign an indemnity in the bank's favour. If necessary, the issuing bank's instructions could be sought by cable before making payment. The exporter may be reluctant to give an indemnity covering a technical discrepancy in the documents, however, because if the market for the goods has changed, the importer might refuse the documents purely on the technical point as an excuse for not taking up the goods. Discrepancies in documents are the biggest problem for the banker in dealing with documentary credits, especially where a weak customer is concerned. The majority of customers, however, would not want to take advantage of a minor discrepancy and refuse to accept documents and be debited for a draft because of one.

The third section of the Documentary Credits Department, the *Transit Section*, deals with credits in respect of goods that do not touch our shores. It would most likely be responsible for back-to-back credits and transferable credits where they relate to re-exports, the London merchant having purchased goods from overseas and having sold them to a foreign buyer.

The section would also be responsible for *transit credits* in respect of goods sold by one foreign country to another and financed through the bank in Britain. These are likely to arise where the importing country has more than ample reserves in sterling in London and wishes its nationals to make use of this sterling in paying for imports from third countries. For instance, a firm in Sweden may have bought goods from Hong Kong to be paid for by way of a documentary credit opened by the London bank in favour of the exporter. This involves three banks, Bank A in Sweden, Bank B in London, and Bank C in Hong Kong. The bank in Sweden opens a credit in favour of the Hong Kong exporter and requests Bank B in London to confirm it, or alternatively asks the London bank to open the credit. The credit provides for drafts in sterling to be drawn on the London bank and these are debited to

Bank A's sterling account when they are paid. Bank C in Hong Kong is a correspondent bank of Bank B and it passes on the credit to the exporter, sends the documents to the Transit Section of Bank B and negotiates the drafts for the exporter. Bank C's account in sterling is credited by Bank B with the value of the drafts.

An alternative arrangement is a *reimbursement credit*, where a bank in the importer's country opens a sterling credit direct with a correspondent bank in the exporter's country and authorizes that bank to draw in sterling on a London bank in reimbursement. The opening bank notifies the London bank of any such reimbursements it has authorized.

EXAMINATION GUIDELINES

An examiner who wishes to set a question, or more than one question, on documentary credits has several options open to him, as follows:

(*a*) A straightforward question requiring a definition of a documentary credit and an explanation of the purpose of the *Uniform Customs and Practice for Documentary Credits.*

(*b*) To require the student to explain in detail one or more of the different types of documentary credit and the requirements of *Uniform Customs* in this connection.

(*c*) A question requiring the student to define a documentary credit and then to go into detail about the commercial documents, again with particular reference to *Uniform Customs.*

(*d*) A question concerning a number of discrepancies in documents and how the bank should react to them.

(*e*) A question requiring the student to compare a documentary credit with a bill for collection as a means of payment.

Clearly the first two types of question relate to the subject matter in this chapter and therefore the examples below come under those two categories. As will be seen from the sample questions, Institute of Bankers' questions under category (*b*) now take the form of mini case studies in which the student is expected to determine which type of instrument is most appropriate to the particular needs of the customer. As far as categories (*c*) and (*d*) are concerned they relate to Chapter 8 and will be dealt with at the end of that chapter.

The comparison type of question in category (*e*) is best dealt with after bills for collection have been covered and therefore they appear at the end of Chapter 9.

The following questions with model answers are all from category (*b*) as it is assumed that the student reader will be able to extract the answers to questions under category (*a*) straight from the text of this chapter. A number of questions of this type are given in the list of other questions that follows the model answers.

Question 1

As manager of your branch, you have arranged an appointment with Mr Dealer, managing director of Counter-Trade Ltd. The account of Counter-Trade Ltd has been with you since incorporation some two years ago and, during that time, has worked in credit to your satisfaction. There is little, if any, strength in either the company's balance sheet or the latest set of management accounts Mr Dealer places before you. He asks you to provide a facility to cover an irrevocable letter of credit for £100 000 in favour of a South American company selling coffee—for which he can demonstrate a firm purchase contract from France. Counter-Trade Ltd's profit margin for this transaction would be 25 per cent gross if the deal goes through.

REQUIRED

(*a*) Your response to Mr Dealer concerning this *specific* proposal, indicating the means by which your bank could help this company to finalize *this* transaction without involving the bank in hazardous liabilities.

(*b*) State briefly the method by which your proposal would operate.

SOLUTION

(*a*) A back-to-back credit is not the answer to this question as it would be far too hazardous a proposition and the question does state that the bank should not be involved in hazardous liabilities.

The answer lies in a transferable, irrevocable and confirmed documentary credit, if of course the French importer is willing to open such a credit. This method would enable Counter-Trade Ltd to finance the transactions without any financial support from the bank, which would obviously not be forthcoming in view of the lack of strength in the company's balance sheet and set of management accounts.

(*b*) The credit should be opened in accordance with Article 54 of *Uniform Customs and Practice for Documentary Credits* (1983 Revision). All that is necessary for the credit to fall within this category would be for it to be marked 'transferable'. Under Article 54 our bank would be authorized, as the bank called upon to effect payment, to make the credit available in whole or in part to one or more other parties (second beneficiaries) if requested by the beneficiary.

Our bank will notify the South American supplier through the agency of a correspondent bank in the nearest town to the supplier, of the terms and conditions of the credit. These must be the same as those in the original credit, with the exception of the amount of the credit, of any unit prices stated therein, the period of validity and the last date for presentation of the documents, any or all of which may be reduced or curtailed. In addition, the percentage for which insurance cover must be effected may be increased in such a way as to provide the amount stipulated in the original credit and the name of the first beneficiary may be substituted for the name of the applicant for the credit.

Counter-Trade Ltd will have the right to substitute their own invoices for those of the South American supplier when the documents are received by us, and obviously these will be for £125 000, i.e. 25 per cent above the original price. Mr Dealer should be warned of the difficulty that will arise if he fails to produce his own invoices immediately the commercial documents have been received by us and that it would therefore be wise to prepare these in advance. Under Article 54 of *Uniform Customs and Practice* we will have the right to deliver the South American Supplier's invoices to the issuing bank if Mr Dealer does not supply his own invoices in time, but we are hardly likely to want to be placed in that position.

When we have claimed reimbursement under the credit from the issuing bank and paid over £100 000 to the South American supplier, the remaining £25 000 less charges will be credited to the account of Counter-Trade Ltd.

Question 2

Lamb & Co. import wool and woollen products from Australia and have recently been asked to provide pre-shipment finance by their suppliers overseas. As their bank manager, you agree to support them in meeting this request. In the past they have experienced difficulties when importing goods from overseas because of the rules covering partial shipments and partial drawings. Your customers understand that these difficulties should not arise in future since you will be able to establish one basic instrument that will cover the two points.

REQUIRED

(*a*) A description of the basic instrument and its method of operation.

(*b*) The reason why the problem of partial shipments/drawings can be overcome without difficulty.

SOLUTION

(*a*) The basic instrument referred to in the question is an irrevocable documentary credit in favour of the Australian suppliers containing the red clause.

This clause authorizes the advising bank in Australia to make advances to the suppliers against an undertaking by us as the issuing bank to reimburse it in respect of such advances whether the goods are shipped or not. The amount of the advances will be deducted from the amount payable under the credit when the goods are shipped. If the goods are not shipped then the advising correspondent bank can claim from us, the UK issuing bank, for the amount of the advances plus interest and charges.

Lamb & Co. must be advised that if the goods are not shipped, their account will be debited with the advances plus charges.

The pre-shipment finance can be either conditional or unconditional. The former calls for documents of title or warehouse warrants to be produced by the shipper before the advances are made whereas the latter requires no such security provision and is of course more risky for both us and our customers.

(*b*) The partial shipment part of the question calls for a reference to Article 44 of *Uniform Customs and Practice* (1983 Revision), which stipulates that partial shipments and/or partial drawings are allowed, unless the credit stipulates otherwise. Lamb and Co. must ensure that in their application for the documentary credit to be opened, they state their wishes in this connection. Partial drawings are allowed only for partial shipments and therefore the credit should specify if both are acceptable or not in order to avoid misunderstanding.

Article 44 states that where goods are transported by sea or by more than one mode of transport, but including carriage by sea, made on the same vessel and for the same voyage, they will not be regarded as partial shipments, even if the transport documents indicating loading on board bear different dates of issuance and/or indicate different ports of loading on board. As in this instance the goods are to be transported by sea and may be loaded up at different ports, they will, by virtue of Article 54, be regarded as one shipment.

Question 3

Your customers, Facings Ltd, import high quality granites, marbles and facing stone from the continent of Europe. They have, in the past, paid for these goods by means of documentary collections routed through your bank sixty days D/A terms. On a previous occasion the goods were found to be severely damaged when they arrived in the UK and your customer refused to pay for them until replacements were received. The suppliers now insist that the customer establish irrevocable letters of credit calling for drafts at sixty days sight on your bank. The customers finding difficulty in obtaining sufficient credit facilities from you to cover the total number of letters of credit likely to be outstanding at any one time. They have asked you if there is a solution to the problem, even though *their suppliers insist that irrevocable letters of credit* must be established in their favour.

REQUIRED

Brief notes on:

(*a*) a solution to the problem that will provide the suppliers with a method of payment that is secure and yet at the same time permits your customer to maintain a high level of imports and give them sixty days' credit;

(*b*) how the payment instrument you describe would operate so as to protect your customers as well as their suppliers.

SOLUTION

(*a*) The instrument that might be acceptable to the continental suppliers is a stand-by letter of credit. This is in effect a guarantee of payment by a bank that the suppliers can fall back on should the normal means of payment prove unsatisfactory. It is not meant to be the normal means of settlement only, as its name suggests, one that is standing by in case of need.

Stand-by letters of credit are provided for in the *Uniform Customs and Practice for Documentary Credits* for the first time in its latest revision (the 1983 revision). They provide a solution to this particular type of problem, where the importer's bank is not willing to extend the facility of having a large number of documentary credits outstanding at one time, and yet the suppliers insist on the protection of documentary credits. Given that they know that if any of the bills drawn on our customers on a sixty-days D/A basis are dishonoured, they will be able to call for payment under the stand-by credit, it is expected that the suppliers will be willing to allow our customer to revert to the old method of payment. This will enable them to maintain a high level of imports and still obtain sixty days' credit.

(*b*) The bank would agree to open any stand-by credit for a specific amount (covering at least one and possibly more than one shipment).

It is essential that our bank should be the presenting bank for bills drawn upon Facings Ltd by overseas suppliers, and we should thus have the commercial documents as well as the drafts channelled through us. The collection orders should specify that in the event of dishonour, bills should be protested in order to protect the suppliers.

The stand-by letter of credit will call for bills of exchange to be drawn on the bank to be accompanied by a copy of the invoice and the dishonoured bill of exchange drawn on Facings Ltd, together with evidence of dishonour (a copy of our letter notifying non-payment would suffice).

Other questions

1. Medico Ltd, a small chemist wholesaler, have from time to time been engaged in exporting relatively small consignments, which they have been able to finance out of their own limited resources. They have now secured a very large export order, with payment at sight on cif terms. A manufacturer in the UK is prepared to provide the goods on similar terms at a reduced price.

(*a*) Describe the two methods by which the transaction could be arranged, using documentary credits only.
(*b*) State which of the two methods entails the lesser risk to Medico and to any intermediary bank involved. Give reasons. (*Inst. of Bankers*)

2. Held & Sons are steel stockholders in London whose account is operated on an overdraft basis. Hitherto they have obtained their stocks in the UK, but they are now forced to look elsewhere for supplies of a specialized steel, for which they have received the following quotations:

	Country	*Price per ton*	*Terms for payment*
(*a*)	Belgium	B. fr.11 030 fob Antwerp	Open account—settlement 1 month after shipment
(*b*)	Spain	S. pts.26 500 c & f London	Draft drawn payable 2 months after shipment D/A (collection charges for buyer)
(*c*)	France	F. fr.1697 cif London	Irrevocable documentary credit payment 3 months after shipment
(*d*)	Germany	DM740 franco buyers' premises	Payment with order

Your customers, Held & Sons, decide to accept the quotation from France for the supply of special steel. The suppliers ask them to arrange, in accordance with *Uniform Customs and Practice for Documentary Credits*, an irrevocable documentry credit that is transferable and confirmed.

(*a*) Describe precisely but briefly what it is that the seller requires.
(*b*) Explain the seller's possible reason for the stipulation that the credit be transferable.
(*c*) In view of the request that the credit be transferable, what factor should your customers consider before proceeding, and what particular document would they be wise to insist should be provided under the documentary credit? (*Inst. of Bankers*)

3. What points should an importer consider when requesting his bank to issue a documentary credit in favour of an overseas beneficiary?

(Inst. of Freight Forwarders)

4. To what extent is payment guaranteed under a documentary credit? Confine your answer to a full appraisal of the beneficiary's position under this method of settlement. *(Inst. of Freight Forwarders)*

5. Explain the purpose and procedure for establishing a back-to-back letter of credit. *(Inst. of Freight Forwarders)*

6. Your customers, Woodwork Ltd, are timber merchants and act either on their own behalf or as agents for timber stockists. They buy hardwood from various parts of the world for on-selling in Western Europe. Inward and outward payments have normally been made by cable transfer (Express International Money Transfer) upon shipment but occasionally by letters of credit.

A recent re-organization in the company has taken place because of their deteriorating trading position. The new finance director, Mr Oakbeam, calls to see you to discuss a new general strategy for the company, and one particular transaction he is trying to arrange, involving a Malaysian supplier and a West German buyer. Payment will be by sight letter of credit and the terms of shipment cif Hamburg. The German buyer has no objection to arranging an irrevocable letter of credit in favour of your customers, who have ascertained that the Malaysian supplier requires to be paid by the same method. The letter of credit is to be issued by a West German bank and will be advised through you. Mr Oakbeam says that when the company has used irrevocable letters in the past there had usually been difficulty with contracts because it had never been able to get its documentation right. Following the recent banking changes, however, he is hoping to arrange for an irrevocable letter of credit to be established in the company's favour that will cater for the needs of Woodwork Ltd as well as those of the Malaysian supplier.

Supply brief notes covering the following:

(*a*) A description of the basic instrument that will satisfy the needs of all parties and an indication of why it will be satisfactory.
(*b*) To what is Mr Oakbeam referring as 'recent banking changes' and how will these changes help in this particular transaction?

(Inst. of Bankers)

7. Antipodes Ltd, customers of yours of many years' standing, have a thriving business. As manager of your branch you have been able to offer

facilities that have been utilized to your complete satisfaction as well as to the benefit of the company. Imports include many products from the antipodes and the company have set up a chain of trusted buying agents to act on their behalf. The agents in the past have been able to offer to the company ninety days D/A terms.

The agents are suffering from cash-flow problems and have asked Antipodes Ltd to finance them on a temporary basis. You have been called in by your customers to discuss the methods that might be available to provide the agents with post-shipment finance and, possibly, pre-shipment finance.

Supply the following:

(*a*) Brief notes describing a basic instrument that would arrange for post- and pre-shipment finance, together with a note of the particular document that, if post-shipment finance is arranged, would afford your customers some degree of protection.

(*b*) Brief notes showing the explanation you would give to Antipodes Ltd on how the instrument would work and its benefit or otherwise to them and their agents. (*Inst. of Bankers*)

8. Bric-a-Brac Ltd have a number of outlets at holiday resorts in various parts of the UK. Traditionally, they have purchased fancy goods from local wholesalers but now find their prices are unattractive. Ceside Crafts of Manila have offered to supply them with a whole range of products but insist upon secure methods of payment at sight on a cif UK port basis. To the benefit of their cash-flow, your customer had in the past been able to obtain sufficient credit (ninety days) from the wholesalers to enable them to sell the goods before having to pay for them.

Supply the following:

(*a*) Brief notes describing a method of payment that would afford Ceside Crafts the protection they need and, at the same time, take account of the cash-flow requirements of Bric-a-Brac Ltd.

(*b*) A brief description of the documents you would expect the sellers to provide for your customers. (*Inst. of Bankers*)

8
DOCUMENTARY CREDITS: II

LIABILITIES AND RESPONSIBILITIES

SO far, little has been said about the documents called for in a documentary credit. Obviously these are of major importance, for the banks involved in documentary transactions are dealing with documents, not goods, and they must ensure that these documents are in order if they are to be certain of obtaining reimbursement for any payments made under a credit. The *Uniform Customs and Practice* is very detailed on the subject of documents, especially transport documents, in order to guide and protect the banker handling documents. A number of articles in the early part of *Uniform Customs and Practice* deal with the liabilities and responsibilities of the parties concerned with documentary credits, and they can be summarized as follows:

1. Banks must examine all documents with reasonable care to ascertain that they appear *on their face* to be in accordance with the credit (Article 15).

2. In all operations, the parties deal in documents and not in goods (Article 4).

3. Payment, acceptance or negotiation against documents that appear on their face to be in accordance with the terms and conditions of the credit binds the party authorizing the bank to do so to reimburse the bank (Article 16).

4. If the issuing bank receives documents that appear on their face not to be in accordance with the terms and conditions of the credit, the bank must determine, on the basis of the documents alone, whether to claim that payment, acceptance or negotiation was not effected in accordance with the terms and conditions of the credit. The bank has a reasonable time to examine the documents and make this decision. Notice of such a claim must be sent to the remitting bank and the

documents must be returned to the bank or held at its disposal (Article 16).

5. Banks assume no liability or responsibility for:

(*a*) the form, sufficiency, accuracy, genuineness, falsification or legal effect of any documents;
(*b*) the conditions stipulated in the documents or superimposed thereon;
(*c*) the description, quantity, weight, quality, condition, packing, delivery, value or existence of goods;
(*d*) the good faith or acts and/or omissions, solvency, performance or standing of the consignor, the carriers or the insurers of the goods or any other person;
(*e*) the consequences arising out of delay and/or loss in transit of any messages, letters or documents, or any errors in transmission of any telecommunication or in translation;
(*f*) the consequences arising out the interruption of their business by Acts of God, riots, or civil commotion. Unless specifically authorized, banks will not effect payment, acceptance or negotiation after expiration under credits expiring during such interruptions of business;
(*g*) the failure of another bank to carry out instructions given to it, even if the bank issuing the instructions has taken the initiative in the choice of the other bank (Articles 17–20).

6. The applicant for the credit is bound by and liable to indemnify the banks against all obligations and responsibilities imposed by foreign laws and usages (Article 20).

7. All instructions to issue, or amend a credit and the credit itself must specify the documents precisely and such terms as 'first class', 'well known', and 'qualified' must not be used to describe the issuers of any documents. If they are included, banks may accept documents as presented without further responsibility (Article 22).

Despite these protective provisions of the *Uniform Customs and Practice*, the banks can very easily slip up in their handling of documentary credits and find themselves liable for negligence.

TRANSPORT DOCUMENTS

Certain documents are called for in a documentary credit as evidence that the goods have been dispatched and that they purport to be of the type and quality ordered. Furthermore, the documents are required both to ensure that the goods are being properly transported and, in the case of bills of lading, in order that the buyer can claim possession of the goods when they arrive.

If goods are being transported by sea the transport document called for is the bill of lading, which is a document of title and has, to some degree, the attributes of a negotiable instrument. The goods are handed over only against surrender of the bill of lading and the holder is *prima facie* the person entitled to receive the goods. Normally bills of lading are issued in sets of three and a fourth copy is kept by the ship's master. When one copy is handed over to claim possession of the goods, the remaining copies become void.

A bill of lading is a document signed by, or on behalf of, a master of a ship, certifying that goods have been received on board in good order for transportation and delivery as specified in the document. An example of a bill of lading is given in Fig. 8.1.

The bill of lading bears the name of the vessel and the port of lading and port of discharge. Space is also provided on the printed form for the name of the firm shipping the goods and for the name of the consignee. The bill is usually consigned to 'Order' and endorsed in blank and a note is made of the person or firm to be notified of the arrival of the goods. Space is also provided for the marks and numbers borne by the consignment, the quantity, the number and type of packages, a description of the goods, and the weight and measurement of the packages. As it is the responsibility of the master of the ship to deliver the goods in the condition in which they are received, they are carefully inspected upon arrival on board, and, if they are not in good condition, a note to this effect is made on the bill of lading. A bill carrying comments which *expressly declare* that goods and/or their packaging were received in a defective condition is called a *dirty* or *foul* bill of lading. A *clean* bill of lading is one which carries no such indication that the goods or their packaging were defective when received on board.

The *Uniform Customs and Practice* stipulates that banks will refuse foul bills of lading or other transport documents unless the credit expressly states clauses or notations which may be accepted (Article 34). Students should carefully note that the clause or notation declaring the defective condition must be superimposed on the transport document, and that it

BILL OF LADING FOR COMBINED TRANSPORT SHIPMENT OR PORT TO PORT SHIPMENT

OVERSEAS CONTAINERS LIMITED

B/L No. 35773729
Booking Ref. 1206575
Shippers Ref.

Shipper
SLEEPEEZEE LTD.,
MORDEN ROAD,
LONDON SW19 3XP
ENGLAND

Consignee
SINGH INTERNATIONAL,
ROHTAK ROAD
NEW DELHI - 110 052
INDIA

Notify Party/Address
SINGH INTERNATIONAL,
ROHTAK ROAD
NEW DELHI - 110 052
INDIA

Place of Receipt
SLEEPEEZEE LTD.,
MORDEN ROAD,
LONDON SW19 3XP
ENGLAND

Ocean Vessel and Voy No
CANDIA 4243

Place of Delivery
NEW DELHI I.C.D. (DRY PORT)

Port of Loading
TILBURY

Port of Discharge
BOMBAY

Marks and Nos; Container Nos.	Number and kind of Packages; description of Goods	Gross Weight (kg)	Measurement (cbm)
OCLU1038299 S I 6733 NEW DELHI VIA BOMBAY NOS 1 - UP	1 X 40 FT CONTAINER CONTAINING DIVAN SETS (107 PIECES)	2997	48.560

"FREIGHT PAID"

SHIPPED ON BOARD "CANDIA"
AT TILBURY 18 FEB 1986
FOR OVERSEAS CONTAINERS LIMITED

ABOVE PARTICULARS AS DECLARED BY SHIPPER

*Total No. of Containers/Packages
CONTAINER 1

Movement
FCL DOOR /FCL DEPOT

Freight and Charges (indicate whether prepaid or collect)

Origin Inland Haulage Charge	PAID ORIGIN
Origin Terminal Handling/LCL Service Charge	PAID ORIGIN
Ocean Freight	PAID ORIGIN
Destination Terminal Handling/LCL Service Charge	DUE DESTN.
Destination Inland Haulage Charge	

Received by the Carrier from the Shipper in apparent good order and condition (unless otherwise noted herein) the total number or quantity of Containers or other packages or units, indicated *, stated by the Shipper to comprise the Goods specified above, for Carriage subject to all the terms hereof (INCLUDING THE TERMS ON THE REVERSE HEREOF AND THE TERMS OF THE CARRIER'S APPLICABLE TARIFF) from the Place of Receipt or the Port of Loading, whichever is applicable, to the Port of Discharge or the Place of Delivery, whichever is applicable. In accepting this Bill of Lading the Merchant expressly accepts and agrees to all its terms, conditions and exceptions, whether printed, stamped or written, or otherwise incorporated, notwithstanding the non-signing of this Bill of Lading by the Merchant. When this document calls for Combined Transport it is a negotiable Combined Transport Document the terms of which are based upon the Uniform Rules for a Combined Transport Document (ICC Publication No. 298)

Place and Date of Issue
LONDON 18 FEB 86

Number of Original Bills of Lading
THREE (3)

IN WITNESS of the contract herein contained the number of originals stated opposite has been issued, one of which being accomplished the other(s) to be void.

ICS
CT B 1
April 78

3.4

For the Carrier
----------EXAMPLE ONLY----------

As Agent(s) only

Fig. 8.1. Bill of lading

must *expressly* declare the condition. In other words, it must state categorically that the goods and or the packaging are defective, e.g. 'several casks leaking', 'timber badly warped and stained'. A clause that states that the goods have been stored next to the ship's boilers only implies that the goods might become defective and does not expressly state that they are defective, and therefore the clause does not make the transport document foul. The applicant for the credit has the right to approve a 'dirty' clause and to condemn a 'clean' clause, but if he wishes to do so he must expressly state his wishes when giving instructions to open the credit. Unless he does this then Article 34 must be firmly applied, i.e. a 'dirty' clause will not be accepted and a 'clean' clause will not be rejected, for a bank must judge a transport document solely by Article 34 and by the specific instructions, if any, contained in the particular credit.

If a credit specifically calls for an on board transport document, bills of lading must show that the goods are loaded on board a named vessel or shipped on a named vessel. This may be evidenced by a notation to the effect dated and signed or initialled by the carrier or his agent (Article 27), this has been done on our specimen bill of lading. Banks refuse a transport document showing the stowage of goods on deck, unless specifically authorized in the credit (Article 28).

Liner waybills are often asked for in a documentary credit instead of bills of lading and may be accepted by a bank if this is the case. However, from a banker's point of view a liner waybill does not give him the control over the goods that a bill of lading provides, for unlike a bill of lading it is not a document of title. A bank may therefore be reluctant to advance money against documents that include a liner waybill. The waybill is evidence of a contract of carriage and a receipt by the shipping company for the goods, but it does not have to be handed over to the shipping company to gain possession of the goods on arrival.

The changing trends in international trade, especially the growth of roll-on/roll-off traffic with Europe, to which nearly half of our goods are exported and from which nearly half of our imports are purchased, has led to the increasing use of documents inferior to the full bill of lading and hence, as security for bank advances, they are less desirable. However, apart from this aspect, the banks freely accept carriers' receipts and other forms of transport document evidencing dispatch or taking in charge of goods that do not conflict with the instructions in the credit. Short-form bills of lading, i.e. simplified forms that do not contain all the details and conditions shown on a full bill of lading, may be accepted unless otherwise stated in the credit.

Unless transhipment is prohibited by the terms of the credit, a transport document indicating transhipment will be accepted if the entire voyage is covered by it. Transport documents incorporating printed clauses stating that the carriers have the right to tranship are acceptable even though the credit prohibits transhipment (Article 29).

The words 'freight paid' or 'freight prepaid', or similar words on shipping documents, constitute evidence of the payment of freight, but such words as 'freight prepayable' and 'freight to be prepaid' do not. Banks will honour documents stating that freight or transportation charges are payable on delivery, if they are consistent with other documents, unless the credit specifies otherwise (Article 31). Note that the specimen bill of lading (Fig. 8.1) has been stamped 'Freight Paid'.

The judgment in the case of *Soproma S.p.A.* v. *Marine and Animal By-Products Corporation* (1966) is of importance in connection with bills of lading. The corporation in New York had sold a consignment of fishmeal to buyers in Italy, and presented the documents for payment under a letter of credit opened in their favour. The credit called for bills of lading marked 'freight prepaid', but the bills were marked 'freight collect'. This was in itself sufficient justification for the buyers to refuse the documents, which indeed they did, but a further factor that concluded the case in favour of the buyers was that the bills of lading were not a good tender because they were not negotiable or transferable documents. They were made out to a named party and not to order and blank endorsed. In this way they did not conform with the credit. They did not permit of endorsements and were not good tender under cif or c & f contracts at common law.

THE INVOICE

A documentary credit will call for an invoice specifying the quality and the quantity of the goods consigned and the unit and total price. This is a *commercial invoice*; for an example see Fig. 8.2. The credit may provide for the invoice to be rendered in duplicate or triplicate, or in even greater numbers, depending upon the needs of the importer and the requirements of his country (e.g. the customs authorities may require some copies of the invoice). The importer may require that the invoices be 'certified invoices', in other words they must be certified by some responsible person to the effect that the goods are in accordance with the description on the invoice. The description of the goods in the invoice must correspond with the description in the credit, whereas in other documents the goods may be described in general terms (Article 41). It is for this reason that the banks ask their customers to describe the goods only briefly when applying for a documentary credit to be opened.

SHIPPING/COMMERCIAL INVOICE AND PACKING LIST

Exporter

Sleepeezee Ltd
Morden Road, London SW19 3XP.
Telephone: 01-540 9171 (15 lines)
Telegrams: "Sleepeezee, London SW19"
Telex: 929309
V.A.T. Reg. No.: 216 3705 82
FROM THE HOUSE OF SIMMONS

Vehicle Bkg. Ref.	CAN		Tariff Heading
Invoice No. and Date (Tax Point) CON.1062 6.12.85		Exporter's Reference Contract No. U.406	
Buyer's Reference Order No.		F/Agent's Ref.	S.S. Co. Bkg. No.

Consignee (If 'Order' State Notify Party and Address)
Singh International,
Rohtak Road
New Delhi - 110 052
India

Buyer (If not Consignee)

Port Account No.

Forwarding Agent/Merchant
Ferry Freighting (Croydon) ltd.
288a, High Street
Croydon CRO 1NG

Coding for H.M. Customs	Destination	ICD	Container	Ro Ro (a) (b)	Flag	Port

Country of Origin of Goods: United Kingdom
Country of Final Destination: INDIA

Receiving Date(s)	Dock, Container base Etc.
Pre-Carriage By	Place of Receipt by Pre-Carrier
Vessel/Aircraft Etc.	Port of Loading
Port of Discharge	Place of Delivery by On-Carrier

Terms of Delivery and Payment: C.I.F. New Delhi

EUR1 Remarks

Insured Value (state Currency)

Name of Receiving Authority

Marks, Nos. and Container No.; No. and kind of Packages; Description of Goods (state Nature of Hazard if any)	Quantity	Per Unit CIF	Amount C.I.F
CCCN Nos. 9404 5500/9404 3000			
165x200cms Olympic Mattresses	3	£127.90	£ 383.70
82x200cms B/Rest 12" Sprung Edge Linked Divans	6	£ 58.90	£ 353.40
90x200cms Olympic zipped Mattresses	4	£ 79.45	£ 317.80
90x200cms B/Rest 12" Sprung Edge Linked Divans	4	£ 60.40	£ 241.60
165x200cms Maxipaedic Mattresses	9	£ 90.40	£ 813.60
82x200cms Maxipaedic 12" Sprung Edge Linked Divan	18	£ 58.90	£1,060.20
165x200cms Saxony Mattress.	1	£164.00	£ 164.00
82x200cms Saxony 12" Sprung Edge Linked Divan	2	£ 62.00	£ 124.00
135x190cms Maxipaedic Mattresses	12	£ 67.00	£ 804.00
135x190cms Maxipaedic 12" Sprung Edge Divan	4	£ 72.40	£ 289.60
90x190cms Maxipaedic Mattresses	20	£ 50.90	£1,018.00
90x190cms Twosome Grey Upper Frames.	3	£ 52.10	£ 156.30
90x190cms Twosome Grey Lower Frames.	3	£ 58.25	£ 174.75

Invoice Total (state Currency): CONTINUED

Total Gross Wt (Kg.)	Total Cube (M³)

Signatory's Company and Telephone Number: Sleepeezee Ltd., 540 9171
Name of Authorised Signatory: M.F.Gibbs
Place and Date of Issue: Merton, England 6.12.85
Signature

SL 365 3/81

Fig. 8.2. Commercial invoice

Before goods can be imported into some countries, *consular invoices* may have to be obtained. These are special forms that are available

SHIPPING/COMMERCIAL INVOICE AND PACKING LIST

Exporter
Sleepeezee Ltd
Morden Road, London SW19 3XP.
Telephone 01-540 9171 (15 lines)
Telegrams "Sleepeezee, London SW19"
Telex 929309
V.A.T. Reg. No. 216 3705 82
Sleepeezee
FROM THE HOUSE OF SIMMONS

Vehicle Bkg. Ref. CAN
Tariff Heading
Invoice No. and Date (Tax Point) CON.1062 6.12.85
Exporter's Reference
Contract No. U.406
Buyer's Reference
Order No.
F/Agent's Ref.
S.S. Co. Bkg. No.

Consignee (If 'Order' State Notify Party and Address)
Singh International,
Rohtak Road
New Delhi - 110 052
India

Buyer (If not Consignee)

Port Account No.

Forwarding Agent/Merchant
Ferry Freighting (Croydon) Ltd.,
288a, High Street
Croydon, CRO 1NG

Coding for H.M. Customs | Destination | ICD | Container | Ro Ro (a) (b) | Flag | Port

Country of Origin of Goods: United Kingdom
Country of Final Destination: INDIA

Receiving Date(s)
Dock, Container base Etc
Pre-Carriage By
Place of Receipt by Pre-Carrier
Terms of Delivery and Payment: C.I.F. New Delhi
Vessel/Aircraft Etc
Port of Loading
EUR1 Remarks
Port of Discharge
Place of Delivery by On-Carrier
Insured Value (state Currency)
Name of Receiving Authority

Marks, Nos and Container No. / No and kind of Packages, Description of Goods (state Nature of Hazard if any)	Quantity	Per Unit	Amount
CCCN Nos. 9404 5500/9404 3000		CIF	C.I.F
90x190cms Twosome Lilac Upper Frames	3	£ 52.10	£ 156.30
90x190cms Twosome Lilac Lower Frames	3	£ 58.25	£ 174.75
90x190cms Spacesaver Mattresses	12	£ 42.85	£ 514.20
107 Pieces as follows:-			
13 @ 165x200x20cms 38.50 Kilos each.			
26 @ 82x200x32cms 29.00 Kilos each.			
4 @ 90x200x20cms 23.75 Kilos each.			
4 @ 90x200x32cms 28.50 Kilos each.			
12 @ 135x190x20cms 33.00 Kilos each.			
4 @ 135x190x32cms 35.50 Kilos each.			
32 @ 90x190x20cms 22.68 Kilos each.			
6 @ 100x200x 9cms 23.30 Kilos each.			
6 @ 95x200x10cms 21.80 Kilos each.			

Invoice Total (state Currency): £6,746.20

C.I.F. New Delhi

Total Gross Wt (Kg): 2997.25
Total Cube (M³): 48.56m³

TERMS:- Nett
METHOD OF PAYMENT:- Payment to be made within 60 days from the arrival of merchandise in India

Signatory's Company and Telephone Number: Sleepeezee Ltd., 540 9171
Name of Authorised Signatory: M.F Gibbs
Place and Date of Issue: Merton, England. 6.12.85
Signature: M.F. Gibbs

SL 365 3 81

Fig. 8.2. Part II

through the country's embassy or consulate in the exporter's country and usually a charge is made; quite a substantial one in the case of some South American embassies. In some cases the exporter's own invoices are authenticated by the embassy or consulate and these are known as *legalized invoices*. They usually have to be countersigned by the chamber of commerce.

Another type of invoice is the *pro forma invoice*, which is really a form of quotation to a potential buyer, inviting him to buy the goods on the terms stated. The invoice clearly states that it is pro forma and if it is accepted the details are normally transferred to a commercial invoice against which payment will be made, although in some cases payment will be made against a pro forma invoice, e.g. where payment for the goods is required before despatch. Pro forma invoices are sometimes required by the buyer in order that he may obtain an import licence and/or exchange control approval to make the payment for the goods, and possibly to prepare a letter of credit.

INSURANCE DOCUMENTS

The *Uniform Customs and Practice* prescribes that insurance documents must be specifically described in the credit, and must be issued and/or signed by the insurance companies or their agents or by underwriters. Cover notes issued by brokers are not acceptable unless specifically authorized in the credit (Article 35). It will be noticed that in the request form for opening a documentary credit (Fig. 7.1), the applicant is required to state specifically what is required, i.e. whether an insurance policy or certificate, and the risks to be covered. The reason why banks are very cautious about insurance is that some types of evidence of insurance, such as certificates and cover notes, have not in the past been favoured by English courts. Where a consignment is covered by a general policy covering a number of shipments, a certificate of insurance will be issued, but a certificate does not contain all the terms of the insurance contract. Furthermore, it is insufficient when claims are made under a policy, because it is usual for an insurance company to require presentation of the policy when claims are made. The credit must expressly state any additional risks that are to be covered, and imprecise terms such as 'usual risks', or 'customary risks' must not be used (Article 38).

Unless otherwise stated in the credit the insurance document must cover 10 per cent above the invoice amount. When the cif value of the goods cannot be determined from the documents on their face, the banks accept as the minimum the amount of the drawing under the credit or the amount of the relative commercial invoice, whichever is the greater. Unless otherwise specified, the insurance document must be expressed in the same currency as the credit (Article 37).

Where the contract between the exporter and the foreign importer is a cif contract, as distinct from an fob contract, it is the exporter's responsibility to insure the goods (see Chapter 4). When an insurance policy is produced, it is usual for it to be made out in favour of the correspondent bank, or if it is made out in favour of the exporter, it will be endorsed in blank, for, like a bill of lading, an insurance policy is freely transferable by endorsement and delivery. The Marine Insurance Act 1906 provides that a marine insurance policy must specify the name of the insurers, the name of the person in whose name the insurance is effected, the nature of the goods insured, and the risk or risks insured against, the sum or sums insured, and the period of insurance.

Banks must refuse insurance documents which bear a date later than the date of loading on board or despatch or taking in charge of goods, unless the credit specifically authorizes their acceptance.

An example of a marine insurance certificate is given in Figs. 8.3(*a*) and 8.3 (*b*).

OTHER DOCUMENTS

Where goods are to be despatched by road, rail or air instead of by sea, the documentary credit will call for a *carrier's receipt* or *railway receipt* or an *air waybill* instead of a bill of lading. All three of these are simply an acknowledgement that the goods have been accepted for delivery to a destination indicated on the receipt. None of these documents is a document of title to goods in the same way that a bill of lading is. An example of an air waybill is given in Fig. 8.4.

A credit may call for a *certificate of origin*, which certifies that the goods were produced in a particular country. This will be necessary where, for instance, goods are being imported from a country that is a member of the EEC, and they are therefore free of import duty. To ensure that these goods have not been channelled through an EEC country to avoid import duty, the certificate of origin is required.

A *certificate of quality* may be required. This is simply a certificate to the effect that the goods despatched are of the quality specified in the contract. It has to be signed by a responsible person at the time and place of shipment.

Documentary credits will be further discussed in Chapters 10 and 13

LLOYD'S

THIS CERTIFICATE REQUIRES ENDORSEMENT IN THE EVENT OF ASSIGNMENT

CLAIMS SETTLEMENT INSTRUCTIONS

1. Lloyd's Agent at Bombay is authorised to adjust and settle on behalf of the Underwriters, and to purchase on behalf of the Corporation of Lloyd's, in accordance with Lloyd's Standing Regulations for the Settlement of Claims Abroad, any claim which may arise on this Certificate.
2. In the event that Clause 1 is not completed claim papers should be sent to: Lyon Traill Attenborough Ltd., Lyon House, 160 Borough High Street, London SE1 1LB.

Certificate of Insurance No. C 6599/

This is to Certify **that there has been deposited with the Council of Lloyd's a continuous Contract effected by** *Lyon Traill Attenborough Ltd.* **of Lloyd's, acting on behalf of** *Ferry Freighting (Croydon) Limited and/or Associated and/or Subsidiary Companies* **with Underwriters at Lloyd's, and that the said Underwriters have undertaken to issue to** *Lyon Traill Attenborough Ltd.* **Policy/Policies of Insurance at Lloyd's to cover, up to** *£100,000* **in all by any one** *steamer or sending by air and/or road and/or rail and/or conveyances or location, Interest as detailed over* **from any port or ports, place or places in** *the United Kingdom* **to any port or ports, place or places in** *the World (***excluding** *Iran, Afghanistan, Lebanon and Nigeria) and/or vice versa, direct or including transhipment, other voyages held covered* **and that** *Ferry Freighting (Croydon) Limited and/or Associated and/or Subsidiary Companies* **are entitled to declare against the said Contract insurances attaching thereto on or after the** *First* **day of** *July, 1984.* **This Certificate is not valid in respect of insurances attaching after the** *Thirtieth* **day of** *June, 1987.*

for the Council of Lloyd's
Dated at Lloyd's, London, 15th June, 1984.

Conveyance 'CANDIA' **From** Tilbury
Via/To **To** New Delhi via Bombay
INSURED VALUE/Currency Seven Thousand, Four Hundred and Twenty Pounds - 82

Marks and Numbers
OCLU 1038299

Interest
1 x 40' Container S.T.C.
DIVAN SETS (107 Pieces)

SPECIMEN

CIF + 10%

We hereby declare for Insurance under the said Contract interest as specified above so valued subject to the special conditions stated below and on the back hereof.

Institute Cargo Clauses (A) or Institute Cargo Clauses (Air) (excluding sendings by Post) as applicable.
Institute War Clauses (Cargo) or Institute War Clauses (Air Cargo) (excluding sendings by Post) as applicable.
Institute Strikes Clauses (Cargo) or Institute Strikes Clauses (Air Cargo) as applicable.
Institute Classification Clause.
Shipped under or on deck, including jettison and washing overboard.
For the purpose of claims for general average and salvage charges recoverable hereunder the subject-matter insured shall be deemed to be insured for its full contributory value.

Underwriters agree losses, if any, shall be payable to the order of FERRY FREIGHTING (CROYDON) LIMITED and/or Associated and/or Subsidiary Companies on surrender of this Certificate.

In the event of loss or damage which may result in a claim under this Insurance, immediate notice should be given to the Lloyd's Agent at the port or place where the loss or damage is discovered in order that he may examine the goods and issue a survey report.

(Survey fee is customarily paid by claimant and included in valid claim against Underwriters.)

SEE IMPORTANT INSTRUCTIONS ON REVERSE

This Certificate not valid unless the Declaration be signed by

FERRY FREIGHTING (CROYDON) LIMITED
and/or Associated and/or Subsidiary Companies.

Dated 18th February 1986

Signed

Authorised Signatory

Brokers: Lyon Traill Attenborough Ltd.,
Lyon House, 160 Borough High Street, London SE1 1LB.

3798

Fig. 8.3(a). Marine insurance certificate

INTEREST

Moulding Compounds, Plastic Sheeting, Synthetic Resins, Co-Polymer Resins and Moulding Compounds, etc., as shipped for Cole Group, ATO Chemical Products Ltd. and Wedge Chemicals Ltd.
Other interests held covered.

"**Approved Interest**" Goods and/or Merchandise deemed to be approved if they attract no special hazard in regard to stowage, handling, packing or during normal methods of transit, or, by their inherent nature, pilferage, leakage, shortage, loss-in-weight, breakage, scratching, bruising, chipping, denting, bending or crushing, or are not liable to perish, deteriorate or suffer any change in quality, or suffer from electrical, mechanical, or any other form of derangement or breakdown.
Other interest including personal and household effects, held covered.

IMPORTANT INSTRUCTIONS IN EVENT OF CLAIM

DOCUMENTATION OF CLAIMS

To enable claims to be dealt with promptly, the Assured or their Agents are advised to submit all available supporting documents without delay, including when applicable:–

1. Original policy or certificate of insurance.
2. Original or copy shipping invoices, together with shipping specification and/or weight notes.
3. Original Bill of Lading and/or other contract of carriage.
4. Survey report or other documentary evidence to show the extent of the loss or damage.
5. Landing account and weight notes at final destination.
6. Correspondence exchanged with the Carriers and other Parties regarding their liability for the loss or damage.

IMPORTANT
LIABILITY OF CARRIERS, BAILEES OR OTHER THIRD PARTIES

It is the duty of the Assured and their Agents, in all cases, to take such measures as may be reasonable for the purpose of averting or minimising a loss and to ensure that all rights against Carriers, Bailees or other third parties are properly preserved and exercised. In particular, the Assured or their Agents are required:–

1. **To claim immediately on the Carriers, Port Authorities or other Bailees for any missing packages.**
2. **In no circumstances, except under written protest, to give clean receipts where goods are in doubtful condition.**
3. **When delivery is made by Container, to ensure that the Container and its seals are examined immediately by their responsible official. If the Container is delivered damaged or with seals broken or missing or with seals other than as stated in the shipping documents, to clause the delivery receipt accordingly and retain all defective or irregular seals for subsequent identification.**
4. **To apply immediately for survey by Carriers' or other Bailees' Representatives if any loss or damage be apparent and claim on the Carriers or other Bailees for any actual loss or damage found at such survey.**
5. **To give notice in writing to the Carriers or other Bailees within 3 days of delivery if the loss or damage was not apparent at the time of taking delivery.**

Note. – **The Consignees or their Agents are recommended to make themselves familiar with the Regulations of the Port Authorities at the port of discharge.**

NOTE.—**The Institute Clauses incorporated herein are deemed to be those current at the time of commencement of the risk.**
It is necessary for the Assured when they become aware of an event which is "held covered" under this Insurance to give prompt notice to Underwriters and the right to such cover is dependent upon compliance with this obligation.
Lloyd's Agents referred to herein are not insurers and are not liable for claims arising on this Certificate. The service of legal proceedings upon Lloyd's Agents is not effective service for the purpose of starting legal proceedings against Underwriters.
This Insurance is subject to English jurisdiction.

Printed by The Carlton Berry Co. Ltd.

Fig. 8.3(b). Marine insurance certificate (reverse)

Set your tabulator stops here **STAPLE DOCUMENTS ABOVE PERFORATION** ← Line-up here →

125 | 4376 7032 | CSR/ECI | 125-4376 7032

Shipper's Name and Address / Shipper's account Number	Not negotiable **Air Waybill** Issued by British Airways London Member of IATA **BRITISH AIRWAYS**
	Copies 1, 2 and 3 of this Air Waybill are originals and have the same validity
Consignee's Name and Address / Consignee's account Number	It is agreed that the goods described herein are accepted in apparent good order and condition (except as noted) for carriage SUBJECT TO THE CONDITIONS OF CONTRACT ON THE REVERSE HEREOF. THE SHIPPER'S ATTENTION IS DRAWN TO THE NOTICE CONCERNING CARRIERS' LIMITATION OF LIABILITY. Shipper may increase such limitation of liability by declaring a higher value for carriage and paying a supplemental charge if required. ISSUING CARRIER MAINTAINS CARGO ACCIDENT LIABILITY INSURANCE
Issuing Carrier's Agent Name and City	Accounting Information
Agent's IATA Code / Account No.	
Airport of Departure (Addr. of first Carrier) and requested Routing	
to / By first Carrier (Routing and Destination) / to / by / to / by	Currency / CHGS Code / WT/VAL PPD COLL / Other PPD COLL / Declared Value for Carriage / Declared Value for Customs
Airport of Destination / Flight/Date (For Carrier Use only) / Flight/Date	

Handling Information

No of Pieces RCP	Gross Weight	kg lb	Rate Class / Commodity Item No.	Chargeable Weight	Rate / Charge	Total	Nature and Quantity of Goods (incl. Dimensions or Volume)

Prepaid	Weight Charge	Collect	Other Charges
	Valuation Charge		
	Tax		
	Total other Charges Due Agent		Shipper certifies that the particulars on the face hereof are correct and that insofar as any part of the consignment contains dangerous goods, such part is properly described by name and is in proper condition for carriage by air according to the applicable Dangerous Goods Regulations.
	Total other Charges Due Carrier		Signature of Shipper or his Agent
Total prepaid		Total collect	
Currency Conversion Rates		cc charges in Dest. Currency	Executed on (Date) at (Place) Signature of Issuing Carrier or its Agent
For Carrier's Use only at Destination		Charges at Destination	Total collect Charges

125-4376 7032

M 197 - 2nd

Printed in the Fed. Rep. Germany

Original 3 - (For Shipper)

Fig. 8.4. Air waybill

in which they are considered from the points of view of the exporter and the importer.

EXAMINATION GUIDELINES

The reader is referred back to the comments on documentary credit examination questions given at the end of Chapter 7.

Question 1

Your customers, Northern Trading Co., are finding it difficult to obtain adequate sources of supply of raw materials for their operation in the UK. They have identified an Australian manufacturer who can meet their needs against secure methods of payment. You have been asked to establish an irrevocable letter of credit in favour of the Australian suppliers but the customers advise you that they do not understand the implications for the company.

REQUIRED

They would like to know:

(*a*) What is an irrevocable letter of credit.
(*b*) The basic documents they should call for and the details they would expect to find in those documents if the bank agreed to establish a letter of credit.
(*c*) Any precautions that the buyers can take to ensure that they receive the goods they have contracted to buy, whilst at the same time satisfying the seller's needs.

State briefly, in note form, what you would tell your customer.

SOLUTION

(*a*) Article 10 of *Uniform Customs and Practice for Documentary Credits* defines an irrevocable documentary credit as a definite undertaking of the issuing bank, provided that the stipulated documents are presented and that the terms and conditions of the credit are complied with:

(i) to make a payment at sight
or (ii) to make a deferred payment
or (iii) to accept a draft drawn by the beneficiary
or (iv) to negotiate a draft drawn by the beneficiary or to arrange for negotiation by another bank.

The article also stipulates that as it is an irrevocable credit, the bank's undertaking can neither be amended nor cancelled without the agreement of the issuing bank, the confirming bank (if any), and the beneficiary.

Thus a documentary credit guarantees payment, either immediately or at an agreed future time, provided the exporter produces all the documents called for in the credit and that they are in order, and that all the other terms and conditions of the credit are fulfilled, and if it is irrevocable it cannot be amended nor cancelled without his approval.

(*b*) The basic documents required are:

(*i*) Invoices in which the description of the goods marries up with the description in the credit. It must show the shipping marks, the number of items, the weight of the goods and the basis for the price, e.g. cif or fob.

(*ii*) An insurance document, either a policy or certificate as specified in the credit. A broker's cover note will not be acceptable. The amount of cover must be for 110 per cent of the cif or invoice value and must be in the same currency as the credit. It must be in a transferable form and cover all the risks specified in the credit. It must not be dated later than the transport document.

(*iii*) A transport document which, as the goods are coming from Australia and comprise bulky raw materials will be a bill of lading. This evidences transportation by sea and three copies with be issued by the master of the vessel. It is a document of title and one copy must be produced in order to take possession of the goods. The bill must indicate that the goods have been loaded on board and, if it is a c & f or cif contract, must be marked 'Freight Paid'. It should be endorsed in blank.

(*c*) A documentary credit provides no guarantee that the goods will be exactly what the importer has ordered as the banks involved are dealing with documents and not in goods and can only match up the descriptions in the credit and the invoice. To overcome this problem, as far as is possible, Northern Trading Co. should be advised to:

(*i*) Ask for a certificate of quality to accompany the shipping documents. It will be signed by a designated reputable company in Australia after they have inspected the goods or a sample of them.

and/or (*ii*) Arrange to pay for only a percentage of the goods through the documentary credit and the remainder after the goods have arrived in the UK and been inspected by them.

(*iii*) It is unlikely that the suppliers will agree to a revocable documentary credit as they have specifically asked for an irrevocable one, but it may be worth asking.

(*iv*) They should take out status reports on the suppliers through the bank and by judicious enquiries through the trade.

Other questions

1. A German importer contracts to purchase 500 tons of linseed oil from a London merchant, for shipment from Buenos Aires, at a price of US $300 per ton cif Hamburg, payment against the appropriate shipping documents to be made under a documentary letter of credit. The London merchant, in turn, buys from a producer in the Argentine on terms that are exactly the same except for the price, this being US $280 per ton.

State briefly what the 'appropriate shipping documents' will consist of and describe the alternative ways of handling the documentary letter of credit side of these deals, indicating any special points to be borne in mind.

(*Inst. of Bankers*)

2. Explain the following terms when applied to bills of lading.

(*a*) clean;
(*b*) stale;
(*c*) forwarding agent's bill;
(*d*) received for shipment.

Which of the above would not be acceptable to banks as tender under a documentary credit and why? (*Inst. of Freight Forwarders*)

3. You have received an irrevocable credit issued by a New York bank on the instructions of your US buyer. The credit is in US dollars and expires on Saturday, 21 February. It calls for documents covering a shipment of ten cases of kitchenware at $500 per case cif.

You present documents to the advising bank on Monday, 23 February. The invoice shows eleven cases of assorted pans but the amount claimed is only for ten cases at the specified price. The insurance, certificate dated 19 February covers all eleven cases for £3437—the sterling value of the invoice amount plus 10 per cent. The forwarding agent's bill of lading, dated 18 February, describes the goods as 'assorted pans'.

(*a*) Give the reasons why the British bank would refuse to negotiate.
(*b*) What action can you take to obtain payment as quickly as possible.

(*Inst. of Export*)

4. Your customers, Junk Galore Ltd, are negotiating to purchase goods from overseas for the first time. They advise you that they wish to purchase electronic calculators and that their suppliers have asked for an irrevocable letter of credit to be established in their favour. Under the terms of the letter of credit, the bills of exchange will be drawn on a UK bank in sterling at ninety days' sight. You are also advised that shipment will be effected by sea and that the price basis is cif UK port. Junk Galore Ltd have a contract to supply a buyer in the south of England within one month of the goods being received in the

UK. Your customers' facilities are fully extended but you would like to assist them in financing this import.

Supply brief notes listing:

(*a*) the points you must consider from the bank's point of view when establishing a letter of credit on behalf of your customers and the protection that may be available in the transaction itself;

(*b*) the practical steps necessary to ensure that at all stages the bank is fully protected. (*Inst. of Bankers*)

5. 'A documentary credit relieves the exporter of most of his anxieties and at the same time affords a degree of protection to the buyer.'

(*a*) What is the value of a documentary credit to an exporter and an importer respectively?

(*b*) Explain how each can obtain the highest degree of protection. (*Inst. of Bankers*)

6. On behalf of your customers, Import Traders Ltd, you recently established an irrevocable documentary letter of credit to cover the purchase of tinned tomatoes. Documents are presented under the credit and comply with the terms in every respect. Import Traders Ltd wish to defer payment because they claim that the goods have been shipped earlier than arranged in the contract between buyer and seller.

What would your answer be to this request? Give reasons and indicate how this dispute could have been avoided. (*Inst. of Bankers*)

7. The bill of lading is said to be one of the most important documents in international trade.

What are its characteristics that justify this statement? What are the requirements of the *Uniform Customs and Practice for Documentary Credits* concerning bills of lading? (*Inst. of Export*)

8. A London banker advises you of the issue of an irrevocable letter of credit in your favour from a Saudi Arabian bank. The relative drafts can be negotiated through the London bank.

Shipment is required by Friday, 24 March (Good Friday), and the credit expires on the same day. The credit calls for documents covering ten copying machines at £200 each cif Bahrain and is for the total value of £2000. Part shipments are not mentioned and the credit states that the insurance is to be covered by the beneficiary. It calls for four invoices and a certificate of origin, the originals of which have to be certified by the Arab/British Chamber of Commerce and legalized by the Saudi Arabian Embassy. A full set of clean, on board, freight paid bills of lading are required. You present documents to the London bank on Tuesday, 28 March. There is a set of three original shipped bills of lading dated 21 March that state that freight is payable in London.

Thinking to assist the buyer, you have sent him one of the original bills of lading with three copy invoices, direct. The cases have been packed in a container and under one of the clauses on the back of the bill lading the shipping company has the option to ship on deck. The bill of lading is claused 'one case damaged'.

The certificate of insurance from your insurance company is for the full invoice value (cif) plus 5 per cent and is dated 25 March (the date on which you received the bill of lading). The insurance certificate describes the goods as 'office machines'.

Owing to a short strike which held up production you are able to ship only eight machines. As the Arab/British Chamber of Commerce and the embassy were closed for one week (religious holiday) you cannot get the legalized documents back in time to present them with the other documents, so you write to the bank explaining the reason for the delay and saying you will forward them as soon as possible.

Would the London banker negotiate the documents 'without recourse' and if not why not? (*Inst. of Export*)

9. Explain the following terms when applied to bills of lading:

(*a*) clean;
(*b*) stale;
(*c*) forwarding agents' bill;
(*d*) received for shipment.

Which of the above would not be acceptable to banks as tender under a documentary credit and why? (*Inst. of Freight Forwarders*)

10. 'Documents presented by UK beneficiaries under documentary credits frequently do not conform to the terms and conditions of the credit.'

Discuss, in detail, the implications of this statement.

(*Inst. of Freight Forwarders*)

9
BILLS OF EXCHANGE

THE DIFFERENT KINDS OF BILL

A BILL of exchange provides a very useful device with which to settle an international trading transaction. From the exporter's point of view, the ideal arrangement is to draw a sight bill of exchange (frequently referred to as a draft) under a documentary credit, and to receive payment of it immediately upon presentation of the documents relating to the shipment and the draft. If the importer is not prepared to make such an arrangement, the next best thing from the exporter's point of view is to draw a *usance*, *tenor* or *term* bill (i.e. a bill drawn payable a number of days or months from its date or from the day it is received for acceptance by the drawee) under a credit and have it accepted by the bank confirming the credit.

When exporters and importers have been trading with one another for some time and have built up a satisfactory trading relationship, they may decide to dispense with documentary credits and rely solely on *documentary bills* to finance their transactions. This means that the exporter will despatch his goods and attach the documents relating to the consignment to the bill of exchange which he draws on the importer. The bill and the commercial documents are then sent through the exporter's bank to the importer's bank (or another bank in the importer's country) for acceptance and/or payment.

Another possibility is for the exporter to draw a *clean bill* on the importer, i.e. a bill without documents attached, and to send the commercial documents direct to the importer. In this way, the exporter has no control over the documents once he has parted with them and must rely upon the good faith of the importer for ultimate acceptance and payment of the bill.

A bill of exchange is defined in the Bills of Exchange Act 1882 as 'an unconditional order in writing, addressed by one person to another, signed by the person giving it, requiring the person to whom it is addressed to pay on demand, or at a fixed or determinable future time, a sum certain in money, to or to the order of, a specified person or to bearer'.

Bills of exchange are still sometimes drawn in sets of three and each set is despatched separately so that if there is any delay in the receipt of the first copy of the bill, the second or third copy can be presented. The bills are identical apart from a reference on the face of the bill to the other copies. Usually this takes the form of: 'At ninety days' sight pay this first bill of exchange (second and third unpaid).' The drawee must be careful to accept only one copy of the bill.

Commercial bills of exchange fall into two categories, *bank bills* and *trade bills.* A bank bill is one that is drawn on or bears the acceptance of a bank, i.e. a commercial bank or a merchant bank. As such, it carries little risk and can be discounted at the finest (i.e. lowest) rate of interest. Bills drawn by and accepted by commercial firms are known as trade bills and those bearing the signatures of firms of first-class repute are fine trade bills and can be discounted at rates of interest only fractionally higher than those for bank bills.

Accommodation bills or *finance bills* are drawn as a way of raising funds. A person, firm or merchant bank lends his or its name as drawee and acceptor of a bill to enable the drawer to raise funds by discounting the bill.

THE PARTIES TO A BILL

The person who draws the bill (i.e. the exporter or the person to whom a debt is due) is called the *drawer.* The person to whom the bill is addressed is called the *drawee*, and the person to whom payment is to be made is the *payee.* Usually the drawer and the payee are the same person (i.e. the firm drawing the bill will instruct the drawee to pay the bill 'to the order of ourselves'), but this is not essentially so.

An example of a bill of exchange is given in Fig. 9.1. This is an example of a draft drawn under an irrevocable documentary credit opened by an importer of die castings in Lombardia in favour of the British exporters, the Tungsten Metal Co. Ltd. The importer's bank is the Bank of Lombardia which has an office in London. The bank's London office have notified the exporters that the credit has been opened in their favour and have undertaken to accept bills of exchange at thirty days' sight drawn on them within the terms of the credit. It is a *usance* bill payable thirty days after sight. The drawers are the Tungsten Metal Co. Ltd, and they are also the payees. The drawee is the Bank of Lombardia, the issuing bank. It will be noticed that the bill of exchange refers to the documentary credit against which it is drawn and also mentioned the nature of the goods for which payment is sought. It is common practice to specify the goods in this way on bills of exchange, though it is by no means essential to do so. Where a bill is accepted by a bank in the UK, and therefore it is likely to find its way into the London discount market, i.e. be sold to a discount house, this type of clausing is desirable because when a clearing bank buys a bill from a discount house it likes to see evidence of an underlying transaction.

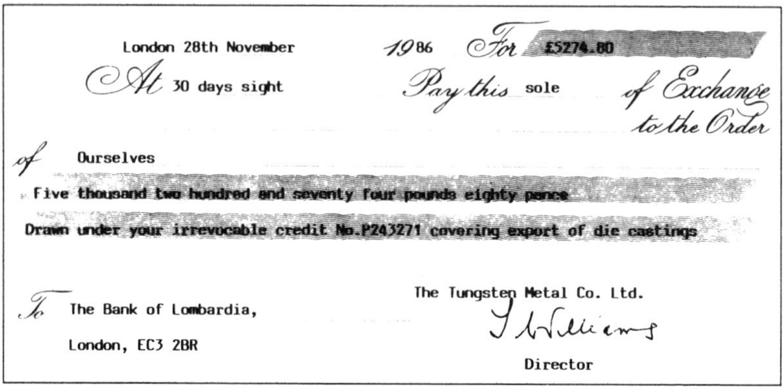
London 28th November 1986 For £5274.80

At 30 days sight Pay this sole of Exchange to the Order

of Ourselves

Five thousand two hundred and seventy four pounds eighty pence

Drawn under your irrevocable credit No.P243271 covering export of die castings

To The Bank of Lombardia,

London, EC3 2BR

The Tungsten Metal Co. Ltd.

J Williams

Director

Fig. 9.1. Bill drawn under a documentary credit

Drawing a bill of exchange is a responsibility, because by virtue of s.55 of the Bills of Exchange Act the drawer 'engages that on due presentation it shall be accepted and paid according to its tenor and that if it be dishonoured he will compensate the holder or any endorser who is compelled to pay it, provided that the requisite proceedings on dishonour are duly taken'.

A term or usance bill needs to be accepted by the drawee. This he does by writing his name across the face of the bill or, more usually, by writing something on the following lines followed by his signature: 'Accepted payable at Cornhill Bank Ltd, 959 Threadneedle Street, London, EC2 6SB.' In accepting a bill of exchange, the acceptor undertakes that it will be paid within the terms of his acceptance. This applies whether or not he has received any consideration. If the drawee fails to accept a bill of exchange when it is presented for acceptance it is said to be dishonoured by non-acceptance.

An endorser of a bill is liable on it to subsequent endorsers and holders of the bill. If, however, an endorser adds the words *sans recours*, or *without recourse,* after his signature, he limits his liability, but the holder of the bill has recourse to other parties to the bill whose liability has not been limited in this way.

THE USE OF BILLS

A bill of exchange is a useful means of settlement in that it:

(*a*) provides written evidence of a debt that can be used in a court of law;
(*b*) enables the exporter to obtain immediate payment, by presentation if it is a sight bill, or by negotiation if it is a usance bill, or, possibly, get an advance against it;
(*c*) enables the importer to delay payment until the bill's maturity.

If a bill of exchange is a *documentary* bill it will be accompanied by the commercial documents relating to the goods for which payment is sought. The exporter presents the documents called for in the contract between the importer and himself to his bank and instructs the bank to deliver them to the importer against either acceptance or payment of the bill. If the documents are to be released against the importer's acceptance of the bill, the bill is called a D/A bill (documents against acceptance) and if upon payment then the bill is a D/P bill (documents against payment). If a bill is a *sight* or demand bill, the documents will be handed over only against payment of the bill. If the bill is a *usance* bill, the documents will be handed over against acceptance or against payment in accordance with the exporter's instructions. The drawee of a bill is entitled to inspect the documents before accepting the bill and this is usually done at the presenting bank's premises, though if he is a customer of repute he may be allowed to inspect them at his own premises with the understanding that he must return them within twenty-four hours unless he accepts the bill. If a bill is a D/P bill, the drawee is usually allowed to inspect them only at the bank.

The documents attached to a documentary bill are, of course, those called for in the documentary credit, if there is one, or those agreed in the contract, and the reader is referred to the previous chapter for detailed comment on the documents that are used in international trade. In some cases, the importer will have no choice but to ask for particular documents to comply with the laws and customs of his country.

If a bill is dishonoured, notice of dishonour must be given to the drawer and to each endorser against whom it is desirable to retain recourse. A foreign bill dishonourd by non-acceptance must be protested for non-acceptance, and if such a bill is dishonoured by non-payment it must be duly protested for non-payment. Failure to protest releases the drawer and endorsers from liability on the bill. In the UK, a bill may be 'noted' for non-acceptance or non-payment as a preliminary step to protesting.

The formal procedure of protest provides proof of presentation and dishonour acceptable in a court of law both in the UK and in foreign countries. In some countries, publicity is given to protested bills to discourage traders from dishonouring bills.

NEGOTIATION AND COLLECTION OF BILLS

The process of selling a foreign bill of exchange to a bank is called negotiation, but negotiation involves much more than simply discounting, which is the term used when a bank buys a domestic bill. There may not in fact be a bill of exchange, simply the commercial documents to be presented to the overseas buyer against payment. If the bank is prepared to buy these documents it will pay over the face value less discount to the exporter. Similarly, if there is a bill of exchange drawn on the buyer it is purchased together with the commercial documents, and the bill and/or the commercial documents are sent for collection by the bank in its own right as owner of them. In effect, the banker advances the value of the bill to his customer until the proceeds are received because he has full recourse against the drawer by virtue of s.55 of the Bills of Exchange Act 1882, and usually takes a signed undertaking from the customer to the effect that he will reimburse the bank if the bill is dishonoured.

A bill that is negotiated is unlikely to have been accepted, whereas a domestic bill that has been discounted will always have been accepted before being offered for discounting, and it will always be a term bill as there is no point in discounting a sight bill which could so easily be presented to the drawee in order to obtain an immediate payment of the face value. A foreign bill for negotiation, on the other hand, may be either a sight or term bill. It will be drawn on a drawee overseas and will be payable overseas.

The price at which a bank will be prepared to negotiate a bill of exchange and/or documents will naturally depend upon the rate of interest that is appropriate at the time and also the length of time to maturity. The bank will not receive the proceeds until the bill has been presented to the drawee and paid and the proceeds have been remitted back. The bank will be out of funds until it gets the proceeds and must charge for this, for the cost of collection and for any additional risks involved.

The bank's attitude to its customer who wishes to negotiate a bill will be affected by the existence of a policy issued by Export Credits Guarantee Department (ECGD), the benefits of which can be assigned to the bank. An ECGD policy gives protection from the insolvency or protracted default on the part of the buyer and many other risks, and covers anything up to 95 per cent of the value of the goods. The Department's facilities are dealt with in detail in Chapter 11. A bank may agree to negotiate a bill of exchange only on condition that an ECGD policy is taken out and assigned to the bank. Quite apart from this form of security, the bank will apply normal lending considerations to the proposition and in the final analysis its decision will be based very much on its assessment of the exporter customer's character and creditworthiness.

A bank is a *holder for value* of a bill it has negotiated and may secure the protection of being a *holder in due course*, which is defined in the Bills of Exchange Act 1882 as a holder of a bill 'who takes it, complete and regular on the face of it and not overdue, in good faith, for valuable consideration and without knowledge of any defect in the title of the person from whom the bill was taken'. Thus the banker has a valid claim against all parties to the bill and collects the proceeds on its own behalf.

In addition to the security of the bill itself, and any other security the bank insists upon, the bank has the security of any documents attached to the bill. The bank may require its customer to sign a *letter of pledge* or *letter of hypothecation* pledging the goods to the bank. The bank may thus be able to sell the goods represented by the documents and will take particular care to ensure that there are no discrepancies in the documents that will delay or prevent payment.

Where funds are not required immediately, or where bills are not sufficiently attractive to the banker for negotiation, they may be handed by an exporter to his bank for collection, when the bank will act as the exporter's agent in collecting the proceeds. If the customer wishes to borrow on the strength of a bill sent for collection, it is unlikely that the banker will advance the full value of the bill and may insist on retaining a margin to be paid over to the customer when the bill is collected. This is common practice and the normal margin is about 10–15 per cent. The extent of the margin must, of course, depend upon the financial standing of the customer, for although the collecting bank has full recourse against its customer, in the last resort, whether or not it makes a loss through dishonour depends upon the customer's ability to pay. The margin may not be necessary if the customer is able to put up sufficient security. He may, for instance, be able to give a pledge over other bills of exchange the bank is collecting for him, or an assignment of his book debts.

In collecting bills of exchange the bank sends the bills (and documents attached, if there are any) to a correspondent bank overseas, instructing that bank to present the bill for acceptance and/or payment and to hand over the documents against acceptance or payment. Apart from default or negligence on the part of its own servants, a collecting bank will make it clear to its customer that it accepts no responsibility for any delays that occur in collecting a bill, nor for any omissions on the part of the bank's agents overseas in looking after the documents, nor any default of any kind. As agent for its customer, the bank must take precise instructions from him and carry them out with care. The British banks therefore require detailed instructions from their customers when they request that a bill of exchange be negotiated or collected. The request form sets out a list of instructions, such as those given below, and the customer is required to indicate which ones are applicable and delete the alternative that is not applicable where an alternative is given:

1. Release documents against acceptance.
2. Release documents against payment.
3. Release goods against acceptance.
4. Release goods against payment.
5. Acceptance/payment may be deferred pending arrival of the goods.
6. Collect all charges from drawees.
7. Charges may be waived if refused.
8. Advise acceptance and due date by airmail/cable.
9. Remit proceeds by airmail/cable.
10. Advise non-acceptance by airmail/cable.
11. Advise non-payment by airmail/cable.
12. In case of need refer to . . .

    (*a*) Follow their instructions without reserve. } Delete as
    (*b*) For assistance only. } required.

13. If unaccepted/unpaid protest.
14. If unaccepted/unpaid do not protest.
15. If documents are not duly taken up on arrival of goods, store goods (if possible in customs or bonded warehouse) and insure against:

    (*a*) fire only } Delete as required.
    (*b*) all available risks }

Claim all charges from drawees, but if not paid by them, they are for our account.

Instructions 3 and 4 apply only where the goods are to be addressed to a bank. This might apply to goods sent by air or by parcel post.

Uniform rules for collections

In the same way that the international banks have a common code of practice for documentary credits, so they have for the collection of bills. This is the *Uniform Rules for Collections*, the English version of which is reproduced in full in Appendix II. These rules were written by a committee of bankers under the aegis of the ICC in the same way as *Uniform Customs and Practice for Documentary Credits.* In the comments that follow the references given are to the appropriate articles of the *Uniform Rules for Collections.*

Like the *Uniform Customs,* the rules for the collection of bills and other instruments are in effect written into a bank's contract with its customer by a statement on the bank's form of application for the collection of bills, that the provisions and definitions in the *Uniform Rules* will apply unless otherwise expressly stated or unless contrary to the provisions of a national, state or local law and/or regulation that cannot be departed from.

The *Rules* make a clear distinction between *financial* documents and *commercial* documents. Financial documents are defined as bills of exchange, promissory notes, cheques, payment receipts or other similar instruments used for obtaining the payment of money. Commercial documents are defined as invoices, shipping documents, documents of title or other similar documents, or any other documents whatsoever, not being financial documents. This distinction between the two types of documents is important when considering the difference between a *clean collection* and a *documentary collection.* The former is concerned with the collection of financial documents not accompanied by commercial documents whereas the latter is the collection of commercial documents, with or without financial documents.

There are five parties concerned with a collection, the customer, the remitting bank, the collecting bank, the presenting bank and the drawee. The customer is the principal who entrusts the operation of collection to his bank, which is the remitting bank. The collecting bank is any bank, other than the remitting bank, involved in processing the collection order, and the presenting bank is the collecting bank making presentation to the drawee—more than one collecting bank may be involved in collecting a bill and it is the bank that actually presents the bill to the drawee for acceptance/payment that is the presenting bank. The drawee is the person specified as the one to whom the financial document and/or commercial documents is to be presented.

A collecting bank must be sent a collection order with the documents concerned, and this must give complete and concise instructions. It will in fact incorporate all the instructions contained in the application form (see p. 150). Banks are only permitted to act upon instructions given in such an order and must advise the remitting bank immediately if they cannot comply with the instructions contained in the order.

Banks are under no obligation to examine the commercial documents and are not responsible for their regularity other than to verify that they appear to be as listed in the collection order. They must advise the party from whom the collection order was received of any documents that are missing (Article 2).

The collection order must bear the complete address of the drawee or of the domicile at which presentation is to be made (Article 8).

Presentation for payment of sight drafts, and of usance drafts for acceptance must be made without delay and usance drafts must be presented for payment not later than the appropriate maturity date. The collection order must state whether documents are to be released against acceptance (D/A) or against payment (D/P). In the absence of instructions, *the documents will be released only against payment* (Articles 9 and 10).

Documents will be released to the drawee only against payment in local currency which can be immediately disposed of in accordance with the instructions in the collection order, or, where payment is to be made in the currency of a country other than the country of payment, against payment in the relative foreign currency which can immediately be remitted in accordance with the instructions in the collection order (Articles 11 and 12). This is important from the point of view of the presenting bank (usually the importer's bank). If there is any doubt as to whether the funds being paid over can be remitted, i.e. if there are exchange control regulations that prohibit the remittance, then the payment must not be accepted. The presenting banker must refuse to hand over the documents, if it is a D/P bill, and notify the remitting bank of the situation.

Article 13 stipulates that partial payments of clean remittances may be accepted if the law in force in the place of payment permits this, and in the case of documentary remittances, only if the collection order specifically authorizes partial payments. The documents will only be released after final payment has been received.

The presenting bank is responsible for seeing that the form of the acceptance appears to be complete and correct, but it is not responsible for the genuineness of any signature or for the authority of any signatory to sign the acceptance (Article 15).

The collection order must give specific instructions regarding protest for non-acceptance or non-payment and should clearly indicate the powers of a case-of-need if one is nominated. If instructions concerning protest are not given, the banks concerned are not responsible for any failure to protest, and whether a case-of-need is nominated or not, in the absence of specific instructions the collecting bank has no obligation to take any action in respect of the goods represented by the documentary remittance (Articles 17, 18 and 19).

Advice of payment or non-payment, acceptance or non-acceptance, must be sent to the place from which the collection order was received without delay; and in the absence of instructions to the contrary, by the quickest mail. Even where specific instructions are given concerning the method of notification, if the bank considers the matter to be urgent, it may advise by other quicker methods at the expense of the customer (Article 20).

If interest is due because it is written into a financial document, e.g. a bill of exchange, as an unconditional and definitive interest clause, it can be waived only if the collection order to authorizes. However, interest collected on the basis of instructions in the collection order and not embodied in the financial document may be waived unless the collection order says otherwise. Refusal to pay interest must be notified to the bank from which the collection order was received (Article 21).

If the collecting bank is instructed to obtain the charges and expenses from the drawee and the drawee refuses to pay them, the commercial paper may be delivered without payment of them, unless the bank is expressly instructed to the contrary (Article 22).

Banks utilize the services of other banks for the account of and at the risk of the customer (the principal). A customer may nominate the collecting bank to be employed, but the remitting bank has the right to direct commercial paper to such a collecting bank through a correspondent bank of its own choice (Article 3).

Goods should not be despatched direct to the address of a bank or consigned to a bank without prior agreement on the part of that bank. Where goods are despatched direct to a bank for delivery to the drawee against payment or acceptance, the bank has no obligation to take delivery of the goods, which remain at the risk and responsibility of the party despatching the goods (Article 6).

Other articles in the *Uniform Rules* absolve the banks from liability or responsibility for the consequences arising out of delays or interruption of their business. All the provisions of the *Rules* are, of course, designed to protect the banks. This is all very well, but the banks must be careful to protect their customers' interests as well if they are to remain customers, and therefore it is essential that the customer should be required to give concise instructions when asking his bank to collect a bill of exchange. If the student carefully compares the *Uniform Rules* with the list of instructions that should be taken from the customer (see p. 150), he will appreciate the need for taking such precise instructions. These instructions must be carefully passed on to the collecting bank in the collection order.

Trust receipts

Where a bank, acting as agent for an overseas bank, receives documents that are to be handed over to an importer against payment, it may be prepared to release the documents before the maturity date of the draft against what is known as a *trust receipt.* Similarly, if the bank is advancing money to the importer to enable him to pay a sight draft, it may take the commercial documents plus a letter of pledge as security, and yet be willing to release the documents to the importer against a trust receipt. In either case it would do this only for an importer of good standing, to enable him to get possession of the goods so that they can be sold. In the wording of the trust receipt, the customer undertakes to land, store, insure and hold the goods as agent for the bank and to pay the proceeds of sale to the bank. He also undertakes to pay sufficient funds to the bank to meet the draft, either from the proceeds of sale or from some other source, at least three days before maturity and to deliver up either the documents or the goods to the bank if called upon to do so.

The customer holds the documents, the goods they represent, and the proceeds of the goods when they are sold in trust for the bank, hence the title *trust receipt.* The bank has this legal document and could sue the customer if he defaults. This would be little comfort to the bank, however, if the customer pledged the documents of title to the goods elsewhere, allowed the goods to become intermingled with his own goods in a warehouse, or failed to pay in the proceeds of sale, made sure they were untraceable and then went into bankruptcy. In the last resort, therefore, the bank must depend upon the soundness of its customer, and will not allow documents to be released against a trust receipt unless the importer is very reliable.

The due date of a bill

Where a bill is payable at a given number of days after sight or date, these days must be calculated precisely, but where it is payable at a given number of months, calendar months are used. A few examples will make the procedure clear. A ninety-day bill dated or sighted on 7 April is payable on 6 July. This is calculated as follows:

	23	days left in April
	31	days in May
	30	days in June
	6	days up to 6 July
	—	
Total	90	days

A three months' bill dated or sighted on 18 May is due on 18 August. No allowance is made for the days lacking in a month, i.e. for those months that have less than thirty-one days. Therefore, a bill dated or sighted on the 31st of the month would become due on the last day of the month whether it was the 28th, 29th, 30th or 31st, e.g. a two months' bill dated 31 July would be payable on 30 September, and a three months' bill sighted 31 January would be payable on 30 April. However, a three months' bill dated 28 February would be payable on 28 May.

If a usance bill is expressed to be payable three months after date, then this period is calculated from the actual date of the bill. If, however, it is payable three months after sight, then the period begins from the date of acceptance, i.e. the day the bill of exchange is sighted by the drawee. As bills are usually accepted the day they are sighted, the date of acceptance is taken as the date of sight.

A bill of exchange is payable on the last day of the payment period unless that day is a Saturday, Sunday or Bank Holiday, in which case it is payable on the next working day.

Exchange clauses

The majority of bills of exchange drawn by British exporters are drawn in sterling, and in order to ensure that no dispute or uncertainty arises as to the rate of exchange to be used when the bill is met by the importer by a payment in foreign currency, an exchange clause is sometimes used. For bills payable in some countries such as Australia, South Africa, Zambia, Bangladesh, India and Pakistan, clauses are very commonly used. If a bill is drawn in a foreign currency there is no need for an exchange clause, for it is then up to the exporter to sell the currency proceeds at the best possible rate of exchange and, furthermore, he can sell the proceeds in the forward exchange market and ascertain in advance precisely what the sterling proceeds will amount to. If the bill is drawn in sterling, he knows how much he should receive in sterling, but will want to ensure that this is not whittled down through loss in exchange, bank charges for commission and interest, and postages and stamp duty.

A very common clause is the *exchange as per endorsement* clause, which is used on bills for negotiation drawn on Australia, South Africa and some other African countries. The wording of the bill includes the clause '*payable with exchange and stamps as per endorsement*'. The rate is endorsed on the back of the bill by the negotiating bank and it is a rate that will produce the sterling amount of the bill plus the interest on the money that has been advanced to the exporter and stamp duty.

Once a bill bearing the 'exchange as per endorsement clause' has been converted into the foreign currency equivalent, the amount of it is written on the face of the bill above the sterling amount and the bill becomes a foreign currency bill. The negotiating banker receives this amount in foreign currency when the bill matures, so that he has, in effect, bought the currency from his customer, paying the sterling amount for it. It is the banker who runs the exchange risk, but he covers himself by selling the currency forward.

Another clause that is used on bills on Australia for negotiation is:

> Payable at the Australian on London sight selling rate at the date of maturity, together with interest at . . . per cent per annum from the date of the draft to the approximate date of arrival of the proceeds in London, together with all bank charges and stamps.

The effect of this clause is similar to that of the first type, in that the exporter receives the face value of the bill without any deductions for interest and other bank charges and stamp duty.

Where bills on Australia are sent for collection, interest charges are not involved and the usual clause is '*payable at the current rate of exchange for sight drafts on London plus stamp duty*'. If bank charges and postage are also to be paid by the importer, the clause will continue '*and all bank charges and postage*'.

There are a number of other exchange clauses used on international bills of exchange and these include the following:

> 'Payable without loss in exchange.'

'Payable with approved banker's cheque on London for full face value.'
'Payable at the collecting bank's selling rate for sight drafts on London at the date of maturity.'

ADVANTAGES OF BILLS

To complete this chapter it would be as well if we summarized the advantages to the exporter and importer respectively, of using a documentary bill of exchange as a method of payment.

Advantages to the exporter

(*a*) Whilst not as secure a method of payment as a documentary credit, the bank's control over the documents, especially with a D/P bill, offers more security than open account terms or a clean bill.
(*b*) An accepted bill is evidence of a debt and may be used in an action in a court of law.
(*c*) He can give a period of credit to the buyer by drawing a usance bill, and yet be able to get immediate finance by negotiating the bill and documents, or by obtaining an advance against the bill if it is sent for collection. But his finance could prove expensive.
(*d*) The presenting bank may be able to press the drawer for payment and be better able to succeed than the exporter himself.

Advantages to the importer

(*a*) It is a cheaper method of payment than a documentary credit, the expense of which inevitably falls on the importer.
(*b*) If the bill is a usance bill he has a period of credit during which he might be able to resell the goods and obtain payment for them.
(*c*) He can take delivery of the goods if it is a D/A bill and ensure that they are what he ordered.
(*d*) He may be able to defer accepting the bill or paying it until after the goods arrive, if this is permitted in the collection order.
(*e*) If he has to pay the bill at sight he may nevertheless be able to obtain credit on the strength of the goods until he has resold them and been paid.

It will be seen that both for the exporter and the importer the use of a bill of exchange makes it possible to obtain finance. Justice has not been done to the question of post-shipment finance in this chapter as it forms the subject of Chapters 10 and 11 where the various means of obtaining finance are examined in detail.

EXAMINATION GUIDELINES

Questions on the use of bills of exchange in international trade are very popular with examiners and in the Institute of Bankers' examination the student can be sure that at least one will occur every time. Most of them are concerned with the collection process and call for some detailed references to the requirements of the *Uniform Rules for Collections.* A close study of these rules is therefore likely to prove well worthwhile. They are relatively short and straightforward, and quite explicit. Study them in the light of the comments and references to the particular Articles in the chapter before working through the following questions.

As mentioned in the Examination Guidelines at the end of Chapter 7, questions requiring the student to compare documentary credits and bills for collection as methods of payment are included at the end of this chapter as the reader should now be in a better position to answer them.

Question 1

A. Clothier, senior director of your customers, Cover-up Ltd, is negotiating for the first time with suppliers abroad to purchase some outer wear garments at present unobtainable in the UK. The terms of payment the sellers have suggested are a ninety days' sight draft D/A with presentation through a UK bank. You understand that the presentation will be subject to *Uniform Rules for Collections* (ICC publication No. 322) and the shipping terms are to be c & f UK port. Your customer believes he will have the opportunity of examining the goods when they are received in the UK and that, if they are not in accordance with specification, he can refuse the goods and will not be liable to pay the sellers, since all charges will be against the goods.

REQUIRED

(*a*) Brief notes on the terms of payment mentioned above.
(*b*) The instructions you would expect to see on the collection order.
(*c*) What you would say to the suggestion by Mr Clothier that, if the goods were not in accordance with specification, the company could refuse to take them up and pay for them.

SOLUTION

(*a*) These terms of payment mean that a draft will be drawn on A. Clothier by the supplier payable at ninety days after sight. The draft and the commercial documents relating to the shipment will be sent with an accompanying collection order from the seller's bank to us as the importer's bank (possibly through the agency of one or more other banks). The collection order will instruct us that the commercial documents are to be released to Mr Clothier against his acceptance of the bill of exchange. His acceptance of the bill will constitute a legal obligation to pay it at maturity, which will be ninety days after the date of the acceptance.

The shipping terms c & f UK port mean that the supplier will be responsible for paying carriage to a UK port and that the price quoted therefore includes that carriage. Marine insurance costs are not included in the price and therefore Mr Clothier would have to arrange and pay for this. The supplier must not only pay the shipping freight but also get the goods to the ship. The buyer is responsible for all charges incurred once the goods have been unloaded at the UK port.

(*b*) The instructions to be contained in the collection order will reflect the requirements of the *Uniform Rules for Collections* and be as follows:

(*i*) The documents are to be released against acceptance of the ninety-day draft.

(*ii*) Whether acceptance of the bill of exchange may be deferred until the arrival of the goods.

(*iii*) If the bill is not accepted by our customer should the bill be protested for non-acceptance, and similarly if the bill is not paid at maturity should it be protested for non-payment?

(*iv*) Whether the advices of acceptance or non-acceptance and payment or non-payment should be sent by airmail or cable.

(*v*) The name of the case of need, if there is to be one, and whether his instructions should be taken without reserve or whether he should be consulted for advice only.

(*vi*) If the bill is paid how are the proceeds to be remitted, by airmail or by cable?

(*vii*) If the charges are for the account of the drawees or not and if they are whether they may be waived.

(*viii*) If the bill is not accepted what is to be done with the goods? Are they to be warehoused and insured at the drawer's expense?

(*c*) The bank must act in accordance with these instructions in the collection order and in accordance with the *Uniform Rules for Collections.* This must be explained to our customer together with a list of the instructions likely to be contained in the order. Article 10 of *Uniform Rules* specifies that with a D/A bill the commercial documents are to be released to the drawee against acceptance and therefore he must accept before he receives the documents that will enable him to inspect the goods. If he then discovers that the goods are not what he ordered he must nevertheless pay the bill of exchange at maturity in accordance with his acceptance and in accordance with the Bills of Exchange Act 1882. It must also be explained to Mr Clothier that if the bill is not accepted, or if it is accepted and then it is not paid, the bank will have no alternative but to protest for non-acceptance or non-payment if the collection order stipulates that this is to be done.

Question 2

Your customers, Import Anything Ltd, purchase goods from the Far East. On 30 September you receive, for presentation to your customers, a ninety days' sight documentary bill of exchange dated 1 September, together with a collection order indicating the following:

(*a*) Subject to *Uniform Rules for Collections* (ICC Publication No. 322).
(*b*) Release documents against acceptance.
(*c*) Protest if unpaid.
(*d*) In case of need contact Far Eastern agents.
(*e*) Collect interest at 10 per cent from date of bill to the due date.

The customers accept the bill of exchange but at maturity decline to pay and offer 50 per cent down, stating that the drawer has agreed to reduce the bill amount because of faulty goods. The customers also claim that in any event interest is *not* payable on the bill and they must therefore refuse to pay any.

REQUIRED

(*a*) A brief explanation of the meaning of (*a*) above
(*b*) your advice to the customers concerning their offer.

SOLUTION

(*a*) The *Uniform Rules for Collections* are a code of practice drawn up by the International Chamber of Commerce in conjunction with a committee of international bankers, and accepted by banks in most parts of the world. This is clearly not a code of law, but the fact that the banks make it clear on the collection order to all parties concerned with a bill of exchange that is sent for collection that the collection is subject to the *Rules* would be good defence at law. The rules are there to assist the banks in collecting bills of exchange and other financial documents, handing over commercial documents against acceptance and/or payment of the financial document, or simply handing over the commercial documents against a straight payment without a financial document.

The *Uniform Rules* are particularly useful to the banks when attempting to resolve misunderstandings and difficulties that arise. As far as some problems are concerned, such as refusal to pay interest as in this question, the *Rules* are quite explicit as to how the presenting bank must react.

(*b*) The bank must not act on the customer's statement that, because the goods are faulty the drawer has agreed to reduce the bill, and must act only on the strength of its mandate, which is the collection order. It is acting as agent for the remitting bank and must obey its instructions contained in that order. One of these instructions is that, if the bill is unpaid, it must be protested and this the bank must do if the bill is not paid in full.

Although there is a case of need named in the collection order, his powers are not stated and therefore the bank must not act upon his instructions, though it can be advised by him.

The bank may decide to accept the 50 per cent payment and place it on suspense account. It should then protest for the remaining 50 per cent and inform the remitting bank by cable and also the case of need.

As far as interest is concerned, as it is mentioned in the collection order, and not presumably in the bill of exchange, it may be waived as the customer refuses to pay it. This is in accordance with Article 21 of *Uniform Rules.* If the interest has been written into the bill of exchange, however, it could not be waived unless the collection order says otherwise.

Question 3

Tall Tale Ltd, wholesale booksellers, wish to import expensive rare books and have come to you for help and advice. They have been given to understand that payment will have to be made to their main suppliers of these books by means of either an irrevocable letter of credit calling for bills of exchange drawn at ninety days sight or a documentary collection through the bank on sight D/P terms.

REQUIRED

(*a*) A description of each method of payment.
(*b*) The advantages and disadvantages of each method.

SOLUTION

(*a*) A documentary letter of credit is defined in Article 2 of *Uniform Customs and Practice for Documentary Credits* (1983 Revision) as an arrangement whereby a bank (the issuing bank), acting at the request and on the instructions of a customer (the applicant for the credit) is to make a payment to the beneficiary or to his order, or is to pay or accept bills of exchange drawn by him, or authorizes another bank to do these things or to negotiate such a bill of exchange.

This is on condition that stipulated commercial documents are presented and that all the terms and conditions of the documentary credit are complied with.

As the documentary credit is to be an irrevocable one, in accordance with Article 10, it cannot be amended nor cancelled without the agreement of the issuing bank, the confirming bank (if any) and the beneficiary.

Thus, by using this method of payment, Tall Tale Ltd would be providing their suppliers with a banker's guarantee of payment, ninety days after the commercial documents and the bill of exchange are presented to the advising bank in the exporter's country, provided all the conditions are met. The advising bank will accept the bill of exchange and it will be payable by them at maturity.

A documentary collection is described in the preamble to *Uniform Rules for Collections*. As the handling by banks, on instructions received, of documents, in order to

(*a*) obtain acceptance and/or payment
or (*b*) deliver commercial documents against acceptance and/or payment
or (*c*) deliver documents on other term and conditions.

The documents referred to in this description are (*a*) financial documents and (*b*) commercial documents. The former are bills of exchange, promissory notes, cheques, etc., and the latter are invoices, shipping documents, documents of title or other similar documents, not being financial documents.

A collection can be either clean or documentary; the former is not accompanied by commercial documents whereas the latter is, although a documentary collection could consist of only the commercial documents, payment being made against them without a bill of exchange.

The collections referred to are to be documentary collections and therefore the commercial documents will accompany the bills of exchange, and as the bills are to be D/P bills, the commercial documents will be handed over to Tall Tale Ltd only against payment. We shall be acting as presenting bank and shall have to obtain the acceptance of Tall Tale Ltd on the ninety-day bills of exchange and then present them to them at maturity for payment.

(*b*) *Letters of credit:* These offer the advantage to Tall Tale Ltd of ninety days' credit plus possession of the documents, and hence access to the goods once they have arrived. They may be able to resell the goods before the payment is made under the credit.

If our customers include a certificate of quality as one of the documents called for in the credit, they will be inspected by a nominated party in the exporter's country before despatch. This will give added protection to our customers because the documentary credit system does not ensure that the quality of the goods is up to expectations, in that the banks handle only the documents and their responsibility lies only in making sure that the description in the invoice matches the description in the credit.

Unless the overseas supplier agrees to meet the bank charges in connection with the documentary credit, this will have to be borne by our customers, and these charges are higher than those for documentary collections.

When opening a documentary credit on behalf of a customer, a bank is undertaking a liability, and therefore it will include that liability amongst others, such as performance bonds, acceptances and forward exchange contracts, in accessing the borrowing capacity of the customer. The use of documentary credits as the method of payment could therefore reduce the ability of the customers to borrow from the bank.

Documentary collections: As mentioned above, the bank charges for documentary collections are less than those for a documentary credit. Our customers could refuse to pay them and they may be waived unless the collection order says otherwise. However there may be a contractual obligation to pay the charges, though they are unlikely to be sued for them.

Similarly the customers may refuse to take up the documents, i.e. refuse to pay the bill of exchange, and leave the goods in the hands of the presenting bank. But again the customers cannot avoid their contractual obligations and may be sued by the suppliers for non-performance of their contract.

There are two disadvantages of D/P collections, firstly, that in order to get hold of the documents the importer must pay for the goods, and this may mean denying himself the credit period. Secondly, the importer has no opportunity to examine the goods before paying.

Other questions

1. 'In all cases, whether the bill is collected or negotiated, it is important that the bank should receive the clearest instructions from the customer.'

What major points would you expect such instructions to cover in the case of a documentary tenor bill of exchange drawn by a UK exporter on his overseas buyer and handed by the exporter to his bank for collection? (*Inst. of Bankers*)

2. Your customers, Home Products Ltd, have received their first enquiry from a merchant in Canada. The enquirer asks for the price to be quoted in sterling 'cif Montreal' and suggests payment terms 'ninety days' sight draft D/A'.

(*a*) How would you explain these terms to the customer?
(*b*) What risks are there in the method of payment suggested?
(*c*) By what method could the buyer obtain ninety days' credit with complete security for your customer? (*Inst. of Bankers*)

3. You are negotiating a contract with overseas buyers to supply machinery valued at £100 000. They have offered to pay by means of a bill of exchange drawn on them at ninety days' sight D/A.

(*a*) Explain the meaning of this offer.
(*b*) What risks do you incur?
(*c*) How can you guard against such risks? (*Inst. of Export*)

4. Bills of exchange are used as a convenient means of collecting a commercial debt under documentary credit as well as under collection procedures.

Describe briefly the differences between the two methods of settlement mentioned in the previous sentence, and state how bills of exchange may be used under each method for settlement purposes. (*Inst. of Freight Forwarders*)

5. The following terms have been quoted to your customer in respect of the purchase of goods from the Far East, by the sellers' London representative, Tom Jones & Co., who operate in an advisory capacity and are not empowered to act on behalf of their principals:

Thirty days' sight D/P
Ninety days' sight D/A plus interest at 10 per cent (bank guaranteed).

(*a*) Explain these terms and how they operate.
(*b*) List the instructions you would expect to receive from the remitting bank abroad, in respect of a collection based on your customer's agreement to the latter quotation.
(*c*) What action would you take if, at maturity, a bill relating to such a collection was presented and your customer requested you to make payment of the principal amount only, because he was not satisfied with the goods? (*Inst. of Bankers*)

6. List the main methods of payment available for exports in order of least risk. What steps can be taken to eliminate or reduce those risks? What are the points to be checked when receiving advice of a letter of credit? (*Inst. of Export*)

7. You have received an order from an overseas buyer who asks for ninety days' credit. What precautions would you take? What method of payment would you suggest? What steps would you take to minimize the risks? (*Inst. of Freight Forwarders*)

8. Your company manufactures machinery of a specialized nature selling in a competitive market. Orders may vary in size from £200 to £20 000.

So far your export trade has been limited and you normally trade on 'open account' terms. Recently, however, your export turnover has increased rapidly and the finance director is concerned about the growing incidence of bad debts and delays in payment by overseas buyers.

What suggestions would you make to your Board for the reorganization of terms and methods of payment taking into account the issues at stake?

(*Inst. of Export*)

9. You are a branch manager and, as a member of the local Export Club, you agree to join a panel of speakers in an open forum discussion of local exporters' problems. The following question is posed by a member of the audience:

> We have recently been approached by a US company to arrange to supply them with deck-fittings for racing yachts. The terms quoted are ninety days after shipment D/A. As it is a buyers' market, and we are unable to vary the terms of shipment, what risks are there in the company accepting this quotation, and can you indicate any remedies?'

In brief note form, cover the points you would make, outlining:

(*a*) the risks to the company; and
(*b*) your recommendations to help the company to overcome some of the difficulties.

(*Inst. of Bankers*)

10. As manager of a branch of a bank in the UK, you learn that the London office of an overseas bank is complaining about the delay in effecting settlement of a documentary collection sent to your branch.

The collection order was accompanied by a thirty days' sight draft on D/A terms and a full set of bills of lading. Protest instructions were not given in the collection order but you were asked to contact the remitting bank if any difficulty arose. The documents, together with the bills of exchange for acceptance, were sent 'in trust' to your respected customers, XYZ. Although forty-five days have passed since the customers received the documents and bills of exchange, you still have not received an acceptance.

You now discover that XYZ Ltd examined the goods and arranged for half to be delivered to a customer. The other half are at present being unloaded at the docks. XYZ Ltd are prepared to pay for half the value of the goods and to negotiate with the suppliers for the balance, since they claim that the goods were not in accordance with the agreed specification.

In brief note form give a statement of:

(*a*) your position under UK law and banking practice;
(*b*) the action you should immediately take.

(*Inst. of Bankers*)

11. As the manager of your branch you call to see a new customer, International Importers Ltd, to discuss with their financial director the various aspects of their importing business and how the branch can help. The financial

director advises you that, apart from a few letters of credit, the majority of imports will be covered on a sixty days' sight bill D/A basis or on 'cash against document' terms. All presentations are apparently routed through banks.

Give brief notes on:

(*a*) any international regulations you may have to be aware of when handling documents in the manner mentioned above;
(*b*) any instructions you would expect to receive from remitting banks;
(*c*) any aspects you can foresee that might cause problems between yourself and your new customer, and your responsibilities to the parties involved in overcoming the difficulties.

(*Inst. of Bankers*)

10
BANKING SERVICES TO EXPORTERS

METHODS OF PAYMENT AND FINANCE

THE two principal services provided for exporter customers by the commercial banks, whether they be clearing banks, merchant banks or foreign banks in the UK, are concerned firstly with the machinery through which payment is received for exports, and secondly with the provision of finance either before or after shipment. Students must therefore expect to find questions on these services in their examination, and it is essential that they be able to distinguish between questions concerned with the means of payment and those concerned with obtaining finance. The student should be able to answer the first type of question from what he has read so far in this book. All that is called for is a knowledge of the various ways through which payment can be received for exports – bills of exchange, documentary credits, banker's drafts, SWIFT, TTs, mail transfers and the importer's own cheque—and the risks involved in each. Obviously, the risk that the buyer may fail to pay for the goods is reduced where control is maintained over delivery of the documents. If credit is to be given to the importer and bills of exchange are used, they provide the exporter with a means of obtaining finance from the banks to bridge the gap between the manufacture and export of goods and the receipt of payment.

The method of payment used must be clearly defined in the contract between the exporter and the importer, and there must be no doubt as to who is to pay the expenses of freight and insurance. As we saw in Chapter 4 if the contract stipulates that the goods are to be supplied fob, then the exporter is responsible for getting the goods on to the ship, and the cost of insurance and freight are the importer's responsibility. If, on the other hand, the contract is a cif contract, then the seller is responsible for paying the cost of insurance and freight.

Where an exporter is in any doubt as to the method of payment to insist on, his bank will advise him. The best arrangement is a confirmed irrevocable documentary credit, which will ensure that he receives payment on delivering the documents to his bank or on a fixed or determinable date thereafter. If it is a documentary acceptance credit, he draws his bills on a UK bank (like the bill in Fig. 9.1) and these are accepted on presentation and then become readily discountable. However, the exporter may have no alternative but to accept a less satisfactory means of payment such as a D/A or D/P bill. These are customary forms of payment for trade with particular areas and for trade in particular commodities, and the exporter will have to fall in line with the custom if he wishes to sell his goods.

Where an exporter is obliged to trade on a D/A or D/P basis then considerable risks are obviously involved. The bill may not be accepted or, if it is accepted, it may not be paid. If it is not accepted then the goods will not be taken up when they arrive at the port of destination and the exporter will have to find another buyer as quickly as possible, and also meet the costs of storage, additional freight, etc. If it is a D/A bill and the bill is not paid then the exporter must make provision for a bad debt because the exporter has lost control of the goods in that the commercial documents will be handed over to the buyer against acceptance of the bill. If it is likely to be fruitful, he may take the necessary legal action in the country concerned, but this will be expensive. Other risks involved are that the exchange rate may move against the exporter by the time payment in a foreign currency is received and that the importer may not be able to pay, even if he has the funds to do so, because of exchange control restrictions imposed by his government.

The exporter can guard against the exchange risk by selling his potential receipts of foreign currency in advance, i.e. by entering into a forward exchange contract in advance or by borrowing the currency, selling it spot for sterling and repaying the loan with the foreign currency receipts when they arrive. Alternatively, if he is also buying goods in the same currency he may avoid the exchange risk by opening a foreign currency account. Many of the other risks can be guarded against through the ECGD and by making enquiries in advance through his bank concerning the status of the importer and the economic situation in his country. These safeguards will be explored more fully later in this and in the following chapter.

WORKING CAPITAL

For a large proportion of exporters finance is no problem, either because they are able to persuade their buyers to open documentary credits that ensure immediate payment or a facility to negotiate bills of exchange, or because they have ample working capital to tide them over until payment is received, which may be several weeks or months after the goods have been shipped. Their working capital may have been reinforced by loans from their banks based on their creditworthiness as manufacturers, quite apart from the export orders they may have in the pipeline. No firm wants to borrow more than it has to, for to do so is expensive, but if an exporting firm finds itself short of capital the first thing it must consider is whether or not it can arrange an overdraft limit or loan arrangement on the security of the firm's assets. If an overdraft is agreed to, it will fluctuate from day to day with the firm's needs and as it is flexible in this way it ensures that borrowing is done only when really necessary. The rate of interest paid on a bank loan or overdraft will depend upon the firm's standing with the bank and may be 2 per cent, 3 per cent or more above the bank's base rate. If the advance is well secured it will attract a lower interest charge than if it were unsecured. The bank looks for some gradual reduction in the limit and complete repayment within a reasonable period of time, as payment (including profit) is received from the sale of goods. However, if the firm's scale of business is continually expanding, and hence also its need for working capital, the bank may be prepared to extend the credit over a longer period and possibly even increase it. The important thing is that the bank should be able to see that the finance is being used wisely and profitably so that repayment of borrowed money is assured.

If the firm has borrowed as much as it can, or as much as it wishes, by way of working capital, it may turn to the various forms of short-term export finance available to it. The most common form of bank finance for exporters is bill finance.

BILL FINANCE

There are a number of ways of obtaining finance from the banks open to the exporter of consumer goods who is in possession of a bill of exchange drawn on the importer (see p. 171). Firstly, he may be able to negotiate the draft with his bank, whether it be with a clearing bank or a merchant bank. Secondly, he could use the draft and the commercial documents as security for an overdraft from his bank for anything up to 85 per cent or 90 per cent of the face value of the draft, depending upon how much he requires and how much the bank is willing to advance. Whether the bill is negotiated or taken by the bank for collection as security for a bill advance, it is usually taken by the bank before it has been accepted. Thirdly, if his bank is a merchant bank, he may be able to obtain an acceptance credit from a merchant bank. When an acceptance credit is opened by the bank, the exporter hands the documentary bill to the bank, together with the ECGD policy, if there is one, and the bank sends the draft for collection. On the strength of the bill lodged with the merchant bank for collection, the exporter is permitted to draw a draft on the bank for a proportion of the face value of the draft. This draft is a usance draft to mature a few days later than the expected date by which the proceeds of the documentary bill are expected to arrive. When the draft drawn on the merchant bank has been accepted by the bank, the draft can be discounted and, being a bank bill it can be discounted at a fine rate of interest.

Whichever of the methods is used, the bank will retain recourse against its customer and will hold the draft and commercial documents as its primary security. The ECGD comprehensive guarantee, if there is one, would be assigned to the bank.

Perhaps the best way of making crystal clear to the reader the advantages of bill finance to the exporter is to consider a past examination question on the subject, and in doing so to discuss more fully the three methods of obtaining finance. Let us take the following Institute of Bankers' question:

> A Midlands hardware manufacturer, who exports part of his output, discovers that continental competition may necessitate his allowing up to 180 days' credit terms to his overseas buyers.
>
> He tells you that he can only do this if he can secure bank finance for his export transactions.
>
> Advise him about the possible sources and methods of finance which might be available to him in London.

In this question, the candidate is asked to comment on the sources and methods of finance available to the *exporter* in London. He is to obtain the finance himself and give the importer 180 days' credit, so therefore a long essay on the advantages to the exporter of a documentary acceptance credit is not called for. Obviously, if the importer is prepared to provide the exporter with this means of obtaining post-shipment finance, he would be quite satisfied. He would be able to present the documents and the 180-day bill to the UK bank that had undertaken in the documentary credit to accept the bill (i.e. the London office of the foreign bank in the importer's country that opened the credit, or its correspondent bank in the City that had added its confirmation). If the documents were in order, the bill would be accepted, and, carrying the acceptance of a bank, it would be readily negotiated by the exporter's bank or by a London discount house at a fine rate of interest.

A comment on these lines would be justifiable in answering a question of this nature, but beyond that the student must confine himself to an answer that assumes that no such documentary credit is opened and that, therefore, the exporter must get what finance he can on the strength of his bill of exchange drawn on the importer.

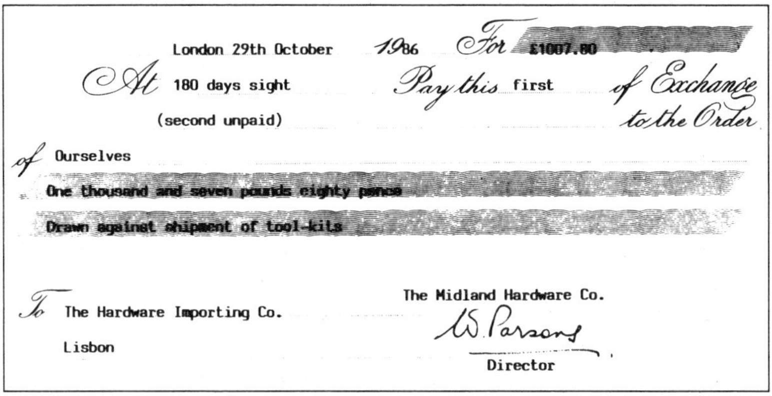
London 29th October 1986 For £1007.80

At 180 days sight Pay this first of Exchange

(second unpaid) to the Order

of Ourselves

One thousand and seven pounds eighty pence

Drawn against shipment of tool-kits

To The Hardware Importing Co.

Lisbon

The Midland Hardware Co.

W. Parsons

Director

Fig. 10.1. Bill drawn on an importer

His bill of exchange is illustrated in Fig. 10.1. It is drawn on the importer himself but has not been accepted by him. What can the exporter who, let us assume, trades as the Midland Hardware Co., do with it? He could ask his bank to negotiate the draft, or he could pledge the draft as security for an overdraft or a special bill advance. If the bank agrees to negotiate the bill, it will in effect buy it, but with recourse to the exporter. It would send the bill and the shipping documents with a collection order to a correspondent bank in the importer's country for presentation for acceptance, and later payment, in its own right. Whether or not the bank would be prepared to negotiate the bill would depend on the creditworthiness of the exporter and their knowledge, if any, of the firm overseas on whom the bill is drawn. As the exporter customer is just about to start trading on a 180-day credit basis and thus has not built up a record of regular sound credit transactions with his buyer, the bank would probably prefer to collect the bill for its customer and advance him a proportion of the face value of the bill. In the last resort, in the event of dishonour of the bill, the bank would have to seek repayment from its customer, so that it would have to consider very carefully whether the Midland Hardware Co. was financially sound enough to be able to pay back the advance out of its own resources. The bank would have the bill as its primary security and would take a letter or pledge from the exporter covering the goods that are being exported, together with the customer's instructions about delivery of the documents to the importer and other matters for inclusion in the collection order.

As the exporter is not new to the business of exporting, he may be used to insuring his shipments through the ECGD. If this is so, he may be willing to assign his ECGD comprehensive guarantee to the bank as additional security.

If the Midlands hardware manufacturer's bank is a merchant bank (which we will call the London Acceptance Co.), he may be able to arrange for an acceptance credit to be opened in his favour. This London acceptance credit may be for, say, 80 per cent of the value of the particular bill drawn on the importer, or on a revolving basis that will enable him to ship goods on a continuous basis, replacing bills drawn under the credit by new ones as the old ones mature. For instance, if the exporter knows he will have £50 000 of exports outstanding on six-months' credit terms at any one time, the merchant bank may open an acceptance credit for £40 000, requiring him to find the other 20 per cent out of his own resources. On the strength of this acceptance credit the exporter could draw bills of exchange on the merchant bank that they will accept. These bills are bank bills and therefore readily discountable with a London discount house. A typical bill of this nature is shown in Fig. 10.2.

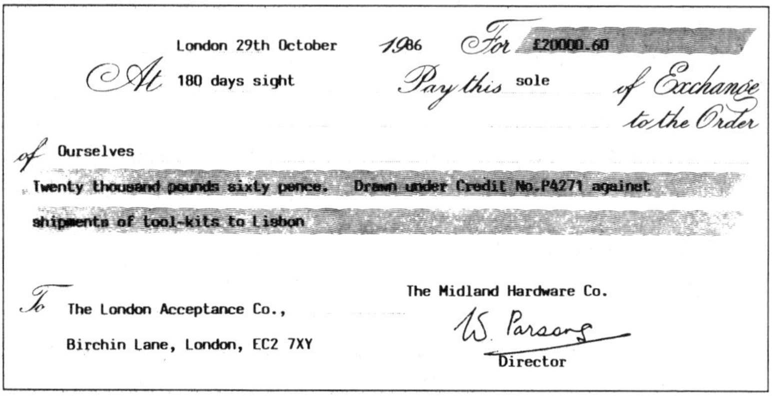
London 29th October 1986 For £20000.60

At 180 days sight Pay this sole of Exchange to the Order

of Ourselves

Twenty thousand pounds sixty pence. Drawn under Credit No.P4271 against shipments of tool-kits to Lisbon

To The London Acceptance Co.,

Birchin Lane, London, EC2 7XY

The Midland Hardware Co.

W. Parsons

Director

Fig. 10.2. Bill drawn under acceptance credit

The London Acceptance Co. would require security in the same manner as a clearing bank would do. They have lent their name by accepting bills drawn by the Midland Hardware Co., and when the bills mature will have to pay them on presentation. In the meantime, they expect their exporter customer to receive payment of the bills he has drawn on foreign importers in a regular manner, so that the amount of debt due to the exporter remains at about £50 000 and does not mount up through default on the part of importers. The merchant bank would require a letter of pledge over the goods and would normally wish to keep the documents under their control (through their agents overseas) until they are handed over to the importers against their acceptance of the bills drawn upon them. Further security would be required in the form of an assignment of the ECGD policy covering the exports concerned if there is one.

Bills drawn under an acceptance credit can be sold in London at a fine rate, i.e. a relatively low rate of discount. To this interest charge must be added the acceptance commission charged by the merchant bank for opening the credit and accepting the bills. There is no hard and fast rule as to what this amounts to, but it is likely to be somewhere between $1\frac{1}{4}$ per cent and 2 per cent per annum.

Although the question is concerned with sources and methods of finance available in London, specific mention is made of bank finance and, therefore, it is not necessary to comment on the facilities available from other institutions in London such as those mentioned in Chapter 12.

CASH AGAINST DOCUMENTS

Where an exporter does not draw a usance bill on the importer but instead trades on *cash against documents* terms or on *open account basis* giving up to six months' credit, he may nevertheless still get finance from his bank to tide him over until the proceeds are received. He would almost certainly be expected to assign his ECGD comprehensive short-term guarantee to the bank.

MEDIUM-AND LONG-TERM FINANCE

The exporter of capital goods is usually expected by the importer to supply his goods on credit terms that extend over a number of years, possibly five or more. Credit beyond six months and less than five years is often referred to as medium-term, and that for more than five years as long-term. The British banks have been able to provide much of the medium- and long-term finance required by such exporters, having been greatly assisted in this by the new types of cover that have been provided by the ECGD. In Britain there is not a government-sponsored credit institution, as there is in some other countries, that provides finance for exporters, and exporters have had to rely on the banks; but the government, through its own department, the ECGD, has been able to bring its influence to bear in persuading the banks to provide ample credit on very reasonable terms through improving the security attached to such advances.

One of these forms of security is the *specific bank guarantee,* which is direct to the bank and not to the exporter and covers 100 per cent of loss through any default. This greatly improves the attractiveness of lending propositions as far as the banks are concerned, for they need not rely on an assignment of the exporter's own ECGD policy, and they have the satisfaction of knowing that the department is sufficiently satisfied with the creditworthiness of the buyer to give the unconditional guarantee. When capital goods are sold, the exporter usually draws bills of exchange or receives promissory notes in a series payable at six-monthly intervals, covering both principal and interest. These are lodged with the bank for presentation when they fall due, and if they are not paid, the bank claims against the ECGD within the terms of the bank guarantee.

The ECGD also provides *buyer credit guarantees,* which cover loans direct to the foreign buyer, not loans to the British exporter, and enable the exporter to be paid in cash, even though the buyer requires medium or long-term credit. Normally, only contracts for £1 million or over will be covered by this type of guarantee, and only then if the department is satisfied that it is in the interest of the UK to provide this credit to the foreign buyer. The guarantee must not cover more than 80 per cent of the purchase price, the buyer being expected to provide 20 per cent of the finance. The UK exporter has to find an institution willing to provide the long-term finance for the importer and must arrange for the guarantee and pay the ECGD charges.

Chapter 11 on the ECGD should be consulted for further information on bank guarantees and buyer credit guarantees.

The banks provide finance to exporters against *specific bank guarantees* at the preferential rates of interest decided upon at regular six-monthly meetings of a committee representing major exporting nations at the Organization for Economic Co-operation and Development (OECD), and the difference between these consensus rates, as they are called, and market rates of interest is made up by the government (see p. 190).

An alternative source of medium-term finance is that of *forfaiting,* which is becoming increasingly popular in respect of trade between the

UK and the continent of Europe. Where the seller has drawn a series of bills of exchange on the buyer, or the buyer has given the exporter a series of promissory notes, a bank may be prepared to forfait them. The same facility might also be made available against guaranteed book debt obligations.

In effect the bank agrees in advance to negotiate the bills or notes provided they are *avalized.* This is the term applied to a guarantee by the importer's bank that the bills or notes will be paid. Such a guarantee is known as an *aval.*

Not only does the bank commit itself in advance to negotiate the bills or notes but also it agrees in advance what the rate of discount and its commitment fee is to be. The exporter is therefore able to work out what his proceeds will be and he can base his price to the buyer on what these will amount to. He is likely to be able to offer the best possible terms to the overseas buyer, knowing that he need not be cautious and make provision for erosion of the proceeds from changes in interest rates or in other expenses of obtaining finance because these factors have been taken care of by the forfaiting process. He gets immediate cash for his exports and is relieved of liability as the bank has no recourse to him. He is relieved of the chore of having to present the bills as they fall due and his overdraft facilities are left available for use in other parts of his business.

FINDING A BUYER

Apart from the provision of the various means of settling international trade debts and financing the shipment of goods, the clearing, merchant or other banks provide a variety of other services which are vital to the exporter.

The banking system is able to provide the exporter with help and advice as to the opportunities for the sale of his type of goods overseas. He must first of all decide on the best countries in which to try to sell his product, and here the banks are able to help through their intelligence departments and international branches. They are able to provide statistics relating to the trade in the particular product with individual countries and show clearly which markets are expanding more rapidly than others. Through the various departments of the international branch, it is possible to get first-hand information about prospects in particular markets, for officers in these departments travel extensively overseas, collecting information about developments in individual countries. Furthermore, through their subsidiary banks and correspondent banks overseas, the banks are able to make enquiries about the potential demand for particular products.

When he has decided upon the best markets for his product, the exporter can obtain information from his bank about the economic and political situation in the countries concerned. A country that is politically and economically unstable is obviously a risky market. A report to the effect that a country's balance of payments is adverse would suggest the possibility of import restrictions, which may preclude an importer from fulfilling his contract, and likewise political unrest might disrupt trade and payments. The risks involved in trading with a particular buyer can, of course, be insured against through the ECGD, but no exporter will be pleased to find that his outlet for a commodity has been cut off and that he has to look for new markets, whilst in the meantime his stocks are building up.

If conditions in the particular market are satisfactory and the exporter decides to go ahead, he can obtain from his bank the names of possible buyers, and agents and distributors, as well as names and addresses of firms and organizations that may be interested in linking up with the British firm to produce the goods concerned. The banks can seek this type of information from their correspondent banks in the country in which the exporter is interested and, furthermore, the banks receive enquiries from this source from time to time concerning foreign importers who want to be put in touch with British suppliers, and they can frequently direct business to their customers.

Having found a buyer for his goods, the exporter can make enquiries through his bank as to the creditworthiness and reliability of the importer. The banks maintain status reports on many hundreds of thousands of firms and individuals, both at home and overseas, and if they are unable to produce a report on a particular foreign trader from their records, they can quickly do so by contacting a correspondent bank in the importer's country. To make sure that there is no change in the financial status of the importer, the exporter should renew the status enquiry every six months or year.

The exporter may find it well worthwhile to visit an overseas market to develop his established business there, or to consider whether or not he is likely to be successful if he starts exporting to that market. He is then able to study the particular requirements of that country, such as the packaging and advertising techniques adopted, and to make contact with existing and potential customers. The banks provide the necessary foreign travel facilities such as traveller's cheques and supplies of foreign currencies required by customers travelling abroad in this way. Furthermore, they will provide introductions through their correspondents overseas from which the customer is able to get on-the-spot help and advice when he arrives at his destination. Such introductions are a great help to the person who has no contacts in the foreign country and who might therefore be at a loss to know where to start looking for the contacts and help that he needs.

There may be trade and exchange restrictions in the country to which the goods are to be consigned, which will impede trade in that market. The banks are able to assist in this matter also by making enquiries through their contacts at home and abroad. They are able to obtain information about tariffs and quotas and exchange control restrictions imposed by foreign governments, and warn their customers of the consequences of these. The British exporter must not assume that because a foreign importer has an import licence it implies automatic authority to acquire the necessary foreign exchange, and he must remember that restrictions may be imposed at any time at short notice, which will prevent the importer from purchasing the goods even though he has contracted to buy them. A British exporter may, therefore, find himself with goods for which there is no market, or with frozen debts in a foreign currency. The ECGD will, of course, give the exporter cover against these risks, but if the exporter has not insured his goods through the ECGD, consultation with the bank about trade and exchange restrictions may save him from incurring a loss.

PERFORMANCE BONDS

An exporter who enters into a large capital project overseas may have to supply the buyers with a guarantee or bond protecting them against non-performance of the contract. If the contract is for £250 000 or more the ECGD may be prepared to issue a guarantee to a bank that provides such a bond for the exporter (see p. 191). The existence of such an ECGD guarantee (for which the exporter pays a premium of course) will encourage a bank to enter into such an undertaking, but of course the exporter's standing may be such that it will be prepared to issue a performance bond without ECGD backing.

There are four types of bonds banks provide for exporters and in all cases a counter-indemnity is taken by the bank from the exporter:

1. Performance bond

This is issued in support of an exporter who has a contract to fulfil. The buyer is given an assurance in the bond that in the event of the bank's customer not completing the contract, the bank will make a payment to the buyer of a sum of money, usually 10 per cent of the contract amount or thereabouts.

2. *Bid or tender bond*

This is issued in support of a bank customer's tender for a contract and is an undertaking that in the event of the customer not taking up the contract, if it is offered to him within the terms of his tender, the bank will pay an agreed sum of money to the beneficiary of the bond, i.e. the company or organization offering the contract. Quite often the bond is issued on behalf of the British bank by a bank overseas.

Once a tender has been accepted and a contract signed the tender bond is cancelled and replaced by a performance bond.

3. *Advance or progress payment bond*

Where the buyer abroad under a capital goods or services contract pays the British contractor sums of money in advance an advance or progress payment bond will guarantee him the refund of some or all of the payment if the contract is not fulfilled. It can apply to a series of progress payments as well as to a single advance payment.

4. *Warranty or retention bond*

As the name suggests, this is a bond that covers a period after completion of the contract during which the contractor has undertaken to maintain the project or goods and to put right any defects that are discovered. The bond guarantees the fulfilment of the undertaking and may be necessary before the final payment under the contract is made by the buyer.

The student will realize that when the exporter receives payments in foreign currency for his exports, his bank will buy the currency from him and credit his account with the proceeds. To avoid loss through fluctuations in exchange rates, the exporter can sell the currency forward if he chooses to do so, and also, if he is wise, give himself the protection of an ECGD currency contracts endorsement (see p. 186).

EXAMINATION GUIDELINES

After reading this chapter the student reader will appreciate that a considerable amount of the subject matter cuts across that to be found in Chapter 11 which deals specifically with ECGD. This is inevitable if the very complex subject of ECGD services is to be dealt with separately. Furthermore, non-recourse finance facilities are left to Chapter 12. The same overlap occurs with examination questions and therefore answers concerning export finance which bring in ECGD in any detail and non-recourse finance have been left to the end of Chapters 11 and 12. This leaves us with questions concerned with bill finance and other forms of bank finance for exporters, excluding medium and long-term finance involving ECGD specific and buyer credit guarantees, and factoring and other forms of non-recourse finance.

Question 1

Floral Charm Ltd, who are customers of your bank, manufacture fancy goods for the UK tourist industry based upon traditional perfumes, soaps and herbs. Following a visit to this country, a group of overseas tourists has written asking them to forward to California a container load of their fancy goods. The proposal is that a container should be shipped to the west coast of America every quarter. The terms of shipment would be fob UK port with payment in dollars thirty days after shipment.

Status reports confirm the prospective buyers to be absolutely satisfactory from both the customer's point of view and that of the bank.

REQUIRED

Brief notes setting out the types of working capital facility your bank could arrange to help your customer to finance this export deal, indicating how the various facilities would work.

NOTE: *Ignore merchant banking, confirming house and factoring finance facilities.*

SOLUTION

(*a*) The bank may be prepared to offer normal unsecured loan or overdraft facilities or increase any that have already been taken up. Alternatively, if the customers have security they are prepared to have charged to the bank, then this would enhance the likelihood of more overdraft or loan facilities. The advance could be in dollars rather than in sterling if the customers prefer.

(*b*) Advances could also be made on the strength of bills sent for collection if that is to be the method of payment. The bank would determine a proportion of the value of the bills up to which it is prepared to lend and would require a certificate of pledge or letter of hypothecation over the goods to which the bills relate. Such advances would be with recourse to the customers who would be wise to take out an ECGD comprehensive guarantee which could be assigned to the bank as extra security.

(*c*) The bank may be prepared to negotiate bills and/or commercial documents drawn on the overseas buyer for the face value less discount but with recourse to Floral Charm. Alternatively, it may negotiate cheques or drafts in US dollars or sterling sent by the buyers in payment.

(*d*) If the buyers are prepared to open a documentary acceptance credit through a bank in the UK, such accepted bills could readily discounted.

Question 2

One of your customers, Capital Contracts Ltd, manufacture large items of capital plant and has obtained an order from a third world country. The company understand that guaranteed payment will be available from a European bank and it asks to discuss with you the various ways in which this method of finance is provided. ECGD cover is not involved and it will take up to five years for payment to be effected.

REQUIRED

A brief description of:

(*a*) the salient features of the method of finance involved;
(*b*) the advantages of the method;
(*c*) the disadvantages.

SOLUTION

(*a*) This is clearly a question about forfaiting and an important clue to this is the fact that *guaranteed* payment will be available from a *European* bank. Where capital goods are being sold under medium-term contracts up to five years, as in this instance, or possibly more, the usual practice is for the buyer to issue a series of bills of exchange on him. If a bank (and particularly a European bank where the practice is common), is willing to avalize the bills or notes, payment of them is guaranteed. Clearly for a bank to add its aval in this way must mean that its customer is undoubted and this type of standing is essential if a UK bank is to forfait bills or note.

Forfaiting involves an undertaking by a bank, possibly as much as eighteen months in advance, to buy such a series of bills or notes at a rate of interest fixed at the outset. The exporter is then able to determine what his net proceeds will amount to. The bank takes on all the risks, i.e. the exchange risk, and the political and economic risks, in that the purchase of the bills or promissory notes is on a non-recourse basis. The most common currencies in which such transactions are carried out are US dollars, Deutschemarks and Swiss francs.

(*b*) The advantages of this method are that the transaction becomes in effect a cash sale, thus keeping his credit facilities at the bank intact and avoiding a contingent liability on his balance sheet.

Furthermore, because he is able to determine his net proceeds in advance, the exporter is possibly able to compete more effectively in tendering for contracts. In this instance he has already obtained the order, but he may be in a better position when he bids for further contracts if he brings the bank in at the outset to determine the costs of forfaiting. As the rate of interest is fixed, the exporter is relieved of the risk of interest rate fluctuations that might occur if he were to borrow the finance required. He is also relieved of the exchange risk in that the bank takes this over when it buys the bills or notes for cash.

The exporter is also relieved of the problem of collecting the six-monthly instalments and of the expenses involved with that process.

(*c*) The disadvantages to the exporter are that the cost of this method of financing is relatively high. In addition to the interest rate he may have to pay a substantial commitment fee, especially if the buyer's country is having economic or political problems.

Other questions

1. Your customers, X Port Ltd, have developed a large export market in various countries for their consumer goods. The terms of sale call for 120 days' credit and, owing to difficult trading conditions, the customers are in danger of becoming short of working capital. You meet the financial director to discuss the various facilities available to the customers to enable them to overcome their shortage of working capital.

Supply the brief reference notes that you would make for record purposes following these discussions with your customers.

(*Inst. of Bankers*)

2. Explain how the clearing banks and merchant banks can provide finance for a UK exporter who is selling overseas on 120 days' credit terms.

(*Inst. of Bankers*)

3. 'Exporters now find themselves competing not only in quality and price, but also in the credit terms they are able to offer the prospective buyer.

'Two further problems for the exporter have arisen from this development. First, there are the risks involved in granting extended periods of credit to foreign buyers.... The second problem for the exporter is simply one of finding the finance to enable him to provide the extended credit terms his foreign buyer needs.'

Discuss these problems, and explain how they are now solved for the UK exporter selling on medium-term credit.

(*Inst. of Bankers*)

4. 'Financially an exporter is concerned with two things, i.e. to obtain payment from the overseas buyer, and to borrow while he is waiting to receive that payment.'

Explain how a UK exporter selling overseas in sterling on ninety days' credit terms can use bills of exchange to solve this twofold problem.

(*Inst. of Bankers*)

5. How can a documentary collection assist the exporter to obtain payment from his buyer and at the same time provide a means of finance? What facilities are provided by the banks in this respect?

(*Inst. of Export*)

6. 'A bill of exchange is a key document in the provision of finance in international trade.' Discuss this statement in the context of a documentary acceptance credit detailing how both contractual parties may derive finance under such a facility.

(*Inst. of Freight Forwarders*)

7. Name the four main types of guarantee or bond banks are requested to issue on behalf of contractors for large overseas projects. Describe the purpose of each.

(*Inst. of Bankers*)

11

EXPORT CREDITS GUARANTEE DEPARTMENT

INTRODUCTION

SINCE 1919, the Export Credits Guarantee Department, a government department, has provided exporters with facilities for insuring their consignments against default on the part of foreign importers and most other risks, apart from normal marine insurance. The Department operates on commercial lines, charging premiums that should provide sufficient income to meet their claims though in recent years it has incurred substantial deficits and has had to be provided with finance from the Treasury. However, over a period of years it is supposed to break even. One small exception to this policy of operating on commercial lines is where, in the national interest and because of abnormal circumstances, insurance cover is provided by the Department on a non-commercial basis. Even in these cases, applications are most carefully vetted.

The ECGD is not directly involved in providing finance for exports, but because the ECGD insures exports, it makes it easier for exporters to obtain finance from other institutions, especially the banks. What would otherwise appear to be too risky a proposition to a bank asked to make an advance, becomes a good banking risk when an ECGD policy is offered as security.

In 1946–7, the figure of business insured by ECGD was £88 million, but by 1984–5 the figure had risen to over £17 000 million.

Basically, the ECGD provides two types of insurance cover, *comprehensive* and *specific.* Comprehensive insurance covers trade of a more or less repetitive nature, often with the same regular buyers, and involving goods being sold for cash or on a short-term credit basis, or on an extended term basis of up to five years. This type of insurance accounts for 75 per cent of the Department's business. Specific insurance is in respect of capital transactions overseas for large engineering projects, which are usually paid for over a lengthy period.

THE RISKS COVERED

ECGD comprehensive policies cover the following types of risk:

(*a*) Insolvency of the buyer.
(*b*) The buyer's failure to pay within six months of due date for goods he has accepted.
(*c*) The buyer's failure to take up goods that have been despatched to him (where not caused or excused by the policy-holder's actions, and where the ECGD decides that the institution or continuation of legal proceedings against the buyer would serve no useful purpose).
(*d*) A general moratorium on external debt decreed by the government of the buyer's country or of a third country through which payment must be made.
(*e*) Any other action by the government of the buyer's country that prevents performance of the contract in whole or in part.
(*f*) Political events, economic difficulties, legislative or administrative measures arising outside the UK that prevent or delay the transfer of payments or deposits made in respect of the contract.
(*g*) Legal discharge of a debt (not being legal discharge under the proper law of the contract) in a foreign currency, which results in a shortfall at the date of transfer.
(*h*) War and certain other events preventing performance of the contract provided that the event is not one normally insured with commercial insurers.
(*i*) Cancellation or non-renewal of a UK export licence or the prohibition or restriction on export of goods from the UK by law (this risk is covered only where the pre-credit risk section of the guarantee applies).
(*j*) In the case of certain public buyers (central, regional, provincial and local government buyers), the ECGD may agree to cover the risk of failure or refusal of the buyer to perform the contract. Each buyer is approved individually.

The ECGD does not provide 100 per cent cover against loss, but expects the exporter to carry a small percentage of loss so that business is not entered into recklessly, without consideration of the financial consequences should the transaction fail to be carried through satisfactorily. Furthermore, if the exporter must bear some of the loss, he will have an interest in maximizing recoveries once a claim has been made against the ECGD. This is important because, even after paying a claim, the Department does not normally interfere in the contract of sale between the exporter and the foreign buyer; as a result, for protection of its interest, it must depend upon the exporter.

All transactions with the Department are kept confidential so that the importer does not become aware that the goods consigned to him are insured through the ECGD, as this might encourage him to default. Only in exceptional circumstances will the Department agree to its interest being disclosed to the buyer.

COVER FOR SHORT-TERM CREDIT

For exports of consumer goods, durables and engineering manufactures sold on up to six months' credit the ECGD offers the *comprehensive short-term guarantee.* The policy-holder normally undertakes to insure his whole export turnover for a period of not less than a year. In some cases the ECGD will accept business on a range of markets selected by the policy-holder but the premiums are normally slightly higher than those paid by policy-holders who insure their whole turnover. Where an exporter selects markets he must, in doing so, offer the ECGD a fair spread of potential good and bad risks.

Normally a comprehensive short-term guarantee covers the exporter from the time the goods are despatched but it is possible for him to obtain cover for the 'pre-credit risk', i.e. from the date of the contract of sale. The goods must be exported within twelve months of contract and the policy-holder must take out the extra cover for all of his export turnover. He cannot select contracts for cover in this way. An additional premium at a flat rate per £100 is payable for this cover.

The procedure with comprehensive guarantees is that once a month the exporter declares to the ECGD the total amount of business he has transacted under each policy. Normally individual contracts do not need to be referred to the Department because either they come within the exporter's discretionary limit or within the limit set for the amount of debt that can be outstanding for a particular buyer. The exporter can sell goods up to £250 to a new buyer at his discretion provided that he has had no adverse information on him. Beyond that he can trade up to £5000 with a buyer provided he has had a satisfactory report on the buyer from a bank or credit information agency or has previously traded with the buyer on a satisfactory basis. This is a revolving discretionary limit which means that he can trade up to this figure of outstandings with the particular buyer. For higher amounts credit limits have to be approved by the ECGD and once they are approved these limits stay in existence unless varied or withdrawn by the ECGD. Within that limit the exporter can automatically consider himself covered by the policy, but he must seek the approval of the ECGD for any higher amount of outstandings. This allows him the maximum flexibility and freedom in the conduct of his day-to-day business. The creditworthiness of buyers can be quickly assessed, for the Department has a reference library of up-to-date information about the status of some hundreds of thousands of buyers throughout the world.

As mentioned above the premiums on comprehensive short-term guarantees are paid in two ways. Firstly a non-refundable premium is paid at the commencement of each year of insurance based on the size of the policy-holder's export turnover, and on the degree of use he makes of the ECGD's credit limit service. All policy-holders pay at least a minimum sum for each year of insurance. Secondly, a premium is payable on exports declared each month at a flat rate per £100 fixed at the commencement of each year of insurance but this is not payable where insurable exports are less than £25 000 a year. Policy-holders who have pre-credit risk cover also pay the additional premium each month at a separate flat-rate.

On comprehensive guarantees, the ECGD covers 90 per cent of the loss where the buyer is insolvent or fails to pay within six months. For the other risks, apart from the buyer's failure to take up the goods, the proportion is 90 per cent if the cause arises before despatch overseas (pre-credit risk), and 95 per cent if it arises after despatch. Where the buyer fails to take up the goods, the exporter must bear the 'first loss' of 20 per cent of the full price and the ECGD bears 90 per cent of the balance. The times of payment of claims depend upon the cause of the loss. For insolvency of the buyer, the payment is made immediately on proof of insolvency. Where there has been protracted default on goods accepted, payment of claims is made six months after the due date of payment, and where the importer has failed to take up the goods, the period is one month after resale. For most other causes, payment is made four months after the due date of payment or the date of the event causing the loss.

Comprehensive guarantees apply not only to contracts in sterling but also to contracts in many other currencies. Where an exporter enters into a forward exchange contract with his bank to sell the foreign currency proceeds to the bank or borrows the foreign currency in anticipation of the receipt of the payment, he can protect himself against a loss resulting from his being unable to fulfil that contract by a *foreign currency contracts endorsement* to his comprehensive short-term guarantee. In the event of a claim under that guarantee the ECGD will pay up to 10 per cent more to the exporter than he would otherwise be entitled to to cover the extra loss incurred through the forward contract. The whole purpose of a forward exchange contract is of course to protect oneself against a loss caused by an adverse change in the exchange rate by the time payment is due to be received, i.e. an appreciation in the value of sterling that will cause the exporter to have to pay over more units of the foreign currency for every pound sterling. However, if the foreign currency is not received because the exporter defaults the contract will have to be closed out, and this may be at a less favourable rate than that at which the forward exchange contract has been agreed. It is this type of loss that the foreign currency contracts endorsement is designed to cover.

Where an exporter has a comprehensive policy for his short-term business, he may take out a self-contained guarantee with its own operational and premium systems. This is known as a *supplemental extended terms guarantee* and covers goods, such as engineering goods, sold on credit terms beyond the normal credit period of six months or, possibly, involving a delivery period beyond twelve months. Under this guarantee the contract should not normally include a delivery period beyond two years and a credit period beyond five years. He must have an established pattern of continuing trade on these terms and may cover all markets, or selected markets. Unlike the basic policy, however, each proposed sale or tranche of cover must be submitted to the ECGD for approval, as there is no discretionary limit.

Another type of supplementary guarantee is the *supplemental stocks guarantee*, to cover the risks involved in *holding* stocks overseas in order to be able to undertake to provide delivery of spares and other goods. A limit is set for stocks in each market and a premium at a flat rate per £100 is paid at the outset on the aggregate of the stock limits held. This cover is an addition to the extended cover available under the normal comprehensive guarantee in respect of sales from stocks held overseas.

If goods of foreign origin are not imported and re-exported, but are shipped direct from one foreign country to another by a British merchant, an *external trade guarantee* can be obtained. Such a policy can cover either all markets or a selected group of markets. It is limited to commodities or manufactures that do not compete with British products. The risks covered by an external trade policy are more limited than under an ordinary comprehensive policy: there is no cover against the buyer's default, but the exporter is covered against 90 per cent of loss occurring through the insolvency of the buyer, or against loss occurring through war, revolution or civil disturbance, or through the failure or refusal of a government buyer to fulfil the terms of the contract. There is no cover for loss before shipment.

A parent or associated company in the UK may obtain a *subsidiaries guarantee* to cover sales of goods by an overseas subsidiary. The ECGD would normally insist upon covering the sale to the overseas subsidiary before covering the sale by the subsidiary. This guarantee follows the general form and content of the comprehensive short-term guarantee. A UK exporter can obtain cover in respect of sales to an *associate company* overseas (i.e. where the UK company has not got a controlling interest) but, whereas political risks are fully covered buyer risks.

An exporter's rights under a comprehensive guarantee may be assigned to his bank either in respect of the whole policy, or for all transactions in specified markets, or for all transactions with a named buyer. Such an assignment provides security for a bank that makes an advance against the buyer's promissory notes or acceptances of bills, or against goods sold on a cash against documents, or on an open account basis. This form of security, though generally safe and worthwhile, suffers from one drawback however, which is that if the failure to pay is because of some fault on the part of the exporter himself ECGD may not pay up under its comprehensive guarantee.

Earnings from invisible exports in the form of technical or professional services, copyright fees, etc., can be covered by ECGD *services guarantees*. Where overseas services are performed on a recurrent basis, cover is obtainable under and ECGD *comprehensive services guarantee* on the same principle as comprehensive policies, with the policy-holder agreeing to insure the whole of his services earnings and declaring his business as he does it. For services business that does not provide any continuing pattern of business, a *specific services guarantee* is issued, which covers all earnings under an individual services contract. The risks covered by services policies are insolvency of the principal, protracted default in payment, delay in transfer of sterling, war and civil disturbances, and any other cause of loss occurring outside the UK and beyond the control of buyer and seller. The proportion of loss covered on the first two risks is 90 per cent, both for the comprehensive and specific types of cover. For the other risks, the proportion is 95 per cent for the comprehensive cover and 90 per cent for the specific type.

COVER FOR MEDIUM- AND LONG-TERM CREDIT

Transactions involving capital goods are covered by ECGD *specific guarantees.* These projects are usually large and involve granting credit for up to five years or more. The exporter cannot give the ECGD the same spread of markets as can the exporter of consumer goods and, therefore, the premiums cannot be based on the spread of risks and are the subject of negotiation between the exporter and the Department. Cover is obtainable from the date of contract or the date of shipment, but as lengthy manufacturing periods are usually involved, contracts policies are more common for capital projects. The premiums are moderate and, even for a contract with a buyer in one of the riskiest markets involving payment over five years with a manufacturing period of two years, the cost should not exceed £5 per £100.

The risks covered by specific policies are the same as those for comprehensive policies, with the exception of the failure of private buyers to take up exported goods. For sales of capital goods to government buyers, the ECGD will cover the risk of default by the buyer at any stage in the transaction. The top percentage is 90 per cent, compared with 95 per cent for comprehensive policies.

Normally, specific policies cover credit up to five years, but in recent years the Department has been permitted to match terms of credit exceeding five years from shipment offered by foreign competitors with official credit insurance or equivalent support.

Negotiations with the ECGD about a specific policy usually commence when the contract for the supply of the capital goods is being negotiated with the buyer. The Department is then able to state whether a policy would be obtainable for the country concerned and the probable cost of the cover. When the negotiations for the contract near completion, the Department will make a firm offer of cover that is normally valid for one month.

Modified specific policies are available for aircraft and ships and a *specific constructional works guarantee* is available to cover both the supply of goods and the performance of services in respect of overseas projects.

As with a comprehensive guarantee an exporter can assign to his bank his rights under all transactions covered by an ECGD specific guarantee. The Department gives formal acknowledgement of such an assignment and provides the bank with copies of relevant policy documents, such as credit limit approvals. For large amounts and credit terms of five years or more, a bank would however, prefer a direct guarantee from the ECGD, and the *specific bank guarantee* is available for this purpose. A bank guarantee is, in fact, supplementary to the normal ECGD cover and is an unconditional guarantee to the exporter's bank that it will pay the bank in the event of non-receipt of money due from the buyer. The bank is given complete security, which is not conditional on the manner in which non-payment arises.

Guarantees are available for individual contracts for the supply of capital goods on credit of not less than two years from shipment. They cover 100 per cent of loss through any default, and payment is made three months after default. The guarantees are operative when the goods have been shipped or accepted, the works have been completed, or the services have been satisfactorily performed. Because a bank guarantee covers 100 per cent of the value of the loan, the exporter must sign a separate recourse agreement to enable the ECGD to recover from him any payments under the guarantee that it would not have made under the terms of the normal insurance policy.

On loans against *specific bank guarantees* and *buyer credit guarantees* (see below), the banks charge the so-called consensus rates of interest. These are guideline rates determined by representatives of the main exporting countries through the OECD and are subject to revision every six months. The rates vary according to the degree of prosperity of the *buyer's country*. For instance from July 1986 the recommended rates for credit periods of between two and five years ranged from 7.4 per cent for relatively poor countries to 9.55 per cent for relatively rich countries. The guidelines also include recommendations for maximum credit periods again favouring poor nations in that for relatively poor the recommendation is ten years whereas for relatively rich ones it is 5–8½ years. Where the rate of interest charged by the bank is below market rates of interest the government makes up the difference by a payment to the bank concerned through the agency of the ECGD. These preferential rates of interest do not apply in respect of contracts with EEC countries.

Another type of ECGD guarantee in respect of medium- and long-term credit is the *buyer credit guarantee*. These guarantees cover loans made by British banks and other financial institutions direct to overseas purchasers to enable them to pay their suppliers on cash terms. These guarantees are intended to assist the financing of large contracts of £1 million or more, and they are issued without recourse to the supplier. Buyer credit guarantees are confined to a maximum of five years' credit, except where it is established that longer terms are necessary to match foreign competition.

It is the responsibility of the UK exporter to find a financial institution prepared to finance the foreign borrower, and he is also responsible for the Department's charges, which are similar to those for specific cover on a similar project. The purchaser is normally required to pay from 15 per cent to 20 per cent of the contract price direct to the supplier out of his own resources, including an adequate down-payment on signature of the contract. The remaining 80–85 per cent is paid to the supplier from the loan made to the buyer by the financial institution and guaranteed by the ECGD as to 100 per cent of capital and interest against non-payment for any reason whatsoever.

Four legal agreements are involved with a buyer credit guarantee. These are a contract between the British supplier and the overseas buyer; a loan agreement between the financing bank and the overseas buyer; a financial agreement given by the ECGD to the financing bank to cover the risk of non-payment of principal or interest; and a premium agreement between the British supplier and the ECGD. The guarantee does not relieve the supplier, lender or borrower of any commercial responsibilities inherent in transactions of this kind. The system of buyer credit guarantees is extended to provide cover for lines of credit to overseas buyers to facilitate the purchaser of a range of capital goods from a number of suppliers, in order to carry out a capital project. Arrangements vary, but typically, the ECGD will give a guarantee to one British bank that will have secured the backing of other banks and will undertake to provide credit up to a specified amount in respect of contracts for British goods or services falling within the terms of the credit agreement. Contract values may be as low as £25 000.

OTHER COVER

In order to encourage banks to provide performance bonds the ECGD will support such bonds by issuing its *performance bond guarantee* (see p. 177 for details of the various types of performance bonds that are called for by overseas buyers). It is also possible for an exporter to obtain ECGD cover for unfair calling of bonds raised without ECGD support. This type of insurance is available for contracts covered by normal ECGD comprehensive and specific guarantees and is an addendum to that guarantee. The ECGD reimburses the exporter for 100 per cent of any loss due to the calling in of a bond if it is shown subsequently that the exporter was not in default in his performance of the contract, or if any failure on his part is due to specified events outside his control. A premium is charged by making a modest increase to the premium per £100 payable on the normal guarantee.

To encourage British investment overseas the ECGD has since 1972 been offering a system of insurance for the potential risks involved. Insurance is available for investments of equity capital in the form of cash, plant or know-how, for loans to overseas enterprises and for certain guarantees of loans raised outside the UK. The investment must be new and the investor must apply for cover before becoming irrevocably committed to invest. The risks that are covered are expropriation, war damage and restrictions on remittances. The insurance covers 90 per cent of loss and the ECGD's commitment is for fifteen years. An overall maximum insured amount is determined at the outset and within this limit the investor proposes a current insured amount at the beginning of each twelve months of the contract of insurance. A premium ranging between 0.7 and 1 per cent is charged annually on the current insured amount and in addition one-quarter of the agreed premium rate has to be paid on the difference between the current insured amount and the maximum insured amount.

EXAMINATION GUIDELINES

The banking student can be certain that an ECGD question will occur in the examination paper every time and indeed this is reasonable in view of the importance of the subject. The banker is expected to know the subject in order to be able to advise his exporter customers and also to be able to insist, where appropriate, on the type of first-class security that the ECGD direct bank guarantees offer and similar, but to a more limited extent, assignments of ECGD guarantees.

Examination questions in the Institute of Bankers' paper are now invariably of the problem type and the student is expected to identify from the details given the type of ECGD cover appropriate in those particular circumstances. It is hoped that the framework answers given below will help the reader in this connection. These answers are deliberately given only in skeleton form because once the type of cover is identified it is simply a question of giving the details of the particular ECGD scheme as recorded in the chapter.

Question 1

Your customer, International Traders Ltd, is a holding company for a number of trading companies engaged in direct exports and imports and in the merchanting trade. The group, which has ECGD cover, including the bank guarantee scheme, is anxious, for balance sheet purposes, to minimize its liability exposure in connection with finance of its exports. It has been asked to quote for a number of export contracts, each valued at several million pounds and requiring medium- to long-term finance.

Explain how such finance might be arranged by the bank at special fixed interest rates to meet the group's requirements. Set out the salient features of this type of financing.

NOTE: *Ignore non-banking sources such as confirming houses or export financing houses.*

SOLUTION

The clues as to what is required here are that:

(*a*) contracts valued at several million pounds on medium to long term are involved;
(*b*) special fixed interest rates are mentioned;
(*c*) the company wants to limit its liability exposure.

These three clues, especially the third one, point us clearly towards *buyer credit guarantees.* By arranging for a bank to lend direct to the buyer, International Traders will be virtually trading for cash and therefore there will be no liability on the balance sheet. The special fixed interest rates are of course the 'consensus rates' recommended through committee at OECD and reviewed every six months, though for each particular guarantee the rate remains fixed at the rate appropriate when the loan is negotiated. Incidentally, you would not be expected to quote the latest consensus rates in detail, though if you can all well and good. The most important thing is to be able to refer to the existence of such rates and how they vary according to the type of country *buying*, and the fact that the government makes up any shortfall between the rate of interest the bank receives and an appropriate market rate of interest.

The main points to be commented upon are:

(*a*) A brief description of what a buyer credit guarantee is.
(*b*) The fact that the exporter must find a bank willing to make the advance and is also responsible for the premium.
(*c*) The size of the premium.
(*d*) The down-payment.
(*e*) The four contracts.
(*f*) Must be for at least £1 million and may be in foreign currency.

Question 2

Your customer, Resurrection Products Ltd, an extremely well-managed company, has recently been formed following a management buy-out. The capital reconstruction means that you are quite prepared to grant facilities to the company to the extent of £750 000 provided that it takes out all the insurance cover appropriate to its business.

The company's business is export-orientated and although it seeks payment against confirmed irrevocable letters of credit wherever possible, it has been asked to quote for business with credit terms in excess of two years. The directors call to see you to discuss putting together a package for a £300 000 contract they are negotiating with an overseas government buying agency.

REQUIRED

Brief notes on:

(*a*) the support your bank can give in connection with this type of business, *excluding* direct financial assistance;
(*b*) any UK government-backed support that may be available to this particular customer.

SOLUTION

The clues as to what is required here are that a large capital contract is involved, the company is financially very sound, they are looking for bank assistance other than financial and with the support of a government-backed scheme. All of these points direct us towards performance bonds (with ECGD backing) and stand-by letters of credit.

The answer should give details of the various types of performance bond and how the ECGD will provide a performance bond guarantee that gives the bank 100 per cent protection if it issues such a bond and has to pay out under it. Reference should also be made to the fact that if the customers have a performance bond that has been supplied without ECGD backing, they may be able to get protection against unfair calling of the bond by an endorsement of their normal ECGD policy and the payment of an additional premium.

Stand-by documentary credits should be described (see p. 103) and comment made concerning the fact that such a credit has a similar effect to a performance bond.

Question 3

Your customers, Capital Plant Ltd, have been able to sell their goods without any need to resort to the facilities offered by long-term credit agencies. They have normally been paid by letter of credit within eighteen months to two years of shipment. They have now been asked to quote for a contract that would require them to ship goods to a country that is insisting upon credit terms in excess of two years. It is understood that the extended terms required will not have the support of the buyer's bank. Your bank might provide finance to the exporter providing there is backing under an appropriate ECGD scheme.

REQUIRED

A brief summary of the appropriate ECGD scheme with an explanation of the position of the relative parties, i.e. the bank, ECGD and the exporter customer.

SOLUTION

Our clues here are that capital goods are involved, credit terms will exceed two years and that there is no support from the buyer's bank. The latter point rules out an ECGD buyer credit guarantee because even if another bank is asked to provide finance under such a guarantee, it is unlikely to agree if the buyer's own bank is not being supportive.

This is clearly a question concerning ECGD specific bank guarantees, but it should be noted that there is a possibility that, as shipments appear to be quite frequent, that a comprehensive extended terms banker's guarantee could be involved. In either case the customers must have normal ECGD cover, either a specific guarantee or a comprehensive extended terms guarantee. Having stated that we can then proceed without further differentiation between the two types of basic contract because the procedures as far as the bank guarantees are concerned are the same.

The main points to be commented upon are:

(*a*) The cover for the bank is 100 per cent of principal and interest.
(*b*) The cover for the exporter is only that provided by his basic cover and, if ECGD has to pay up under the banker's guarantee, it will look to the exporter for the difference between the two rates of cover.
(*c*) The finance is provided at the consensus rates of interest. The bank has the interest made up by the government.
(*d*) The exporter must pay the premiums for both the basic cover and the bank guarantee.
(*e*) There is usually a down-payment of 15 or 20 per cent.
(*f*) Usually the finance is against a series of bills of exchange or promissory notes at six-monthly intervals.
(*g*) The loan may be in sterling or in foreign currency.

Question 4

The finance director of your customers, Sleep Well Ltd, calls to see you to discuss a developing export trade selling the company's night attire range. During your discussions you learn that the company has been successful in obtaining orders from two very large American chain stores. Payment is to be made against presentation of thirty days' sight bills of exchange. The finance director has already contacted the ECGD and the company has taken out an ECGD comprehensive short-term guarantee policy.

Sleep Well Ltd are already operating on overdraft and the financial director asks whether, as cash-flow problems may arise in the future, you would consider providing finance for the exports *against the protection of the ECGD guarantee (policy) itself.*

REQUIRED

A brief explanation of:

(*a*) the various methods whereby this might be done;
(*b*) the risks the bank will face if it relies wholly on the security offered;

(*c*) why 100 per cent advances will not be available;

N.B. This question has been modified in view of the withdrawal of ECGD direct short-term guarantees to the banks since the question was set.

SOLUTION

This question is quite clearly about ECGD comprehensive guarantees and how they can be used as support for borrowing from a bank. The examinee is required to show how such a guarantee may be assigned to the bank in a number of ways and to comment on the extent to which the bank is likely to be willing to lend to its customer.

The following points need to be covered:

(*a*) The assignment may be of all proceeds due to the exporter, or proceeds of claims relating to a particular market, or claims relating to particular bills. They must of course be bills that are being collected through our bank.

(*b*) The bank is taking the risk that if the failure of the buyer to pay arises through some fault on the part of the exporter (i.e. he has not fulfilled his contract in some way), the ECGD will not pay up under the guarantee.

(*c*) Maximum cover under an ECGD comprehensive guarantee is 95 per cent and could be considerably less, depending upon the cause of non-payment. The bank will not be prepared to lend more than the amount of this cover (probably not more than 90 per cent at the most), and in any case its decision as to how much to lend will be based on other factors as well to do with the general creditworthiness of its customer. It cannot be compelled to lend.

Other questions

1. What are the principal features of the ECGD facilities that concern banks? (*Inst. of Bankers*)

2. 'Much trade, particularly in consumer goods, is done on either D/A collection or open account terms.'

You are required to explain:

(*a*) what these credit terms mean;
(*b*) what risks they involve for the exporter;
(*c*) how he can protect himself against such risks. (*Inst. of Bankers*)

3. A large construction contract has been obtained overseas and there are several contractors involved in the total project of which you are one.

How can protection against credit and other risks be obtained and finance provided for the project? (*Inst. of Export*)

4. You have arranged to cover the whole of your export turnover with the ECGD by means of a comprehensive short-term guarantee.

(*a*) What are the risks covered by this guarantee?
(*b*) In what way could this guarantee enable you to obtain finance?

(*Inst. of Export*)

5. ECGD's comprehensive business in 1977–78 represented 82 per cent of its total business. Describe the 'comprehensive short-term guarantee', including in your answer information on the following: risks covered; percentage cover for the exporter; selected markets. (*Inst. of Freight Forwarders*)

6. (*a*) What is the principal function of the ECGD?
(*b*) What are the methods by which export finance may be made available with ECGD assistance? (*Inst. of Freight Forwarders*)

7. Your customers, Overseas Contractors Ltd, are engaged in large export contracts overseas, and they seek your advice and help on the following matters. (*Each a separate question.*)

1. Describe and explain briefly:
(*a*) the possible risks involved in such operations that are additional to those faced by a similar contractor engaged purely in the domestic market;
(*b*) provisions directly available in the UK to protect a company against these additional risks. It is not intended that your answer should include methods whereby these risks are simply transferred to a party providing finance.

2. Overseas Contractors Ltd are not highly capitalized in relation to their turnover and are therefore finding it difficult because of recourse problems to persuade ECGD to issue further guarantees on their behalf to their bankers in order to obtain finance.

What assistance can ECGD provide in these circumstances, subject to the willingness and co-operation of the other contracting party? Set out in your answer the salient points of any such facility. (*Inst. of Bankers*)

12
OTHER SERVICES TO EXPORTERS

FINANCE WITHOUT RECOURSE

THERE are a large number of firms and institutions in London that provide the exporter with the means of financing the export of goods without recourse to himself. The nature and scope of these services vary a great deal, but the firms and institutions can be grouped into broad categories and that has been done in this chapter.

Factoring

In recent years *factoring* has increased in importance in the UK. There are several large factoring organizations, offering a comprehensive service, in Britain, and the larger British banks have acquired interests in such companies and are thus able to offer factoring services in addition to or in place of normal banking services. Factoring houses provide the seller with 100 per cent credit insurance by taking over his invoices as the goods are supplied, and collecting payment without recourse. The exporter can have some cash immediately he hands over his invoices to the factoring house or wait for payment at an agreed future date. In either case, he receives the face value of the invoices less the factor's charges.

This type of financing is obviously an advantage to the exporter, especially if he is short of working capital. In effect, he sells his goods for cash by selling his invoices to the factor. Furthermore, he is in a better position to pay his creditors immediately and receive any discounts that are offered for prompt payment. Obviously, the factor must make a charge to cover the risk he is taking on, i.e. the risk of non-payment on the part of the foreign importer. But, nevertheless, the exporter may well consider the expense worthwhile if it will relieve him of worry and of a shortage of capital. Another advantage of factoring is that it provides a sales accounting service, the book-keeping being done by the factoring house, and the exporter simply hands over his invoices against payment. A more economical method of factoring is for the exporter to hand over his invoices and have the advantage of the factor's accounting service, but to wait for some time for payment, borrowing from the bank in the meantime if necessary. This reduces but does not eliminate the charges made by the factoring house because if it pays over cash immediately upon receipt of invoices, it may have to borrow in order to do so or use funds that could be gainfully employed elsewhere.

Factoring houses have overseas branches through which arrangements can be made to collect payments from foreign importers. Through their close links with banks they present bills of exchange and other credit instruments and obtain status reports on foreign importers. On the basis of these status reports, the factor sets a limit for each overseas buyer and permits the exporter to supply goods up to this limit and submit his invoice to the factor. Not unreasonably, the factoring house requires that its name shall be disclosed to the buyer. This is necessary, as the factor buys the invoices without recourse and must, therefore, collect the debt in its own right.

Through their relationships with a large number of importers and exporters, the factoring houses are frequently able to secure overseas buyers and agents for exporter clients. Factors prefer to deal with clients who can offer a sizeable and growing amount of business and might insist on a minimum turnover of possibly £100 000.

Confirming and export houses

Another method of securing payment for goods immediately upon despatch without recourse on the part of the seller, is to supply the goods to a *confirming house.* A confirming house is a company that secures orders for goods from foreign importers and passes on these orders to manufacturers, adding its confirmation to the order, which means that the confirming house assumes responsibility for the debt. Confirming houses are sometimes known as *indent houses.* Foreign importers indent for specific types of goods and may even name the particular brand required. It is the job of the confirming house to order and obtain the goods from the manufacturer and arrange for them to be shipped. The manufacturer has the advantage of being able to consult the confirming house near at hand about any problems that arise, instead of having to communicate with the foreign importer, as he would have to do if he was fulfilling an order received direct from the overseas buyer.

Another type of institution used by the exporter is the *export house.*

This is rather like a confirming house, but instead of acting as the importer's agent, it is the exporter's agent. There are a variety of these houses in existence, most of them specializing in the marketing of particular types of goods or selling goods in particular markets. They usually take over the packing, shipping and insurance of the goods and are able to assist in establishing a network of distributors for the goods overseas. Some export houses buy the manufacturer's goods and sell them at a profit.

International credit unions

There are a number of *international credit unions* through which it is possible for the exporter to arrange for the importer to receive credit and thus be able to pay cash for the goods. These unions consist of a number of European finance houses or banks which introduce instalment credit business to their foreign partners on a reciprocal basis.

The members of the organizations provide credit for the importers of a wide range of vehicles, capital goods and some kinds of domestic equipment. The British exporter notifies the British finance house or bank that is a member of that credit union of the name of the importer and details of his credit requirements, and he notifies his buyer that this has been done. The finance house or bank in the importer's country is informed and its representative meets the importer and negotiates the terms of the credit he requires. If the importer is a distributor, the institution will arrange to offer medium-term credit to his retail buyers and will discuss with the distributor the short-term finance he needs. If he is a buyer, then a medium-term credit is arranged for him. The bank or finance house in Britain is notified when the credit is arranged and informs the exporter that this has been done and that he may proceed with the despatch of the goods. It collects payment from the union member in the importer's country and the exporter is paid in full in accordance with his normal terms of contract.

Where money is temporarily scarce, or rates of interest are high in the importer's country, it may be expedient for the financial institution in the exporter's country to lend the money, with perhaps the guarantee of the other union member. As far as the exporter is concerned, however, the effect is the same: he secures the necessary credit for his customer *without cost or recourse to himself.*

Examples of international credit unions are Export Finance International, European Credit Union, and Eurocredit. These are associated with Forward Trust Ltd, Bowmaker Ltd, and Lloyds and Scottish Finance Ltd, respectively. They are all connected with continental financial institutions and Export Finance International also has correspondents in Australia and South Africa.

GOVERNMENT ASSISTANCE

British Overseas Trade Board

The Department of Trade and Industry offer a very comprehensive range of services, both to the importer and the exporter. The facilities offered to the exporter are carried out by the various sections of the department and other government departments and since 1971 have been the responsibility of the British Export Board, later renamed the British Overseas Trade Board (BOTB).

The BOTB consists of businessmen and representatives of the Department of Trade and Industry, the Foreign and Commonwealth Office and the ECGD. The services directed by the Board include guidance to the exporter on his individual export problems, including advice on marketing and advertising a product abroad, which may involve departments in investigating the suitability of the product for foreign tastes and customs. With the help of officials overseas, the Department of Trade and Industry and the Foreign and Commonwealth office are able to supply information about business conditions, local production and imports, the degree of competition, and local tastes and trading methods. Help with overseas publicity is available, together with advice on participating in trade fairs overseas. Introductions are made to potential agents, buyers and firms prepared to manufacture the product overseas under licence. Status reports on these foreign firms can be obtained through the department, but these are concerned with the standing of the potential importer or agent, not with his creditworthiness. Reports on creditworthiness are obtainable through a bank or credit reporting agency. Occasionally, disputes that have arisen between British firms and overseas buyers are resolved amicably in conjunction with British commercial officers overseas.

Through commercial officers and trade commissioners, it is possible to make introductions and appointments, and collect information for the exporter who is going on an overseas business visit before he arrives in the country concerned. Local publicity of the visit can often be arranged.

Before the manufacturer contracts to sell his goods to a particular country, he must ascertain whether or not a tariff will be imposed on them and whether there are any import regulations. The regulations may include requirements concerning certificates of origin, consular invoices and fees, trade and merchandise marks, and imports of samples. This information is obtainable through the Department of Trade and Industry. It is also possible to obtain small samples of goods manufactured overseas, in order to test the strength of foreign competition.

The Export Services and Promotions Division of the BOTB provides a computerized *Export Intelligence Service* through which the individual subscriber receives items of information related to the firm's individual interests and needs and a great deal of background information. The types of information provided by the service include export opportunities and market pointers and reports, agents looking for British principals, calls for tender, overseas buyers visiting the UK, opportunities for co-operation with overseas manufacturers, changes in tariff and import regulations overseas, international aid and loan arrangements, trade agreements, overseas trade fairs, British Weeks and store promotions, reports on the economic and trading position in overseas countries, national and other development plans and notification of events and government legislation. Similar information is published in the weekly journal *British Business* together with details of changes in tariffs, customs, import regulations, export success stories and reports of recent export orders; details of fact-finding trade missions and itineraries of British businessmen going overseas. There are occasional supplements dealing with particular export markets or services and lists of trade fairs, British Weeks and store promotions overseas.

The facilities available in the Statistics and Market Intelligence Library are invaluable to the exporter. This contains many thousands of volumes giving trade, production and other economic data on overseas countries as well as foreign trade and telephone directories and catalogues published by overseas firms.

MARKET ENTRY GUARANTEE SCHEME (MEGS)

Since 1978 the BOTB have been operating a scheme to help small manufacturing firms to cope with the financial risks involved in breaking into an overseas market. This scheme, the Market Entry Guarantee Scheme, enables the exporter to obtain half of the costs of an approved market venture from the BOTB to be recouped by the Board by a levy on sales receipts. This then is tantamount to a loan of 50 per cent of the costs involved, but it goes beyond that inasmuch as in the event of the venture being unsuccessful the loss involved is shared between the BOTB and the exporter. If at the end of an agreed period sales have not been achieved to the extent expected, no further levy payments have to be made, thus sharing the loss. A premium has to be paid for this guarantee.

EXAMINATION GUIDELINES

Questions covering the subject matter of this chapter fall under two categories:—

1. Those concerned with factoring and other non-recourse finance
2. Those concerned with non-financial assistance through government departments and other organizations.

Sometimes questions involve a combination of these two areas, but once the examiner's requirements have been identified, the answers are fairly straightforward and therefore the answers that follow are again only frameworks around which details can be filled in from the text of the chapter.

Question 1

The O.K. Company Ltd, which has been trading for some years, is well managed, but is short of working capital. The managing director, who is also responsible for financial matters, comes to see you to discuss various methods of obtaining finance to cover new export contracts (goods are sold on ninety-day bill terms). The company has recently taken out an ECGD comprehensive policy.

As the manager of your bank, you do not wish to extend the company's facilities any further without a completely reliable guarantee from an independent body. You explain the bank's position and outline a source of finance that might be available through the bank, as well as other sources of non-bank finance that might be available and should satisfy your customer's needs.

REQUIRED

Brief notes on each of the scheme discussed showing their salient features.

SOLUTION

The fact that the question states that the bank does not wish to extend the company's facilities any further without *a completely reliable* guarantee from an independent body rather rules out the possibility of lending the company further funds on the strength of an assignment of its ECGD comprehensive guarantee. This is because of the fact that if the reason for non-payment by the buyer can in anyway be attributed to a fault on the part of the exporter, the ECGD will not pay up under the guarantee.

The question is clearly about sources of non-recourse export finance and one of these, factoring, is likely to be available through the bank because all of the main clearing banks have factoring house subsidiaries. This is indeed the most likely way in which the customers will resolve their problem.

In addition to factoring the answer should refer to the services of:

(*a*) confirming houses;
(*b*) export houses;
(*c*) international credit unions.

Question 2

One of your customers, Plant Propagations Ltd, makes arrangements for a director, A. Grafton, to call to see you to discuss an enquiry the company has had from one of the Arabian Gulf States. The proposal is that your customers should supply a range of plants to landscape a new hotel, office and shopping arcade complex in the Gulf. The enquiry emanates from the main contractor, a resident company in the Middle Eastern country in question. Your customers do not necessarily need finance.

REQUIRED

Brief notes showing the help, other than financial, available to the customers from yourself and other interested agencies.

SOLUTION

The answer to this question falls into two parts

1. What services can the bank offer?
2. What other services may be useful?

Under (1) the answer should contain references to:

(*a*) Providing a political and economic report on the country concerned, together with comments on exchange control restrictions, if any, in the country concerned.
(*b*) Providing a status report on the buyer.
(*c*) Providing information on the appropriate method of payment.
(*d*) Do the customers need any professional help in packing and despatching abroad? If so the bank may be able to put them in touch with an appropriate forwarding agent.
Can they meet the contract or will they need the names of others who can help?
(*e*) If Mr Grafton is going to visit the country concerned the bank will provide travel facilities and provide letters of introduction if required.

(*f*) The question of finance could be touched upon, even though we are told it may not be required. There may possibly be a need for a performance guarantee of some sort—performance bond, stand-by credit.

Under (2) the answer should contain references to:

(*a*) The services of the BOTB.
(*b*) The possibility of help from the local chamber of commerce, a trade association or export club.
(*c*) ECGD services, should they be desirable.

Other questions

1. Your customers. Armchair Sales Ltd, have built up a successful business but have always been short of working capital. Their sales are solely in the UK and recently there has been a shortage of home demand.

At a recent trade fair they received enquiries from a number of overseas companies who have now placed firm orders. You have ascertained that the only way that your customers could obtain the business would be to offer similar terms to those applicable to the existing UK business, namely open account. A number of European currencies will be involved.

The company's finance director seeks your advice asking for details of a scheme that would help them to obtain immediate cash against export receivables and at the same time give some measure of foreign exchange cover.

Briefly describe the possibilities open, outlining a *single* scheme that would assist your customer.

2. Explain the alternatives available to a UK exporter of consumer goods sold on ninety days' credit terms who wants 'without recourse' finance.

(*Inst. of Bankers*)

3. 'A comprehensive range of facilities is now available to the United Kingdom exporter for the finance of export credit.'

Describe the facilities available within this 'comprehensive range' in respect of UK exports of:

(*a*) consumer goods sold on short-term credit;
(*b*) major capital goods sold on long-term credit. (*Inst. of Bankers*)

4. What are the main sources of non-recourse post-shipment finance available to the UK exporter trading on up to 180 days' credit terms? Describe fully one of them. (*Inst. of Export*)

5. You are approached by a factoring company who suggest that you should use their services for the development of your export business. You have so far been quite satisfied with the services and facilities provided by your bank. What

matters would you take into consideration to judge whether such a service would be of any advantage to you?

(*Inst. of Export*)

6. Describe the services provided to an exporter by a factoring company. In what circumstances is such a service worthwhile?

(*Inst. of Export*)

7. Your customers, NBC Ltd, a medium-sized concern with a good record, have asked what government help there might be to assist them to enter overseas markets.

(*a*) Describe the scheme currently available from the UK government.
(*b*) Apart from finance, what help can UK banks give to new exporters.

(*Inst. of Bankers*)

13
BANKING SERVICES TO IMPORTERS

PAYING FOR IMPORTS

As for the exporter, the banks provide two principal services to the importer, a method of payment and the provision of finance to enable him to import the goods and then sell them on credit terms. The methods of payment that can be used in international trade have already been considered in detail and need no further comment, but the ways in which these methods can be used to provide the importer with finance must be examined more fully.

Importers are able to obtain bank finance on either a secured or unsecured basis for use as working capital in the same way as exporters. The extent to which they are able to borrow on a normal loan or overdraft basis must of course depend upon their creditworthiness, and the same comments concerning the cost of such borrowing and the principles concerning repayment mentioned at the beginning of Chapter 10 apply. As the importer receives payments for goods that are sold, possibly manufactured goods incorporating imported raw materials or parts, or commodities, the proceeds are paid into his account, thus reducing his overdraft or loan. The bank will expect the importer's current account balance to fluctuate as payments are received and payments made.

If the importer is able to persuade the overseas exporter to give him a period of credit this will ease the pressure on his working capital, but he must be careful that he is not required to pay the interest cost of this period or, if he does, that it is not excessive. There may be a stipulation in the contract, for instance, that he must pay the costs of negotiating a bill of exchange drawn on him or there may be an exchange clause written into a bill of exchange drawn on him which stipulates that he must pay interest and charges. If he can avoid paying such costs then he would be wise to do so, but if he cannot he must consider carefully whether he could get the finance more cheaply in the UK, in which case he could undertake to pay for the goods against the documents.

From the importer's point of view the best arrangement is for the seller to supply the goods and let him pay later, and not charge him for the time-lag. This would mean that they would be trading on open account or by means of a D/A bill; in other words he (the importer) would be taking advantage of trade credit in the way that he would probably do if he were buying the goods on the home market. By doing so the importer might be able to reduce his bank borrowing or alternatively use his working capital in some other way so as to increase his profit, e.g. to buy additional stocks of goods the price of which is likely to increase.

The overseas supplier may be prepared to grant a period of credit, but only on condition that the importer opens a documentary credit in his favour and an offer to open such a credit may well encourage the supplier to agree to give the importer time to pay. The costs involved will usually fall on the importer, but they will be modest compared with the bank interest charges that might otherwise have to be met if he were to borrow in order to pay cash against documents. Obviously it must be the importer and not the exporter who arranges the credit. He must approach his bank and, if they are satisfied with his creditworthiness, they will act on his behalf and undertake to pay the exporter for him against a term bill of exchange. It is quite common practice for foreign exporters to require the British importer to give them the benefit of a documentary acceptance credit of a London bank rather than the credit of a local bank in their country opened at the request of a London bank. They are then able to draw bills on the London bank that are readily negotiable. An example of such bill is given in Fig. 13.1. The cost of the draft, i.e. the bank's charges for negotiating it, could be added to the invoice amount and thus paid by the importer if the exporter objected to paying them.

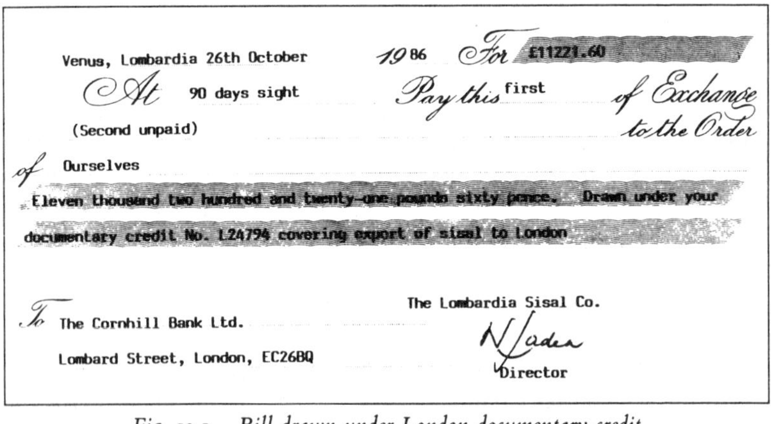
Venus, Lombardia 26th October 1986 For £11221.60

At 90 days sight Pay this first of Exchange

(Second unpaid) to the Order

of Ourselves

Eleven thousand two hundred and twenty-one pounds sixty pence. Drawn under your documentary credit No. L24794 covering export of sisal to London

To The Cornhill Bank Ltd.

Lombard Street, London, EC26BQ

The Lombardia Sisal Co.

Director

Fig. 13.1. Bill drawn under London documentary credit

For imports from the Far East, and some other parts of the world, it is usual for the exporter to draw his bill on *the importer* under a documentary credit which provides for the bill to be negotiated by a bank in the exporter's country, in local currency. The British importer arranges for the credit to be opened by his bank or possibly the London office of an Asian bank. The bank in the exporter's country, having negotiated the bill, sends the bill and the shipping documents to the bank in London, which presents the draft to the importer for acceptance. Where this has been arranged through an Asian bank in London, the goods may be stored on the importer's behalf until the bill is paid by him. This would apply, of course, if it was stipulated that documents should be released against payment, but if it was agreed that the documents should be released against acceptance the importer would be able to take possession of the goods before paying the draft and supply them to the ultimate buyer.

If the foreign supplier agrees to draw a bill on the importer without a documentary credit that provides for its negotiation or acceptance, he may, nevertheless, be able to negotiate it locally or obtain an advance on the strength of the bill lodged for collection. But he will have to rely solely on the good name of the buyer, however, for he will have to part with the documents before payment of the bill.

If the exporter insists on drawing a sight draft instead of a tenor draft under a documentary credit, then the importer may still be able to obtain credit. He may be able to persuade his bank to make a *merchandise advance* (often referred to as a *produce loan*) against the security of the shipping documents. If his bank is a merchant bank and not a commercial bank, the importer may be permitted to draw a tenor *reimbursement draft* under a London acceptance credit, using the proceeds from discounting it to meet the sight draft drawn under the credit.

Instead of requiring the exporter to draw a bill on him, the importer may remit the invoice amount to the exporter, using the proceeds of the reimbursement draft for the purpose. The merchant bank may insist on doing this for the importer through an agent overseas against the documents of title to the goods. It will be appreciated that whether the finance is obtained from a clearing bank or a merchant bank, the bank will probably insist on having control of the shipping documents as security and as a means of repayment, and will require the importer to sign a certificate of pledge or letter of hypothecation giving the bank power to sell the goods if it is necessary to do so. The bank will require a full set of bills of lading endorsed in blank or to the order of the bank and an insurance document with sufficient cover and endorsed in blank or to the bank. The goods will have to be stored in the bank's name and the insurance cover extended and the bank will hold the warehouse receipt. The bank will release the goods to the importer as reductions are made in the loan or the importer may be allowed to take possession of the goods to enable him to deliver them to the buyer. If this is allowed, the bank will require its customer to sign a trust receipt and thus pledge himself to act as agent and trustee for the bank in dealing with the goods (see p. 154).

The bank will normally lend only a proportion of the invoice value of the goods and the size of this proportion will depend upon a number of factors in addition to the importer's creditworthiness. The factors can be summarized as follows:

(*a*) Have the goods been resold? If, so, what is known about the prospective buyer and when can payment be expected?
(*b*) If the goods have yet to be sold, how difficult is it likely to be to find a buyer?
(*c*) When can repayment of the loan be expected? This question is of course closely related to (*a*) and (*b*)
(*d*) If the bank has to sell the goods, what is the lowest price it can expect to get for them?
(*e*) Are the goods perishable?
(*f*) Is it costly to handle and store the goods and are there any special marketing problems involved with them?
(*g*) Is any security being offered in addition to the goods?
(*h*) How does the sum to be advanced compare with the importer's own stake in his business?
(*i*) How much does the importer want to borrow? He will obviously not borrow more than he requires.

A back-to-back documentary credit would not provide the period of credit the importer needs, because the ultimate buyer is not paying for the goods under a documentary credit immediately they arrive in the UK. A back-to-back credit is issued only when the merchant has already sold the goods and persuaded the buyer to open a documentary credit in his favour. The second credit (in favour of the original supplier of the goods) is opened on the strength of this credit opened by the buyer, and there must be a minimum of delay in getting the documents from the supplier, switching invoices and presenting the documents to the bank opening the original credit. A back-to-back credit would be useless to an importer who, as an examination question may describe, needs finance covering a period of say, four or six months from the date of shipment, to bridge the gap between the date of shipment and the time when the goods finally arrive and are processed and sold. If the goods are sold to a buyer in the UK, then payment is likely to be made after the arrival of the goods, possibly by cheque, in the way that goods are normally supplied and paid for on the domestic market.

FINDING A SUPPLIER

An importer's bank can assist him in finding foreign suppliers of goods he wishes to buy. Correspondent banks are continually seeking buyers in the UK for their customer's goods, and banks are able to pass on the names of such suppliers to potential importers. The British banks will always make specific enquiries through overseas banks when requested to do so, and having found a source of supply, will obtain a status report for their importer customer on the potential exporter concerned. The status report would be concerned with the supplier's creditworthiness and ability to fulfil his contract.

If the importer travels overseas to make contacts, or develop contacts, he will, of course, be assisted by his bank. He will be provided with introductions through correspondent banks from whom he is able to obtain help and advice on arrival in the country concerned. The necessary traveller's cheques, foreign currencies, etc. would also be supplied by the importer's bank.

EXAMINATION GUIDELINES

There is really only one subject area for examination questions to cover the subject matter of this chapter and that is how a bank may be prepared to provide finance for an importer who has to pay for his goods immediately and yet will have to wait some time before he receives payment from the company he has resold them to. Just one sample question will suffice to show what is involved in answering such a question.

Question 1

A UK importer purchasing goods on a sterling basis has agreed with his suppliers that settlement will be made against presentation of shipping documents through his bankers. The importer would like ninety days' credit before payment, but the suppliers insist on payment against documents. On the assumption that the goods are readily saleable, how could you, as his banker, assist the importer with the provision of ninety days' finance against the security of the goods?

SOLUTION

We are told that the goods are readily saleable, which is one of the key factors in deciding the extent to which we are prepared to help our importer customer. Ideally we would have liked the goods to have actually been resold and to know the name of the buyer in order that we could check his credit standing. However, that is not the case and we must make our own assessment of how long it will take to resell the goods and what the forced-sale value of the goods would be if we were obliged to sell them in order to recoup our advance to the importer. In the final analysis we are dependent upon our importer customer's creditworthiness and business ability because we do not want to have to fall back on our security, i.e. the imported goods, against which we will make the advance.

Bearing all the points in mind, we must decide just how much we are prepared to lend the importer. We will certainly not be prepared to lend 100 per cent of the value of the goods, unless he has some additional form of security to offer. Much will depend of course on just how much he needs to borrow.

Having agreed to lend against the security of the goods, we will want to have possession of the commercial documents and to have the goods warehoused and insured in the bank's name when they arrive. The bill of lading and the insurance document should be indorsed in blank or made over to the bank. The warehouse receipt will be held by the bank. In addition, our customer will be required to sign a letter of pledge or letter or hypothecation in order that the bank will be in a position to sell the goods should it be necessary to do so.

As payment(s) is received for the goods so they will be released, but it may be extremely difficult for our customer to sell the goods without actually having possession of them, and he may well press us to allow him to have access to them. If we prepared to do this we will do so against the importer's signature on a trust receipt in which he acknowledges that he will be acting as agent for the bank when handling the goods. He promises to hand over the sale proceeds to the bank or, alternatively, to return the documents or the goods to the bank. Such an undertaking does give us some reassurance, but there are considerable dangers in allowing our customer to handle the goods, which are, after all, our security. These dangers are that he may sell the goods and abscond with the proceeds or go into bankruptcy. He may pledge the goods elsewhere or alternatively, he may mix the goods in with others so that it would be very difficult to identify the particular goods that were imported and reclaim them. This would be particularly difficult if the goods were machine parts that had been assembled into machines.

Despite the risks involved, goods are released against trust receipts without difficulties arising but the bank will only take the risks if it has a good regard for its customer and his reliability.

Other questions

1. A British wool merchant has to pay his Melbourne supplier immediately the greasy wool is shipped, although he will not receive the resale proceeds until four months later, i.e. after the wool has arrived in the UK, has been scoured and combed into tops, and the tops have been delivered to and paid for by a Bradford spinner.

Advise the British wool merchant on the banking facilities available to him in the UK for handling this transaction. (*Inst. of Bankers*)

2. Explain how a bill of exchange can be used to provide a UK importer with short-term finance after his overseas supplier has been paid against shipping documents. (*Inst. of Bankers*)

3. A London importer has purchased a quantity of canned salmon from a supplier in Japan and resold it to a Birmingham wholesaler on terms that mean that he must wait for payment from the Birmingham wholesaler until after the goods have arrived in the UK, although he will have to pay his Japanese supplier in sterling immediately the goods are shipped.

Describe how the London importer's bank could help him to effect settlement and at the same time provide him with the necessary finance. (*Inst. of Bankers*)

4. Explain how a London bank or accepting house can make short-term finance available to a British importer against the security of his imports. (*Inst. of Bankers*)

5. How could a UK bank:

(*a*) assist a British importer to pay his overseas supplier against documentary evidence of the shipment of the goods;

(*b*) provide the importer with three months' credit against the security of the goods' (*Inst. of Bankers*)

6. Your customers, Importers Ltd, ask you to help with the finance of an import of goods into the UK from Japan, repayment to come from the proceeds of the sale to the ultimate buyer three months after arrival of the goods.

How could your bank help, using the goods as security, when payment to Japan has to be made as soon as possible after despatch from Japan, either by irrevocable letter of credit or documentary sight collection? (*Inst. of Bankers*)

7. An importer has ordered a consignment of goods but has been unable to obtain any credit terms from his supplier and will have to pay cash against a sight draft. He will therefore need some financial assistance to pay for the goods and have time to dispose of them. Using the goods as security, how could the bank provide him with the necessary finance? What would be the procedure and on what points would the bank require satisfactory information? How would the bank protect itself? (*Inst. of Export*)

APPENDIX 1
UNIFORM CUSTOMS AND PRACTICE FOR DOCUMENTARY CREDITS (1983 REVISION)

A. GENERAL PROVISIONS AND DEFINITIONS

ARTICLE 1

These articles apply to all documentary credits, including, to the extent to which they may be applicable, standby letters of credit, and are binding on all parties thereto unless otherwise expressly agreed. They shall be incorporated into each documentary credit by wording in the credit indicating that such credit is issued subject to *Uniform Customs and Practice for Documentary Credits*, 1983 revision, ICC Publication No. 400.

ARTICLE 2

For the purposes of these articles, the expressions 'documentary credit(s)' and 'standby letter(s) of credit' used herein (hereinafter referred to as 'credit(s)'), mean any arrangement, however named or described, whereby a bank (the issuing bank), acting at the request and on the instructions of a customer (the applicant for the credit),

(*a*) is to make a payment to or to the order of a third party (the beneficiary), or is to pay or accept bills of exchange (drafts) drawn by the beneficiary, or

(*b*) authorizes another bank to effect such payment, or to pay, accept or negotiate such bills of exchange (drafts),

against stipulated documents, provided that the terms and conditions of the credit are complied with.

ARTICLE 3

Credits, by their nature, are separate transactions from the sales or other contract(s) on which they may be based and banks are in no way concerned with or bound by such contract(s), even if any reference whatsoever to such contract(s) is included in the credit.

ARTICLE 4

In credit operations all parties concerned deal in documents, and not in goods, services and/or other performances to which the documents may relate.

ARTICLE 5

Instructions for the issuance of credits, the credits themselves, instructions for any amendments thereto and the amendments themselves must be complete and precise.

In order to guard against confusion and misunderstanding, banks should discourage any attempt to include excessive detail in the credit or in any amendment thereto.

ARTICLE 6

A beneficiary can in no case avail himself of the contractual relationships existing between the banks or between the applicant for the credit and issuing bank.

B. FORM AND NOTIFICATION OF CREDITS

ARTICLE 7

(*a*) Credits may be either

(*i*) revocable, or
(*ii*) irrevocable.

(*b*) All credits, therefore, should clearly indicate whether they are revocable or irrevocable.

(*c*) In the absence of such indication the credit shall be deemed to be revocable.

ARTICLE 8

A credit may be advised to a beneficiary through another bank (the advising bank) without engagement on the part of the advising bank, but that bank shall take reasonable care to check the apparent authenticity of the credit which it advises.

ARTICLE 9

(*a*) A revocable credit may be amended or cancelled by the issuing bank at any moment and without prior notice to the beneficiary.

(*b*) However, the issuing bank is bound to:

(*i*) reimburse a branch or bank with which a revocable credit has been made available for sight payment, acceptance or negotiation, for any payment, acceptance or negotiation made by such branch or bank prior to receipt by it of notice of amendment or cancellation, against documents which appear on their face to be in accordance with the terms and conditions of the credit;

(*ii*) reimburse a branch or bank with which a revocable credit has been made available for deferred payment, if such branch or bank has, prior to receipt by it of notice of amendment or cancellation, taken up documents which appear on their face to be in accordance with the terms and conditions of the credit.

ARTICLE 10

(*a*) An irrevocable credit constitutes a definite undertaking of the issuing bank, provided that the stipulated documents are presented and that the terms and conditions of the credit are complied with:

(*i*) if the credit provides for sight payment—to pay, or that payment will be made;

(*ii*) if the credit provides for deferred payment—to pay, or that payment will be made, on the date(s) determinable in accordance with the stipulations of the credit;

(*iii*) if the credit provides for acceptance—to accept drafts drawn by the beneficiary if the credit stipulates that they are to be drawn on the issuing bank, or to be responsible for their acceptance and payment at maturity if the credit stipulates that they are to be drawn on the applicant for the credit or any other drawee stipulated in the credit;

(*iv*) if the credit provides for negotiation—to pay without recourse to drawers and/or bona fide holders, draft(s) drawn by the beneficiary, at sight or at a tenor, on the applicant for the credit or on any other drawee stipulated in the credit other than the issuing bank itself, or to provide for negotiation by another bank and to pay, as above, if such negotiation is not effected.

(*b*) When an issuing bank authorizes or requests another bank to confirm its irrevocable credit and the latter has added its confirmation, such confirmation constitutes a definite undertaking of such bank (the confirming bank), in addition to that of the issuing bank, provided that the stipulated documents are presented and that the terms and conditions of the credit are complied with:

(*i*) if the credit provides for sight payment—to pay, or that payment will be made;

(*ii*) if the credit provides for deferred payment—to pay, or that payment will be made, on the date(s) determinable in accordance with the stipulations of the credit;

(*iii*) if the credit provides for acceptance—to accept drafts drawn by the beneficiary if the credit stipulates that they are to be drawn on the confirming bank, or to be responsible for their acceptance and payment at maturity if the credit stipulates that they are to be drawn on the applicant for the credit or any other drawee stipulated in the credit;

(*iv*) if the credit provides for negotiation—to negotiate without recourse to drawers and/or bona fide holders, draft(s) drawn by the beneficiary, at sight or at a tenor, on the issuing bank or on the applicant for the credit or on any other drawee stipulated in the credit other than the confirming bank itself.

(*c*) If a bank is authorized or requested by the issuing bank to add its confirmation to a credit but is not prepared to do so, it must so inform the issuing bank without delay. Unless the issuing bank specifies otherwise in its confirmation authorization or request, the advising bank will advise the credit to the beneficiary without adding its confirmation.

(*d*) Such undertakings can neither be amended nor cancelled without the agreement of the issuing bank, the confirming bank (if any), and the beneficiary. Partial acceptance of amendments contained in one and the same advice of amendment is not effective without the agreement of all the above named parties.

ARTICLE 11

(*a*) All credits must clearly indicate whether they are available by sight payment, by deferred payment, by acceptance or by negotiation.

(*b*) All credits must nominate the bank (nominated bank) which is authorized to pay (paying bank), or to accept drafts (accepting bank), or to negotiate (negotiating bank), unless the credit allows negotiation by any bank (negotiating bank).

(*c*) Unless the nominated bank is the issuing bank or the confirming bank, its nomination by the issuing bank does not constitute any undertaking by the nominated bank to pay, to accept, or to negotiate.

(*d*) By nominating a bank other than itself, or by allowing for negotiation by any bank, or by authorizing or requesting a bank to add its confirmation, the issuing bank authorizes such bank to pay, accept or negotiate, as the case may be, against documents which appear on their face to be in accordance with the terms and conditions of the credit, and undertakes to reimburse such bank in accordance with the provisions of these articles.

ARTICLE 12

(*a*) When an issuing bank instructs a bank (advising bank) by any teletransmission to advise a credit or an amendment to a credit, and intends the mail confirmation to be the operative credit instrument, or the operative amendment, the teletransmission must state 'full details to follow' (or words of similar effect), or that the mail confirmation will be the operative credit instrument or the operative amendment. The issuing bank must forward the operative credit instrument or the operative amendment to such advising bank without delay.

(*b*) The teletransmission will be deemed to be the operative credit instrument or the operative amendment, and no mail confirmation should be sent, unless the teletransmission states 'full details to follow' (or words of similar effect), or states that the mail confirmation is to be the operative credit instrument or the operative amendment.

(*c*) A teletransmission intended by the issuing bank to be the operative credit instrument should clearly indicate that the credit is issued subject to *Uniform Customs and Practice for Documentary Credits*, 1983 revision, ICC Publication No. 400.

(*d*) If a bank uses the services of another bank or banks (the advising bank) to have the credit advised to the beneficiary, it must also use the services of the same bank(s) for advising any amendments.

(*e*) Banks shall be responsible for any consequences arising from their failure to follow the procedures set out in the preceding paragraphs.

ARTICLE 13

When a bank is instructed to issue, confirm or advise a credit similar in terms to one previously issued, confirmed or advised (similar credit) and the previous credit has been the subject of amendment(s), it shall be understood that the similar credit will not include any such amendment(s) unless the instructions specify clearly the amendment(s) which is/are to apply to the similar credit. Banks should discourage instructions to issue, confirm or advise a credit in this manner.

ARTICLE 14

If incomplete or unclear instructions are received to issue, confirm, advise or amend a credit, the bank requested to act on such instructions may give preliminary notification to the beneficiary for information only and without responsibility. The credit will be issued, confirmed, advised or amended only when the necessary information has been received and if the bank is then prepared to act on the instructions. Banks should provide the necessary information without delay.

C. LIABILITIES AND RESPONSIBILITIES

ARTICLE 15

Banks must examine all documents with reasonable care to ascertain that they appear on their face to be in accordance with the terms and conditions of the credit. Documents which appear on their face to be inconsistent with one another will be considered as not appearing on their face to be in accordance with the terms and conditions of the credit.

ARTICLE 16

(*a*) If a bank so authorized effects payment, or incurs a deferred payment undertaking, or accepts, or negotiates against documents which appear on their face to be in accordance with the terms and conditions of a credit, the party giving such authority shall be bound to reimburse the bank which has effected payment, or incurred a deferred payment undertaking, or has accepted, or negotiated, and to take up the documents.

(*b*) If, upon receipt of the documents, the issuing bank considers that they appear on their face not to be in accordance with the terms and conditions of the credit, it must determine, on the basis of the documents alone, whether to take up such documents, or to refuse them and claim that they appear on their face not to be in accordance with the terms and conditions of the credit.

(*c*) The issuing bank shall have a reasonable time in which to examine the documents and to determine as above whether to take up or to refuse the documents.

(*d*) If the issuing bank decides to refuse the documents, it must give notice to that effect without delay by telecommunication or, if that is not possible, by other expeditious means, to the bank from which it received the documents (the remitting bank), or to the beneficiary, if it received the documents directly from him. Such notice must state the discrepancies in respect of which the issuing bank refuses the documents and must also state whether it is holding the documents at the disposal of, or is returning them to, the presentor (remitting bank or the beneficiary, as the case may be). The issuing bank shall then be entitled to claim from the remitting bank refund of any reimbursement which may have been made to that bank.

(*e*) If the issuing bank fails to act in accordance with the provisions of paragraphs (*c*) and (*d*) of this article and/or fails to hold the documents at the disposal of, or to return them to, the presentor, the issuing bank shall be precluded from claiming that the documents are not in accordance with the terms and conditions of the credit.

(*f*) If the remitting bank draws the attention of the issuing bank to any discrepancies in the documents or advises the issuing bank that it has paid, incurred a deferred payment undertaking, accepted or negotiated under reserve or against an indemnity in respect of such discrepancies, the issuing bank shall not be thereby relieved from any of its obligations under any provision of this article. Such reserve or indemnity concerns only the relations between the remitting bank and the party towards whom the reserve was made, or from whom, or on whose behalf, the indemnity was obtained.

ARTICLE 17

Banks assume no liability or responsibility for the form, sufficiency, accuracy, genuineness, falsification or legal effect of any documents, or for the general and/or particular conditions stipulated in the documents or superimposed thereon; nor do they assume any liability or responsibility for the description, quantity, weight, quality, condition, packing, delivery, value or existence of the goods represented by any documents, or for the good faith or acts and/or omissions, solvency, performance or standing of the consignor, the carriers, or the insurers of the goods, or any other person whomsoever.

ARTICLE 18

Banks assume no liability or responsibility for the consequences arising out of delay and/or loss in transit of any messages, letters or documents, or for delay, mutilation or other errors arising in the transmission of any telecommunication. Banks assume no liability or responsibility for errors in translation or interpretation of technical terms, and reserve the right to transmit credit terms without translating them.

ARTICLE 19

Banks assume no liability or responsibility for consequences arising out of the interruption of their business by Acts of God, riots, civil commotions, insurrections, wars or any other causes beyond their control, or by any strikes or lockouts. Unless specifically authorized, banks will not, upon resumption of their business, incur a deferred payment undertaking, or effect payment, acceptance or negotiation under credits which expired during such interruption of their business.

ARTICLE 20

(*a*) Banks utilizing the services of another bank or other banks for the purpose of giving effect to the instructions of the applicant for the credit do so for the account and at the risk of such applicant.

(*b*) Banks assume no liability or responsibility should the instructions they transmit not be carried out, even if they have themselves taken the initiative in the choice of such other bank(s).

(*c*) The applicant for the credit shall be bound by and liable to indemnify the banks against all obligations and responsibilities imposed by foreign laws and usages.

ARTICLE 21

(*a*) If an issuing bank intends that the reimbursement to which a paying, accepting or negotiating bank is entitled shall be obtained by such bank claiming on another branch or office of the issuing bank or on a third bank (all hereinafter referred to as the reimbursing bank) it shall provide such reimbursing bank in good time with the proper instructions or authorization to honour such reimbursement claims and without making it a condition that the bank entitled to claim reimbursement must certify compliance with the terms and conditions of the credit to the reimbursing bank.

(*b*) An issuing bank will not be relieved from any of its obligations to provide reimbursement itself if and when reimbursement is not affected by the reimbursing bank.

(*c*) The issuing bank will be responsible to the paying, accepting or negotiating bank for any loss of interest if reimbursement is not provided on first demand made to the reimbursing bank, or as otherwise specified in the credit, or mutually agreed, as the case may be.

D. DOCUMENTS

ARTICLE 22

(*a*) All instructions for the issuance of credits and the credits themselves and, where applicable, all instructions for amendments thereto and the amendments themselves, must state precisely the document(s) against which payment, acceptance or negotiation is to be made.

(*b*) Terms such as 'first class', 'well known', 'qualified', 'independent', 'official', and the like shall not be used to describe the issuers of any documents to be presented under a credit. If such terms are incorporated in the credit terms, banks will accept the relative documents as presented, provided that they appear on their face to be in accordance with the other terms and conditions of the credit.

(*c*) Unless otherwise stipulated in the credit, banks will accept as originals documents produced or appearing to have been produced:

(*i*) by reprographic systems;
(*ii*) by, or as the result of, automated or computerized systems;
(*iii*) as carbon copies,

if marked as originals, always provided that, where necessary, such documents appear to have been authenticated.

ARTICLE 23

When documents other than transport documents, insurance documents and commercial invoices are called for, the credit should stipulate by whom such documents are to be issued and their wording or data content. If the credit does not so stipulate, banks will accept such documents as presented, provided that their data content makes it possible to relate the goods and/or services referred to therein to those referred to in the commercial invoice(s) presented, or to those referred to in the credit if the credit does not stipulate presentation of a commercial invoice.

ARTICLE 24

Unless otherwise stipulated in the credit, banks will accept a document bearing a date of issuance prior to that of the credit, subject to such document being presented within the time limits set out in the credit and in these articles.

DI Transport documents (documents indicating loading on board or despatch or taking in charge)

ARTICLE 25

Unless a credit calling for a transport document stipulates as such document a marine bill of lading (ocean bill of lading or a bill of lading covering carriage by sea), or a post receipt or certificate of posting:

(*a*) banks will, unless otherwise stipulated in the credit, accept a transport document which:

(*i*) appears on its face to have been issued by a named carrier, or his agent, and

(*ii*) indicate despatch or taking in charge of the goods, or loading on board, as the case may be, and

(*iii*) consists of the full set of originals issued to the consignor if issued in more than one original, and

(*iv*) meets all other stipulations of the credit.

(*b*) Subject to the above, and unless otherwise stipulated in the credit, banks will not reject a transport document which:

(*i*) bears a title such as 'Combined transport bill of lading', 'Combined transport document', 'Combined transport bill of lading or port-to-port bill of lading', or a title or a combination of titles of similar intent and effect, and/or

(*ii*) indicates some or all of the conditions of carriage by reference to a source or document other than the transport document itself (short form/blank back transport document), and/or

(*iii*) indicates a place of taking in charge different from the port of loading and/or a place of final destination different from the port of discharge, and/or

(*iv*) relates to cargoes such as those in Containers or on pallets, and the like, and/or

(*v*) contains the indication 'intended', or similar qualification, in relation to the vessel or other means of transport, and/or the port of loading and/or the port of discharge.

(*c*) Unless otherwise stipulated in the credit in the case of carriage by sea or by more than one mode of transport but including carriage by sea, banks will reject a transport document which:

(*i*) indicates that it is subject to a charter party, and/or

(*ii*) indicates that the carrying vessel is propelled by sail only.

(*d*) Unless otherwise stipulated in the credit, banks will reject a transport document issued by a freight forwarder unless it is the FIATA Combined Transport Bill of Lading approved by the International Chamber of Commerce or otherwise indicates that it is issued by a freight forwarder acting as a carrier or agent of a named carrier.

ARTICLE 26

If a credit calling for a transport document stipulates as such document a marine bill of lading:

(*a*) banks will, unless otherwise stipulated in the credit, accept a document which:

(*i*) appears on its face to have been issued by a named carrier, or his agent, and
(*ii*) indicates that the goods have been loaded on board or shipped on a named vessel, and
(*iii*) consists of the full set of originals issued to the consignor if issued in more than one original, and
(*iv*) meets all the other stipulations of the credit.

(*b*) Subject to the above, and unless otherwise stipulated in the credit, banks will not reject a document which:

(*i*) bears a title such as 'Combined transport bill of lading', 'Combined transport document', 'Combined transport bill of lading or port-to-port bill of lading', or a title or a combination of titles of similar intent and effect, and/or
(*ii*) indicates some or all of the conditions of carriage by reference to a source or document other than the transport document itself (short form/blank back transport document), and/or
(*iii*) indicates a place of taking in charge different from the port of loading, and/or a place of final destination different from the port of discharge, and/or
(*iv*) relates to cargoes such as those in Containers or on pallets, and the like.

(*c*) Unless otherwise stipulated in the credit, banks will reject a document which:

(*i*) indicates that it is subject to a charter party, and/or
(*ii*) indicates that the carrying vessel is propelled by sail only, and/or
(*iii*) contains the indication 'intended', or similar qualification in relation to

(*a*) the vessel and/or the port of loading—unless such document bears an on board notation in accordance with Article 27(*b*) and also indicates the actual port of loading, and/or
(*b*) the port of discharge—unless the place of final destination

indicated on the document is other than the port of discharge, and/or

(*iv*) is issued by a freight forwarder, unless it indicates that it is issued by such freight forwarder acting as a carrier, or as the agent of a named carrier.

ARTICLE 27

(*a*) Unless a credit specifically calls for an on board transport document, or unless inconsistent with other stipulation(s) in the credit, or with Article 26, banks will accept a transport document which indicates that the goods have been taken in charge or received for shipment.

(*b*) Loading on board or shipment on a vessel may be evidenced either by a transport document bearing wording indicating loading on board a named vessel or shipment on a named vessel, or, in the case of a transport document stating 'received for shipment', by means of a notation of loading on board on the transport document signed or initialled and dated by the carrier or his agent, and the date of this notation shall be regarded as the date of loading on board the named vessel or shipment on the named vessel.

ARTICLE 28

(*a*) In the case of carriage by sea or by more than one mode of transport but including carriage by sea, banks will refuse a transport document stating that the goods are or will be loaded on deck, unless specifically authorized in the credit.

(*b*) Banks will not refuse a transport document which contains a provision that the goods may be carried on deck, provided it does not specifically state that they are or will be loaded on deck.

ARTICLE 29

(*a*) For the purpose of this article transhipment means a transfer and reloading during the course of carriage from the port of loading or place of despatch or taking in charge to the port of discharge or place of destination either from one conveyance or vessel to another conveyance or vessel within the same mode of transport or from one mode of transport to another mode of transport.

(*b*) Unless transhipment is prohibited by the terms of the credit, banks will accept transport documents which indicate that the goods will be transhipped, provided the entire carriage is covered by one and the same transport document.

(*c*) Even if transhipment is prohibited by the terms of the credit, banks will accept transport documents which:

(*i*) incorporate printed clauses stating that the carrier has the right to tranship, or

(*ii*) state or indicate that transhipment will or may take place, when the credit stipulates a combined transport document, or indicates carriage from a place of taking in charge to a place of final destination by different modes of transport including carriage by sea, provided that the entire carriage is covered by one and the same transport document, or

(*iii*) state or indicate that the goods are in a Container(s), trailer(s), 'LASH' barge(s), and the like and will be carried from the place of taking in charge to the place of final destination in the same Container(s), trailer(s), 'Lash' barge(s), and the like under one and the same transport document.

(*iv*) state or indicate the place of receipt and/or of final destination as 'CFS' (container freight station) or 'CY' (container yard) at, or associated with, the port of loading and/or the port of destination.

ARTICLE 30

If the credit stipulates despatch of goods by post and calls for a post receipt or certificate of posting, banks will accept such post receipt or certificate of posting if it appears to have been stamped or otherwise authenticated and dated in the place from which the credit stipulates the goods are to be despatched.

ARTICLE 31

(*a*) Unless otherwise stipulated in the credit, or inconsistent with any of the documents presented under the credit, banks will accept transport documents stating that freight or transportation charges (hereinafter referred to as 'freight') have still to be paid.

(*b*) If a credit stipulates that the transport document has to indicate that freight has been paid or prepaid, banks will accept a transport document on which words clearly indicating payment or prepayment of freight appear by stamp or otherwise, or on which payment of freight is indicated by other means.

(*c*) The words 'freight prepayable' or 'freight to be prepaid' or words of similar effect, if appearing on transport documents, will not be accepted as constituting evidence of the payment of freight.

(*d*) Banks will accept transport documents bearing reference by stamp or otherwise to costs additional to the freight charges, such as costs of, or disbursements incurred in connection with, loading, unloading or similar operations, unless the conditions of the credit specifically prohibit such reference.

ARTICLE 32

Unless otherwise stipulated in the credit, banks will accept transport documents which bear a clause on the face thereof such as 'shippers load and count' or 'said by shipper to contain' or words of similar effect.

ARTICLE 33

Unless otherwise stipulated in the credit, banks will accept transport documents indicating as the consignor of the goods a party other than the beneficiary of the credit.

ARTICLE 34

(*a*) A clean transport document is one which bears no superimposed clause or notation which expressly declares a defective condition of the goods and/or the packaging.

(*b*) Banks will refuse transport documents bearing such clauses or notations unless the credit expressly stipulates the clauses or notations which may be accepted.

(*c*) Banks will regard a requirement in a credit for a transport document to bear the clause 'clean on board' as complied with if such transport document meets the requirements of this article and of Article 27(*b*).

D2 Insurance documents

ARTICLE 35

(*a*) Insurance documents must be as stipulated in the credit, and must be issued and/or signed by insurance companies or underwriters, or their agents.

(*b*) Cover notes issued by brokers will not be accepted, unless specifically authorized by the credit.

ARTICLE 36

Unless otherwise stipulated in the credit, or unless it appears from the insurance document(s) that the cover is effective at the latest from the date of loading on board or despatch or taking in charge of the goods, banks will refuse insurance documents presented which bear a date later than the date of loading on board or despatch or taking in charge of the goods as indicated by the transport document(s).

ARTICLE 37

(*a*) Unless otherwise stipulated in the credit, the insurance document must be expressed in the same currency as the credit.

(*b*) Unless otherwise stipulated in the credit, the minimum amount for which the insurance document must indicate the insurance cover to have been effected is the cif (cost, insurance and freight . . . 'named port of destination') or cip (freight/carriage and insurance paid to 'named point of destination') value of the goods, as the case may be, plus 10 per cent. However, if banks cannot determine the cif or cip value, as the case may be, from the documents on their face, they will accept as such minimum amount the amount for which payment, acceptance or negotiation is requested under the credit, or the amount of the commercial invoice, whichever is the greater.

ARTICLE 38

(*a*) Credits should stipulate the type of insurance required and, if any, the additional risks which are to be covered. Imprecise terms such as 'usual risks' or 'customary risks' should not be used; if they are used, banks will accept insurance documents as presented, without responsibility for any risks not being covered.

(*b*) Failing specific stipulations in the credit, banks will accept insurance documents as presented, without responsibility for any risks not being covered.

ARTICLE 39

Where a credit stipulates 'insurance against all risks', banks will accept an insurance document which contains any 'all risks' notation or clause, whether or not bearing the heading 'all risks', even if indicating that certain risks are excluded, without responsibility for any risk(s) not being covered.

ARTICLE 40

Banks will accept an insurance document which indicates that the cover is subject to a franchise or an excess (deductible), unless it is specifically stipulated in the credit that the insurance must be issued irrespective of percentage.

D3 Commercial invoice

ARTICLE 41

(*a*) Unless otherwise stipulated in the credit, commercial invoices must be made out in the name of the applicant for the credit.

(*b*) Unless otherwise stipulated in the credit, banks may refuse commercial invoices issued for amounts in excess of the amount permitted by the credit. Nevertheless, if a bank authorized to pay, incur a deferred payment undertaking, accept, or negotiate under a credit accepts such invoices, its decision will be binding upon all parties, provided such bank has not paid, incurred a deferred payment undertaking, accepted or effected negotiation for an amount in excess of that permitted by the credit.

(*c*) The description of the goods in the commercial invoice must correspond with the description in the credit. In all other documents, the goods may be described in general terms not inconsistent with the description of the goods in the credit.

D4 Other documents

ARTICLE 42

If a credit calls for an attestation or certification of weight in the case of transport other than by sea, banks will accept a weight stamp or declaration of weight which appears to have been superimposed on the transport document by the carrier or his agent unless the credit specifically stipulates that the attestation or certification of weight must be by means of a separate document.

E. MISCELLANEOUS PROVISIONS

Quantity and amount

ARTICLE 43

(*a*) The words ‘about’, ‘circa’ or similar expressions used in connection with the amount of the credit or the quantity or the unit price stated in the credit are to be construed as allowing a difference not to exceed 10 per cent more or 10 per cent less than the amount or the quantity or the unit price to which they refer.

(*b*) Unless a credit stipulates that the quantity of the goods specified must not be exceeded or reduced, a tolerance of 5 per cent more or 5 per cent less will be permissible, even if partial shipments are not permitted, always provided that the amount of the drawings does not exceed the amount of the credit. This tolerance does not apply when the credit stipulates the quantity in terms of a stated number of packing units or individual items.

Partial drawings and/or shipments

ARTICLE 44

(*a*) Partial drawings and/or shipments are allowed, unless the credit stipulates otherwise.

(*b*) Shipments by sea, or by more than one mode of transport but including carriage by sea, made on the same vessel and for the same voyage, will not be regarded as partial shipments, even if the transport documents indicating loading on board bear different dates of issuance and/or indicate different ports of loading on board.

(*c*) Shipments made by post will not be regarded as partial shipments if the post receipts or certificates of posting appear to have been stamped or otherwise authenticated in the place from which the credit stipulates the goods are to be despatched, and on the same date.

(*d*) Shipments made by modes of transport other than those referred to in paragraphs (*b*) and (*c*) of this article will not be regarded as partial shipments, provided the transport documents are issued by one and the same carrier or his agent and indicate the same date of issuance, the same place of despatch or taking in charge of the goods, and the same destination.

Drawings and/or shipments by instalments

ARTICLE 45

If drawings and/or shipments by instalments within given periods are stipulated in the credit and any instalment is not drawn and/or shipped within the period allowed for that instalment, the credit ceases to be available for that and any subsequent instalments, unless otherwise stipulated in the credit.

Expiry date and presentation

ARTICLE 46

(*a*) All credits must stipulate an expiry date for presentation of documents for payment, acceptance or negotiation.

(*b*) Except as provided in Article 48(*a*), documents must be presented on or before such expiry date.

(*c*) If an issuing bank states that the credit is to be available 'for one month', 'for six months' or the like, but does not specify the date from which the time is to run, the date of issuance of the credit by the issuing bank will be deemed to be the first day from which such time is to run.

Banks should discourage indication of the expiry date of the credit in this manner.

ARTICLE 47

(*a*) In addition to stipulating an expiry date for presentation of documents, every credit which calls for a transport document(s) should also stipulate a specified period of time after the date of issuance of the transport document(s) during which presentation of documents for payment, acceptance or negotiation must be made. If no such period of time is stipulated, banks will refuse documents presented to them later than twenty-one days after the date of issuance of the transport document(s). In every case, however, documents must be presented not later than the expiry date of the credit.

(*b*) For the purpose of these articles, the date of issuance of a transport document(s) will be deemed to be:

(*i*) In the case of a transport document evidencing despatch, or taking in charge, or receipt of goods for shipment by a mode of transport other than by air—the date of issuance indicated on the transport document or the date of the reception stamp thereon whichever is the later.

(*ii*) In the case of a transport document evidencing carriage by air—the date of issuance indicated on the transport document or, if the credit stipulates that the transport document shall indicate an actual flight date, the actual flight date as indicated on the transport document.

(*iii*) In the case of a transport document evidencing loading on board a named vessel—the date of issuance of the transport document or, in the case of an on board notation in accordance with Article 27(*b*), the date of such notation.

(*iv*) In cases to which Article 44(*b*) applies, the date determined as above the latest transport document issued.

ARTICLE 48

(*a*) If the expiry date of the credit and/or the last day of the period of time after the date of issuance of the transport document(s) for presentation of documents stipulated by the credit or applicable by virtue of Article 47 falls on a day on which the bank to which presentation has to be made is closed for reasons other than those referred to in Article 19, the stipulated expiry date and/or the last day of the period of time after the date of issuance of the transport document(s) for presentation of documents, as the case may be, shall be extended to the first following business day on which such bank is open.

(*b*) The latest date for loading on board, or despatch, or taking in charge shall not be extended by reason of the extension of the expiry date and/or the period of time after the date of issuance of the transport document(s) for presentation of document(s) in accordance with this article. If no such latest date for shipment is stipulated in the credit or amendments thereto, banks will reject transport documents indicating a date of issuance later than the expiry date stipulated in the credit or amendments thereto.

(*c*) The bank to which presentation is made on such first following business day must add to the documents its certificate that the documents were presented within the time limits extended in accordance with Article 48(*a*) of the *Uniform Customs and Practice for Documentary Credits*, 1983 revision, ICC Publication No. 400.

ARTICLE 49

Banks are under no obligation to accept presentation of documents outside the banking hours.

Loading on board, despatch and taking in charge (shipment)

ARTICLE 50

(*a*) Unless otherwise stipulated in the credit, the expression 'shipment' used in stipulating in earliest and/or a latest shipment date will be understood to include the expressions 'loading on board', 'despatch' and 'taking in charge'.

(*b*) The date of issuance of the transport document determined in accordance with Article 47(*b*) will be taken to be the date of shipment.

(*c*) Expressions such as 'prompt', 'immediately', 'as soon as possible', and the like should not be used. If they are used, banks will interpret them as a stipulation that shipment is to be made within thirty days from the date of issuance of the credit by the issuing bank.

(*d*) If the expression 'on or about' and similar expressions are used, banks will interpret them as a stipulation that shipment is to be made during the period from five days before to five days after the specified date, both end days included.

Date terms

ARTICLE 51

The words 'to', 'until', 'till', 'from', and words of similar import applying to any date term in the credit will be understood to include the date mentioned. The word 'after' will be understood to exclude the date mentioned.

ARTICLE 52

The terms 'first half', 'second half' of a month shall be construed respectively as from the 1st to the 15th, and the 16th to the last day of each month, inclusive.

ARTICLE 53

The terms 'beginning', 'middle', or 'end' of a month shall be construed respectively as from the 1st to the 10th, the 11th to the 20th, and the 21st to the last day of each month, inclusive.

F. TRANSFER

ARTICLE 54

(*a*) A transferable credit is a credit under which the beneficiary has the right to request the bank called upon to effect payment or acceptance or any bank entitled to effect negotiation to make the credit available in whole or in part to one or more other parties (second beneficiaries).

(*b*) A credit can be transferred only if it is expressly designated as 'transferable' by the issuing bank. Terms such as 'divisible', 'fractionable', 'assignable', and 'transmissible' add nothing to the meaning of the term 'transferable' and shall not be used.

(*c*) The bank requested to effect the transfer (transferring bank), whether it has confirmed the credit or not, shall be under no obligation to effect such transfer except to the extent and in the manner expressly consented to by such bank.

(*d*) Bank charges in respect of transfers are payable by the first beneficiary unless otherwise specified. The transferring bank shall be under no obligation to effect the transfer until such charges are paid.

(*e*) A transferable credit can be transferred once only. Fractions of a transferable credit (not exceeding in the aggregate the amount of the credit) can be transferred separately, provided partial shipments are not prohibited, and the aggregate of such transfers will be considered as constituting only one transfer of the credit. The credit can be transferred only on the terms and conditions specified in the original credit, with the exception of the amount of the credit, of any unit prices stated therein, of the period of validity, of the last date for presentation of documents in accordance with Article 47 and the period for shipment, any or all of which may be reduced or curtailed, or the percentage for which insurance cover must be effected, which may be increased in such a way as to provide the amount of cover stipulated in the original credit, or these articles. Additionally, the name of the first beneficiary can be substituted for that of the applicant for the credit, but if the name of the applicant for the credit is specifically required by the original credit to appear in any document other than the invoice, such requirement must be fulfilled.

(*f*) The first beneficiary has the right to substitute his own invoices (and drafts if the credit stipulates that drafts are to be drawn on the applicant for the credit) in exchange for those of the second beneficiary, for amounts not in excess of the original amount stipulated in the credit and for the original unit prices if stipulated in the credit, and upon such substitution of invoices (and drafts) the first beneficiary can draw under the credit for the difference, if any, between his invoices and the second beneficiary's invoices. When a credit has been transferred and the first beneficiary is to supply his own invoices (and drafts) in exchange for the second beneficiary's invoices (and drafts) but fails to do so on first demand, the paying, accepting or negotiating bank has the right to deliver to the issuing bank the documents received under the credit, including the second beneficiary's invoices (and drafts) without further responsibility to the first beneficiary.

(*g*) Unless otherwise stipulated in the credit, the first beneficiary of a transferable credit may request that the credit be transferred to a second beneficiary in the same country, or in another country. Further, unless otherwise stipulated in the credit, the first beneficiary shall have the right to request that payment or negotiation be effected to the second beneficiary at the place to which the credit has been transferred, up to and including the expiry date of the original credit, and without prejudice to the first beneficiary's right subsequently to substitute his own invoices and drafts (if any) for those of the second beneficiary and to claim any difference due to him.

Assignment of proceeds

ARTICLE 55

The fact that a credit is not stated to be transferable shall not affect the beneficiary's right to assign any proceeds to which he may be, or may become, entitled under such credit, in accordance with the provisions of the applicable law.

The *Uniform Customs and Practice for Documentary Credits* were proposed by the ICC Commission on Banking Technique and Practice.

This Commission brings together bankers from throughout the world with the object of:

(*a*) defining, simplifying and harmonizing the practices and terminology used in international banking;
(*b*) expressing the views of bankers before relevant international organizations, in particular the United Nations Commission on International Trade Law (UNCITRAL);
(*c*) serving as a forum for bankers to discuss common problems.

Each ICC National Committee may appoint members of the Banking Commission, and of the twenty other ICC Commissions covering most subject areas of interest to international business.

APPENDIX 2

UNIFORM RULES FOR COLLECTIONS

GENERAL PROVISIONS AND DEFINITIONS

A. These provisions and definitions and the following articles apply to all collections as defined (*B*) below and are binding upon all parties thereto unless otherwise expressly agreed or unless contrary to the provisions of a national, state or local law and/or regulation which cannot be departed from.

B. For the purpose of such provisions, definitions and articles:

1.

(*a*) 'Collection' means the handling by banks, on instructions received, of documents as defined in (*ii*) below, in order to

(*i*) obtain acceptance and/or, as the case may be, payment, or,

(*ii*) deliver commercial documents against acceptance and/or, as the case may be, against payment, or,

(*iii*) deliver documents on other terms and conditions.

(*b*) 'Documents' means financial documents and/or commercial documents:

(*i*) 'financial documents' means bills of exchange, promissory notes, cheques, payment receipts or other similar instruments used for obtaining the payment of money;

(*ii*) 'commercial documents' means invoices, shipping documents, documents of title or other similar documents, or any other documents whatsoever, not being financial documents.

(*c*) 'Clean collection' means collection of financial documents not accompanied by commercial documents.

(*d*) 'Documentary collection' means collection of

(*i*) financial documents accompanied by commercial documents;

(*ii*) commercial documents not accompanied by financial documents.

2. The 'parties thereto' are:

(*a*) the 'principal' who is the customer entrusting the operation of collection to his bank;

(*b*) the 'remitting bank' which is the bank to which the principal has entrusted the operation of collection;

(*c*) the 'collecting bank' which is any bank, other than the remitting bank, involved in processing the collection order;

(*d*) the 'presenting bank' which is the collecting bank making presentation to the drawee.

3. The 'drawee' is the one to whom presentation is to be made according to the collection order.

C. All documents sent for collection must be accompanied by a collection order giving complete and precise instructions. Banks are only permitted to act upon the instructions given in such collection order, and in accordance with these rules.

If any bank cannot, for any reason, comply with the instructions given in the collection order received by it, it must immediately advise the party from whom it received the collection order.

LIABILITIES AND RESPONSIBILITIES

ARTICLE 1

Banks will act in good faith and excercise reasonable care.

ARTICLE 2

Banks must verify that the documents received appear to be as listed in the collection order and must immediately advise the party from whom the collection order was received of any documents missing.

Banks have no further obligation to examine the documents.

ARTICLE 3

For the purpose of giving effect to the instructions of the principal, the remitting bank will utilize as the collecting bank:

(*a*) the collecting bank nominated by the principal, or, in the absence of such nomination,

(*b*) any bank, of its own or another bank's choice, in the country of payment or acceptance, as the case may be.

The documents and the collection order may be sent to the collecting bank directly or through another bank as intermediary.

Banks utilizing the services of other banks for the purpose of giving effect to the instructions of the principal do so for the account of and at the risk of the latter.

The principal shall be bound by and liable to indemnify the banks against all obligations and responsibilities imposed by foreign laws or usages.

ARTICLE 4

Banks concerned with a collection assume no liability or responsibility for the consequences arising out of delay and/or loss in transit of any messages, letters or documents, or for delay, mutilation or other errors arising in the transmission of cables, telegrams, telex, or communication by electronic systems, or for errors in translation or interpretation of technical terms.

ARTICLE 5

Banks concerned with a collection assume no liability or responsibility for consequences arising out of the interruption of their business by Acts of God, riots, civil commotions, insurrections, wars, or any other causes beyond their control or by any strikes or lockouts.

ARTICLE 6

Goods should not be despatched direct to the address of a bank or consigned to a bank without prior agreement on the part of that bank.

In the event of goods being despatched direct to the address of a bank or consigned to a bank for delivery to a drawee against payment or acceptance or upon other terms without prior agreement on the part of the bank, the bank has no obligation to take delivery of the goods, which remain at the risk and responsibility of the party despatching the goods.

PRESENTATION

ARTICLE 7

Documents are to be presented to the drawee in the form in which they are received, except that remitting and collecting banks are authorized to affix any necessary stamps, at the expense of the principal unless otherwise instructed, and to make any necessary endorsement or place any rubber stamps or other identifying marks or symbols customary to or required for the collection operation.

ARTICLE 8

Collection orders should bear the complete address of the drawee or of the domicile at which presentation is to be made. If the address is incomplete or incorrect, the collecting bank may, without obligation and responsibility on its part, endeavour to ascertain the proper address.

ARTICLE 9

In the case of documents payable at sight the presenting bank must make presentation for payment without delay.

In the case of documents payable at a tenor other than sight, the presenting bank must, where acceptance is called for, make presentation for acceptance without delay, and where payment is called for, make presentation for payment not later than the appropriate maturity date.

ARTICLE 10

In respect of a documentary collection including a bill of exchange payable at a future date, the collection order should state whether the commercial documents are to be released to the drawee against acceptance (D/A) or against payment (D/P).

In the absence of such statement, the commercial documents will be released only against payment.

PAYMENT

ARTICLE 11

In the case of documents payable in the currency of the country of payment (local currency), the presenting bank must, unless otherwise instructed in the collection order, only release the documents to the drawee against payment in local currency which is immediately available for disposal in the manner specified in the collection order.

ARTICLE 12

In the case of documents payable in a currency other than that of the country of payment (foreign currency) the presenting bank must, unless otherwise instructed in the collection order, only release the documents to the drawee against payment in the relative foreign currency which can immediately be remitted in accordance with the instructions given in the collection order.

ARTICLE 13

In respect of clean collections partial payments may be accepted if and to the extent to which and on the conditions on which partial payments are authorized by the law in force in the place of payment. The documents will only be released to the drawee when full payment thereof has been received.

In respect of documentary collections partial payments will only be accepted if specifically authorized in the collection order. However, unless otherwise instructed, the presenting bank will only release the documents to the drawee after full payment has been received.

In all cases partial payments will only be accepted subject to compliance with the provisions of either Article 11 or Article 12 as appropriate. Partial payment, if accepted, will be dealt with in accordance with the provisions of Article 14.

ARTICLE 14

Amounts collected (less charges and/or disbursements and/or expenses where applicable) must be made available without delay to the bank from which the collection order was received in accordance with the instructions contained in the collection order.

ACCEPTANCE

ARTICLE 15

The presenting bank is responsible for seeing that the form of the acceptance of a bill of exchange appears to be complete and correct, but is not responsible for the genuineness of any signature or for the authority of any signatory to sign the acceptance.

PROMISSORY NOTES, RECEIPTS AND OTHER SIMILAR INSTRUMENTS

ARTICLE 16

The presenting bank is not responsible for the genuineness of any signature or for the authority of any signatory to sign a promissory note, receipt, or other similar instrument.

PROTEST

ARTICLE 17

The collection order should give specific instructions regarding protest (or other legal process in lieu thereof), in the event of non-acceptance or non-payment.

In the absence of such specific instructions the banks concerned with the collection have no obligation to have the documents protested (or subjected to other legal process in lieu thereof) for non-payment or non-acceptance.

Any charges and/or expenses incurred by banks in connection with such protest or other legal process will be for the account of the principal.

CASE-OF-NEED (PRINCIPAL'S REPRESENTATIVE) AND PROTECTION OF GOODS

ARTICLE 18

If the principal nominates a representative to act as case-of-need in the event of non-acceptance and/or non-payment the collection order should clearly and fully indicate the powers of such case-of-need.

In the absence of such indication banks will not accept any instructions from the case-of-need.

ARTICLE 19

Banks have no obligation to take any action in respect of the goods to which a documentary collection relates.

Nevertheless in the case that banks take action for the protection of the goods, whether instructed or not, they assume no liability or responsibility with regard to the fate and/or condition of the goods and/or for any acts and/or omissions on the part of any third parties entrusted with the custody and/or protection of the goods. However, the collecting bank must immediately advise the bank from which the collection order was received of any such action taken.

Any charges and/or expenses incurred by banks in connection with any action for the protection of the goods will be for the account of the principal.

ADVICE OF FATE, etc.

ARTICLE 20

Collecting banks are to advise fate in accordance with the following rules:

(*a*) Form of advice—all advices or information from the collecting bank to the bank from which the collection order was received, must bear appropriate detail including, in all cases, the latter bank's reference number of the collection order.

(*b*) Method of advice—in the absence of specific instructions the collecting bank must send all advices to the bank from which the collection order was received by quickest mail but, if the collecting bank considers the matter to be urgent, quicker methods such as cable, telegram, telex, or communication by electronic systems, etc. may be used at the expense of the principal.

(*c*)

(*i*) Advice of payment—the collecting bank must send without delay advice of payment to the bank from which the collection order was received, detailing the amount or amounts collected, charges and/or disbursements and/or expenses deducted, where appropriate, and method of disposal of the funds.

(*ii*) Advice of acceptance—the collecting bank must send without delay advice of acceptance to the bank from which the collection order was received.

(*iii*) Advice of non-payment or non-acceptance—the collecting bank must send without delay advice of non-payment or advice of non-acceptance to the bank from which the collection order was received.

The presenting bank should endeavour to ascertain the reasons for such non-payment or non-acceptance and advise accordingly the bank from which the collection order was received.

On receipt of such advice the remitting bank must, within a reasonable time, give appropriate instructions as to the further handling of the documents. If such instructions are not received by the presenting bank within ninety days from its advice of non-payment or non-acceptance, the documents may be returned to the bank from which the collection order was received.

INTEREST, CHARGES AND EXPENSES

ARTICLE 21

If the collection order includes an instruction to collect interest which is not embodied in the accompanying financial document(s), if any, and the drawee refuses to pay such interest, the presenting bank may deliver the document(s) against payment or acceptance as the case may be without collecting such interest, unless the collection order expressly states that such interest may not be waived. Where such interest is to be collected the collection order must bear an indication of the rate of interest and the period covered. When payment of interest has been refused the presenting bank must inform the bank from which the collection order was received accordingly.

If the documents include a financial document containing an unconditional and definite interest clause the interest amount is deemed to form part of the amount of the documents to be collected. Accordingly, the interest amount is payable in addition to the principal amount shown in the financial document and may not be waived unless the collection order so authorizes.

ARTICLE 22

If the collection order includes an instruction that collection charges and/or expenses are to be for account of the drawee and the drawee refuses to pay them, the presenting bank may deliver the document(s) against payment or acceptance as the case may be without collecting charges and/or expenses unless the collection order expressly states that such charges and/or expenses may not be waived. When payment of collection charges and/or expenses has been refused the presenting bank must inform the bank from which the collection order was received accordingly. Whenever collection charges and/or expenses are so waived they will be for the account of the principal, and may be deducted from the proceeds.

Should a collection order specifically prohibit the waiving of collection charges and/or expenses then neither the remitting nor collecting nor presenting bank shall be responsible for any costs or delays resulting from this prohibition.

ARTICLE 23

In all cases where in the express terms of a collection order, or under these rules, disbursements and/or expenses and/or collection charges are to be borne by the principal, the collecting bank(s) shall be entitled promptly to recover outlays in respect of disbursements and expenses and charges from the bank from which the collection order was received and the remitting bank shall have the right promptly to recover from the principal any amount so paid out by it, together with its own disbursements, expenses and charges, regardless of the fate of the collection.

INDEX

Newton Compton Editores

20/abril/2025

Querido Máximo,

No sabemos si habrás decidido esperar o no a cumplir tus 13 añitos cuando hayas abierto este regalo, pero de cualquier forma esperamos que lo disfrutes y que siempre recuerdes que te queremos mucho y te llevamos en el corazón.

Felicidades lindura ♡ ♡

(desde tu tierra natal, Galicia)

Este libro es una obra de ficción. Todos los personajes, sucesos y organizaciones son fruto de la imaginación del autor y se han utilizado con fines meramente ficticios.

Título original: *Death And The Conjuror*

Primera edición: marzo de 2025

Newton Compton Editores es un sello de Antonio Vallardi Editore S.u.r.l.
Pl. Urquinaona, 11, 3.° 1.ª izq. Barcelona, 08010 (España)
www.newtoncomptoneditores.com

Gruppo editoriale Mauri Spagnol S.p.A.
www.maurispagnol.it

ISBN: 978-84-10080-36-2
Código IBIC: FA
DL: B 16.341-2024

Diseño de interiores:
David Pablo

Composición:
Sergi Godia

Impreso en marzo de 2025 en Puntoweb s.r.l., Ariccia (Roma), en Italia.

Tom Mead

La verdad sobre el caso del psiquiatra desaparecido

Traducción de Tatiana Marco Marín

Newton Compton Editores
Barcelona, 2025

Para mi madre y mi padre.
Y en recuerdo de J. D. C (1906-1977)

Dramatis personae

Doctor Anselm Rees, un psiquiatra
Doctora Lidia Rees, su hija
Floyd Stenhouse, un músico (Paciente A)
Della Cookson, una actriz (Paciente B)
Claude Weaver, un escritor (Paciente C)
Benjamin Teasel, un productor teatral
Lucy Levy, una actriz
Marcus Bowman, un financiero mujeriego
Tweedy, un editor
Pete Hobbs, un operario de ascensor
Olive Turner, una ama de llaves
George Flint, un inspector de policía
Jerome Hook, un sargento de policía
Joseph Spector, un embaucador profesional

ACTO I

El cuento del robo

(Viernes, 11 de septiembre de 1936)

«En el teatro se necesitan brazos largos».
Sarah Bernhardt, *Memories of My Life*

I

Algo fuerte

En el Teatro Pomegranate, los ánimos estaban tan caldeados como las lámparas de aceite.

–¿Habéis visto mi pendiente? –preguntó Lucy Levy.

El tramoyista se limitó a mirarla con la boca abierta, pero no le contestó.

La señorita Levy chasqueó la lengua. Se dirigió a todos aquellos que trabajaban entre bastidores, agachándose para pasar por debajo de los travesaños, rodeando los carritos de vestuario, pestañeando con sus párpados de color gris oscuro y haciendo muecas con esos petulantes labios rosas que tenía. Aun así, no había ni rastro del pendiente.

Aquel era el último ensayo de *La dama Muerte* antes de la noche del estreno, por lo que el ambiente estaba tan tenso como las cuerdas de un piano. La señorita Levy, que era la segunda protagonista femenina, llevaba las últimas dos semanas teniendo problemas para mantener la compostura conforme se acercaba el gran momento. Y seguía sin haber ni rastro del pendiente.

Lucy salió de detrás del escenario y se dirigió hacia el centro de la escena con los tacones repiqueteando sobre la madera desnuda.

–Della, si me has mangado el pendiente…

–¡Cuidado! –exclamó una voz procedente de entre bambalinas.

Se trataba de Benjamin Teasel.

Lucy estuvo a punto de caerse de cabeza por una trampilla abierta. Se detuvo en el último momento con el pie suspendido en el aire.

–Sí, eso podría haber sido bastante desagradable –dijo una segunda voz.

Dos hombres salieron de entre bastidores por el lado contrario del escenario. Teasel iba vestido con el traje verde estilo Norfolk que se ponía para subrayar su autoridad. El otro tipo era mayor que él e iba ataviado de forma un tanto escandalosa con una capa negra forrada de seda carmesí.

La señorita Levy se tomó un momento para recuperar el aliento. Miró a Teasel pestañeando y, después, se giró hacia el otro hombre.

–¿Y quién es usted?

–Lucy, no seas maleducada –la reprendió Teasel, ya que le gustaba interpretar el papel del maestro crítico–. Este es Joseph Spector.

Dijo el nombre como si ella ya tuviera que saber quién era aquel anciano.

–Un placer –contestó Spector con una sonrisa.

Era una sonrisa cadavérica. El hombre parecía pertenecer a una época pasada. Su traje, que era de terciopelo negro, poseía el glamur deslucido de la próspera década de 1890. Él tenía el rostro arrugado como una hoja de papel de carta convertida en pelota. Sin embargo, tenía unos ojos de mirada profunda y del azul más pálido que hubiese visto jamás. Aunque sus andares y su forma de vestir eran propios de un hombre muy anciano, su voz era suave y, en cierto sentido, inocente. A Lucy le pareció alguien que podría salirse con la suya en cualquier crimen.

–Tan solo estamos haciendo la puesta a punto del truco del tercer acto –le explicó él–. Si es tan amable de abandonar el escenario…

Y Lucy Levy, que seguía sin aliento y con un pendiente perdido, salió de allí sin mediar palabra. Sin embargo, se demoró lo suficiente como para oír a los dos hombres intercambiar murmullos.

–Dios mío –gruñó Teasel–, juro que, un día de estos, voy a matarla.

–Tan solo está emocionada. Además, si la dejas a su aire, puede que acabe haciéndolo ella misma –dijo Spector mientras se arrodillaba junto a la trampilla–. ¿Todo listo ahí abajo? –preguntó.

–Sí, señor –respondieron.

Spector soltó una sonrisita y, después, le guiñó un ojo a Teasel.

–Veamos qué tal, ¿te parece?

Se produjo una pequeña pausa antes de que una espantosa figura de cera emergiera en silencio de la trampilla. El rostro macabro contemplaba el auditorio vacío y tenía las manos contorsionadas en forma de garra.

–Excelente –comentó Spector–, aunque tal vez debamos ajustar el tiempo.

–A mí me ha parecido que estaba bien –dijo Teasel.

–Tiene que ser cuestión de un instante, Benjamin. Quiero que los espectadores griten en sus asientos. ¿Tal vez podríamos echarle un poco más de aceite al mecanismo?

–No hay tiempo. Tenemos que ponernos con el monólogo de Della del segundo acto. ¿Dónde está?

Escarmentado, Joseph Spector se dirigió hacia la parte trasera del escenario. Del bolsillo interior se sacó una cajetilla de tabaco que contenía diez cigarrillos negros y estrechos. Se colocó uno entre los dientes y lo encendió. Después, exhaló una voluta de humo fragrante en dirección al aire mohoso. Lucy Levy lo contemplaba desde un rincón ensombrecido que estaba enclavado en el laberinto de pasillos que había entre bastidores. Sin que la vieran, observó a aquel tal Joseph Spector.

Era difícil determinar su edad. Dependiendo de la iluminación, aparentaba tener desde cincuenta hasta ochenta años. Como todos los magos, se prestaba a la confusión. Ella no lo sabía, pero «Joseph Spector» no era su nombre real; era un alias procedente de otra vida, de su carrera como mago de teatro. Sin embargo, aunque se había retirado de las actuaciones más de una década atrás, se había esforzado por conservar su famoso juego de manos.

En ese momento, el mago se dirigió a la puerta de la entrada de artistas. El portero le sonrió y, haciendo tintinear las llaves, le dejó salir a la calle lateral. Lucy lo siguió pero no atravesó la puerta de inmediato, tal como había hecho él. En su lugar, miró al portero y, con un dedo en los labios de forma amenazadora, abrió la puerta solo una rendija y se asomó. Fuera, vio a Della Cookson, que estaba sentada de forma ridícula sobre un cubo de basura con el disfraz completo de su personaje.

–Della –dijo Spector–, ¿qué haces aquí fuera?

La estrella le sonrió.

–Bueno, tenía que ir a alguna parte, ¿no?

Incluso Lucy tenía que admitir que, con respecto a su cara, Della Cookson era sensacional. Desde las cejas negras y arqueadas hasta el hoyuelo ensombrecido de la barbilla, el más mínimo gesto podía despertar un torbellino de emociones. Y con el rostro enmarcado por una cascada de cabello castaño cobrizo, bien podría haber salido de una fotografía. Describirla como una «gran estrella» hubiera sido equivocado, ya que era diminuta, pero en sus gestos y expresiones había una expansividad y una vitalidad casi sobrenaturales.

Sin embargo, al igual que muchos artistas, sufría de melancolías periódicas que la incapacitaban (a veces, durante semanas) y que le habían granjeado cierta reputación. Aquel día tenía un aspecto lóbrego gracias a la piel pálida y los labios carmesí de una tuberculosa en decadencia.

–Ni siquiera es la noche del estreno y ya nos están crucificando –dijo mientras levantaba un periódico cuyo titular rezaba «Espectáculo de miedo de mal gusto».

–Nunca pensé que fueras el tipo de persona que se toma esas cosas como algo personal, Della –dijo Spector.

–Para ti es fácil de decir, no es a ti a quién están criticando sin motivo.

–Has de saber que este espectáculo se basa en mis trucos y mis espejismos –prosiguió el anciano–. Para mí, son como mis hijos. Los he estado cultivando durante muchos, muchos años.

Della le dedicó una sonrisa triste y cambió de tema de conversación.

–¿Cuántos años tienes en realidad, Joseph? Me lo he estado preguntando.

–¡Oh! Al menos quinientos. Recuerdo claramente la Armada Invencible. Arruinó mi décimo cumpleaños.

Della se rio con educación.

–Ay, los magos... No sois capaces de dar una respuesta directa, ¿verdad?

–Desde luego que no. Por eso me contrató Teasel. A él no le

sirven las respuestas directas. Hay que reconocer que *La dama Muerte* es una historia escabrosa, por lo que requiere la *mise-en-scène* más elaborada que el hombre haya visto jamás. Eso es lo que la hace perfecta para un recinto como este, que está recién reformado y tiene tanto espacio glorioso por rellenar. Si Benjamin no puede llenarlo con un espectáculo semejante, nadie podrá.

–El bueno de Benjamin Teasel... –dijo Della con un mal disimulado veneno en el tono de voz–. ¿Por qué te ha mandado aquí fuera? Pensaba que eras vital para el ensayo con todos esos monstruos tuyos apareciendo por debajo de las tablas del suelo.

–Tal vez fuese vital hace dos meses, pero se podría decir que estos días soy consciente de mi propia superfluidad.

–Debe de ser raro ver a otras personas haciendo tus trucos.

–«Surrealista» sería una palabra más adecuada. Sin embargo, no está exento de cierto placer. Después de todo, los trucos siguen funcionando y eso ya es algo, ¿no?

Della dio un trago de una petaca.

–¿Quieres un trago?

El hombre se la quitó.

–¿Qué lleva?

Ella se encogió de hombros.

–Prefiero no saberlo.

Tras un instante, la curiosidad de Spector se impuso.

–Ah, ¿y por qué no?

Dio un sorbito. El alcohol le quemó la parte posterior de la garganta y le dejó un rastro ardiente en el gaznate. Tosió de forma seca y rugiente.

–Es algo fuerte –dijo.

Della se rio.

–Joseph, no les hables de esto a los demás, por favor. Me refiero a lo de beber. Son solo los nervios de la noche del estreno. Lo dejaré en cuanto empecemos con las funciones.

Spector le sonrió, pero no respondió. Se despidió con rapidez y se escabulló, dejando atrás el teatro. Tan cerca de la noche del estreno (que, a aquellas alturas, quedaba a apenas unas horas), se las podrían arreglar bien sin él. Lanzó una última mirada al cartel que había en la fachada (DELLA COOKSON EN *LA DAMA MUERTE)* antes de desaparecer entre la multitud de almas errantes del Strand. Con el cuello subido contra el cortante viento otoñal, no era más que otra mancha gris que caminaba hacia Saint Martin-in-the-Fields.

Con una sonrisa afilada, Lucy Levy cerró la puerta de la entrada de artistas.

II

La dama Muerte

El cielo al otro lado de la ventana de la casa de Dollis Hill se había vuelto de un monstruoso color morado. El atardecer lanzaba un manto de sombras sobre Londres. El doctor Anselm Rees estaba sentado en su escritorio, tomando notas, mientras el Paciente A yacía en el diván de cuero que estaba en la otra punta de la habitación con la mirada fija en la moldura del techo. Estaba contando una historia.

–No puedo moverme y estoy ahí tumbado sin aliento y paralizado cuando, de pronto, aparecen unos ojos que me observan en la oscuridad. Miro a mi alrededor, intentando ver algo, cuando la puerta se abre de golpe y una figura oscura se desliza al interior de la habitación y se coloca a los pies de mi cama.

–Esa figura... ¿De quién se trata?

El doctor Rees hablaba con un acento muy suave.

–De mi padre. –Rees asintió. Era tal como había imaginado–. Pero, de algún modo, es un poco diferente, como un fantasma.

–Su padre... me refiero a su padre de verdad... ¿sigue vivo?

–Sí. Hace unos meses que no lo veo ni hablo con él, pero está vivito y coleando.

–¿No tiene ningún miedo o ansiedad con respecto a su salud?

–Nada que pueda determinar. Pero en el sueño está ahí, al pie de mi cama, mirándome sin pestañear. Lleva una especie de túnica parecida al hábito de un monje. Me siento casi como si estuviera tumbado en un altar de sacrificios a punto de ser asesinado como ofrenda a algún dios pagano.

–¿Y entonces?

–Entonces, se lleva las manos a la túnica y la rasga, dejando a la vista su pecho desnudo. Y yo... –El Paciente A se detuvo un momento para recobrar la compostura. Aquella era una historia que le resultaba muy difícil de contar–. Y veo por primera vez lo que le ha pasado. –El doctor Rees contempló a su paciente, expectante, con la punta de la pluma suspendida sobre la página. El joven continuó–. Su caja torácica se ha convertido en... una boca. El pecho se le abre como una mandíbula y veo un montón de dientes resplandecientes y afilados como una cuchilla. Y en el interior del pecho, donde debería tener el corazón, hay una... lengua.

El Paciente A interrumpió su monólogo mientras los ojos se le llenaban de lágrimas.

–¿Así acaba el sueño? –insistió Rees.

–No, no. Pero no creo que pueda contarle nada más ahora mismo.

–Lo entiendo. Terminemos aquí la sesión. Aunque tengo algunas teorías sobre la naturaleza simbólica de este sueño.

–¡Padre!

El Paciente A se puso en pie de un salto.

–¿Quién ha sido? –gritó–. ¿Quién llama?

–Solo es mi hija, Lidia –dijo el doctor Rees–. Está en el piso de arriba. –Se acercó hasta la puerta y la abrió de golpe antes de hablar en dirección al pasillo–. ¿Qué ocurre, Lidia?

–Marcus está aquí –respondió ella–. Su automóvil acaba de doblar la esquina.

–¡Ah! –dijo el doctor mientras se volvía hacia su paciente–. Entonces, llámeme mañana y continuaremos nuestra discusión. Mientras tanto, le haré otra receta de Veronal.

–No conozco a su hija –dijo el Paciente A de forma ausente.

–No. Ahora mismo no atiende a pacientes, pero posee un conocimiento psiquiátrico formidable y está trabajando en una serie de artículos para el *New Statesman* –dijo Rees mientras se inclinaba sobre el escritorio y garateaba la receta en el bloc de notas.

Después, arrancó la hoja y se la tendió al joven.

–Si no es demasiada molestia –se aventuró a decir el Paciente A–, me marcharé por el ventanal.

–Por supuesto. Entiendo que quiere que nuestras citas sean confidenciales. Permítame...

Al decir eso, el anciano doctor se dirigió hacia el ventanal francés y se sacó una llave de la bata. Abrió las ventanas y dejó que su paciente saliera al jardín. Al otro lado del estrecho saliente de piedra se encontraba la tierra dura de un austero macizo de flores.

El Paciente A no era tan joven como aparentaba. En torno a sus ojos pálidos había cierto cansancio del mundo. Estaba recién afeitado y vestía de forma descuidada con un traje de *tweed* que no era de su talla y que se le abultaba sobre la barriga. Era músico de profesión, uno de los mejores violinistas que hubiera conocido la Filarmónica. Su nombre real (porque en algún momento había que mencionarlo) era Floyd Stenhouse. Floyd se llevó sus malos sueños y su receta y se escabulló a toda prisa a través del jardín y la verja trasera.

Había algo un poco extraño en sus andares mientras se alejaba a grandes zancadas por Dollis Hill Road. Por supuesto, cualquiera que le echara un vistazo al pasar por su lado lo tomaría por uno de esos encantadores ingleses excéntricos con tanta personalidad en el rostro e inteligencia en los ojos juntos y profundos. Sin embargo, el verdadero motivo para aquel paso casi desequilibrado era el peso en el bolsillo de su gabardina. Con la mano enterrada en dicho bolsillo, sentía el tacto frío de la empuñadura. Era un recuerdo de la guerra, un regalo de su tío: un revólver.

Dollis Hill era un barrio de las afueras con calles anchas y serpenteantes que estaban bordeadas por casas eduardianas y setos exuberantes. El hogar de los Rees estaba construido con robustos ladrillos rojos y la fachada de estilo italiano estaba enmarcada por esquinas de piedra ornamentadas y salpicada por tres hileras de ventanas de guillotina con marcos blancos. A la puerta principal se accedía por un tramo de escalones de piedra que procedían de la calle. No se diferenciaba demasiado de la casa que el Doctor Rees había dejado atrás en Viena.

Anselm Rees había abierto su negocio en el noroeste de Londres en cuanto había llegado al país, cinco meses atrás. Hasta entonces, había pasado toda su vida en Viena, pero, por motivos tanto personales como políticos, había tomado la dolorosa decisión de emigrar. Ahora era un hombre mayor con un dolor de dientes palpitante y una vista que se nublaba. Sin embargo, su mente seguía tan afilada como un cuchillo, su ingenio igual de rápido y su célebre sentido de la moda tan chic como siempre. No le había costado encontrar su lugar entre la alta sociedad londinense. Cuando había desembarcado del *HMS Magnificent* en los muelles de Southampton a finales de febrero, había lucido sombrero de copa y frac. Había bajado a grandes zancadas por la pasarela del brazo de la única criatura en la Tierra a la que apreciaba más que a sí mismo: su hija, Lidia.

Aquel día, cuando padre e hija habían pisado tierra firme inglesa, los *flashes* se habían disparado. Lidia, con su melena recta a la altura de la barbilla y negra como el azabache y su forma de vestir moderna (abalorios en el cuello y una inclinación especial por el *tweed* masculino en contraste con las pieles), salía bien en todas las fotografías. Tenía la piel del rostro tersa y los rasgos seductores de Louise Brooks. Sin embargo, su voz era suave y tenía un acento plagado de sílabas lánguidas y ondulantes.

Al propio Rees tampoco se le había dado mal encandilar a los nativos. Había dejado claro que no tenía intención de aceptar nuevos pacientes, pero apenas había pasado un mes cuando incumplió su promesa. De hecho, había aceptado a tres pacientes: dos hombres y una mujer. Mantenía sus identidades en el más estricto secreto, aunque los tabloides habrían pagado mucho dinero por aquella información. En sus cuadernos se refería a ellos como Pacientes A, B y C. Por supuesto, a pesar de que no los veía, Lidia sabía quiénes eran. Es importante señalar que nunca dijo ni una sola palabra al respecto.

El doctor Rees cerró y atrancó la ventana. Excepto por el leve olor del sudor producido por el miedo, era como si no hubiese recibido ninguna visita. Cuando le dio la espalda al cristal, se sobresaltó al descubrir a Lidia en el umbral de la puerta con las manos en las caderas.

El estudio se encontraba en la parte trasera de la casa. Era una habitación amplia, cuadrada y de techos altos que estaba iluminada con lámparas colgantes de cristal, cubierta por alfombras turcas y repleta de estanterías con libros encuadernados en piel: clásicos multilingües y textos especializados de medicina, todos ellos con ediciones prístinas. La estancia era austera, pero, al mismo tiempo, tenía cierto aire hogareño, como si estuviera habitada sin estarlo en realidad. Sus puntos más destacados eran un escritorio *Biedermeier* barnizado, un sofá estilo diván con muchos cojines de terciopelo (para los pacientes) y una chimenea de piedra gris. En el rincón más alejado había un baúl de viaje de madera de teca. Se mirara donde se mirara, el baúl era una presencia constante en la periferia del campo visual. Acechaba desde allí como si fuese un ataúd ligeramente siniestro.

–No estás vestido –dijo Lidia.

–Sí lo estoy.

–No para ir al teatro.

Anselm Rees suspiró.

–Lo había olvidado por completo.

–Bueno, más vale que te des prisa. Marcus está aquí y saldremos en quince minutos, ya sea contigo o sin ti.

Por los pelos, pero lo consiguieron. Anselm Rees bajó las escaleras dando pisotones y ataviado con la ropa para la velada. Con un único minuto de margen, se recolocó la pajarita.

–Buenas noches, señor –dijo Marcus Bowman.

El doctor lo miró de arriba abajo. El joven era alto y larguirucho, un poco arácnido, y vestía un traje a rayas y una estridente pajarita roja. Llevaba el bigote de las estrellas de cine y el cabello negro brillante y engominado hacia atrás. Tenía los ojos húmedos y denotaban tan poca inteligencia como los de un perro.

Aquel insólito trío se dirigió al vehículo de Bowman (un Austin estilo *landaulet* de color amarillo abejorro) y pusieron rumbo al Pomegranate.

Durante el trayecto, el doctor Rees observó que la pareja era muy desigual. Desde luego, Lidia era muy hermosa, pero una agitadora y una intelectual. Marcus Bowman procedía de una larga estirpe de financieros y había asistido a uno de los colegios privados más elegantes, pero era tan soso y vacuo como un globo a medio inflar. Conducía su automóvil de manera imprudente y se vestía como si fuera alguna especie de mujeriego. Al doctor Rees le resultaba difícil pensar en él con algo que no fuera desdén.

Lidia era terriblemente rápida a la hora de adaptarse a sus nuevas circunstancias. Con veintiséis años, acababa de terminar su doctorado en Psicología. Sin embargo, sus teorías se distanciaban de las de su padre en puntos intrigantes. Incluso se podría decir que existía una rivalidad profesional entre ellos. Si bien la joven también sabía cómo divertirse. Era lo bastante osada como para aventurarse a entrar sin acompañante en algunos de los clubes nocturnos más estilosos de Londres. Allí, su belleza y sus modales misteriosos y continentales llamaban la atención de forma considerable. Uno de sus favoritos era el Palmyra Club, en el Soho, donde las bebidas eran baratas y el *jazz* ruidoso de un modo casi insoportable. Había sido allí donde había conocido a Marcus Bowman, el hombre que pronto se convertiría en su prometido.

Marcus Bowman era uno de los llamados «Bright Young Things», aquellos jóvenes adinerados que vivían en la más absoluta extravagancia. Tenía una leve sobremordida con unos molares especialmente prominentes, parecidos a los de una ardilla, y una nuez bulbosa que le daba el aspecto gracioso de un boceto mal dibujado. Se vestía como el *bon viveur* que era: con pantalones de golf y, de normal, una bolsa de golf colgada del hombro. Por no hablar del bigote, que, en una ocasión, había sido objeto de un artículo en el *Top-Storey Chap* sobre el cuidado masculino. Parecía caer con pereza sobre su labio superior del mismo modo en que él solía tumbarse sobre los muebles en lugar de sentarse en ellos. Cuando hablaba, lo hacía con la jerga afectada de los burgueses ingleses de pura cepa y cada frase estaba remarcada por un «¿Qué de qué?» o un «¡Digo yo!».

Y, aun así, parecía que Marcus hacía feliz a Lidia...

Las calles bullían con la emoción vespertina de los aficionados al teatro que se habían reunido a las afueras del Pomegranate para la noche del estreno. Marcus aparcó el automóvil y el trío se bajó del mismo. Anselm leyó en el cartel el título de la obra, *La dama Muerte*, con un suspiro. Las puertas del teatro se abrieron de par en par. El vestíbulo estaba atestado de gente charlando, brindando con sus vasos y hojeando los programas. Anselm no estaba de ánimo para socializar y se dirigió a su asiento de mal humor. Lidia lo acompañó mientras Marcus compraba cigarrillos en el puesto de la concesión.

–¿Qué ocurre, papá? Pareces decaído.

–Oh... Estoy bien –dijo el anciano–. Tan solo estoy cansado.

–¿De qué? –le preguntó su hija.

–Creo que fue el doctor Johnson el que dijo: «El hombre que está cansado de Londres está cansado de la vida». ¿Responde eso a tu pregunta? –contestó con una media sonrisa.

En ese momento, un anciano con una capa forrada de seda y con aspecto de malhechor salido de una novelucha barata les pidió permiso y se deslizó para pasar por delante de ellos en la fila de asientos. Rees observó al tipo un instante antes de volver a centrar su atención en el escenario. Miró el reloj. Faltaban unos cinco minutos para que se abriera el telón.

–¿Quién es la tal Helen Cookson? –preguntó Marcus.

–Della Cookson –le corrigió Lidia–. Es una de las mejores actrices de nuestra época. Deja de ser tan ignorante, Marcus.

Y, tras decir aquello, se abrió el telón.

El primer acto llegó y se fue. Lucy Levy fue una presencia vivaracha y Della mantuvo a la audiencia encandilada durante su primera aparición. Incluso el viejo y malhumorado doctor Rees se adelantó en su asiento cuando apareció en escena. Un breve intermedio precedió al segundo acto, en el que se pusieron más cosas en juego. Hubo más sorpresas y más risas y el tipo con capa que había junto a ellos parecía especialmente encantado con algunos de los efectos escénicos.

El intermedio entre el segundo acto y el tercero fue más largo, así que Rees se aventuró a salir al bar. En cuanto hubo puesto un pie fuera, una voz a sus espaldas pronunció su nombre.

–Perdóneme por entrometerme, pero ¿es usted el doctor Anselm Rees?

El hombre se dio la vuelta.

–Así es. ¿En qué puedo ayudarle?

–Soy Teasel, Benjamin Teasel. Soy el productor y director de este Grand Guignol.

El promotor estaba resplandeciente con su corbata negra. Con el puño ligeramente tembloroso, sostenía un martini.

–En tal caso, debo darle la enhorabuena. Su trabajo está teniendo un gran efecto en la audiencia.

–Es usted muy amable, muchas gracias. –El hombre inclinó la cabeza con humildad calculada–. Espero no molestarle, pero quería extenderles una invitación a usted y a su hija.

–¿Ah, sí?

–Para mañana por la noche. Una fiesta en mi casa, en Hampstead. Pensé en esperar a que llegaran las primeras críticas, por eso montaremos el jolgorio mañana por la noche –le explicó.

–Entonces, ¿es usted optimista?

Teasel soltó una carcajada.

–¡Mire a su alrededor, doctor! Contemple el océano de rostros sonrientes y parlanchines. Eso, amigo mío, es la audiencia de un espectáculo que va para largo. Pero quiero esperar hasta que las reseñas digan lo mismo. Entonces, podré disfrutar de las bebidas y la música sin el miedo a los periódicos del día siguiente...

–Ya veo... Es una proposición interesante, pero me temo que ya tengo planes para mañana por la noche.

–¿De verdad? Vaya, qué lástima. Me hubiera encantado oír la interpretación de un psiquiatra de este dramita diabólico. Bueno, tome mi tarjeta de todos modos, por favor. Por si cambia de opinión. ¡Oh, Edgar! ¡Edgar Simmons! –Otro invitado había llamado la atención de Teasel–. Edgar, ¿dónde te has estado escondiendo estos últimos meses?

Y el productor desapareció entre un mar de admiradores.

Rees no se mostraba reacio a las veladas ocasionales, después de todo, eran un hervidero inevitable de posibles clientes. Sin embargo, había algo en Teasel que le había desagradado. El mismísimo aire que lo rodeaba apestaba a la sordidez del mundo del espectáculo. Se estremeció un poco y regresó al auditorio. Llegó a su asiento justo a tiempo de que comenzara el tercer acto.

–¿Quién era ese con el que estabas hablando? –quiso saber Lidia.

–Benjamin Teasel. Ha dirigido este... gran espectáculo. Quiere que vaya a una fiesta mañana por la noche.

–Santo cielo... No hay manera de librarse de ellos, ¿verdad? Menudos parásitos...

Al oír el nombre de Teasel, el hombre de la capa aguzó el oído. En ese momento, parecía a punto de entrometerse en la conversación de la familia Rees. Sin embargo, el telón se levantó.

El tercer acto fue aquel en el que los diferentes aspectos de la obra convergieron al fin. Hubo un truco con una trampilla especialmente macabro que pilló por sorpresa incluso al doctor. La audiencia ahogó un grito. Cuando cayó el telón, los aplausos fueron instantáneos y afectuosos. Algunos incluso se pusieron en pie cuando Della Cookson apareció para la ovación final.

La actriz caminó hacia el frente bajo un foco, hizo una reverencia y recibió un fastuoso ramo de flores de parte de un admirador que estaba en la primera fila. Se mantuvo de pie y con lágrimas en los ojos mientras recibía la adulación del público. Como se suele decir que ocurre con los retratos, había algo en ella que hacía que pareciera que estaba mirando fijamente y de forma individual a cada miembro del auditorio. Pero aquello no eran más que ilusiones. En realidad, aquella noche solo había un hombre al que miraba, cuyo rostro había reconocido al instante: el doctor Anselm Rees.

Mientras salían, un acomodador le tendió una nota. Las personas de la audiencia que lo rodeaban estaban volviendo a salir al vestíbulo y al bar mientras charlaban amistosamente sobre el entretenimiento de aquella noche. Rees se detuvo y desdobló el papel.

–Marchaos sin mí –les dijo a Marcus y a Lidia.

–Pero ¿cómo volverás a casa?

–Tomaré un taxi. No te preocupes por mí.

Después, se perdió entre la multitud.

Otra acomodadora estaba lista para escoltarlo detrás del bar y hacia la parte de detrás del escenario.

–Por aquí, señor –le dijo mientras mantenía la puerta abierta para que pasara.

Rees entró y se encontró en otro mundo. Los tramoyistas estaban celebrándolo y el director de escena estaba hojeando una copia destrozada del guion mientras hacía cambios rápidos y brutales con un lápiz puntiagudo. El doctor siguió a la acomodadora por un largo pasillo que conducía al camerino de la estrella. Llamaron a la puerta.

–Un momento –dijo una voz desde el interior.

Rees esperó.

Entonces, la estrella del espectáculo, Della Cookson, abrió la puerta. Sin embargo, para el doctor Rees, era la Paciente B.

Estaba radiante y su saludo fue luminoso, pues le dio un beso afectuoso en la mejilla. Le pidió que se sentara en su silla frente al espejo donde se maquillaba antes de cerrarle la puerta en las narices a la acomodadora.

–¿Qué le ha parecido la obra, doctor?

–Mi hija es una admiradora de los *thrillers* –contestó, incómodo, mientras la miraba a los ojos a través del espejo–. Oh, parece que se le ha caído algo, Della.

–¿Dónde?

Rees señaló algo que resplandecía sobre la alfombra.

–Ahí. ¿Qué es? –Se agachó para recoger el objeto–. Solo es una joya.

Se la tendió a la actriz, que se la metió en el bolsillo de su kimono. Se trataba de un único pendiente de oro.

La mujer se acomodó y comenzó a desmaquillarse.

–¿Por qué me ha pedido que viniera, Della?

La Paciente B suspiró y contempló su rostro en el espejo. Entonces, lentamente, se volvió hacia él.

–Porque he hecho algo horrible, doctor.

ACTO II

El cuento de la mentira

(Del 12 al 14 de septiembre de 1936)

«En la magia, hoy en día, como siempre, el efecto es lo que cuenta. El método o los métodos que se utilicen son siempre secundarios».

Dai Vernon

«Me complace decir que a la mayoría de la gente le gusta la habitación cerrada. Pero este es el maldito problema: incluso sus partidarios dudan a menudo».

John Dickson Carr, *El hombre hueco*

ENTREACTO I

El hombre del abrigo largo y negro

(Sábado, 12 de septiembre de 1936)

Igual que los artistas asolados por la pobreza de la París revolucionaria, Claude Weaver solía escribir sus novelas en un ático.

El ático en cuestión, que se encontraba sobre su casa de dos pisos en Hampstead, había sido modificado para acomodar varias librerías y un escritorio. Su esposa solía afirmar de forma hiperbólica que rara vez salía de allí; que prefería su compañía a la de ella. Eso, en su mayor parte, no era cierto. Salía con frecuencia, solo que prefería que ella no se diera cuenta.

Weaver era por naturaleza un hombre intrascendente, de esos con los que se cruzaría por la calle sin dirigirle una sola mirada. Si le hubiera conocido, le habría resultado callado, sumiso e incluso tímido. Nunca ofrecía entrevistas. Nunca aparecía en los almuerzos literarios ni en las veladas benéficas.

Teniendo eso en cuenta, su esposa, Rosemary, parecía decidida a sacarlo de su cómodo nido y empujarlo a la luz del día. Era una mujer inteligente y a menudo inescrutable. Sin embargo, no había logrado entender que la soledad de él era un componente vital de su creatividad. Así habían comenzado todos los problemas.

La mañana del 12 de septiembre, como siempre, él estaba sentado en su escritorio del ático con la máquina de escribir y un montón de papel en blanco frente a él. Aquel día, las palabras no le salían. Tenía una cita antes de la comida, pero había decidido escribir durante un par de horas antes de eso.

Aquello le estaba resultando más difícil de lo esperado. Había algo que le estaba distrayendo. Se puso en pie, estiró las extremidades doloridas y paseó de un lado a otro del ático. Había un pequeño ventanal redondo que proyectaba un estrecho haz de luz sobre el escritorio. Sin embargo, también le ofrecía unas vistas decentes de la calle. Se acercó a él y miró hacia afuera con la nariz casi pegada al cristal. Fue entonces cuando vio al hombre del abrigo negro.

¿Cuánto tiempo había pasado? Tal vez una semana. Una semana desde que Weaver se había percatado por primera vez de aquella presencia indefinible, de que alguien lo perseguía. Ahora, las horas de vigilia las pasaba consumido por una sensación casi sobrenatural de miedo. Pensó en *El Horla*, de Maupassant, y, por primera vez, empezó a preguntarse si de verdad se estaba volviendo loco. Su paranoia era tal que Rosemary estaba empezando a darse cuenta, y eso era algo que no podía permitir. Hasta ahora, había conseguido contenerlo, pero la mañana del día 12 había mirado por casualidad por la ventana del ático y, por primera vez, había visto al hombre del abrigo negro.

Había poco más que decir de aquel tipo a excepción de que se trataba de un hombre. Permanecía de pie en la acera de enfrente, completamente inmóvil y mirando hacia su ventana. Llevaba un abrigo largo y la parte superior de su rostro quedaba ensombrecida por el ala ancha del sombrero. Lo único que podía distinguir era que iba bien afeitado.

Weaver bajó haciendo ruido dos tramos de escaleras y abrió de golpe la puerta delantera. No sabía qué iba a hacer si el hombre se dirigía a él, pues no había pensado tanto. Tal vez albergase la idea errada de enfrentarse a aquel tipo o de afrontar su miedo. Sin embargo, la calle estaba vacía. El hombre había desaparecido.

Weaver cerró la puerta con cuidado y se encerró a sí mismo dentro junto con las hojas color tierra que el viento otoñal había arrastrado al interior.

III

Tres llamadas telefónicas

En Dollis Hill, el día comenzó con una llamada de teléfono. Anselm Rees, que se había levantado tarde, estaba en su escritorio y descolgó el auricular.

–¿Doctor Rees?

Reconoció la voz del teléfono como la del Paciente C, que en su día a día era una especie de novelista. Claude Weaver era el nombre de aquel tipo. Rees se había mostrado decidido a no buscar sus obras.

–Señor Weaver –dijo el psiquiatra con la voz teñida de impaciencia–, parece haberse saltado nuestra cita de esta mañana.

–Lo siento, ha ocurrido algo y no voy a poder llegar. Pagaré por la sesión, por supuesto, pero no puedo ir a verle hoy.

–¿Hay alguna razón para que sea así?

–Lo siento.

Y, tras decir aquello, el Paciente C colgó el teléfono. Mientras sacudía la cabeza y mascullaba para sí mismo, Rees alcanzó su libro de citas y pasó las páginas hasta el día en cuestión. Encontró el nombre «Paciente C» y trazó una línea sobre él con la pluma.

–Señora Turner –dijo–, mi paciente de esta mañana ha cancelado su cita. ¿Qué debería hacer para ocupar el tiempo?

El ama de llaves entró en el estudio afanosamente con una bandeja de té. Olive Turner era el ama de llaves en casa de los Rees desde el día que cruzaron el umbral de la misma. Era una mujer meticulosa que algunos consideraban sin gracia. Sin embargo, el doctor Rees observaba en ella un afecto discreto y un ingenio que le encantaban. Ni que decir tiene que, además, era muy habilidosa en su trabajo. La casa siempre estaba en perfecto orden y la comida guisada a la perfección.

–El artículo –le dijo ella con una severidad fingida.

El artículo en cuestión era uno que, supuestamente, estaba escribiendo para una apreciada revista de psiquiatría. Un artículo que incluso su propio autor creía que era tan aburrido como una partida de ajedrez retransmitida por la radio. Le resultaba difícil concentrarse cuando sus tres pacientes habían demostrado ser casos de estudio fascinantes.

Sonrió en dirección a Olive.

–Ya sabe que valoro su concisión, señora Turner. Por eso la contraté: nada de palabrería superflua.

Olive Turner le dedicó una leve sonrisa.

–Bueno, es usted el que ha preguntado.

En ese momento, el breve silencio se vio interrumpido de nuevo por el sonido del teléfono. La señora Turner dejó la bandeja sobre la mesita de cristal que había en el centro de la sala mientras el doctor contestaba a la llamada.

–Rees al teléfono. ¿Quién llama?

Por encima del tintineo de la vajilla, Olive pudo distinguir una voz difusa al otro lado de la línea, pero eso fue todo.

–Ya veo –dijo el doctor en dirección al aparato–. ¿Puede contarme más?

Más de la misma locución difusa. Olive, que ya no ocultaba su curiosidad, se irguió para escuchar.

–Ya veo –repitió el doctor mientras miraba en dirección al ventanal francés–. Eso parece... problemático. –Otra pausa, esta vez más larga–. Sí –asintió el hombre con una nota de rotundidad en la voz–. Le estaré esperando.

Entonces, colgó el teléfono.

Olive Turner recordaría aquella segunda conversación telefónica aquella noche y lamentaría haber permitido que sus modales se interpusieran en el camino de una historia. Como muchas de las conversaciones escuchadas y recordadas a medias, la segunda llamada iba a demostrar ser decisiva.

Lidia Rees soltó un grito. Al girar una página de la versión encuadernada en piel de *Die Elixiere des Teufels*, la esquina de una hoja le había hecho un corte en el pulgar, creando un hilillo de sangre que goteó sobre la página. Se chupó el dedo intentando alejar el dolor y centrarse en lo escrito, pero era demasiado tarde: se había desconcentrado.

Gruñó, cerró el tomo de golpe y lo devolvió a su estantería. Estaba trabajando en su habitación del segundo piso. Aquel era un día que había decidido dedicar al estudio. Pronto pondría en marcha su propia consulta de psiquiatría y ya estaba pensando muy seriamente en crear una lista de pacientes deseables.

Había buscado de forma consciente entre la alta sociedad londinense; se entiende que como una mera observadora. En su opinión, el fenómeno de la clase alta inglesa presentaba una dicotomía cultural fascinante. Los ancianos del grupo, como si fueran los de una tribu paleolítica, eran el modelo a seguir de un sentido del decoro social arbitrario. Pero una guerra brutal había resquebrajado la fachada de seguridad que los había rodeado durante tanto tiempo. Los límites entre las clases estaban desapareciendo de forma sistemática y ese revestimiento de decoro se estaba haciendo añicos.

Independientemente de su clase, la generación más joven (aquellos que habían cumplido la mayoría de edad durante o después de la Gran Guerra) estaba desarrollando un gusto por el anarquismo. Por supuesto, a nivel político (el socialismo estaba en alza), pero también en su forma de abordar el arte, la música y todo lo demás.

Aquel era el derrotero que estaban tomando las teorías de Lidia. Ya había esbozado el primer borrador de un artículo que, de forma provisional, se llamaba «La teoría de lo inglés». Se preguntó si no sería un título demasiado general y pomposo. Sabría más cuando comenzara a trabajar con su primer paciente o, más bien, con su primer paciente de verdad.

La ensoñación llegó a su fin de forma abrupta cuando alguien llamó a la puerta del dormitorio.

–Adelante –dijo mientras seguía chupándose el pulgar.

Se trataba de Olive Turner.

–Hay una llamada para usted, señorita Rees.

–Qué curioso –dijo Lidia–. No he oído sonar el teléfono.

–No ha dejado de hacerlo en toda la mañana, señorita.

A pesar de sus múltiples peticiones, el ama de llaves no era capaz de referirse a la joven señorita como «Lidia».

–¿Y bien? ¿Quién llama?

–El señor Marcus Bowman.

Lidia suspiró.

–Dile que no puedo hablar con él. O, mejor aún, dile que he salido.

–Creo que llama para confirmar la hora a la que pasará a recogerla esta noche. Entiendo que todavía piensa salir con él.

Marcus había conseguido reservar para ellos una mesa en el Savoy. Llevaba mucho tiempo prometiendo invitarla a probar la mejor cocina londinense, pero los frecuentes compromisos para jugar al golf habían echado por tierra sus planes. Ahora, la reserva estaba hecha al fin y la cita fijada.

–Ah, sí. Supongo que saldré con él esta noche. –Entonces, dio un paso ligeramente predatorio hacia el ama de llaves–. Dile que saldré con él. Puede recogerme a las ocho. Por favor, que no llegue tarde.

Lidia le dedicó una sonrisita. Fue una sonrisa que, al día siguiente, Olive Turner recordaría y se preguntaría qué había significado.

IV

La noche en cuestión

–Marcus.

Lidia saludó a su novio con una sonrisa atractiva y depredadora.

–¡Ah del barco! –dijo él mientras se inclinaba en el umbral de la puerta para darle un beso casto en la mejilla.

Aún era pronto (todavía no habían dado las ocho), pero el cielo ya estaba del color de la fruta picada: oscuro y opresivo. Lidia iba ataviada con un vestido de noche de raso y un collar con un rubí en torno al cuello. La joya estaba acomodada entre sus clavículas y resplandecía bajo la luz de las farolas de la calle.

–Te invitaría a pasar –dijo ella–, pero la señora Turner está enfrascada en la limpieza de la casa. No creo que le fuese a hacer mucha gracia.

Aquello era mentira: Olive Turner había terminado de limpiar varias horas antes. En ese momento estaba en la cocina, esforzándose por preparar la cena del doctor.

La joven salió a la calle y estaba a punto de cerrar la puerta a sus espaldas cuando Anselm Rees apareció en el pasillo, asomándose por detrás de su hombro izquierdo.

–Buenas noches, Marcus –dijo.

–Buenas noches, señor.

–Llegaremos tarde a cenar, papá –dijo Lidia con una informalidad forzada–. Marcus va a conducir hasta el centro.

–De hecho –replicó el joven–, había pensado que podíamos tomar un taxi y dejar aquí mi automóvil. Así podremos disfrutar más de la noche.

–Lo que tú prefieras, querido.

Lidia enhebró el brazo de Marcus y dejó que la condujera hasta la acera. Con el brazo libre, el hombre paró un taxi que pasaba por allí. Anselm Rees se quedó en la puerta observando cómo la joven pareja trepaba dentro y se perdía en medio de la noche con un rugido.

Una vez que los hubo perdido de vista, regresó al comedor, se sentó solo en la mesa y dio un sorbo de jerez.

–Actúa de forma un poco extraña, ¿no es así? –preguntó Olive mientras dejaba frente a él un plato humeante de estofado de ternera.

–Es mi hija –replicó el doctor Rees–. ¿De qué otro modo esperaba que actuara? –dijo bromeando, aunque había cierta verdad en ello.

A las nueve en punto exactamente, Olive le llevó un refrigerio tardío. Para entonces, él se había retirado a su estudio y, cuando el ama de llaves llamó a la puerta, contestó:

–Espere un momento.

Ella oyó cómo se levantaba de su silla, se acercaba en su dirección arrastrando los pies y giraba la llave en la cerradura. Después, abrió la pesada puerta de caoba. Tenía el ceño un poco fruncido, como si estuviera preocupado, pero, más allá de eso, no había nada en su comportamiento que la inquietase.

Le tendió la tabla de quesos (el doctor permaneció impasible en el umbral de la puerta; era evidente que no quería que pasara) y él le dio las gracias. Entonces, le dijo que tenía que pedirle un favor.

–Olive, esta noche, más tarde, voy a recibir una visita. Lo más probable es que se dirija a la puerta principal, así que no quiero que se alarme cuando llegue. Solo deje que pase e indíquele dónde se encuentra el estudio.

–Señor, ¿no quiere que lo acompañe yo misma?

–No. –Aquella fue una orden firme; una de las pocas que solía darle Anselm Rees–. Solo déjele entrar y dígale dónde puede encontrarme. Después, váyase a la cama.

Olive abrió la boca para hacer otra pregunta, pero Rees se retiró con la tabla de quesos y le cerró la puerta en las narices. El cerrojo giró de forma ruidosa. Ella regresó a la cocina ligeramente ofendida.

Dos horas después, justo a las once en punto, una triste lluvia otoñal comenzó a repiquetear contra la ventana. Olive seguía sentada en la cocina, arrebujada con su bata y bebiendo una taza de chocolate caliente mientras leía el periódico bajo la luz de la lámpara de gas. La noche seguía avanzando con lentitud.

Poco después de que el reloj marcara las once y cuarto, alguien llamó a la puerta delantera, haciendo que Olive se despertara sobresaltada de su letargo. Se puso en pie y salió fatigosamente de la cocina al pasillo. Allí, recortada contra el cristal esmerilado, vio una figura. Sintió una oleada repentina de miedo, así que colocó la cadena de la puerta antes de abrirla un poco para poder ver al visitante.

–¿Sí? –dijo en lo que era poco más que un susurro.

–¿Puedo pasar? –respondió el hombre.

Llevaba un sombrero de fieltro calado sobre la frente y el cuello y la barbilla cubiertos por una bufanda gruesa que amortiguaba sus palabras. Olive no podía discernir muchos más detalles.

–¿Quién llama?

–Vengo a ver al doctor Rees.

Olive apretó los dientes y recordó las instrucciones del doctor. A regañadientes, quitó la cadena de la puerta y le dejó entrar al pasillo.

–¿Me da el sombrero y el abrigo, señor?

–No, gracias –contestó el hombre con un tono de voz grave y ronco.

Se dirigió de inmediato a las escaleras.

–¡Señor! –protestó ella–. Si busca al doctor Rees, su oficina está al final de ese pasillo. Es la última puerta a la derecha.

El extraño se detuvo y le lanzó una mirada impaciente antes de alejarse a grandes zancadas por la dirección que le había indicado. Olive se quedó observando mientras el desconocido llegaba ante la puerta del estudio, llamaba con decisión y lo dejaban pasar.

Tras un instante, no pudo contener la curiosidad. Se arrastró por el pasillo hasta el estudio. Como era de esperar, estaba cerrado y la llave puesta en la cerradura, pero no pudo resistirse a apoyar la oreja contra la madera durante unos segundos.

–No parece sorprendido de verme –dijo la voz del desconocido.

–En absoluto –respondió el doctor–. Le he estado esperando.

–¿De verdad?

Siguió un silencio breve pero inquietante. Cualquier palabra quedó oculta por el estruendo del corazón de Olive. Entonces, el extraño volvió a hablar.

–Su ama de llaves nos está espiando.

La mujer sintió que podía morirse allí mismo, en el pasillo. La oleada de adrenalina y la punzada de terror que sintió en el pecho bien podrían resultarle letales. Ahogando un grito, se escabulló de allí.

Necesitó una copita de brandi para calmarse. Sentada a solas en la cocina, el corazón seguía palpitándole con fuerza. Había algo muy desconcertante en aquel desconocido. Mientras tanto, la lluvia seguía cayendo y golpeando la ventana hasta crear un ritmo propulsor como el de los tambores tribales.

Aguzó el oído cuando oyó que se abría la puerta del estudio y que el desconocido se marchaba. Había pasado más o menos media hora desde que había llegado. Tras abrir la puerta de la cocina con cuidado, observó a través de la rendija cómo el extraño (que volvía a estar cubierto por el sombrero, la bufanda y el abrigo) se abría paso hasta la puerta delantera. Su instinto era seguirlo y decirle: «Le acompaño a la salida, señor», pero no se atrevió a hacerlo.

Se arrastró por el pasillo para poder ver cómo abría la puerta el hombre y salía a la calle. La puerta se cerró de golpe tras él. Contempló cómo su figura se alejaba y se perdía de vista. Después, corrió a su escondite y echó el cerrojo dos veces.

A continuación, se dirigió al estudio del doctor. Llamó a la puerta de madera y dijo:

–¿Va todo bien ahí dentro, señor?

–Bien, bien –contestó él, aunque la respuesta fue demasiado apresurada para el gusto de Olive.

–¿Está seguro, señor? ¿Quiere que le traiga algo? ¿Una copa?

–No, gracias. Eso es todo.

Olive se quedó allí de pie un instante. Después, abordó el asunto.

–¿Puedo preguntarle quién ha venido a verle esta noche, señor?

Se produjo una pausa. Al otro lado de la madera podía oír una respiración.

–Un viejo amigo, nada más –susurró él–. Buenas noches.

El ama de llaves se dio la vuelta para marcharse. Decidió que, en ese momento, sí que se marcharía a la cama. Mientras se dirigía a la escalera, el silencio fantasmal de la casa y el repiqueteo percutor de la lluvia fueron interrumpidos por el sonido del teléfono. Olive chilló, asustada, y frenó en seco. Se acercó al que colgaba de la pared del pasillo, pero llegó demasiado tarde. El aparato había dejado de sonar.

Oyó cómo el doctor descolgaba la extensión que había en el estudio y gruñía con una voz que apenas resultaba reconocible.

–¿Qué ocurre? –Hubo una pausa–. Ya veo. –Su tono se suavizó–. ¿Y entonces?

Olive retomó su posición junto a la puerta del estudio con la oreja pegada a la fría madera. Oyó el rasgar familiar de la pluma del doctor sobre el bloc de notas. Estaba tomando varias anotaciones apresuradas. Casi se sintió tentada de tomar el aparato del pasillo y escuchar la conversación. Pero, por supuesto, aquel comportamiento hubiera estado totalmente fuera de lugar.

–Bien, eso está bien –dijo el doctor–. Pero, ahora, será mejor que duerma. De verdad, es muy tarde para hablar de esto. Venga a verme mañana. A las diez en punto. Entonces, podremos entrar en detalles. Muy bien. Buenas noches.

En ese momento, colgó el teléfono.

Olive se abrió paso de nuevo hasta las escaleras. Mientras subía el primer escalón, recordó que se había dejado el libro que estaba leyendo en la mesa de la cocina. Con un suspiro, se dio la vuelta.

Finalmente, libro en mano, recorrió por última vez el pasillo en dirección a las escaleras.

–¡Ay, señor! –exclamó, sobresaltada.

El libro se le escapó de las manos y golpeó las baldosas del suelo. En el cristal esmerilado se recortaba una silueta que estaba llamando con delicadeza a la puerta. ¿Un segundo visitante?

–¿Quién anda ahí? –preguntó.

–¡Déjeme entrar!

La voz era femenina.

–¿Quién es? –insistió ella.

–¡Está lloviendo! Por favor, déjeme entrar.

Olive se arrastró hasta la puerta y, con una mano temblorosa, estiró el brazo y descorrió el cerrojo. Entonces, abrió la puerta de un tirón y la mujer entró en la casa. Se trataba de la actriz Della Cookson.

–Gracias a Dios –suspiró Della.

–¡Señorita Cookson! ¿Qué se le ofrece a esta hora?

–Necesito ver al doctor Rees. Por favor, es una emergencia.

Olive se quedó plantada un instante con las manos en las caderas y dando golpecitos en el suelo con el pie.

–Bueno, veré qué puedo hacer, pero no le prometo nada. El doctor sigue trabajando en su estudio, pero de normal no atiende a los pacientes tan tarde. Será mejor que pase.

La condujo hasta el estudio y se detuvo frente a la puerta. Cerró el puño para volver a llamar y lo hizo con tres golpes estridentes.

Esperaron.

–¡Doctor Rees! –exclamó Olive–. ¡Tiene una visita!

Los hombros de Della Cookson subían y bajaban junto con su respiración agitada. Aquel era el único sonido más allá de la lluvia. Olive volvió a pegar la oreja a la madera.

–¿Doctor Rees? –preguntó de nuevo.

–Por favor –dijo Della–. Tengo que verle. Es imperativo.

El ama de llaves golpeó la puerta. Después, se arrodilló y miró por el ojo de la cerradura, pero, como era de esperar, la imagen quedaba obstruida por la dichosa llave. Se inclinó hacia delante hasta que la nariz casi le tocaba el suelo para intentar mirar por debajo de la puerta. Lo único que pudo distinguir fue un estrechísimo haz de luz.

–Algo va mal –dijo.

El ama de llaves dejó a Della sola en el pasillo y fue hasta la cocina. Regresó apenas medio minuto después con un lapicero y una hoja de papel. Era un viejo truco, tan antiguo que apenas será necesario esclarecerlo en estas páginas. Coló la hoja de papel por debajo de la puerta y metió el lapicero en el ojo de la cerradura. Prestó atención al ruido de la llave al caer al otro lado antes de tirar de la hoja de papel para recogerla. Se trataba de un pequeño juego de manos que conocía bien gracias a su atenta lectura de novelas de ficción barata.

Se puso en pie con dificultad, abrió la puerta y se precipitó al interior. Della la siguió de cerca. De entrada, no parecía que hubiese nada fuera de lugar dentro de la habitación. Las luces resplandecían y había papeles esparcidos por el escritorio. La silla del doctor estaba orientada hacia los ventanales y él mismo yacía en ella, desplomado.

Olive se colocó frente a él y lo miró a la cara. El corazón le latió con tanta fuerza que apenas oyó gritar a Della.

El doctor Anselm Rees yacía muerto en aquella silla. Su rostro era una máscara blanca y un horrible tajo carmesí le atravesaba la garganta. La sangre se le había derramado por la parte delantera y parecía dibujar un babero. Tenía los ojos medio abiertos y vidriosos y las manos cruzadas en un gesto paciente sobre el regazo.

–¡Cierre la puerta! –dijo Olive.

–¿Qué? –tartamudeó la actriz.

–¡La puerta! No quiero que su hija llegue a casa y lo vea así.

Della hizo lo que le pidió, cerró la puerta del estudio y las encerró en su interior con el cadáver. El ama de llaves ya tenía el teléfono en la mano.

–Dos, tres, uno de Dollis Hill –anunció–. Han asesinado al doctor Anselm Rees.

Mientras proporcionaba varios detalles, miró en torno a la habitación y se dio cuenta de algo.

–Las ventanas están cerradas –dijo mientras colgaba el auricular.

–¿Cómo?

Della sonaba sorprendida.

–Las ventanas están cerradas por dentro.

Para demostrarlo, agarró una de las manillas y la sacudió. No se movió. Además, la llave sobresalía de la cerradura.

–¿Y qué?

–¿Cómo se ha escapado el asesino?

–¿Qué quiere decir?

–No ha podido salir por el pasillo, ya que yo he estado ahí todo el tiempo. Y no hace ni cinco minutos... Puedo decirle que no hace ni cinco minutos el doctor estaba vivito y coleando dentro de esta habitación, porque lo he oído hablando por teléfono.

Della pensó en ello.

–No pueden estar cerradas.

Estiró la mano y agarró ella misma una de las manillas. Sin embargo, las ventanas no cedieron.

–Están cerradas por dentro –dijo Olive–. Igual que la puerta.

La actriz se dio la vuelta y contempló el cadáver. Se había hundido en la silla como una marioneta de mano sin nadie que la manejara.

En el rincón más apartado de la estancia se encontraba el baúl de madera. Olive miró a Della a los ojos e hizo un gesto con la cabeza en su dirección. La actriz frunció el ceño, incrédula. El ama de llaves se encogió de hombros como si quisiera decir: «¿En qué otro sitio podría estar?».

Ambas mujeres se arrastraron sobre la alfombra mullida en dirección al baúl. Olive miró a Della y se llevó un dedo a los labios. Agarró el atizador de la chimenea y lo levantó por encima de su cabeza. Entonces, le hizo un gesto rápido a la otra mujer.

Della se inclinó hacia delante y abrió el baúl de un tirón.

Olive soltó con fiereza un grito de batalla mientras blandía el atizador como si fuera una raqueta de tenis. Sin embargo, lo único que golpeó fue el aire. Ambas miraron dentro del baúl, que estaba totalmente vacío.

–Muy bien. Entonces, ¿dónde está? –preguntó Della.

Olive soltó el atizador, que cayó sobre la alfombra con un golpe.

–No lo sé –contestó.

–Necesito un trago –dijo la actriz. El ama de llaves no respondió–. No, lo digo en serio: necesito un trago.

–Hay jerez en el armario –replicó Olive de forma ausente.

–¿No hay nada más fuerte?

–En la cocina tengo brandi.

–Lléveme allí –respondió Della–. Necesito salir de esta habitación.

Olive se dio por vencida.

–Tal vez tenga razón. Aquí no podemos hacer nada.

Ambas salieron de la habitación y Olive abrió la marcha hasta la cocina, no sin antes cerrar la puerta del estudio a sus espaldas, encerrando de nuevo al difunto doctor Rees.

Las dos se sintieron un poco mejor tras una copita de brandi. No menos horrorizadas, pero sí más preparadas para encargarse de las cuestiones prácticas de la situación.

–Lo que no entiendo es dónde puede haber ido el asesino –dijo Della.

–A ninguna parte –contestó Olive–. No hay ningún sitio al que ir.

V

El nacimiento

Para cuando el inspector George Flint llegó a casa de los Rees, la lluvia se había convertido en una llovizna moribunda. Lo acompañaron hasta la habitación del asesinato, donde Anselm Rees, que cada vez tenía un aspecto más parecido al de una vela medio derretida, seguía sobre su silla.

–Un auténtico desastre –dijo Flint a nadie en particular.

Era cierto: a Rees casi le habían cortado la cabeza de un solo tajo. La expresión calmada que había en su rostro muerto era suficiente para aparecer en las pesadillas incluso de un perro viejo y con heridas de guerra como Flint.

La actitud del inspector hacia el crimen era filosófica: si bien, en general, estaba en contra de él, seguía pudiendo considerarlo una necesidad social. Pensemos en el asesinato, por ejemplo. La mayoría de ellos eran asuntos sórdidos que ocurrían en callejones sin ningún tipo de misterio o magia. De normal, el culpable era quienquiera que estuviese más unido a la víctima. Pero, en los últimos años, cada vez había sido más consciente de un pujante subgénero del crimen que se había esparcido por la ciudad como la niebla. Se trataba de los crímenes imposibles. Típicamente, eran asuntos de la alta sociedad en los que hombres en habitaciones cerradas eran asesinados bajo circunstancias irrealizables o en los que, por ejemplo, se encontraba un cuerpo estrangulado en un campo nevado con un único conjunto de huellas que retrocedían desde el cadáver. El asesinato como un rompecabezas.

Costaba darse permiso para involucrarse de manera emocional en un caso como ese. Se debía conservar una distancia intelectual. Para resolver un crimen de ese tipo, se necesitaba una clase de cerebro especial que Flint, sencillamente, no poseía, por lo que se hacía necesario buscar las respuestas en otra parte.

–¿Algún rastro del arma?

–No –contestó Jerome Hook.

Era la mano derecha de Flint, un joven desgarbado muy apto para el trabajo preliminar.

–Así que el asesino se la ha llevado con él. O, por el contrario, la ha escondido en algún lugar de esta habitación. ¿Algún avance con la búsqueda del primer visitante de la noche? El que ha asustado a la señora Turner…

–Todavía no, hay algunos compañeros investigando el asunto.

–Bien. En cuanto sepa algo, hágamelo saber. ¿Y qué hay de esta habitación? No me diga que nos encontramos ante una de esas tonterías de «habitaciones herméticamente cerradas»…

–Eso me temo, señor. Tanto Olive Turner como Della Cookson han confirmado que la puerta del estudio estaba cerrada por dentro. Y, como puede comprobar usted mismo, el ventanal también.

–Pero el asesino ha tenido que marcharse por ahí. Si hubiese salido al pasillo por la puerta, Olive lo habría visto, en eso estamos de acuerdo. Eso significa que ha tenido que salir por las ventanas y, después, usar algún tipo de truco para cerrarlas desde el exterior.

–Me temo que no es posible, señor. Mire, cuando ha ocurrido el asesinato, llevaba un rato lloviendo, y justo al otro lado del ventanal hay un parterre que conduce al jardín. El agua lo ha dejado hecho un lodazal, por lo que nadie podría haber salido por ese camino sin dejar huellas. Y, como puede ver, no hay ninguna.

Sí que había huellas en el jardín (huellas de hombre), pero no se acercaban ni a la casa ni a las ventanas, así que alguien había estado aquella noche en el jardín durante la tormenta, pero, quienquiera que hubiera sido, era imposible determinar si había estado allí antes, durante o después del asesinato. Incluso podría haber sido cosa de un policía torpe mientras husmeaba por allí. Cosas más raras se habían visto.

–Ya veo. –Flint entrelazó los dedos y observó el cadáver–. Así que tenemos un asesino que se ha esfumado como un fantasma.

¿Estamos seguros del todo de que Rees estaba vivo cuando se ha marchado el hombre misterioso?

–Sí. Ha hablado con Olive a través de la puerta y se le ha oído recibiendo una llamada telefónica.

–Así que el asesinato ha ocurrido en los pocos minutos que han transcurrido entre la partida del visitante y la llegada de Della Cookson. ¿Es esa nuestra teoría?

–Eso parece, señor.

–¿Y sabemos por qué la señorita Cookson ha venido a una hora tan tardía de la noche?

Hook se encogió de hombros.

–Está en la sala de estar, esperando a que la interroguen. El ama de llaves está con ella.

Della estaba resplandeciente sobre un diván antiguo. Parecía sacada de uno de los carteles de sus obras. Aunque Flint se sintió brevemente fascinado, consiguió recuperar su gesto habitual de evaluación impasible.

–Era usted paciente del doctor Rees, ¿no es así?

Ella apretó los dientes.

–Sí, llevaba más o menos un mes viniendo a verle.

–¿Por qué motivo?

–No veo por qué debería contestar a eso. No tiene nada que ver con lo que ha ocurrido aquí esta noche, eso se lo aseguro.

Flint ladeó la cabeza de forma amigable.

–Está en su derecho, pero, por favor, tenga en cuenta que vamos a tener acceso total a las notas del doctor, así que bien podría contárnoslo.

Sin embargo, los labios de la mujer permanecieron sellados.

Olive Turner estaba sentada junto a la ventana, mirando hacia fuera con el rostro de un blanco fantasmal. Se sobresaltó un poco cuando Flint se acercó a ella.

–Lo siento –dijo–. Estoy algo agitada.

–No pasa nada, es del todo comprensible. Tan solo quería hacerle un par de preguntas mientras todavía tiene frescos los acontecimientos de esta noche.

El ama de llaves sacudió vagamente una mano.

–Pregunte.

–El visitante, el hombre que ha venido a ver al doctor Rees antes de que haya llegado la señorita Cookson… ¿Está del todo segura de que era alguien que no había visto nunca antes?

–Sí. Era un desconocido. Todo en él, su cara, su voz… Era casi como si se hubiera disfrazado, como si hubiera intentado de forma activa ocultar quién era.

–¿Y por qué podría ser eso?

Olive volvió la mirada vidriosa hacia él.

–¿Cómo iba a saberlo?

–Usted ha dicho que el doctor Rees lo estaba esperando. ¿Le ha dado el doctor alguna pista sobre cuál podría ser el motivo del encuentro?

–Ninguna en absoluto. Pero he supuesto que se trataba de un paciente. El doctor guardaba con mucho celo su lista de pacientes.

–¿Y solía atenderlos por la noche de manera habitual?

–No. Mantenía un horario de visitas muy estricto, por eso he sospechado.

–¿Y ha habido algo en el comportamiento de dicho hombre que le haya alarmado?

La mujer lo meditó un momento.

–Ha actuado como un animal herido. Había algo nervioso y excéntrico en él, como si no fuera posible adivinar qué iba a hacer a continuación. Y no conocía la casa.

–¿Por qué dice eso?

–Cuando le he dicho que el doctor lo esperaba en su estudio, se ha dirigido a las escaleras. Un visitante recurrente habría sabido que el estudio se encuentra en el primer piso. Es lógico.

–Mmm… –Flint se dio un golpecito en la barbilla con un dedo índice calloso–. Esa es una observación muy útil. Gracias, señora Turner.

Flint dejó a la mujer y se dirigió de nuevo al estudio. Su sargento, Jerome Hook, lo acompañó mientras tomaba notas en su libreta.

–Muy bien –comenzó a decir–, vamos a recrear las actividades del doctor. Estaba trabajando en sus notas. ¿Sabemos qué estaba escribiendo?

–Estaba trabajando en un artículo para *The Alienist Review*. Las notas están incompletas. De hecho, se cortan en medio de una frase, como si lo hubieran interrumpido.

–Entonces, podemos suponer que estaba trabajando en eso cuando Olive le ha traído el refrigerio. Y ha sido entonces cuando le ha dado esa orden tan extraña: «Solo déjele entrar y dígale dónde puede encontrarme». ¿Por qué haría algo así? ¿Alguna sugerencia?

Hook meditó la pregunta.

–No quería que Olive oyera la conversación. Ninguna parte de la misma. Tal vez tenga tendencia a escuchar a escondidas.

–Podría ser. Sabemos que ha pegado la oreja a la puerta del estudio al menos una vez. Bien. Entonces, ella deja la tabla de quesos y se marcha. Después, a las once y cuarto, oye al visitante llamando a la puerta. No sabemos qué está haciendo el doctor mientras tanto, pero podemos suponer que se está comiendo el refrigerio y trabajando en el artículo. Así que llega su visita. Rees le deja pasar al estudio y se encierran en el interior. Se encargan de sus asuntos en secreto y, entonces, el visitante se marcha. Olive presencia su partida. Ella va hasta el estudio, pero el doctor no le deja entrar en la sala. Sin embargo, sabemos que está vivo porque habla con ella a través de la puerta. ¿Qué ocurre a continuación? Olive sube las escaleras y, entonces, oye a Della llamando a la puerta principal...

–No, se equivoca –le interrumpió Hook–. Se está olvidando de la llamada telefónica.

–Así es. El teléfono suena a las once y cuarenta y cinco. ¿Hemos rastreado ya la llamada?

–Sí –contestó el sargento mientras hojeaba su cuaderno de notas–. Me ha costado un poco, pero yo mismo he hablado con la chica de la centralita. La llamada procedía de un piso en Dufresne Court que está registrado a nombre de Floyd Stenhouse, el músico. Era uno de los pacientes del doctor.

Flint gruñó. No tenía oído musical y, por lo tanto, no escuchaba música.

–Stenhouse. Hablaré con él en breve. Bien, ¿qué más? Olive, que Dios bendiga su alma curiosa, escucha la conversación. Entonces, regresa a la cocina para recoger el libro y, cuando vuelve a salir al pasillo, ve a Della Cookson en la puerta. Por lo tanto, el asesinato ha tenido que ocurrir durante los dos minutos o así que han transcurrido entre el final de la conversación telefónica y la llegada de la actriz. ¿Le encaja?

–Sí, señor.

Flint sonrió.

–Pero, al mismo tiempo, es del todo imposible.

Mientras pronunciaba aquellas palabras, Lidia Rees y Marcus Bowman llegaron a casa. Al oír la conmoción del pasillo, Flint salió a su encuentro. Marcus balbuceaba y se retorcía con excesiva incomodidad ante la presencia de aquellos policías de rostro severo, pero Lidia permaneció totalmente calmada.

–¿Ha ocurrido algo? –preguntó.

–Eso me temo –respondió el inspector–. ¿Es usted Lidia Rees?

–Sí, soy yo.

Flint hizo un gesto solemne con la cabeza.

–Entonces, me temo que tengo malas noticias para usted. ¿Podemos hablar en alguna parte?

Lidia parecía tranquila mientras conducía al inspector escaleras arriba hasta su habitación. Flint se colocó a su lado mientras se sentaba en el tocador y empezaba a quitarse las joyas.

–Señorita Rees, su padre ha muerto.

–Ya veo…

–Lamento decirle que ha sido asesinado. En su oficina.

–¿Uno de sus pacientes?

El policía pareció un poco sorprendido por aquella pregunta.

–¿Eran violentos?

–Bueno, ¿de qué otra cosa podría tratarse? ¿De un robo?

–Supongo que lo que tengo que preguntarle, señorita Rees, es si sabe por qué alguien querría hacerle daño a su padre.

Lidia se contempló a sí misma en el espejo. Por primera vez, Flint se dio cuenta de que tenía los ojos llenos de lágrimas.

–¿Cómo ha muerto? –preguntó ella.

Tenía la voz fría y clara.

–Le han cortado la garganta.

–¿Y tienen algún sospechoso?

–Todavía no. Por eso necesito preguntarle si se le ocurre algún motivo por el que alguien quisiera hacerle daño. –Lentamente, ella negó con la cabeza–. ¿Había notado algo raro en su comportamiento? ¿Parecía preocupado o asustado?

–Mi padre nunca tenía miedo.

–¿A quién esperaba esta noche?

Ella meditó aquella pregunta.

–A nadie. Al menos, que yo sepa.

–¿No tenía ninguna cita de la que usted fuera consciente?

–Si fuese así, se lo diría.

Flint suspiró, pensativo.

–Pero ha recibido dos visitas esta noche.

Lidia apartó la vista de su reflejo, se giró y fulminó con la mirada al inspector.

–¿Quiénes eran?

–Un hombre con gabardina. La señora Turner le ha dejado pasar.

–Pero ¿quién era?

–No lo sabe. Era un hombre que no había visto antes. ¿Se le ocurre a usted quién podría ser?

–Si pudiera, se lo diría. Créame.

–Ha estado un rato con su padre en el estudio. La señora Turner no sabe de qué han hablado. El doctor Rees parecía querer mantener las circunstancias de la reunión en secreto.

Lidia se encogió de hombros.

–Ya veo... No, mi padre no me mencionó nada de todo esto. ¿Cree que ese hombre es el asesino?

–Sería la suposición más conveniente, pero tenemos motivos para pensar que su padre estaba vivo todavía cuando se ha marchado. Aunque, como es evidente, tendremos que hablar con ese tipo, sea quien sea.

–¿Y quién era el segundo visitante?

–¿Eh?

–Ha mencionado que mi padre ha tenido dos visitas esta noche.

–La segunda visita ha sido su paciente Della Cookson.

Lidia apretó la mandíbula.

–Della... lleva varios meses viniendo a verle.

–Bueno, ha aparecido muy tarde, angustiada. Estaba desesperada por ver a su padre. Había algo de lo que tenía que hablar con él. ¿Tiene alguna idea de qué podría ser? La dama se muestra un poco evasiva al respecto.

Ella sacudió la cabeza.

–Ojalá lo supiera. Della es un caso interesante.

–¿Hablaba su padre con usted sobre sus pacientes?

–Por supuesto. A título meramente profesional.

–¿Por qué querría hablar con él? ¿Puede ofrecerme una idea general?

Siguió una pausa larga en la que Flint fue capaz de echar un vistazo de reojo a la habitación. Había estanterías repletas de libros y un armario enorme, además de la lujosa cama de cuatro postes. Sin embargo, de algún modo, parecía vacía y sin alma, a pesar de todos los meses que habían habitado en ella.

–¿Cree que ha sido ella la que ha matado a mi padre?

–Creemos que el asesinato ha tenido que ocurrir en algún momento entre la partida del visitante masculino no identificado y la llegada de Della.

–Entonces, no puedo contárselo. Mi padre jamás consentiría que quebrantásemos la confidencialidad terapéutica, ni si quiera si eso fuese a ayudar a resolver su asesinato.

–Vamos a revisar sus notas, Lidia. Veremos todo lo que haya que ver.

–Estoy segura de que será así, pero, de todos modos, valoro mi integridad. Mi padre jamás permitiría que la devaluara al proporcionarle información irrelevante.

Flint asintió.

–De acuerdo. Y, para ser totalmente sincero, me interesa más el visitante masculino. Hasta que lo identifiquemos, no tendremos la oportunidad de atrapar al asesino. Así que, si se le ocurre algo que pueda compartir con nosotros, lo que sea, cualquier información o detalle, por pequeño que sea, se lo agradecería mucho. –Se puso en pie–. La dejo sola, señorita Rees –dijo.

Se dirigió hacia la puerta. Después, como si se le acabara de ocurrir, volvió a darse la vuelta.

–Ah, una última cosa. Supongo que no hay ningún tipo de entrada oculta al estudio de su padre, ¿verdad?

–¿Qué quiere decir?

–Más allá de la puerta del pasillo y los ventanales, ¿hay alguna otra manera en la que una persona pudiera entrar o salir de la habitación?

–No, no hay nada parecido.

Flint asintió. Era la respuesta que esperaba.

–Muchas gracias, señorita.

Entonces, la dejó a solas.

Mientras bajaba las escaleras, el inspector Flint oyó a Marcus Bowman haciéndole preguntas al sargento Hook.

–¿Qué es lo que ha ocurrido? ¿Qué es lo que quieren? ¿Qué han hecho con Lidia? ¿Dónde está?

–Está perfectamente, señor Bowman –replicó el inspector–. Es solo que ha sufrido una conmoción. Eso es todo.

Bowman se dirigió a las escaleras.

–Entonces, déjeme que la vea. Necesito hablar con ella…

Flint colocó la palma de la mano en el centro del pecho del joven para retenerlo.

–Todavía no, caballero. Tengo que hacerle algunas preguntas.

–¿Qué ocurre? ¿Qué ha pasado?

–El doctor Anselm Rees está muerto, señor. Asesinado. Lo han matado en la última hora. –Aquello hizo que Marcus se callara–. Tengo que preguntarle dónde ha estado esta noche.

–He estado con Lidia. Todo el tiempo. Ella se lo confirmará. Dios mío, ¿no estará intentando decirme que cree que yo…?

–¿Dónde han estado?

–En el Savoy. Hemos… hemos cenado allí.

–¿Y después?

Se produjo un silencio incómodo.

–En un club del Soho.

–¿En cuál?

–El Palmyra.

–¿Y a qué hora se han marchado?

–A-ahora mismo. Quiero decir…, hace unos minutos. Hemos

tomado un taxi para venir aquí. Le he di-dicho que la acompañaba a casa.

–Muy caballeroso por su parte, señor.

Bowman lo miró con cara de tonto.

–Bueno, eh… Verá, es que había dejado mi automóvil aquí.

Flint llevó aparte al sargento Hook.

–Quiero que lo interrogue. Quiero que registre la casa en busca de la más mínima pista. Una huella de zapato. Una huella dactilar en el polvo. No deje que se le escape nada. Voy a regresar a la comisaría. –Hizo una pausa–. Después, tendré que visitar a alguien.

–Sí, señor. ¿A quién, señor?

Varias horas después, sobre las diez de la mañana, Londres dormitaba bajo un lodazal de llovizna cuando el inspector Flint salió del coche de policía en Putney. El pub The Black Pig se alzaba frente a él en todo su ruinoso esplendor. Tras limpiarse las botas llenas de barro en el felpudo, se dirigió al interior.

La camarera le hizo un gesto silencioso en dirección al cuartito trasero. Flint era un rostro familiar, por lo que sabían a quién estaba buscando. Atravesó una puerta baja hasta la habitación contigua, donde unos sillones raídos habían sido colocados de manera artística sobre las tablas del suelo y frente a un hogar apagado. Desde la repisa de la chimenea lo observaba la cabeza apolillada de un ciervo.

Joseph Spector estaba sentado a solas, barajando un mazo de cartas de forma ausente. Flint se sentó frente a él.

–Parece agotado –dijo el viejo mago sin levantar la mirada–. Me parece que esta mañana no se ha afeitado.

–Llevo trabajando desde media noche.

Spector alzó la mirada de golpe.

–Un asesinato, ¿verdad? ¿Alguien a quien conozca?

–Un psiquiatra. El doctor Anselm Rees.

–¿Rees está muerto? ¿Y quién lo ha matado?

Flint entrelazó los dedos. Era lo que hacía para demostrar que el asunto a tratar era serio.

–¿Por qué cree que estoy aquí sentado?

–Ya veo…

Spector se recostó y estiró los brazos por encima de la cabeza. Los nudillos torcidos le crujieron como si fueran ramitas. Soltó un bostezo.

–Será mejor que me lo cuente todo.

Flint le hizo un resumen detallado de los acontecimientos de la noche anterior y un retrato riguroso de los principales protagonistas: Lidia Rees y Marcus Bowman, el ama de llaves Olive Turner y la actriz Della Cookson.

Cuando se habían conocido varios años atrás, el inspector Flint había tratado a Spector con la cautela que reservaba para los estafadores más inteligentes. Después de todo, el hombre era un renombrado devoto de lo macabro y mantenía una de las bibliotecas más completas sobre crimen y lo sobrenatural. Sin embargo, era esa misma otredad que rodeaba a Spector lo que lo convertía en el perfecto ayudante en casos de crímenes imposibles. La parte útil de conocer a un mago es aprender cómo se hacen los trucos.

Él mismo no se habría denominado un «ermitaño», pero, en aquellos momentos, Spector solía limitarse a visitar unos pocos lugares favoritos. Llevaba viviendo en la curiosa casita de Jubilee Court (un lugar de aspecto gótico que, gracias a las luces que resplandecían por sus ventanas, se asemejaba a una calavera vacía) más tiempo del que nadie podía recordar. Sin embargo, la mayoría de las veces podían encontrarlo allí, en la salita de The Black Pig, aquel pub mal iluminado, con vigas bajas y travesaños en las ventanas, por no mencionar los grifos de latón y la burbujeante máquina de cerveza que había detrás de la barra. Algunos dirían que era lúgubre, pero, como bien sabe cualquier mago, la ausencia de luz es la mejor aliada del estafador.

–Muy bien –dijo Joseph Spector–. Entonces, con respecto al ama de llaves…, Olive Turner, ¿confiamos en ella?

–Sí, así es.

–¿Por qué?

–Por varios motivos. En primer lugar, porque no tendría nada que ganar al matar al doctor Rees. En su testamento tan solo había una disposición simbólica a su nombre. A duras penas valdría la pena matar a alguien por eso. En segundo lugar, porque tan solo lleva trabajando en la casa cinco meses. No creo que eso sea tiempo suficiente para albergar un resentimiento letal. Hemos determinado con bastante certeza que el doctor Rees y ella no se conocían antes de que el hombre se estableciera en Inglaterra la primavera pasada. Y, en tercer lugar –continuó Flint–, y, para mí, este es el factor decisivo, porque Della Cookson llegó a la casa después de que ocurriera el asesinato y Olive la dejó pasar. Si acabara de matar a su patrono, ¿cree que habría hecho algo así?

–Tiene razón. Sus dos primeros argumentos no sirven de nada, pero el tercero tiene cierto peso. Entonces, ¿qué hay de esa habitación cerrada? Cuénteme los detalles.

–Hay dos formas de entrar: la puerta y los ventanales. Ambos estaban cerrados por dentro.

–¿Eso es todo?

–Sí. Confíe en mí: hemos revisado la habitación una y otra vez.

–¿Ni rastro del arma?

–Nada.

–¿Y no había manera de que la puerta se hubiera cerrado desde el exterior?

–En absoluto. En ambos casos, la llave estaba en la cerradura.

–¿Alguna posibilidad de que alguien hubiera trasteado con los cristales de los ventanales?

–Ninguna. Por lo que a mí respecta, a Anselm Rees le rebanaron el cuello en una habitación perfectamente cerrada.

Joseph Spector le dedicó una sonrisa.

–Mi crimen favorito. ¿Algún otro rasgo notable de la habitación que tenga que saber?

–Lo habitual. Un escritorio. Librerías. Ah, y un baúl.

–¿Qué tipo de baúl?

–Uno grande de madera. Pero lo registraron y estaba vacío.

–Ya veo... Tendré que examinarlo yo mismo. Pero, por favor, continúe.

–Encontramos dos conjuntos de huellas en el jardín trasero de la finca, pero ninguno de ellos se acercaba a la casa, así que a duras penas podemos establecer una unión entre ellas y el asesinato.

–¿Algo más?

–Hemos estado intentando sonsacarle detalles a Della Cookson, pero no cede. Tal vez pudiera intentarlo usted.

–Bueno, yo puedo ofrecerle una coartada para ella. Estuvo en casa del productor Benjamin Teasel la mayor parte de la velada. Hasta más o menos las once en punto. Todos estuvimos allí tras el espectáculo.

–¿Algún tipo de fiesta?

–Sí. Teasel está obsesionado con ese tipo de acontecimientos. Le encanta la música, bailar, el alcohol y el humo de los cigarrillos.

–No habría creído que ese fuese su tipo de ambiente, Spector.

El mago sonrió, cortó la baraja en dos y, después, volvió a unirla. Flint no tenía forma de saberlo, pero el anciano acababa de llevar a cabo una mezcla estilo faro impecable al intercalar a la perfección ambas mitades de la baraja.

–Le sorprendería lo que aguanta un viejo con tal de lograr un público atento.

–¿Y cuánto tiempo estuvo ella en la fiesta?

–No puedo estar seguro del todo, pero sé que a las diez y media estaba allí y que para las once ya se había marchado.

–¿Tomó un taxi?

–Eso creo. Debería señalar que la casa de Teasel está en Hampstead.

Flint asintió.

–Así que habría tardado al menos veinte minutos en llegar a la casa de Dollis Hill. Y llegó justo después de la llamada de teléfono.

–La llamada de teléfono –repitió Spector–. Sí, volveremos a eso. Por ahora, me interesa más Della Cookson. ¿La han registrado?

–Hemos mirado su bolso. Ni que decir tiene que se ha mostrado reticente. Pero no llevaba nada de interés. ¿Por qué? No creerá que ha sido ella, ¿verdad? Quiero decir…, no es posible que haya entrado al estudio para matar al doctor. Y, si lo hubiera hecho, ¿por qué iría después a la puerta delantera?

–Permítame que lo interrumpa –intervino Spector–. Si bien admito que es poco probable que haya podido matar al doctor Rees en las circunstancias que describe, creo que deberíamos tener cuidado antes de subestimar el papel que ha podido interpretar en el caso. –Flint abrió la boca pero no dijo nada–. Lo que quiero decir es... –continuó el mago–. ¿Tiene alguna manera de saber el motivo real detrás de su visita de anoche? –El inspector sacudió la cabeza lentamente–. ¿Tiene alguna idea de por qué se convirtió en paciente del doctor, para empezar? Anteanoche fue la noche del estreno de su nueva obra, *La dama Muerte*. La llevan a cabo en el Pomegranate y resulta que yo he trabajado en la producción. Parece encaminada a convertirse en un éxito. Así que, anoche, tras la segunda actuación, el productor celebró una fiesta en su casa. Todo el elenco estaba presente junto con el autor, el director y varias figuras de alto rango de ese mundillo. Lo que quiero decir, inspector Flint, es que en esa fiesta ocurrió algo que puede que arroje una nueva luz sobre el asesinato.

–¿Va a contarme el resto o no?

Spector sonrió.

–Benjamin Teasel es productor. Su vida depende de si el espectáculo sigue adelante o no. Y resulta que sé que, esta mañana, Teasel estaba hablando de cancelar la actuación de esta noche. Así que espero que eso le dé una idea de lo serio que es el asunto.

–¿Más serio que un asesinato?

–Para Benjamin, sí. Durante la fiesta se produjo un robo en su casa.

–¿Y qué tiene eso que ver con Della Cookson?

–¿No ha leído todavía las notas del doctor? –Flint sacudió la cabeza–. Es cleptómana, una ladrona compulsiva. Es un secreto a voces en el Pomegranate y el problema se había vuelto tan grande que buscó la ayuda del doctor Rees. Como comprenderá, esto es totalmente extraoficial –añadió a modo de paréntesis–, pero, anoche, antes de visitar al doctor, Della robó algo de un valor casi inestimable.

–Cuénteme –dijo Flint.

Así que Spector se lo contó. Comenzó relatando todo lo que había visto por sí mismo junto con lo que otros presentes le habían contado.

La fiesta en casa de Benjamin Teasel había resultado casi pútrida en su decadencia. El punto central había sido una pirámide de copas de champán y un trío de *jazz* que tocaba en el otro extremo de la sala mientras los miembros del joven elenco y la compañía de *La dama Muerte* bailaban los unos con los otros en un remolino de extremidades.

A Teasel le encantaba hacer el papel de anfitrión y se había vestido para la ocasión con un batín rojo brillante para que no hubiera ninguna posibilidad de que se perdiera entre la multitud. Por lo general, se situaba de forma posesiva junto a los miembros más importantes de la compañía y los atrapaba en una maraña de conversaciones de la que no podían escapar por sí solos. Como es natural, se había centrado en Della Cookson.

Mientras tanto, Spector se había situado en el rincón más alejado del salón de baile mientras se fumaba sus cigarrillos y despojaba a Teasel de varias copas de licor. Aunque el mago se enorgullecía de sus habilidades observacionales casi insólitas, tenía que admitir que la noche de la fiesta no había sido su mejor momento. Cuando se habían acercado a él, se había concentrado demasiado en entretener a sus compañeros con varios trucos viejos de cartas y monedas como para prestar toda su atención a Teasel y a Della.

Estaba seguro de que, en algún momento, Benjamin Teasel y Della Cookson habían abandonado la fiesta y habían subido al piso superior. Habían estado fuera unos diez minutos y entonces, al regresar, la actriz se había despedido de forma apresurada y se había marchado de la fiesta de manera definitiva. Eso había sido a las once en punto más o menos. Teasel había parecido un poco perplejo ante la partida repentina de su protagonista, aunque no tanto como una hora más tarde, justo a medianoche, cuando se había descubierto el robo.

Se había dirigido a grandes zancadas a la parte delantera de la sala y había mandado parar al trío de *jazz* con un gesto abrupto de las manos.

–¡Damas y caballeros! –había rugido por encima de los murmullos de la multitud–. Nadie va a salir de aquí. Se ha producido un robo.

–¿Y qué se llevó? –quiso saber Flint.

–Solo un objeto. Un cuadro. *El nacimiento*, obra del Español Loco, Manolito Espina.

–¿Y por qué está tan seguro de que fue Della la que se lo llevó?

–Es una suposición. Fue la única que abandonó la fiesta y, por lo tanto, la única a la que no registraron.

–¿No es posible que un ladrón entrara en la casa desde el exterior?

–Todas las puertas y ventanas estaban bien cerradas. Excepto en el caso de la puerta principal. Sin embargo, Teasel había puesto allí a dos criadas para que recibieran a los rezagados. Ambas aseguraron que no había habido ningún intruso.

–Bueno, desde luego, es algo muy extraño.

–De hecho, esta mañana, justo antes de que haya llegado usted, he estado hablando con Benjamin Teasel. Está más que decidido a recuperar su posesión.

–¿Qué le ha dicho?

–Quiere que investigue el caso.

Flint se recostó en su asiento, incrédulo.

–¿Por qué?

Spector se encogió de hombros.

–Confía en mí. Sabe que tengo cierta mano con estas cosas.

–¿Le ha dicho algo más?

–Sí. Me ha dado su versión de los acontecimientos de anoche.

–Ven conmigo, quiero mostrarte algo.

Con una Della Cookson achispada del brazo, Benjamin Teasel salió del salón de baile donde la fiesta estaba en todo su apogeo. La condujo por unas escaleras de caracol hasta una pequeña habitación secundaria. De un cordón que llevaba al cuello colgaban un par de llaves: una grande y otra pequeña. Abrió la puerta con la grande.

–¿Por qué me has traído aquí arriba, Benny? –preguntó Della en medio de la oscuridad con un susurro juguetón.

–Voy a enseñarte algo. Algo que sé que te va a gustar. Después de todo, eres una persona con mucha cultura y sensibilidad.

La luz de la luna se colaba a través de una única ventana dentro de aquella habitación de invitados escasamente amueblada. Con un gruñido de dolor, Teasel se arrodilló junto a la estrecha cama individual y de debajo de ella sacó un baúl grande de madera. Abrió dicho baúl con la llave pequeña que llevaba al cuello y levantó la tapa.

–Mira –dijo mientras hacía un gesto para que Della se acercara.

Y allí, con el palpitar y el escándalo provocado por el *jazz* y el baile que transcurría a sus pies, la actriz contempló por primera y última vez el tesoro de Benjamin Teasel. Mirándolos desde el interior del baúl forrado de terciopelo había un cuadro rectangular con un marco dorado de madera.

–Dios mío –dijo Della.

–Lo sé… –contestó él, radiante de orgullo–. ¿No es precioso?

Intentar describir una obra semejante es, inevitablemente, una tarea inútil. El arte se encuentra en algún punto entre el sujeto y el lienzo. Sin embargo, el cuadro representaba a una mujer joven con un bebé en brazos. El rostro de la mujer era liso como la porcelana y su piel estaba dotada del resplandor rosáceo del júbilo y la inocencia beatífica. El niño, con los ojos cerrados y la boca en medio de un grito, estaba representado a la perfección. Casi podías oír su llanto.

–*El nacimiento,* de Manolito Espina –anunció Teasel–. ¿No es divino? –Della estaba mirando el cuadro con fijación–. Perdona el gesto de grandiosidad de un viejo tonto, pero no podía resistirme a la oportunidad de compartirlo con alguien que de verdad fuese a apreciarlo.

–¿Cómo lo has conseguido? –preguntó la actriz.

–En uno de mis viajes –respondió él–. De una persona que no

tenía mucha idea del auténtico valor de la obra. ¿Y bien, Della? ¿Qué tienes que decir?

–Es... deslumbrante –le dijo sin apartar los ojos del lienzo–. ¿Qué vas a hacer con él?

–¿Que qué voy a hacer? Della, es mío. No tengo que hacer nada con él.

–¿No vas a compartirlo o a exponerlo o algo así?

–Nunca expondría algo así, sería demasiado vulgar. Desvirtuaría lo que en esencia es una experiencia religiosa. Y en cuanto a compartirlo..., bueno, lo estoy compartiendo contigo ahora mismo.

–¿Y vas a dejarlo aquí, debajo de la cama?

–Puede que tú no lo sepas, Della, querida –comenzó a decir Teasel–, pero este cuadro está vivo. Respira. Por eso lo guardo en esta habitación y en este baúl. Esta es la única habitación de la casa que tiene el aire adecuado. El cuadro es una cosita malhumorada a la que no le gustan ni los rayos de sol ni los cambios de temperatura. Ambas cosas harían que se resquebrajara y se doblara. Pero, bajo la luz de la luna, resulta sencillamente sublime.

Della estaba de acuerdo. Con aquel marco de madera de un color dorado turbulento no cabía ninguna duda: era auténtico.

A Teasel se le arrugaron las comisuras de los labios como si estuviera satisfecho. Había conseguido el efecto deseado.

–Dame tu veredicto sincero.

–Eh... –comenzó a decir ella.

Entonces, se tambaleó hacia un lado y rozó a Teasel con el codo. Él cerró el baúl de golpe e introdujo con fuerza la llave en la cerradura. Con un giro rápido de la muñeca, *El nacimiento* quedó a salvo. Entonces, volvió a colgarse ambas llaves del cuello y centró toda su atención en su protagonista.

–¡Querida! ¿Qué ocurre?

–Nada –contestó ella con suavidad–. Nada de nada.

Tenía la mirada fija en el baúl.

Teasel la condujo escaleras abajo de vuelta a la fiesta. No sin antes cerrar con llave la puerta que estaba a su espalda.

–Creo que voy a dar la noche por terminada –dijo Della por encima del estruendo de la banda.

–Si eso es lo que quieres, corazón... –dijo el hombre.

Ella enrolló los brazos en torno a su figura pequeña y rotunda y le dio un beso en la mejilla.

Joseph Spector la alcanzó cuando iba de camino a la puerta.

–¿Ocurre algo, Della?

–Tengo que ir a ver a alguien –dijo ella.

–¿Va todo bien?

Pero ya se había marchado. La puerta se cerró tras ella. Todavía no estaba lloviendo y en las calles reinaba un silencio sepulcral. Spector oyó sus tacones repiqueteando sobre la piedra mientras se alejaba.

Manolito Espina, que había fallecido en 1820, era tan conocido por su ignominiosa caída en la locura durante la última década de su vida como por los lienzos que le habían sobrevivido. Su cuadro más célebre, *El patio del fin del mundo*, se encontraba actualmente en la National Gallery. Incluso en el momento presente seguía causando indignación entre los sectores más conservadores de la sociedad. ¡Que una pieza de tal naturaleza hubiera sido colocada en un entorno tan propicio...!

El epíteto que se había granjeado en vida y que todavía mancillaba su legado era «el desquiciado», «el demente». La gente tendía a olvidar que Espina no era un simple esquizofrénico y la imagen que se tenía de él como un loco babeante había sido difícil de disipar. Sin embargo, *El nacimiento* había sido el resultado de sus felices años de juventud, de una época anterior a que la locura se posara sobre su vida. Los rasgos de los personajes resultaban tan suaves y delicados que uno casi podría estirar la mano y tocarlos.

La idea que la mayoría de la gente tenía de Manolito Espina era la del ermitaño loco que embadurnaba los lienzos de oscuridad y depravación. Sin embargo, la adquisición de Teasel era obra de un artista más joven y sensible. El bebé que estaba llorando en brazos de su madre, la sensación real de afecto maternal que desprendían los ojos de la mujer y que, de algún modo, trascendían al simple material y a la pintura... En aquel momento, la gente asociaba a Espina con carne destrozada y hecha jirones y castigos bíblicos, con los horrores de la Inquisición o, por otro lado, con un torbellino de espíritus oscuros y malvados. Sin embargo, algo así implicaba desatender su capacidad para capturar las fragilidades humanas más benignas. Emoción y afecto, amor en estado puro, como un corazón a pecho descubierto. Los sujetos de *El nacimiento* eran anónimos, lo cual solo servía para aumentar esa sensación de milagro etéreo y hacer que uno se preguntase si, después de todo, el español loco estaba tan loco de verdad.

Los únicos hechos comprobados eran que Teasel había poseído el cuadro hasta la noche anterior y ahora ya no. Había estado encerrado en una caja dentro de una habitación. Solo había una llave para la habitación y otra para la caja, y ambas habían colgado de una cadena en torno al cuello del productor. Las llaves habían resplandecido bajo las lámparas mientras el anfitrión bailaba con sus invitados. Y, entonces, como en un truco de magia, ambas llaves habían desaparecido junto con el cuadro.

La fiesta se había interrumpido y se había llamado a la policía. Se había contado y registrado a todo el mundo, a todos y cada uno de los invitados. Aquello había causado una indignación considerable. Incluso Spector había tenido que soportar semejante humillación. Sin embargo, el cuadro había desaparecido. Y la única invitada que no había estado presente había sido Della Cookson.

Cuando Spector hubo terminado de relatarle todos estos acontecimientos al inspector, Flint se quedó sentado un momento, mirando de forma pensativa la cabeza de ciervo que había sobre la chimenea.

–¿Y qué hay del marco? –preguntó el policía.

–Oh, ha desaparecido todo. No hay ni rastro ni del cuadro ni del marco –dijo el viejo mago con un tono casi alegre–. La ventana estaba cerrada por dentro, pero, de todos modos, era demasiado pequeña como para haber sacado el cuadro. En resumidas cuentas, teniendo en cuenta el marco de madera dorada, *El nacimiento* tiene unos sesenta centímetros de alto y treinta de ancho.

La ventana del dormitorio apenas tiene unos veinte centímetros. ¿Con qué nos deja eso? Nos deja con el hecho de que tuvieron que bajar el cuadro por alguna de las escaleras. Si lo hubieran bajado por las escaleras del servicio, tendrían que haber atravesado el salón de baile hasta la puerta principal. Me cuesta creer que pasara desapercibido incluso hasta para el más ferviente de los fiesteros. Eso nos deja con la escalera principal, que está en el vestíbulo. Pero durante toda la fiesta hubo siempre una criada a los pies de la misma. Y, sin duda, el espectáculo de uno de los invitados cargando con un cuadro enorme y valioso habría llamado la atención. Supongo que comprenderá que esto resulta en un problema bastante espinoso. Creo que estará de acuerdo conmigo.

–Tendré que interrogar a Teasel –dijo Flint.

–No se lo recomiendo.

–¿Por qué?

–Porque se cerrará en banda. Recuerde que es posible que consiguiera el cuadro de algún modo poco escrupuloso. Ni siquiera quería que la gente supiera que lo tenía, así que, si un inspector aparece en su puerta parloteando sobre un asesinato, le puedo asegurar que saldrá corriendo a voz en grito en busca del primer abogado que encuentre.

Flint gruñó.

–Tal vez tenga razón. Por lo que me está contando, tengo la impresión de que no ha conseguido asegurarlo. Pero ¿qué tiene todo esto que ver con la muerte de Rees?

–No lo sé. Probablemente, nada. Sin embargo, lo que es innegable es que anoche Della Cookson estuvo en la escena de no uno, sino de dos crímenes importantes: un robo de arte y un asesinato imposible. Así que estoy seguro de que tendrá muchas cosas que contarnos. –Spector se sacó un cigarrillo de detrás de la oreja, se lo puso entre los labios y lo encendió con una cerilla–. Pero creo que es mejor que esperemos a que llegue el momento adecuado. Conozco a Della y se parece bastante a un cervatillo o cualquier otra criatura del bosque similar. Si nos acercamos demasiado o con demasiado ímpetu, saldrá corriendo.

–Qué irritables son ustedes, la gente del teatro, ¿no? –comentó Flint con un gesto irónico en los labios.

–Bueno –dijo el mago–, será mejor que nos pongamos en marcha, ¿no cree?

–¿Adónde iremos?

Spector tomó su mazo de cartas y, con una sacudida de los dedos, las hizo desaparecer.

–¿Cómo que adónde? A Dollis Hill, por supuesto –dijo.

VI

Der Schlangenmann

La casa de los Rees estaba repleta de oficiales uniformados. El cadáver había desaparecido, pero la alfombra del despacho del difunto doctor estaba manchada de sangre seca y del aire colgaba un aroma cobrizo. Flint y Spector, que iba ataviado con su capa y su bastón plateado, escudriñaron la habitación a la luz del día. Pero, como era de esperar, solo pudieron llegar a una conclusión: la puerta había estado cerrada cuando el doctor había muerto. Las ventanas, también. Y, una vez cerradas, habían sido impenetrables. Spector incluso echó un vistazo al baúl de madera vacío, pero no había nada que ver.

–¿Dónde está la hija del doctor? –preguntó.

–En la sala de estar.

–¿Podría hablar con ella?

–Por supuesto.

Flint lo condujo fuera del estudio hasta la salita adyacente. Con su figura recortada contra el ventanal salpicado de lluvia, Lidia Rees resultaba discreta y escultural.

–¿Y quién es usted? –preguntó.

–Soy Joseph Spector –contestó el anciano–. Lamento mucho su pérdida.

–Gracias por su preocupación. Ya le había visto antes, ¿verdad? En el teatro, hace dos noches.

Con los ojos claramente secos y mostrándose casi clínica en su análisis de los acontecimientos de la noche, la joven respondió las preguntas de Spector de forma abierta.

–Si entiendo bien la situación –dijo Lidia con frialdad–, mi padre fue asesinado en circunstancias que no son posibles. Fue víctima de algo siniestro. Se podría decir que lo mató un fantasma.

–Bueno –replicó el mago con un tono claro y sofisticado–, eso es lo que hemos venido a determinar.

–Marcus y yo estuvimos juntos toda la velada. Salimos a cenar y después a tomar unas copas al Palmyra.

–Ya veo. Así que fueron a cenar… ¿Dónde?

–Al Savoy. Llegamos a las ocho. Tendrán la reserva anotada en sus registros y no creo que le vayan a faltar testigos. Estuvimos allí más o menos hasta las diez. El *maître d'hôtel* podrá darle una idea más acertada de las horas. En el Savoy nos subimos directos a un taxi. Me temo que no tengo el número, pero tal vez el portero pueda ayudarle.

–Y, de ahí, ¿directos al Palmyra?

–Correcto. Fue un viaje de diez minutos y, sin duda, el portero del club podrá dar fe de nuestra llegada.

–¿Cuánto tiempo estuvieron allí?

–Al menos hasta media noche. Me temo que no puedo estar segura, pero Marcus corroborará mi coartada, así como yo la suya. Volvimos a casa juntos. El resto ya lo conoce.

–Ya veo. ¿Qué puede contarnos usted de los pacientes de su padre?

–Tenía tres, solo tres. A menudo, mi padre comenta… comentaba sus casos conmigo –se corrigió a sí misma–. También tenía acceso a sus notas. Se trataba de una cuestión meramente profesional, ya me entiende. No conocía a ninguno de ellos a nivel personal.

–Pero sin duda los veía, ¿no?

–Nunca estuve presente durante las sesiones.

–¿Y quién era el primero?

–El Paciente A, como mi padre lo llama en sus notas, es Floyd Stenhouse, el concertista. Fue el primero que vino en busca de mi padre cuando llegamos a este país. La Paciente B es Della Cookson, a quien ya conoce. El Paciente C es el novelista Claude Weaver. Vino por su esposa, que estaba preocupada por el estado de su salud mental.

–¿Podría darme algún detalle sobre los tratamientos que ofrecía el doctor?

–Las notas de mi padre son muy meticulosas. Lo tiene todo ahí. Más allá de eso, no hay mucho más que yo pueda contarle.

–¿Nada personal? ¿Ninguna observación, por pequeña que sea?

–Perdóneme –dijo Lidia–, pero mi mente no funciona de forma adecuada.

–¿Nada en absoluto? ¿Ninguna señal de animosidad, irritación o capacidad de ejercer violencia?

Ella miró a Spector fijamente.

–Revise las notas. Si la respuesta ha de estar en alguna parte, será ahí.

–Discúlpeme por decir esto –insistió el mago–, pero parece usted muy tranquila y calmada teniendo en cuenta las circunstancias.

Lidia lo contempló sin pestañear.

–La triste verdad del asunto es que mi padre murió hace mucho tiempo. La parte de él que podía pensar y sentir cayó muerta muchos años antes incluso de que nos marcháramos de Viena. Su muerte corporal no ha sido más que una secuela inevitable.

–¿Qué quiere decir con eso?

Ella suspiró y se preparó para abordar lo que resultaba evidente que era un asunto problemático.

–En Viena, los periódicos lo llamaban «*Der Schlangenmann*». «El Hombre Serpiente».

–¿A quién?

–Era uno de los pacientes de mi padre, un caso muy inquietante. Por supuesto, ocurrió hace muchos años. Yo solo tenía diez.

–Disculpe –les interrumpió Flint–, pero ¿es esto relevante para el asesinato de su padre?

–Estoy segura de que sí. El Hombre Serpiente estaba obsesionado con un sueño recurrente en el que lo aterrorizaba una serpiente inmensa. Mi padre diagnosticó adecuadamente que estaba sufriendo de paranoia filial. La serpiente era su hija y el sueño indicaba una unión insana e insidiosa entre ambos. Todo esto es de dominio público, ya que mi padre publicó muchas notas sobre el caso.

–¿Y cree que el Hombre Serpiente fue el causante del asesinato de anoche?

Lidia lo miró pestañeando y se mordió el labio.

–¿Era capaz de hacer algo así?

La joven suspiró.

–Esto es un problema tanto de psicología como de patología. Lo que tienen que tener en cuenta es que mi padre era un virtuoso de la mente y que, con toda probabilidad, él ya se hubiese planteado todos y cada uno de los pensamientos que les están atravesando la cabeza mientras hablamos. Están siguiendo el camino exacto que él trazó para ustedes.

Flint se recostó en su asiento.

–¿Quiere decir que es una especie de doble farol? ¿Que creó un crimen imposible para ocultar el hecho de que no se trataba de un crimen en absoluto?

Ella se encogió de hombros.

–El detective es usted. Lo único que puedo decirle es que mi padre está muerto. Sin embargo, el caso del Hombre Serpiente tiene cierta simetría bilateral con las circunstancias actuales, ¿no le parece? *Der Schlangenmann* se cortó la garganta, inspector. Un único tajo transversal causado con una navaja de afeitar. Sin embargo, la violencia y el salvajismo puro de ese único corte fue suficiente para casi decapitarlo. ¿Puede imaginarse el tormento que llevaría a alguien a cometer semejante abominación contra sí mismo?

–No –contestó Flint con una solemnidad estridente–, me temo que no puedo.

–Mi padre sí –añadió Lidia–. Tal vez debería pensar en ello.

Poco después, dejaron sola a Lidia. Estaba claro que no tenía nada más que contarles.

–Quiero ver al ama de llaves –le dijo Spector a Flint en susurros mientras salían del estudio.

La encontraron en la cocina. Se estaba esforzando mucho por fingir que los acontecimientos de la noche anterior no eran más que una pesadilla. Daba vueltas de un lado para otro limpiando el polvo, poniendo teteras a hervir y, en general, haciendo un gran trabajo a la hora de parecer ocupada.

Olive Turner tenía un rostro que podía describirse como amable. Tenía los ojos oscuros y profundos y el labio superior un poco curvado, lo que le daba un aspecto de serenidad casi bíblica. Tenía unos cincuenta años, era una viuda sin hijos, se vestía con trajes voluminosos y chaquetas de lana y se peinaba con rizos muy apretados. En su aspecto y su porte había una modestia que se contradecía con su estridente acento del este de Londres, conocido afectuosamente entre sus amigos como «graznido de pescadera».

Cuando al fin la hubo convencido de que se sentara a la mesa de la cocina, Spector comenzó a interrogarla con amabilidad.

–¿Le gusta su patrona?

–¿La señorita Rees? Sin duda. Es una jovencita dulce e inteligente.

–Nos ha contado que anoche salió con su novio. ¿Es cierto?

–Sí. Él la había llamado antes.

–¿Por teléfono?

–Sí.

–¿Y habló usted con él?

–Así es, la señorita Rees no quería hablar con él, así que yo tomé el mensaje.

Spector frunció el ceño.

–¿No le pareció eso un poco extraño?

–Bueno, ahora que lo menciona, sí. Pero, en fin, es una chica peculiar. Es difícil comprenderla, ¿sabe lo que quiero decir?

–¿Le pareció que estaba enfadada?

–Un poco, pero, bueno, siempre parece bastante airada. Es su forma de ser. Ya sabe cómo son estos europeos... Que Dios los bendiga.

–Pero, cuando él llegó a recogerla, ¿no dio ningún indicio de ello?

–Yo no estaba presente, señor. Estaba en la cocina, preparando la cena del doctor.

–¿Qué cenó?

–Ternera, señor. Y patatas.

–¿Se lo comió todo?

–Sí, señor. Y el queso que le llevé como tentempié también.

–Bien, señora Turner, voy a hacerle una pregunta y no quiero que se alarme, pero necesito que sea sincera y me conteste con todo el detalle que pueda.

El ama de llaves tragó saliva.

–Haré todo lo que sea posible por ayudar.

–Necesito que me hable del hombre que visitó la casa anoche.

Los ojos de la mujer se oscurecieron como si fueran nubes de tormenta.

–Lo único que puedo decirle, señor, es que espero no volver a verlo en lo que me queda de vida.

VII
Dufresne Court

Spector y Flint se marcharon de forma apresurada de Dollis Hill. El mago afirmaba haber visto todo lo que tenía que ver. Sin embargo, también parecía extrañamente insatisfecho.

–Bueno, ¿cómo seguimos adelante? –preguntó el inspector una vez que hubieron regresado al vehículo.

Spector meditó la respuesta.

–Ha mencionado usted algo sobre una llamada telefónica.

–¿Se refiere a la de Floyd Stenhouse? ¿El paciente A? Llamó a la casa y habló por teléfono con el doctor Rees apenas un minuto o dos antes del asesinato.

Spector asintió.

–Bien, vamos a visitarlo a continuación –dijo mientras se alejaban a toda velocidad.

Cuando no estaba de gira mundial con la Filarmónica, Floyd Stenhouse vivía en un apartamento de estilo *art decó* en Dufresne Court, cerca de los jardines de Cranley. La fachada del edificio no parecía más que una losa lúgubre e impersonal, como una imagen distópica sacada de una película de Murnau.

Dufresne Court era un bloque de sesenta apartamentos apilados en seis pisos. La fachada curvada daba a Quarterhouse Square. Estaba construida con ladrillos beis y decorada con parteluces brutalistas. Se trataba de una residencia de lujo en la que un hombre podía perderse a sí mismo o esconderse del mundo. La dirección de Stenhouse se encontraba en el cuarto piso. Desde la acera exterior, Spector alzó la vista e intentó encontrar la ventana indicada, lo cual acabó siendo una tarea inútil, ya que resultó que el apartamento de Stenhouse daba al patio empedrado que estaba en la parte trasera del edificio y no se veía desde la calle.

Spector y Flint entraron en el recibidor cubierto de mármol. El inspector se dirigió con decisión hacia el mostrador principal. Desde allí, el portero los observaba tras su libro de registros.

–¿Puedo ayudarlos, caballeros?

–Sí puede –contestó Flint mientras dejaba con fuerza sobre el mostrador su tarjeta de identificación–. Hemos venido a ver a Floyd Stenhouse.

–¿Está esperando su visita, señor?

El tipo parecía muy tranquilo.

Flint se inclinó hacia delante y arrugó con los codos las hojas del libro de registros.

–No sea tonto. ¿Dónde está?

–Cuatro, cero, ocho. Cuarto piso.

Spector también se inclinó hacia él.

–¿Y cómo se llama usted, señor?

El portero se sobresaltó de manera casi cómica, como si fuese la primera vez que le hacían semejante pregunta.

–Royce –contestó–. Me llamo Royce.

Spector chasqueó los dedos y de la nada sacó una tarjeta de visita.

–Dígame un número, Royce. Del uno al diez. Rápido, sea bueno.

Desconcertado, el hombre dijo:

–Siete.

–¡Ah! –El mago parecía complacido–. Eso pensaba. –Le dio la vuelta a la tarjeta con los dedos para revelar que, en la parte trasera, escrito a mano, estaba el número siete. Se la tendió al portero–. Guárdesela como recuerdo de este día, Royce.

Después, se alejó como si nada.

–¿Qué ha sido eso? –le preguntó Flint mientras se dirigían hacia el ascensor.

–Elemental, si me perdona la flagrante apropiación: una pizca de grafito bajo la uña del pulgar.

–No, lo que quiero decir es: ¿por qué quería hablar con el portero?

–Arrogancia. Es una enfermedad muy extendida entre los porteros de los bloques de apartamentos de la clase alta. He descubierto que viene bien pillarlos por sorpresa de vez en cuando.

Flint había empezado a notar algo interesante sobre Joseph Spector. El «viejo» parecía volverse más viejo o más joven dependiendo de con quién estuviera hablando y de cuál fuese la opción que le ofreciera una mayor ventaja. Era una transformación sutil y casi imperceptible, pero tremendamente efectiva. Relajaba los hombros y enderezaba la columna. Podía ganar hasta unos ocho centímetros de altura. Pero lo que resultaba todavía más inquietante era que su rostro se volvía más joven. Las arrugas se esfumaban y los ojos pálidos se le oscurecían. Entonces, ese bastón plateado suyo se convertía en un mero accesorio de moda. En otras ocasiones, se encogía y marchitaba y su fragilidad física se volvía más pronunciada. Incluso era posible que su voz desarrollara un trasfondo tembloroso que resultaba incómodo. Verdaderamente excepcional. Podía envejecer varias décadas delante de tus propios ojos. En muchos sentidos, aquel era el truco más fascinante que el inspector le había visto hacer jamás.

El muchacho del ascensor parecía un refugiado procedente de uno de los más estimados hoteles estadounidenses. Llevaba un uniforme rojo con ribetes dorados y un sombrerito sin ala atado a la cabeza con una correa. Tendría unos dieciséis años y rebotaba sobre los pies con aire jovial mientras los dejaba acceder a sus dominios.

–¿Tienen amigos en el edificio? –les preguntó con alegría mientras subían.

Flint miró al muchacho con la mandíbula apretada. Spector, por el contrario, se mostró más sociable.

–Venimos a visitar a un caballero que vive en el cuarto piso: el señor Stenhouse.

–Aaah –dijo el chico–. Eso lo explica todo.

–¿Qué es lo que explica? –preguntó Flint con aspereza.

–Han venido a llevárselo, ¿no? Siempre he dicho que está chalado.

–¿Por qué dices eso?

–Es un... ¿Cómo lo llaman? Un ermitaño. Le da miedo el mundo y todo lo que hay en él. Nunca entenderé cómo alguien como él puede sobrevivir en Londres.

–¿Cómo te llamas, jovencito?
–Pete Hobbs, señor.
–¿Y cuánto tiempo llevas trabajando aquí?
–Un año, más o menos, señor.
–¿Puedes contarnos algo específico sobre su comportamiento?
Pete Hobbs entrecerró los ojos y se quedó mirando a la nada en una pantomima de seria reflexión.
–Tiene unas costumbres muy asentadas. Por ejemplo, la semana pasada, vinieron a arreglar el ascensor. ¡Caramba! Cualquiera hubiera dicho que era el fin del mundo. El señor Stenhouse tuvo una buena bronca con los de recepción: no dejaba de gritar sobre las molestias que le estaban ocasionando.
–¿Algo más?
–Es un tacaño, no da propinas. También toca el puñetero violín a todas horas, si me perdonan la forma de hablar.
Flint y Spector intercambiaron una mirada divertida.
–¿Y eso es todo? –preguntó el inspector.
–Con todos mis respetos, señor, creo que eso ya es más que suficiente.
Con un estruendo, el ascensor llegó a su destino. Pete abrió la jaula de un tirón y se quedó a la espera mientras los pasajeros salían. Casi como si se le acabara de ocurrir, el mago le entregó media corona.
–Es usted muy amable, señor –dijo el chico–. Que Dios le bendiga.
–Bueno, ¿qué opina? –le preguntó Spector al otro hombre en voz baja mientras recorrían el pasillo el uno al lado del otro.
–Creo que ese Stenhouse parece un candidato ideal para el tratamiento de Rees.
Llamaron a la puerta del apartamento 408.
–¿Quién es? –respondieron desde el interior.
–El inspector Flint, señor. De Scotland Yard.
La puerta se abrió una rendija. El hombre que los recibió, el Paciente A, no era en absoluto lo que Spector había esperado. Para empezar, porque era alto. Tanto hablar de su fragilidad emocional había hecho que el mago se hiciera una imagen mental

de una figura casi de gnomo acechando entre las sombras. Sin embargo, aquel tipo medía más de un metro ochenta y estaba un poco encorvado, aunque tenía las extremidades estrechas y angulares, como la decoración del edificio.

Su rostro, redondo como un plato, era bastante apuesto en un sentido muy poco imaginativo. Era lo que un niño pequeño dibujaría si le pidieran que dibujara a un héroe o a una estrella del cine. Sin embargo, le faltaba definición o expresión y, además, pestañeaba demasiado con esos ojos oscuros y un poco juntos.

–¿La policía? ¿Qué quieren?

–Creo que era usted paciente del doctor Anselm Rees.

Stenhouse tomó aire con brusquedad.

–«Era»... –repitió.

–Sí. Me temo que al doctor Rees le ha ocurrido algo. De hecho, lo han asesinado.

Cualquiera que fuera la reacción que Spector había esperado, no había sido esa. El músico se limitó a apartarse para dejarles pasar a su apartamento.

–Siento informarle de este modo, señor –prosiguió Flint–. Ocurrió anoche.

–«Asesinado»... –repitió Stenhouse, pronunciando la palabra con un deleite casi palpable.

–Por lo que, como es natural, necesitamos interrogar a todos los pacientes del difunto doctor para poder hacernos una idea de quién podría haber querido hacerle algo así.

Entonces, el dique estalló y Stenhouse dejó escapar un torrente de verborrea ilimitada.

–Caballeros, deben perdonarme; no estoy acostumbrado a recibir visitas a esta hora y las noticias que me traen no son solo sorprendentes, sino profundamente inquietantes para mí a un nivel muy personal. Se trata de un crimen atroz, lo peor de lo peor, y quiero que sepan que haré todo lo que pueda para ayudarlos a atrapar a ese malnacido. Sea lo que sea, solo tienen que pedírmelo. Verán, el doctor Rees era un héroe para mí, un ídolo, el único hombre al que confiaría mis sueños, mis secretos y los horrores de mi desdichado cerebro...

Flint lo interrumpió.

–Ocurrió anoche, en torno a la media noche. ¿Dónde se encontraba usted?

Stenhouse se quedó petrificado.

–«En torno a la media noche»... –repitió. Aquellas repeticiones eran un tic alarmante–. A media noche estaba aquí, en la cama.

–¿Hay alguien que pueda corroborarlo?

Al músico le tembló el párpado.

–¿Qué quiere decir con eso? Les estoy diciendo la verdad. Estaba aquí, en la cama. De hecho...

En ese momento, perdió el hilo.

–¿Sí? –insistió Spector.

–Justo antes de las doce... hice una llamada de teléfono.

–¿Qué puede contarnos de la llamada?

–Llevo mucho tiempo sufriendo pesadillas. Pero no son pesadillas normales. Temo las horas tras el crepúsculo. El doctor Rees me ha estado ayudando a encontrarles sentido. Tanto a las pesadillas como a mi cerebro. Anoche me fui a la cama sobre las once. Tuve un sueño muy inquietante del que me desperté sobre las once y media. Estaba tan alterado que de inmediato telefoneé al doctor. Fue algo impetuoso por mi parte, lo admito, pero necesitaba hablar con alguien.

–Así que habló con él a las once y media... ¿Cómo le pareció que se encontraba?

–Totalmente normal. Un poco preocupado de que le hubiera llamado tan tarde, pero admito que es algo comprensible.

–Entonces, para confirmar... –dijo el inspector–, ¿no tiene ninguna manera de demostrar que estuvo aquí solo toda la noche?

Stenhouse se mostró insultado.

–Puede preguntarle al chico del ascensor, Pete. Él les dirá que no salí para nada.

–Bueno, nos dirá que no usó el ascensor, pero, sin duda, un gran edificio moderno como este poseerá tanto un ascensor como una escalera.

El músico habló con los dientes apretados.

–Entonces, hablen con el portero. O con el asistente nocturno.

Les dirán que no salí, que estuve aquí toda la noche. Además, deben de tener el registro de la llamada telefónica.

Flint asintió.

–Por favor, no nos malinterprete –dijo, mostrándose conciliador de pronto–, tan solo necesitamos esclarecer todos los hechos. No pretendo ofenderle.

–Bueno, pues debería tener cuidado con cómo le habla a la gente. De entre todas las personas del mundo, yo jamás haría nada que le causara algún daño al doctor Rees. De verdad, él era el único que podría haberme ayudado. Era un hombre tan noble... Como todos los vieneses. Una vez fui allí con la Filarmónica. Una ciudad maravillosa.

–En cuanto a la conversación telefónica... –intervino Spector, intentando volver a encarrilar la conversación–. ¿Puede contarnos algo específico que le dijera el doctor? ¿Algo fuera de lo normal o que le resultara raro de algún modo?

Stenhouse lo meditó.

–Me regañó por llamar tan tarde, pero también estuvo de acuerdo en que el sueño era interesante. Tomó nota para que pudiéramos hablar de ello más tarde. Y me invitó a visitarlo mañana..., es decir, hoy.

–¿Y en qué consistía el sueño?

–¿Qué tiene que ver eso con todo lo demás?

Spector dibujó una sonrisita avergonzada.

–Simple curiosidad. Estoy seguro de que no tiene importancia.

–El sueño queda entre el doctor Rees y yo. No quiero discutirlo con ustedes y tampoco pueden obligarme a hacerlo sin una orden judicial.

–Creo que nos costaría incluso con una orden –comentó Flint.

–Muy bien. Ahora, por favor, déjenme solo. No me encuentro bien.

–¿Ha hecho renovaciones en casa recientemente, señor Stenhouse? –preguntó Spector mientras miraba el apartamento.

Un pequeño despertador redondo que había junto a la ventana le llamó la atención. Pensó que estaba en un lugar curioso. ¿Acaso Stenhouse tenía tendencia a quedarse dormido junto a la ventana?

–¿Renovaciones?

–Me ha parecido oler a pintura.

–Una alucinación olfativa –dijo el músico–. Un psiquiatra podría ayudarle con eso.

Flint y Spector abandonaron el apartamento poco después mientras Stenhouse se servía un *whisky* escocés de una bandeja que tenía en un mueble cercano. El hombre se lo bebió de golpe y, cuando volvió a dejar el vaso, no hizo ningún ruido, sino que lo posó en silencio sobre la suavidad de un posavasos.

Cuando se disponían a salir de Dufresne Court, Flint se desvió hacia el mostrador principal.

–¿Estaba usted de servicio anoche? –le preguntó al portero.

–Así es, señor –replicó Royce.

–¿Vio a Floyd Stenhouse en algún momento de la velada?

–¿Al señor Stenhouse? Me parece que no.

–¿No bajó al recibidor para nada?

–No que yo viera. Ahora que me acuerdo..., anoche estuvo tocando en un concierto. Volvió a casa sobre las diez en punto.

–¿Subió directamente a su apartamento?

–Sí, señor.

–¿Y no volvió a bajar?

–No, señor.

–¿Hay alguna otra manera de que hubiera podido salir del edificio sin que lo vieran?

–Diría que no. Eso le habría obligado a pasar por las cocinas o por la lavandería. Cualquiera le habría visto y resulta que sé que, a lo largo de toda la noche, hubo personal trabajando en ambas salas.

Flint asintió, satisfecho, y salieron del edificio.

–Entonces, ¿qué tenemos? –preguntó el inspector.

–Varios hilos desparejados. Para empezar, el cuadro de Benjamin Teasel que, al parecer, robó Della Cookson. Aunque no tenemos ni idea de cómo lo sacó delante de las narices de todo el mundo.

–Ajá. ¿Y qué me dice de todas esas tonterías sobre el Hombre Serpiente?

–No lo sé... Cuesta ignorar las similitudes entre ambas muertes, a pesar de que estén separadas por varios países y décadas. Sin embargo, va a ser difícil establecer algo hasta que no descubramos más sobre ese caso. Por ejemplo: ¿se ha planteado que ese tal Hombre Serpiente podría haber dejado atrás familiares que podrían haber culpado a Rees del suicidio del pobre hombre?

–¿Y qué hay de lo que nos ha dicho Lidia? ¿Cree que su padre era lo bastante inteligente o estaba lo bastante loco como para poner en marcha un plan de suicidio semejante?

–Sinceramente, no, pero me he equivocado en otras ocasiones.

Spector continuó andando.

–¿Y qué viene a continuación? –preguntó Flint al fin–. ¿Della Cookson?

–Todavía no. Hemos conocido al Paciente A. Ambos hemos tenido nuestros encontronazos con la Paciente B. Ya es hora de que conozcamos al Paciente C, ¿no le parece?

VIII
El Paciente C

–La triste realidad es que, últimamente, mi marido no ha sido él mismo –dijo Rosemary Weaver.

Estaban sentados en su salón, que tenía unas decoraciones de color verde oliva y un ambiente húmedo y mohoso, y Joseph Spector pensó que jamás había visto una habitación tan fea. Los Weaver vivían en Hampstead y, por casualidad, su casa se encontraba a unas pocas calles de la de Benjamin Teasel.

Sonriendo, Rosemary Weaver les sirvió el té. Tras un inicio nebuloso, el día se había tornado luminoso y despejado. La lluvia de la noche anterior había dejado cierta frescura en el aire.

–¿En qué sentido «no ha sido él mismo»? –preguntó Spector.

–Ha estado callado, reservado. Y hace poco me confesó cierto miedo extraño.

–¿Y de qué miedo estaríamos hablando?

La mujer se inclinó hacia delante. Su voz era un susurro.

–Que tal vez esté perdiendo la cabeza. –Spector y Flint intercambiaron una mirada–. Puedo asegurarles que yo nunca he creído que fuera cierto –insistió ella–. Claude siempre ha sido aprensivo y últimamente ha tenido muchas cosas en la cabeza.

–¿Por eso empezó a visitar al doctor Rees?

–Fue idea mía. Yo me encargo de la mayoría de los negocios de mi marido. Fui yo la que organizó la primera sesión y sigo de cerca sus progresos.

–¿Alguna vez mostró su esposo lo que a usted podrían haberle parecido tendencias violentas?

La señora Weaver se rio abiertamente.

–¡Caballeros! Mi marido es el alma más benevolente que conocerán jamás. No se dejen confundir por esas novelas suyas. Se le da muy bien evocar un ambiente de miedo y suspense, pero en su día a día es un caballero inglés muy educado. Bastante tímido y modesto. Detesta ser el centro de atención.

–¿Puedo preguntarle dónde está ahora?

–En el jardín, pero regresará enseguida.

–Ya veo… Mientras tanto, solo tengo una pregunta más.

–Adelante.

–¿Sabe dónde se encontraba anoche su esposo?

La sonrisa del rostro de la mujer se extendió hasta convertirse en un rictus similar al de una máscara.

–En una reunión con su editor. Pero, sin duda, no me estará diciendo que sospecha que mi marido puede estar involucrado en la muerte del doctor, ¿no? –Al ver el gesto de Flint, explicó–: Mi esposo y yo lo hemos leído en los periódicos de esta mañana.

–Señora, estamos obligados a seguir todas las vías de investigación –contestó el inspector con una pomposidad practicada–. ¿Quién es el editor?

–Se llama Tweedy. A mí nunca me ha gustado. Es bastante vulgar, tal como suelen ser esos nuevos ricos.

En ese momento, para alivio de todos, Claude Weaver entró en la habitación. A diferencia de Stenhouse, su presencia era tranquila y calmada. Iba en mangas de camisa y de los labios le colgaba un cigarrillo. Estaba quedándose calvo y era huesudo, pero su rostro tenía cierto atractivo rubicundo. No pareció sorprendido por la presencia de aquellos dos desconocidos.

–Oh –dijo.

Se hicieron las presentaciones y rápidamente pusieron al escritor al corriente de la situación. Estaba sentado junto a su esposa, asintiendo con lentitud mientras dejaba caer las cenizas del cigarro en una taza de té.

–Su esposa nos ha contado que anoche tuvo una reunión con su editor –comentó Flint.

–Así es, con Tweedy.

–Ya veo… –dijo el inspector mientras tomaba nota en su cuaderno–. Y llevaba una temporada asistiendo a sesiones con el doctor Rees, ¿no es así?

Weaver se aclaró la garganta y, por primera vez, se puso rígido.

–Bueno, sí... Pero, en realidad, es un tema del que no me siento cómodo hablando.

–Puedo garantizarle que esto es absolutamente confidencial. Nuestra única preocupación es atrapar al asesino del doctor. Durante sus sesiones con él, ¿conoció algún detalle de su vida personal?

–Ninguno. Era todo un profesional y se limitaba al asunto que nos ocupaba.

–Sé que es una posibilidad muy remota, pero supongo que nunca le dijo nada que indicara que podía temer por su vida o que tuviera enemigos, ¿verdad?

–Bueno, ¿cómo sería eso posible? Apenas acababa de llegar a este país. Me atrevería a decir que las únicas personas con las que había tratado eran sus pacientes y el resto de habitantes de su casa.

–¿Vio a su hija en algún momento?

–Sí. Aunque solo era cuestión de toparnos en el pasillo y cosas así. Es una joven encantadora –dijo mientras apartaba la mirada de su esposa con determinación. Después, añadió–: Si bien un poco caprichosa.

–¿Y le pareció alguien capaz de ejercer violencia?

–Escuchen –dijo Weaver mientras se inclinaba hacia delante con los codos apoyados en las rodillas–, si algo he aprendido de las sesiones con el pobre doctor Rees, es que cualquiera es capaz de hacer cualquier cosa.

La señora Weaver intercedió en aquel momento.

–En los últimos tiempos, mi marido ha tenido que hacer frente a muchas cosas. Su salud mental no ha sido la mejor.

El escritor se aclaró la garganta.

–Mi esposa siente que tiene que defenderme, pero lo cierto es que he hecho las paces con mis limitaciones. Soy un hombre con predilección por la soledad. Eso puede resultar difícil cuando se tiene una carrera como la mía. Pero, por otro lado, puede tener grandes ventajas. El doctor Rees fue capaz de mostrarme que podía llegar a un acuerdo aceptable conmigo mismo.

–Pero en este caso no estamos hablando solo de misantropía –intervino la señora Weaver–. Cuéntaselo, Claude.

El hombre suspiró. Se quedó un momento sentado, serenándose.

–¿Alguna vez han oído hablar del «estado de fuga»?

Flint sacudió la cabeza con lentitud, pero Spector dijo:

–¿Se refiere a la disociación y las lagunas mentales?

–Correcto. –Se preparó para hablar y continuó–: Es algo que he estado experimentando a lo largo del último año. No es necesario que les diga que es muy preocupante.

–Aunque no es poco habitual –señaló el mago–. Especialmente entre escritores. Sin duda, se acordará de la señora Christie, que desapareció durante once días y volvió a aparecer sin recordar nada. Creo que eso fue en 1926, más o menos cuando publicó *El asesinato de Roger Ackroyd*. Algunos especularon que fue un truco publicitario para promocionar la novela.

–¿«*Ackroyd*»? –preguntó Flint–. Sí, ese lo he leído. Todo el asunto me pareció un timo.

–¿De verdad? –dijo el mago de forma ausente–. Yo me inclino a pensar que es una obra maestra.

–Conocemos a la señora Christie –dijo Rosemary–. Tanto mi esposo como ella ocupan posiciones bastante importantes en el Detection Club.

–¿Cómo se manifiestan sus estados de fuga? –preguntó Spector mientras se inclinaba hacia delante como si, por primera vez, tuviera interés en la conversación.

–Empezaron en enero del año pasado –explicó Weaver–. Aparecí en Bermondsey sin tener ni idea de cómo había llegado allí. Se suponía que tenía que estar en una reunión con Tweedy en ese momento, pero, como es obvio, nunca llegué. Cuando me recuperé, me encontré un billete de tren en el bolsillo y una cartera de cerillas de Robinson's. Ya sabe, del club de caballeros. Como es natural, me quedé preocupado e intenté seguir mis propios pasos. Sin embargo, fui incapaz de hacerlo. No pude encontrar a nadie que me hubiese visto o que hubiese hablado conmigo. Esas pocas horas son un vacío, se han esfumado.

–¿Y le ha vuelto a ocurrir desde entonces?

–Unas pocas veces. Todas ellas inofensivas. Es como acabar piripi y despertarse a la mañana siguiente con un dolor de cabeza terrible. Pero yo no bebo, así que esos estados de fuga han contribuido mucho a dañar mi paz mental, por no mencionar la preocupación que le han causado a mi esposa. No podía escribir. No podía pensar. No podía viajar muy lejos ni nada por el estilo por miedo a perder la noción de mí mismo una vez más.

Flint se aclaró la garganta.

–Pero, para que quede absolutamente claro, señor: supongo que es usted capaz de explicar dónde estuvo cuando asesinaron al doctor, ¿verdad?

Weaver volvió a caer en el buen humor que era típico en él.

–Creo que eso puedo garantizárselo, inspector. Mi buena fe es excepcional, pero estoy seguro de que usted lo va a investigar a fondo.

Flint le devolvió la sonrisa con cautela.

–Eso puede apostarlo, señor.

IX

Notas del caso

–Todo este asunto es un desastre –dijo Flint mientras ambos salían de casa de los Weaver–. Casi me tienta creer en la teoría del suicidio.

Joseph Spector se rio abiertamente.

–Ay, la teoría del suicidio… Sin duda, es muy creativa, eso lo admito. Aunque no es muy práctica. Ya se habrá dado cuenta de que Lidia no nos ha explicado la desaparición del arma. O el hecho de que, al parecer, el visitante masculino salió de la casa y no regresó. Si el visitante hubiese sido el propio Rees, ¿cómo volvió a entrar en el estudio? No podría haber ido hasta el ventanal francés porque, en aquel momento, la lluvia todavía caía con fuerza y hubiera dejado un rastro de huellas en el barro.

–No empiece a sermonearme a mí, viejo. No es mi teoría. Pero he de decir que es mejor que cualquiera de las cosas que se nos han ocurrido a usted o a mí hasta ahora.

–Sí que señala algo interesante con respecto al tal Hombre Serpiente –añadió el mago de forma pensativa–. Y es que hay cierta simetría entre los casos. Al menos a nivel superficial. Tendré que leer sobre ello.

–Tome. –Flint le tendió el tomo forrado de cuero que Lidia le había prestado–. Lléveselo. Desde luego, yo no tengo intención de leérmelo. –Spector tomó el libro y se lo metió dentro de la chaqueta–. Otro misterio es qué demonios ve Lidia Rees en Marcus Bowman –continuó el inspector–. El tipo es un completo zoquete, además de lisonjero, ya que nos ponemos.

–Bueno, no creo que vayamos a comprender nunca los caprichos del corazón humano. Soy mago, pero ninguno de los trucos que he creado ha sido tan duradero e irresoluble.

–No se trata de su cuenta bancaria, eso se lo aseguro. Bowman procede de una familia adinerada de las de toda la vida, pero es derrochador y no está bien formado. Bueno, estudió en Oxford, pero, según mi experiencia, la educación es algo más que aparecer por clase todos los días. Los Bowman tienen una larga historia y ese fondo fiduciario suyo lo ha sacado de muchos problemas en los últimos tiempos.

–¿Qué tipo de problemas?

–Es propenso al lujo. ¿Ha visto ese automóvil amarillo enorme que tiene? Bueno, probablemente no le sorprenderá descubrir que le gusta apostar. Su juego es el póker. Bueno, no es su juego. Lleva unos seis meses sin conseguir una victoria decente, así que las pérdidas se le acumulan.

–Mmm –dijo Spector–. En ese caso, su necesidad repentina de casarse con una debutante rica tiene un poco más de sentido.

–Pero eso sigue sin explicar qué le ve ella. ¿Qué tiene él para ofrecer a una mujer como Lidia Rees?

–Imagino que poder desafiar a su padre. Marcus es el vulgar resultado de una clase alta moribunda. No habría llegado a ninguna parte sin su apellido. No tiene una educación de la que presumir ni habilidades o ingenio. Simboliza el polo opuesto de las ideas políticas y el intelecto de ella. ¿Sabemos cómo está dividida la herencia del doctor Rees en su testamento?

–No está dividida. Todo es para Lidia. Todo: la casa, el dinero, los libros...

Spector pensó en aquello un momento.

–Entonces, si suponemos que lo mataron por su dinero, eso nos deja con una sospechosa viable.

–Pero Lidia no tiene deudas y tampoco le faltaba de nada. A menos que el estado de las deudas de Marcus Bowman sea peor de lo que pensábamos inicialmente –propuso Flint–. Tal vez él quiera apresurar la boda para hacerse con la herencia de Lidia.

–Dudo que ella fuese a caer en un truco así, Flint.

–Tal vez no, pero Marcus se tiene a sí mismo en muy alta estima. No tengo dudas de que también tiende a sobrestimar sus propias habilidades. Tal vez pensó que podría convencerla de que matar a su padre era la mejor opción para ambos.

–Una especie de *folie à deux*... Bueno, cosas más raras se han visto. Pero ¿qué me dice de sus coartadas?

–Hasta donde yo sé, cada uno de ellos corrobora la coartada del otro. No debería costarnos demasiado desacreditarlos.

Los llevaron en coche de policía hasta Scotland Yard. Durante el trayecto, Flint se mostró callado y taciturno mientras miraba por la ventana. Spector se había sumergido en el libro.

Aquella secuencia de casos prácticos detallados era la piedra angular de la reputación como psiquiatra de Anselm Rees. Había aparecido en inglés por primera vez en 1925 con unas ediciones encuadernadas en piel que fueron lectura obligada en todos los salones de París, Londres y cualquier otra capital cultural. De entre el conocimiento teórico se desprendía una salacidad chismosa en referencia a las vidas sexuales de los sujetos anónimos. Era bien sabido que todos los pacientes del doctor eran de alta cuna y buena educación, personas de reputación y, en algunos casos, poder considerable. Sin embargo, no se sabía quiénes eran. Rees no tenía reparos en compartir los detalles más íntimos sobre sus infancias y vidas sexuales, pero jamás había revelado sus identidades. Por lo tanto, recibían nombres informales en clave que, normalmente, estaban relacionados con la naturaleza de sus neurosis. La traducción en inglés hablaba de una tal «Señorita Aracne», cuya aracnofobia era resultado de un incidente desagradable de su niñez. También estaba el «Maniquí del Sastre», un hombre adulto al que no se podía convencer de que se presentara en los bailes de debutantes a causa de un incidente de juventud en el que le habían descubierto probándose los corsés de su madre. Después estaba «*Der Schlangenmann*».

–Yo no veo cómo es posible que ese tal Hombre Serpiente pueda tener algo que ver con el asesinato –dijo Flint. Tal vez estuviera hablando consigo mismo–. Lo que quiero decir es que estamos hablando de alguien que murió hace años, ¿no? Ni siquiera era inglés. Además, ¿cómo es que Lidia sabe tanto sobre él? Tan solo tenía diez años cuando ocurrió...

–Está olvidando que Lidia era tanto hija como estudiante del doctor Rees. Ha estudiado sus fracasos junto con sus triunfos, así que se podría decir que los conoce tan bien como el mismísimo difunto doctor.

–Pero, más allá de la causa de la muerte, que he de admitir que es una sorpresa, en realidad no hay nada que conecte los dos casos. Es un país diferente y un continente diferente y todo ocurrió hace tanto tiempo…

–Sí, tiene razón, pero estamos tratando con personas obsesivas, inspector. Tiene que recordarlo. Para ellos, el tiempo no significa nada.

Cuando llegaron a Scotland Yard, Joseph Spector había terminado su lectura. Mientras subían las escaleras, le hizo un resumen al inspector.

–El difunto doctor era un escritor excelente. En pocos párrafos puede hacerte sentir como si tú mismo estuvieras sentado en la sala de la terapia. Ahora sé muchas cosas sobre el Hombre Serpiente. Como es evidente, más de las que el pobre hombre sabía sobre sí mismo. Sin embargo, no conozco su nombre, y esa es la información que necesitamos si queremos establecer los lazos entre ambos casos.

–Entonces, ¿cree que están relacionados?

–Es eso o que alguien quiera que creamos que existe tal relación. En cualquier caso, cuanto más sepamos sobre el Hombre Serpiente, mejor.

–Bueno, a mí me parece que lo que estamos buscando es a un intruso, alguien que no termine de encajar en este escenario. ¿Está totalmente seguro con respecto a Della Cookson?

–Puedo garantizar que estuvo en casa de Benjamin Teasel hasta más o menos las once. Sin embargo, la casa de Teasel está en Hampstead, por lo que habría tardado en torno a una media hora en llegar a Dollis Hill en taxi.

–Mmm –Flint estaba perplejo–. Entonces, fue directa de un cóctel para pijos a la casa de su psiquiatra. Y, presuntamente, se desvió un momento para depositar el cuadro robado en algún lugar secreto. ¿Por qué cree que fue a Dollis Hill?

–No tengo ni idea. ¿Se lo ha preguntado a ella?

–Claro que le hemos preguntado, pero le estoy preguntando qué cree usted. Tiene cierta agudeza para estas cosas.

Spector sonrió.

–Muy amable por su parte. Y, sea ella la culpable o no, el cuadro parece ser un problema totalmente diferente. Pero, en cuanto a su visita a Rees…, ¿tal vez fuese una cita establecida con antelación?

Flint negó con la cabeza.

–No había nada en los cuadernos del doctor que indicara que fuese así. Aunque sí sabemos que estaba esperando a alguien.

–Cierto. Todo este tiempo ha asumido que el visitante misterioso y sin identificar era el visitante que el doctor estaba esperando, cuando, de hecho, la suya podría haber sido la visita inesperada, mientras que Della podría haber sido desde el principio su auténtica cita.

–Pero seguro que si Della hubiese sido la visitante que estaba esperando el doctor Rees se lo habría dicho a Olive Turner.

Spector se encogió de hombros.

–Tal vez sí o tal vez no.

Eso pareció poner fin a la conversación.

–He estado pensando y se me ha ocurrido que el único que en realidad no encaja en todo este asunto es Marcus Bowman –comenzó Flint.

–Sí, entiendo lo que quiere decir.

–Es un financiero, lo que en el lenguaje de los pijos quiere decir que no hace demasiado, que es un ricachón. Pasa la mayor parte de su tiempo bebiendo y jugando al golf. Su relación con Lidia Rees es bastante desconcertante, pero también me pregunto qué tiene que ver con toda esta saga de psiquiatras, artistas, etcétera.

–Bueno, estoy de acuerdo en que es difícil comprender qué atractivo tiene para Lidia Rees. Más allá de cierta locura juvenil, claro está. Creo que mi mejor suposición es que es el polo totalmente opuesto de su padre, la mismísima antítesis del intelectual estirado.

–Exacto. –Flint sacudió un dedo como si su socio al fin hubiese dado con algo útil–. Puede que ahí haya algo, ¿no cree?

–Es difícil de saber… No lo sabré seguro hasta que conozca al hombre en cuestión.

–Bueno, está de suerte –dijo Flint–, porque nos está esperando en mi oficina.

Habían acordado aquella cita la noche anterior. Marcus Bowman, que había insistido en que no podía permanecer en la casa de Dollis Hill bajo el mismo techo que un cadáver, había recibido permiso para marcharse con la condición de que se presentara en Scotland Yard a la mañana siguiente para dar una declaración completa. No hace falta decir que no le había gustado la cita que le habían dado para las nueve en punto y que había conseguido regatear hasta lograr un hueco a las doce del mediodía. En realidad, cuando apareció, eran las doce y media.

Se acomodó en la oficina de Flint, despatarrado en una silla como si fuera el dueño del lugar. El inspector se quedó de pie, con los brazos cruzados, señor de sus dominios. Spector se sentó con discreción en un rincón mientras barajaba un mazo de cartas. Sin embargo, prestó atención a cada palabra.

–¿Alguna vez conoció a alguno de los pacientes del doctor Rees? –preguntó Flint.

Una pregunta general para poner en marcha el asunto.

–Nunca tuve el placer, pero estoy seguro de que son un grupo interesante.

Había cierta burla en su tono de voz.

–¿Nunca se topó con ninguno de ellos cuando entraba y salía de la casa?

–No estoy seguro de qué clase de idea se ha hecho, pero nunca he entrado y salido mucho de Dollis Hill. Si le digo la verdad, no creo que el viejo Anselm llegara a tomarme demasiado cariño.

–¿No? Pero sí que ha estado allí en varias ocasiones desde que se comprometió con Lidia, ¿no?

Bowman se encogió de hombros.

–Principalmente para recogerla para ir a cenar, tomar una copa de vino y cosas así, ya sabe…

–¿Alguna vez se ha encontrado con Della Cookson?

–¿Della…?

–Cookson.

–Es actriz, ¿no? Creo que no. Aunque, ahora que lo menciona, la vi en la obra de teatro de la otra noche.

–Era una de las pacientes del difunto doctor. ¿Dice que nunca se encontró con ella en ninguna de sus visitas a la casa?

Bowman volvió a encogerse de hombros de forma afable.

–En cualquier caso, si le digo la verdad, me resulta difícil contestarle a la pregunta, ya que tengo muy mala memoria para las caras.

Flint lo observó con detenimiento y sin compasión.

–¿Qué me dice de Floyd Stenhouse?

–Ni idea. Estoy bastante seguro de que habría recordado a cualquiera con un nombre así.

–¿Y a Claude Weaver?

–Es escritor, ¿verdad? Me parece recordar que Lidia me ha hablado sobre uno de sus libros. *Thrillers* y asesinatos sangrientos, ¿no? Tal vez deberían estar preguntándole a él quién mató al viejo.

–Pero ¿no lo llegó a conocer?

–Me temo que no tengo demasiado interés en la literatura. Nunca he sido un gran lector. Creo que todo se remonta a mis días en el colegio privado. Intentaban obligarte a que te gustara, lo que hacía que, más adelante, te resultara muy poco atractivo, ¿no le parece?

–Me temo que no lo sé, señor –contestó Flint, aunque, siendo sincero, podía empatizar con el joven en aquel asunto–. Tal vez pueda contarme cómo conoció a Lidia Rees.

Bowman se recostó en el asiento como si se estuviera preparando para contar una historia que le complacía mucho compartir.

–Fue en el Palmyra, en el Soho. ¿Lo conoce? Como dirían los estadounidenses: es un garito animado. Buena música.

–¿Les presentaron?

–Más bien nos topamos el uno con el otro. Creo que en sentido literal, aunque no tengo tan buena memoria.

–¿Y van a casarse?

–El próximo año, si todo va bien.

–¡Felicidades! –Flint se encontró con la mirada de Spector y le guiñó el ojo–. Y bien, ¿puede contarme cómo transcurrió la velada de anoche?

–Fuimos al Savoy –contestó Marcus Bowman–. Hacen una comida maravillosa. Fletán.

–¿Y después?

El joven arrugó el rostro, haciendo ademán de estar recomponiendo todo.

–Después de eso, fuimos al Palmyra. Ahora somos clientes habituales. Tenemos muchos recuerdos felices allí.

–Ajá –dijo Flint–. ¿Cuánto tiempo estuvieron allí?

–Hasta que regresamos a casa. Fuera la hora que fuera. No estoy seguro.

–¿Y estuvieron juntos todo el tiempo?

–Por supuesto. ¿Está insinuando algo?

El inspector insistió.

–¿Y no pararon en ningún lugar de camino?

–No, para nada. Tomamos un taxi desde el Savoy hasta el Palmyra y, después, tomamos otro en el Palmyra para volver a Dollis Hill, dejar a Lidia en casa y recoger mi automóvil.

–Supongo que no recordará el número del taxi que les llevó de vuelta a Dollis Hill.

–Mire, ¿de qué va todo esto? Alguien se ha cargado al viejo y es muy triste y todo eso, pero ¿de verdad merece la pena todo este jaleo?

–No estoy seguro de que a su prometida fuera a gustarle lo que ha dicho, señor Bowman.

–Cierto, tal vez no –dijo el joven. Después, en voz más baja, como si hablara para sí mismo, añadió–: Aunque también puede que sí.

El camarero del Palmyra Club se mostró sorprendentemente amable cuando Flint y Spector entraron por la puerta. Después de todo, el club había sido escenario de muchas redadas policiales a lo largo de su larga e histórica existencia y el tipo fue rápido a la hora de servirles algo de beber (a cuenta de la casa, por supuesto) y de identificar fotografías de Lidia Rees y Marcus Bowman.

–Sí, estuvieron aquí –dijo.
–¿A qué hora llegaron?
–No podría asegurarlo, pero calculo que debí de servirles sobre las diez.
–¿Volvió a verlos?
–Por supuesto. Estuvieron aquí un buen rato, sin duda. Estuvieron bailando y causaron un buen escándalo en la pista de baile.
–¿Qué tipo de escándalo?
–Ah, bueno, ya sabe..., tonterías de borrachos. Estuvieron patinando sobre champán derramado, tal como suele hacer la gente joven.
Flint miró a Spector de reojo.
–Eso no es propio de Lidia.
–Pero sí parece propio de Marcus Bowman.
A esas alturas, empezaba a anochecer.
–Vamos –dijo Flint–, tengo que volver a Scotland Yard e intentar entender todo este sinsentido. ¿Tiene que ir a algún sitio?
–Creo que a casa –contestó el mago–. Tengo que hacer algunas lecturas.

Aquella noche, acomodado en un sillón junto al fuego en su pequeña residencia de Jubilee Court, Spector comenzó a leer las notas que el doctor Anselm Rees había dejado atrás.

Aquellos no eran los casos prácticos publicados, que ya había repasado con interés. Ahí no había ningún Hombre Serpiente. Aquellas eran las notas manuscritas que había tomado el doctor desde su llegada a Londres. Los sujetos eran los Pacientes A, B y C. En cuanto hubo descifrado los garabatos del médico, leyó lo siguiente:

> El Paciente A (un hombre con un prodigioso talento musical) es también un individuo que carga con un poderoso sentimiento de culpabilidad. ¿De dónde procede dicha culpabilidad? No soy capaz de encontrar nada evidente en su historia personal reciente que le haya generado semejante carga psicológica. Tal vez se trate del peso que su inmenso talento musical le ha

puesto sobre los hombros (he de confesar que yo mismo soy un admirador y tenía en mi haber varios discos para gramófono de sus obras antes incluso de conocerlo). Entiendo que sus padres no tenían nada especial. Eso hace que su papel como prodigio resulte todavía más sorprendente. Sin embargo, es torpe en situaciones sociales, solitario y con poco interés en los asuntos románticos. Tengo entendido que en el pasado hubo una prometida que murió hace varios años, pero se muestra reticente a hablar de este asunto.

El motivo por el que acudió a mí en primer lugar fueron sus pesadillas (o, como él las llama, sus demonios nocturnos). Estoy convencido de que la clave de su trauma reside en esos sueños. El centro de atención parece ser su padre, que aparece a menudo como personaje de dichos cuadros oníricos. Sin embargo, las situaciones son tan estrafalarias y extrañas que casi parecen desafiar cualquier explicación.

¿Por qué tiene que ser este joven tan diferente? Su cerebro es una maraña de símbolos e ideas. Se entrelazan y se conectan entre sí, pero tampoco tienen principio ni fin. Tal vez, si escribo esos sueños, me revelen su significado.

–Clotilde –dijo Spector–, venga aquí. –La criada obedeció y esperó pacientemente de pie mientras él localizaba un pasaje específico del cuaderno–. Escuche esto –añadió. Se aclaró la garganta y comenzó a leer en voz alta–: «En el sueño estoy sentado junto a un lago. Frente a mí hay un caballete y un lienzo a medio terminar. Estoy pintando. Es pronto por la mañana y hay una niebla ligera sobre la superficie del agua. Y de pronto, como si me golpearan el pecho con un puño, siento un miedo tremendo y repentino. Miro el lienzo y me doy cuenta de que no es un cuadro del lago, sino de una figura encapuchada que porta una lámpara. La figura me observa desde el lienzo. Entonces, alzo la vista y veo que, de algún modo, el lago está cambiando. Las nubes se arremolinan sobre mi cabeza y parecen muy enfadadas. Poco a poco, la figura emerge del agua. Sujeta la lámpara ardiente, que, sin embargo, no arroja ninguna luz. No puedo verle el rostro, pero sé que me está mirando y siento tantísimo miedo en el corazón...». –Spector terminó la lectura y cerró el cuaderno de golpe–. Bueno, Clotilde, ¿qué opina?

El rostro de la criada resultaba suave bajo el resplandor ambiental del fuego y, aun así, su gesto era obstinado. La joven llevaba al servicio del mago lo que parecía toda una vida y, en todos aquellos años, jamás había pronunciado una sola palabra.

–Eso era el Sueño Uno, nombrado con mucha imaginación, del cuaderno del doctor Rees –explicó el hombre–. Lo adscribe al Paciente A, es decir, Floyd Stenhouse. ¿Qué piensa al respecto?

Sin embargo, Clotilde, quizá sabiamente, permaneció callada.

En la siguiente sección del cuaderno, Spector leyó:

> La Paciente B es una especie de persona a medias. Su forma de actuar en situaciones sociales parece totalmente adquirida, como si no tuviera impulsos o reacciones auténticas propias. Su único instinto real es el de supervivencia. Con respecto a esto, uno podría decir que nació para ser actriz, que, en realidad, nunca deja de actuar. Detrás de la enrevesada fachada emocional, existe una ausencia impúdica. Se trata de eso o de un muro tan impenetrable que subsume todo lo que se puede reconocer como humano en su interior.
>
> Esta sensación de vacío se manifiesta de una forma literal en el sentido de que, si bien disfruta de una vida cómoda (incluso lujosa), soporta una compulsión insuperable de robar. Me ha confesado que esta tendencia resultó aparente por primera vez durante su niñez. Recuerda haber robado una estilográfica resplandeciente de la mesa de su maestra y haber tenido problemas para ocultar su alegría mientras la desafortunada profesora registraba los pupitres de todas las alumnas. Sin embargo, nuestra Paciente B era demasiado astuta incluso a tan corta edad. En un momento de distracción, arrojó la pluma por la ventana abierta. La osadía del crimen despertó en sus compañeras una perversa admiración y nunca tuvo que rendir cuentas. Tiene muchas historias sobre incidentes similares a lo largo de su adolescencia y los primeros años de la adultez.

Desde luego, parece que su encanto superficial la ha salvado de pasar muchos apuros en la vida y no hace falta señalar que le ha proporcionado una base incalculable para su carrera en los escenarios.

En los últimos tiempos, nuestras conversaciones se han inclinado hacia un hastío profundo del que no parece capaz de desprenderse. Aunque ella no lo ha dicho abiertamente, entiendo que, ahora mismo, hay un hombre en su vida. La evidencia más destacada de ello fue una única referencia espontánea a un «nosotros» en lugar de un «yo». He adquirido la costumbre de dejar pequeños objetos por toda la oficina durante nuestras sesiones, no tanto para pillarla como para acercarla a un reconocimiento del lado oscuro de su naturaleza. En nuestra sesión más reciente, serví un vaso de agua para ella y otro para mí y, mientras dejaba el vaso frente a ella, me di cuenta de que tenía la mano sobre un mechero dorado que había dejado sobre el cristal de la mesita de café. Cuando se dio cuenta de que la había pillado, se quedó petrificada. Le pregunté qué era lo que le estaba pasando por la cabeza. Ella me miró con cara de póker y se limitó a decir: «Nada». Entonces, apartó la mano. Cuando se acabó la sesión, me di cuenta de que el mechero había desaparecido. No sé cuándo lo tomó.

Más recientemente, he intentado sumergirme en su pasado y su vida familiar para poder hacerme a la idea de sus relaciones interpersonales. He de confesar que he tenido poco éxito en este asunto. Sin embargo, me gustaría tomar nota de un incidente que ocurrió en mi sesión más reciente con ella y que me ofreció una instantánea espontánea de su psique.

La sesión había concluido. La Paciente B, que valora su privacidad pero tampoco insiste demasiado en el asunto, estaba a punto de abandonar mi casa y salir a la calle. De camino, se topó (y me refiero en sentido literal) con un visitante masculino que estaba entrando. El tipo es un visitante frecuente, un pretendiente de mi hija que, en cuanto se hubo disculpado de manera profusa, la miró directamente a la cara y la reconoció. «¡Vaya, Paciente B!», exclamó antes de balbucear una retahíla

> de producciones teatrales. El joven no entiende mucho de sutilezas y semejante demostración habría reducido a cualquier otro paciente menos imperturbable a la consistencia de la gelatina. Sin embargo, la Paciente B se mostró difusa e incluso gélida en su aprobación. Antes de excusarse y parar un taxi, le dio las gracias con amabilidad, pero con poco entusiasmo. Mientras el pretendiente de mi hija permanecía desconcertado, ella se marchó discretamente.
>
> Lo que me resultó interesante de este pequeño encuentro es que el hombre llevaba un reloj de bolsillo de oro colgando del bolsillo del chaleco, una ostentosa afectación que es una garantía para llamar la atención. Sin embargo, cuando la Paciente B se subió al taxi, vi que el visitante masculino todavía tenía el reloj. Eso plantea cuestiones muy interesantes con respecto a los límites de la afinidad de mi paciente por el oro. ¿Por qué llevarse el mechero, cuando ya la habían pillado una vez en el acto de robar, pero no el reloj? ¿Podría tener algo que ver con la evidente admiración que el tipo siente por ella y su conocimiento sobre sus pasadas producciones en los teatros de Londres? ¿Cuál es la relación entre su carrera y el robo? Es una cuestión que hay que investigar más a fondo.

Sin embargo, Rees no había llegado a vivir lo suficiente para hacerlo.

Se estaba haciendo tarde. Spector cerró los ojos un momento y escuchó el crepitar de la chimenea. Le quedaba todavía mucho por leer, pues ni siquiera había llegado todavía al Paciente C. Sin embargo, sentía que, de algún modo, tan solo estaba eludiendo la cuestión principal, que la respuesta al asesinato del doctor estaba en alguna otra parte. Decidió que, a esas alturas, dormir era la mejor opción para él. Después de todo, el doctor seguiría muerto por la mañana, el cuadro seguiría desaparecido y los secretos de esa habitación cerrada seguirían tan impenetrables como siempre.

X

Una breve reflexión sobre el problema de la habitación cerrada

(Lunes, 14 de septiembre de 1936)

A la mañana siguiente, mientras iba de camino a visitar a Spector, Flint hizo una parada en Bloomsbury, que era donde tenía su oficina Ralph Tweedy, el editor de Claude Weaver. No tenía cita con él, pero la simple mención de un asesinato fue suficiente para que lo llevaran hasta el valioso despacho del editor.

El tipo era más joven de lo que el inspector había esperado. Tenía el rostro insufriblemente liso. Flint pensó que aquel era un hombre que no había conseguido nada por sus propios méritos, un niño mimado como Marcus Bowman.

–Creo que uno de sus autores es un hombre llamado Claude Weaver, ¿no es así?

El editor prendió una cerilla y encendió con ella la punta de su cigarro.

–Así es. Claude es uno de los mejores del sector. ¿Conoce su obra?

–Me temo que no, pero no se preocupe, mi pregunta no tiene que ver con eso.

–Oh.

Tweedy retomó su asiento con el cigarro sujeto entre los dedos rechonchos.

–No. Quiero preguntarle sobre la cena que tuvo con el señor Weaver hace dos noches.

–¿Hace dos noches? El día 12... –dijo Tweedy de forma distraída–. En realidad, sería mejor que le preguntara este tipo de cosas a mi secretaria.

–Ya lo hemos hecho. En su agenda tenía una cita para cenar con Claude Weaver. ¿Es eso correcto?

–Si estaba ahí apuntado, tiene que ser correcto –contestó él mientras daba una calada al cigarro hasta que la punta resplandeció con un tono naranja–. De hecho… Espere un momento. Sí, creo que ya me acuerdo. Claude quería reunirse conmigo para hablar del contrato para su última novela.

–¿Se reunieron a las ocho?

El hombre se encogió de hombros.

–Más o menos.

–¿Fue en Brown's?

–Es donde nos reunimos siempre. Hacen una trucha estupenda.

–¿Y cuánto tiempo estuvieron juntos?

–Oh, un buen rato.

Se produjo una breve pausa mientras el humo dibujaba una espiral ascendente en dirección al ocioso ventilador del techo.

–Necesito que sea más específico.

El editor soltó un gemido.

–Dos horas, tal vez tres. De verdad, esto resulta muy desagradable.

–Lo que necesito saber es a qué hora se marchó Claude Weaver del restaurante.

–¿Qué hora le ha dicho él? Claude tiene mejor memoria para estas cosas que yo.

Flint lo contempló con los ojos entrecerrados.

–Si no supiera que es imposible, diría que está intentando ocultarme algo, señor Tweedy.

El editor se rio.

–Créame, esa no es mi intención.

Otra pausa.

–¿Sabía que Weaver estaba viendo a un psiquiatra?

–No, eso no lo sabía –respondió el otro hombre–. Aunque no me sorprende en absoluto.

–¿Por qué no?

–Es un tipo extraño y no es fácil congeniar con él. Ya sabe cómo son los escritores. Demasiado introvertidos y alejados del mundo real.

–¿Y de qué hablaron?

–¿Durante la cena? De lo habitual. Se estaba acercando la fecha límite para la entrega de su última novela.

–¿De qué trata?

El editor le dedicó una media sonrisa, como si estuviese admitiendo la derrota.

–Ahora que lo menciona, trata de un psiquiatra.

–¿Y hablaron de ello durante tres horas?

El joven se recostó, pensativo. Los únicos sonidos dentro de aquella habitación eran el crujido de la silla y el crepitar del cigarro.

–Si quiere que sea sincero del todo, no. Esa fue la noche que Claude se puso enfermo.

–¿Enfermo? Es la primera vez que alguien me menciona esto. ¿En qué sentido se puso enfermo?

–Se sintió indispuesto mientras comíamos. Se excusó, fue al lavabo dando tumbos y... Sí, ahora me acuerdo. Ese fue el último momento en que le vi.

–¿Quiere decir que no regresó?

–No es algo tan inusual como parece, inspector. En mi negocio, uno se acostumbra a todo tipo de pecadillos artísticos.

–¿A qué hora se marchó?

–Bueno, fue en mitad de la cena, así que es probable que en torno a las diez.

–¿Se había quejado antes de encontrarse mal?

–En absoluto. Me estaba hablando de la novela, repasando la escaleta de un capítulo (que prácticamente es el único tema que le emociona), cuando, de pronto, se quedó congelado, como si hubiera visto algo por encima de mi hombro, pero no había nada.

–¿Le dijo usted algo? ¿Algo que pudiera haber malinterpretado?

–Creo que lo que le dije fue... –El joven se detuvo a pensar un momento–. ¡Eso es! Le estaba hablando del nuevo teletipo que tenemos en el taller. –Ante la mirada desconcertada de Flint, continuó–. Es un aparato puñeteramente bueno que nos será de mucha ayuda si alguna vez decidimos aventurarnos con los libros de bolsillo. Por supuesto, Claude no es lo que se dice un admirador del auge de la literatura popular. De eso era de lo que estábamos hablando. No estaba siendo una discusión acalorada ni nada similar, tan solo un intercambio totalmente educado. Claude estaba intentando convencerme de que las ediciones de bolsillo no eran más que copias baratas de los auténticos, de que tal vez pudieran engañar a los incultos, pero que los literatos siempre distinguirían un Claude Weaver auténtico de uno falso.

–Y fue entonces cuando se puso enfermo.

El editor asintió.

–Fue entonces cuando se le puso ese gesto en la cara... Entonces, salió dando tumbos del restaurante, mascullando algo sobre lo enfermo que se sentía, y ya nunca regresó.

–¿Y eso fue a las diez en punto?

–Las diez o las diez y media. No estoy seguro.

–Weaver nos dijo que estuvo con usted toda la velada.

La sonrisa del joven era insufrible.

–En tal caso, el señor Weaver se equivoca.

Mientras se dirigía de nuevo a la residencia de los Weaver, Flint parecía llevar un resorte en los pies. Había decidido que Spector podía esperar unos minutos más mientras él hacía otra visita domiciliaria. En aquella ocasión, no se molestó en llamar al timbre, sino que golpeó la puerta con el puño.

Una criada le dejó pasar y, antes de que la mujer pudiera protestar, fue directo hasta el salón, donde se encontró con un Claude Weaver de aspecto confundido.

–Señor Weaver, sabemos que la noche del asesinato no estuvo toda la velada con su editor. ¿Por qué nos mintió?

El novelista se puso en pie de golpe.

–¿De qué está hablando?

–Nos ha dicho que a mitad de la cena usted se puso enfermo, que se perdió en la noche dando tumbos y que no vio hacia dónde se marchó.

Weaver parecía afectado.

–No sé nada de todo eso...

–Podemos comprobarlo con el personal del restaurante...

–¡No! No dudo de lo que dice, inspector. Lo que quiero decir es que no tengo recuerdo de eso.

Flint lo observó detenidamente.

–¿Qué intenta decirme, señor Weaver?

–Recuerdo el restaurante. Recuerdo la cena. Después, recuerdo llegar a casa...

–¿A qué hora fue eso?

–No lo sé, me fui directo a la cama.

–Entonces, déjeme que me aclare... ¿No puede dar cuenta de sus movimientos la noche que Anselm Rees murió?

–Su-supongo que no.

–¿Visitó a Anselm Rees en algún momento de esa noche?

–No lo creo.

–Pero ¿no puede asegurarlo?

Weaver apretó la mandíbula y se sentó más erguido, estoico.

–No, no puedo asegurarlo.

Flint no tenía manera de saberlo, pero aquella mañana Spector también había dado un pequeño rodeo. Había parado en casa de Benjamin Teasel para analizar el problema del cuadro desaparecido. Teasel estaba fuera, pero las dos criadas que habían permanecido en la puerta toda la noche del robo sí estaban presentes. Se llamaban Hilda y Paulette y formaban una pareja muy cómica. Con los uniformes a juego y los delantales con volantes, se parecían mucho a un par de pimenteros. No mostraban nada de la modesta dignidad y la gracia que poseía la criada propia de Spector.

–Señoritas –dijo el mago. Las dos criadas se miraron con una sonrisita mal disimulada–, me gustaría que me contaran todo lo que puedan sobre la noche de la fiesta del señor Teasel.

–Por supuesto, señor –dijo Hilda–, haremos lo que podamos.

–El señor está tremendamente disgustado –explicó Paulette–. Se está convirtiendo en un embrollo terrible.

–Muy bien. Entonces, ¿qué me dicen de la fiesta? Teasel les dio instrucciones de que recibieran a los invitados, ¿correcto?

–Así es, señor –dijo Hilda–. Nos encomendaron esa tarea a cuenta de que el señor Townsend tenía la noche libre. –Townsend, el ayuda de cámara de Teasel, tenía una buena coartada y, por lo tanto, había quedado excluido de la investigación–. Solo que el señor no confiaba en que pudiéramos hacerlo solas, así que nos puso en pareja.

–Ya veo… ¿Y estuvieron en el recibidor todo el tiempo?

–Así es, señor. –Fue el turno de Paulette–. Dejamos entrar a todos los que llevaban invitación, todos los que encajaban en este lugar.

–¿Y vieron a alguien sospechoso?

–No, señor, a nadie. Ya le digo que nadie podría haber robado el cuadro. No dejamos pasar a ningún ladrón y ya se demostró que no había sido ninguno de los invitados, ¿no?

–¿Están seguras de que no hay ninguna otra manera de que el ladrón hubiera podido colarse en la casa por su cuenta?

–Sin duda, señor. La puerta trasera estaba cerrada con llave. Y la puerta lateral. Las ventanas estaban también todas cerradas.

–¿Vieron a algún invitado que subiera al piso de arriba en algún momento durante el transcurso de la velada?

–¡Oh, sí! ¡Todo el tiempo! Verá…, tenían que subir para usar el… ya sabe qué.

–¿El baño?

Paulette soltó una risita y asintió.

–Así que sería imposible que me dijeran quién podría haberse colado en esa habitación para robar el cuadro…

–Bueno, si hubieran bajado de nuevo con él, sin duda los habríamos visto –explicó Hilda–, pero nadie cargaba con nada. Eso puedo asegurárselo.

–¿Es posible que alguien de la fiesta, es decir, alguno de los invitados, se hubiera escabullido, hubiera abierto una de las ventanas para dejar entrar al ladrón y, después, hubiera regresado a la fiesta?

–No, señor –replicó Paulette.

–¿Y por qué no?

–Porque el resto de las habitaciones estaban bien cerradas. El señor Teasel es muy exigente con eso de que la gente se pasee por el piso de arriba.

–Así que las únicas habitaciones del piso superior que estaban abiertas eran…

–El ya sabe qué. Tiene una ventana, pero no se abre. Nunca se ha abierto; al menos, no desde que yo estoy aquí.

–Ya veo. Así que nos quedan las escaleras o nada.

–Así es, señor.

–¿Qué me dicen de esto? ¿Podrían haber sacado el cuadro de la casa de algún otro modo? ¿Había alguna otra puerta por la que podrían haber salido?

Las criadas sacudieron la cabeza en perfecta sincronía.

–No, señor. Tan solo está la entrada del servicio, que se encuentra en la parte trasera, pero también estaba bien cerrada. Y antes de que pregunte: no faltaba ninguna llave.

–Así que tuvieron que llevarse el cuadro por la puerta delantera...

–Pero nadie lo pasó por delante de nosotras –le aseguró Hilda–. Eso puedo confirmárselo.

Las jóvenes se mostraron dispuestas (tal vez, demasiado) a mostrarle la escena del crimen. Lo condujeron por las escaleras de caracol hasta la puerta que se encontraba al final. Hilda la abrió.

–Ahora, el señor la deja abierta –le explicó–. Dice que, dado que ya no está el cuadro, no tiene demasiado sentido cerrarla.

Spector examinó la habitación con detenimiento. Era tal como había esperado: la ventana era demasiado pequeña para que hubieran sacado el cuadro por allí. Naturalmente, también hubiera sido imposible que alguien entrara o saliera por ella.

En el rellano había una ventana grande que daba a la calle, pero no se abría; no había ni cerrojo ni pasador. El cristal estaba fijado a la pared, sin más. Otro callejón sin salida.

En un último intento de encontrarle sentido a todo aquello, Spector se dirigió al «ya sabe qué». En el baño no había nada especialmente distintivo. No había ni accesorios sueltos ni anomalías en las tuberías que pudiera ver. Y, cómo no, la ventana estaba muy bien cerrada por una combinación de suciedad y óxido. No cedió.

El mago bajó las escaleras, frustrado con su falta de progreso. Para aquel entonces, tendría que haber estado desbordado de ideas. Se dejó caer en un sillón del salón y Hilda le sirvió otra taza de té.

–Está trabajando también en la muerte de ese doctor, ¿verdad, señor? –le preguntó Paulette con delicadeza–. Menudo caso...

–Tiene razón, jovencita... Menudo caso.

Durante los siguientes minutos, las criadas intentaron en vano sonsacarle algún detalle sangriento. El mago se acordó de Jonathan Harker, el personaje de *Drácula*, la novela de Stoker, que había sido acosado por unas vampiresas desesperadas por una gota de sangre.

Reanimado por el té (que no había estado nada mal), comenzó a levantarse del asiento. Fue un proceso lento y laborioso, pero al final, con una criada a cada brazo, consiguió ponerse en pie de nuevo.

–Les doy las gracias a ambas –dijo mientras se llevaba la mano al ala del sombrero–. No envejezcan, señoritas. Dudo que la experiencia fuera a agradarles.

Desbordantes de sonrisas y con gestos educados de la cabeza, volvieron a acompañarlo a la salida. Se estremeció un poco y se ciñó la capa todavía más en torno al cuerpo pulcro y anguloso.

Era casi la hora de la comida cuando el inspector Flint regresó a The Black Pig, en Putney. Encontró a Joseph Spector en su sillón habitual junto a la ventana de la salita. En aquella ocasión, estaba jugueteando con un soberano que, por supuesto, era falso. Le estaba dando vueltas entre los dedos nudosos con una destreza sorprendente. Tanto es así que el inspector se detuvo a observarlo un instante en lugar de interrumpir su espectáculo.

Entonces, con una sonrisa, el mago se metió la moneda en el bolsillo.

–Por favor, siéntese –dijo.

–Tengo noticias –le dijo Flint.

–Yo también.

–Yo primero... La coartada de Weaver se ha hecho añicos. Asegura que sufrió una de sus fugas mientras cenaba con su editor. El editor dice que salió del restaurante dando tumbos como si estuviera en trance.

Spector se estaba mordiendo el pulgar, pensativo.

–Sí, ya había supuesto que ese podría ser el caso.

–¿Qué quiere decir? Sin duda, ¡esto echa por tierra todo! Si Weaver no puede demostrar dónde estaba, podría haber ido a Dollis Hill fácilmente, con fuga o sin ella.

–Sí, pero... ¿cómo entró en el estudio? –Flint abrió la boca y, después, la volvió a cerrar–. Creo que ha llegado el momento de que desmontemos el problema de la habitación cerrada –continuó Spector.

–Pero ¿qué hay de Weaver?

–Weaver puede esperar. Si ni siquiera ha sido capaz de proporcionar una coartada coherente, me cuesta creer que hubiera podido orquestar esta ingeniosa desaparición de una habitación que estaba sellada desde dentro.

Flint suspiró con suavidad.

–Puede que tenga algo de razón.

Spector comenzó a hablar.

–Bien... Nuestro amigo en común, el señor John Dickson Carr, ha escrito un estudio bastante completo sobre el problema de la habitación cerrada en su libro *El hombre hueco*. Esta mañana, además de hacer una breve visita a la casa de Benjamin Teasel, he tenido la oportunidad de volver a leer la parte relevante. En ella, Carr nos proporciona siete categorías generales. Veamos...

»En primer lugar, la muerte accidental. En otras palabras, que el tajo en la garganta de Anselm Rees fuese resultado de algún percance desafortunado. Tal vez se le resbalara la mano con el abridor de cartas mientras estaba repasando la correspondencia del día. Poco probable, pero no imposible en las circunstancias adecuadas. De todos modos, creo que podemos dejar de lado esta opción, ¿no cree?

»En segundo lugar, que la víctima haya sido inducida a suicidarse por algún tipo de droga. O mediante el hipnotismo. Si bien no quiero descartarla sin más y, además, todavía no disponemos del informe *post mortem* del doctor Rees, creo que podemos decir sin temor a equivocarnos que la respuesta se encuentra en otra parte.

»En tercer lugar, que se use algún tipo de trampa mecánica en la habitación. Como una navaja de afeitar con un resorte, por ejemplo. Tras un registro exhaustivo de la habitación, sabemos que podemos descartar esta opción. No hay artilugios ni paneles ocultos.

»En cuarto lugar, un suicidio amañado para que parezca un asesinato. Esta es la solución que ha propuesto Lidia Rees, así que, ahora mismo, no me detendré más en ella.

»En quinto lugar, que el asesino suplante a la víctima tras haberla matado, creando así confusión con respecto a la hora de la muerte. Esto es posible. Después de todo, cuando el visitante se hubo marchado, Olive Turner solo oyó al doctor a través de la puerta. Es decir: no lo vio. Así que podría ser que la voz que escuchó fuese en realidad la del asesino. Sin embargo, eso no nos ayuda a identificar ni al asesino ni al visitante. Tampoco nos permite explicar cómo el asesino fue capaz de abandonar la habitación sin dejar rastro.

»En sexto lugar, que el asesino consiga atacar a la víctima desde fuera de la habitación. R. Austin Freeman y su doctor Thorndyke propusieron un ejemplo interesante de esta opción, pero no veo cómo podría aplicarse al caso de Rees a menos que el asesino hubiera tenido alguna especie de arco y una flecha a la que pudiera unirse una navaja de afeitar.

»En séptimo y último lugar, que la víctima no esté muerta en el momento en el que la encuentran y que, sencillamente, lo parezca; que esté inconsciente o drogada de algún modo y que la maten después de ser encontrada. Una vez más, esto no es posible en nuestro caso. Rees estaba medio decapitado, así que no había duda de que, cuando lo encontraron, estaba muerto.

»Estas son las categorías para una habitación cerrada, tal como se plantean en el libro del señor Carr.

–Bueno, ¿y dónde nos deja todo esto? –preguntó Flint.

No tenía ni idea de quién podía ser el tal Carr, pero, en aquel asunto desastroso, le parecía tan posible sospechoso como cualquier otro.

–Es algo en lo que reflexionar, nada más –contestó Spector–.

Tenemos que ser metódicos. Hasta donde sé, hay otros dos problemas que tenemos que resolver antes de que avancemos más con el enigma de la habitación cerrada.

–¿Solo dos?

El mago asintió.

–El primero es el acertijo de la coartada impenetrable. No existe algo semejante, aunque la de algunos de nuestros personajes principales se acerca bastante. Sabemos que Floyd Stenhouse estaba en su casa. ¿Cómo lo sabemos? Porque los trabajadores pueden atestiguar que no salió de su apartamento. También está ese asuntillo de la llamada telefónica que le hizo al doctor justo antes del asesinato. Esto ha quedado confirmado por la centralita y concuerda a la perfección con los fragmentos de conversación que Olive Turner oyó a través de la puerta.

»¿Quién va después? Della Cookson. Muchos testigos aseguran que, sin duda, asistió a la función de *La dama Muerte* y, del mismo modo, que de allí fue a la fiesta en casa de Benjamin Teasel, en la que yo también estuve presente. También está el asunto del cuadro robado, pero hablaremos de eso en otro momento. Sabemos que se marchó de dicha fiesta sobre las once y media en un estado de cierta agitación. También podemos suponer que, después, fue directa a casa del doctor. Llegó a la puerta delantera del hogar de los Rees en unos quince minutos y Olive Turner la dejó pasar. Eso nos deja con muy poco margen de tiempo para que hubiera entrado y salido de la casa tras haber cometido un asesinato espantoso sin haberse derramado ni una sola gota de sangre sobre el vestido de fiesta de seda.

»Nuestra tercera sospechosa es Lidia Rees. Sabemos que fue a cenar al Savoy y que, de allí, fue al Palmyra Club. ¿Cómo lo sabemos? Porque es lo que dice Marcus Bowman. Del mismo modo, ella garantiza la coartada de él. Pero no es solo eso; también tenemos la evidencia de los empleados del Savoy, del taxi que dejó a la pareja en el Palmyra y de varios camareros del club. Suelo desconfiar de las parejas en las que uno proporciona la coartada del otro, pero tal vez podamos dar su inocencia por sentada basándonos en los testimonios de los testigos y en el hecho de que tanto el Savoy como el Palmyra Club están a varios kilómetros de la casa de los Rees.

»Así que llegamos a Claude Weaver, el novelista conocido por sus enormes desvanecimientos tipo fuga. Aunque se ha esforzado mucho, no ha conseguido darnos una coartada viable. El editor no está dispuesto a corroborarlo y la esposa no puede hacerlo. Eso nos conduce a una conclusión que parece inevitable: que Weaver es el único que podría haber matado a Anselm Rees. Las pruebas son puramente circunstanciales, ya que no hay nada que indique que hubiese enemistad entre ambos hombres. Tan solo se trata de que el escritor no puede dar cuenta de su paradero la noche del asesinato. Pero, si de verdad lo hizo (y recuerde que he dicho «si»), eso sigue dejándonos con otro acertijo que parece irresoluble: ¿cómo entró y salió de la casa sin dejar rastro?

»Sin embargo, hay otro aspecto de este misterio que he olvidado mencionar: el visitante misterioso que solo vio Olive Turner y que se presentó allí para una enigmática última sesión con el doctor. ¿Qué sabemos de este visitante? Solo que era alguien que el ama de llaves no había visto nunca y que parecía decidido a ocultar su identidad. Se trataba de alguien que el doctor conocía o al que, al menos, estaba esperando, ya que le había dicho a Olive que se preparara para una visita aquella noche. Sin embargo, no sabemos de qué hablaron. Tan solo sabemos que el visitante se marchó antes del asesinato y de la llamada de Stenhouse. En tal caso, ¿es la presencia de dicho visitante relevante para el caso o no? Más allá de Della Cookson, ninguno de los otros dos pacientes fue visto llegando o marchándose por la puerta principal. Ni ninguna otra persona, más allá del desconocido. Eso significa que lo más probable es que el asesino entrara a la casa a través de los ventanales del estudio del doctor, pero eso es imposible por dos motivos muy claros. En primer lugar, la tormenta. La lluvia comenzó antes de las nueve, mucho antes del asesinato, por lo que tendría que haber un rastro claro de huellas que indicara la ruta de acceso del agresor. En segundo lugar, los ventanales, que estaban cerrados desde el interior. ¿Cómo lo sabemos? Porque Olive Turner los comprobó cuando entró en la habitación y Della

Cookson también. Más allá de eso, la llave estaba en la cerradura, también en el interior. Así que el asesino no pudo haber entrado siguiendo esa ruta a menos que tuviera una manera de borrar sus huellas o de trucar el cerrojo desde fuera de algún modo. ¿Le parece un resumen efectivo del asunto?

–Así es.

–Muy bien. Pongámonos manos a la obra. El asesino no podría haber salido de la casa por la puerta porque tanto Olive como Della lo habrían visto; no podría haber salido por los ventanales porque sus huellas habrían estado a la vista de todo el mundo en el barro y, además, las ventanas estaban cerradas por dentro.

»Hemos acotado el momento del asesinato a un breve periodo de cinco minutos entre la llamada telefónica de Floyd Stenhouse y el momento en el que Olive consiguió entrar en la habitación. Bien, hombres más importantes que yo han debatido sobre el asesinato en una habitación cerrada, pero, por nuestro propio interés, déjeme que presente unas pocas ideas básicas que pueden aplicarse a nuestro problema particular. Por supuesto, todo el asunto gira en torno a una ilusión. La cuestión es determinar dónde reside la misma.

»Primer punto: la puerta no estaba cerrada, tan solo lo parecía gracias a algún truco. Tal vez estuviese manipulada desde el exterior. Esto es más fácil de conseguir con cerrojos o cerraduras. Por ejemplo, todos conocemos ese asunto con el cubito de hielo que se coloca entre el cerrojo y el cerradero de modo que se vaya derritiendo poco a poco hasta que el cerrojo encaje a la perfección en su sitio una vez que el asesino ya ha salido de la habitación. Del mismo modo, se pueden usar cuerdas y alambres para dejar el cerrojo sellado desde fuera y después deshacerse de ellos cortándolos con una hoja o quemándolos con un mechero o algo similar. En nuestro caso, esto no es posible, ya que no hay cerrojo. Este es el clásico escenario de «la llave en la cerradura». Lo mismo ocurre con los ventanales, que también tenían la llave puesta. Entonces, ¿cómo lo hicieron? ¿Tal vez con un imán? Necesitamos investigarlo más.

»Segundo punto: que haya habido algún engaño con respecto

al tiempo y el asesinato se cometiera antes o después de la hora registrada. En nuestro caso, esto es imposible por dos motivos. Para empezar, sabemos que Rees estaba vivo unos momentos antes porque se le oyó manteniendo una conversación telefónica con Stenhouse. El propio músico puede corroborarlo. Y, por supuesto, no podrían haberlo matado antes, ya que no hay manera de confundir una muerte causada por una navaja de afeitar. La única manera en la que podría haberse hecho sería si hubiesen utilizado una grabación para hacer ver que Rees estaba vivo cuando, en realidad, lo habían matado ya. Y tenemos tanto los registros telefónicos, que establecen la hora y duración de la llamada, como el testimonio de Stenhouse, que determina que el doctor estaba vivo a la hora en cuestión. Además de eso, dentro de la habitación no hay ni rastro de equipos de grabación que se hubieran podido usar para llevar a cabo semejante truco. De todos modos, es algo en lo que pensar.

»Tercer punto: tal vez el asesino nunca llegara a salir de la habitación. Cosas más raras se han visto. Además, todos conocemos el famoso baúl de madera que podría contener un cuerpo humano con facilidad. Pero, claro, Olive lo abrió y determinó que no había nadie dentro. La habitación estaba vacía. Entonces, ¿dónde se metió el asesino?

»Esto nos lleva al punto cuatro: ¿y si nunca llegó a entrar en la habitación? Se conocen asesinatos que han sido causados dentro de una habitación cerrada desde una localización externa. De normal, se trataría de una muerte relacionada con un arma de fuego. Por ejemplo, una pistola inmóvil accionada a distancia. Estoy pensando especialmente en una historia de Melville Davisson Post, tal vez la conozca. Eso sería casi imposible con el método utilizado para matar al doctor Rees. Fue un ataque muy personal, muy físico, no se trata de un crimen que de algún modo hubiera podido ser automatizado. Hablando en sentido figurado: hay huellas humanas por todas partes.

»Sin embargo, el punto cinco nos ofrece una posible solución: ¿y si la víctima se hubiese visto incitada de algún modo a matarse? Podría lograrse con algunos trucos. Por ejemplo, que la víctima cayera en una trampa que lo estrangulara o lo apuñalara como puede ser una daga con resorte. Acuérdese de Wilkie Collins y esa extraña cama suya. O incluso que no fuera un asesinato, sino un ejemplo desconcertante de suicidio que los testigos han confundido con un asesinato. Es posible que un hombre pudiera cortarse la garganta con una navaja de afeitar y, si estuviera lo bastante enfadado o loco, tal vez incluso que pudiera causarse la clase de daño que sufrió Rees. Sin embargo, eso nos dejaría con todavía más misterios. Si el doctor se suicidó, ¿qué ocurrió con el arma? Sabemos que se trataba de una navaja y las navajas están hechas de metal. No podemos eludir el hecho de que se registró la habitación y no se encontró ni rastro de una.

–Bueno, ahí lo tiene –dijo Flint–: ha expuesto el problema. Ahora, ¿qué tal si me da alguna solución?

–El principio de la navaja de Ockham afirma que la solución que requiere menos conjeturas es, con toda probabilidad, la correcta.

–¿Y qué solución es esa?

La sonrisa del mago era vulpina.

–Vamos a seguir planteándolo de manera metódica. –Sacó tres cartas boca abajo. Después, le dio la vuelta a la primera y reveló a la reina de corazones–. Della Cookson. No podemos afirmar que tenga motivos, pero estaba presente en la escena del crimen y sabemos que está intentando ocultarnos algo. –Le dio la vuelta a la siguiente carta: la sota de diamantes–. Floyd Stenhouse. Motivo: incierto. Aunque tampoco tuvo la oportunidad, ya que hemos establecido una coartada para el momento de la muerte. –Al fin, la última carta: el rey de bastos–. Claude Weaver. Motivo: incierto. Sin embargo, sí tuvo oportunidad de hacerlo. Además, ya nos ha mentido en una ocasión sobre su paradero la noche del asesinato. ¡Ah, claro! –exclamó de pronto mientras se sacaba un par de cartas del bolsillo del pecho–. Se me olvidaba algo. –Colocó esas dos cartas adicionales junto a las otras y mostró que se trataba de un par de comodines–. Tenemos los comodines: Marcus Bowman y Lidia Rees. Son la coartada el uno del otro, pero, al mismo tiempo, Olive Turner lo habría sabido de inmediato si uno de los dos hubiera estado en la casa aquella noche.

Además, sabemos que estaban en la otra punta de Londres para cuando ocurrió todo.

–¿Alguna vez ha pensado que tal vez Olive Turner esté encubriendo a Lidia? –le interrumpió Flint.

–¿Por qué motivo? No estamos hablando de una empleada de la familia de toda la vida. Olive lleva cinco meses trabajando en la residencia de los Rees. No tiene vínculos con Lidia; al menos, nada que pudiera justificar escudarla de un cargo de asesinato. No, no, Flint. Estos son nuestros comodines, son anomalías. Y por supuesto, por último, aunque no menos importante...

Se metió una mano en las profundidades del bolsillo del pantalón y sacó una última carta. La colocó junto a los comodines. No llevaba ninguna imagen, tan solo un signo de interrogación en color cobre.

–Aquí tenemos a nuestro visitante sin rostro, al que nadie ha visto después ni ha podido identificar.

Recogió las seis cartas y comenzó a barajarlas.

XI

El Hombre Serpiente, desenmascarado

Cuando ambos hombres se separaron un poco más tarde, resultó evidente que Flint estaba desanimado por el resultado de la exposición de Spector. Sin embargo, el mago parecía entusiasmado de pronto. Le dijo al inspector que se dirigía al Pomegranate para intentar conseguir información sobre Della Cookson. Aquello era verdad a medias, pues, de camino al teatro, paró en casa de los Rees para una breve entrevista con Lidia.

Cuando Olive Turner lo condujo al interior, la joven se había instalado en el despacho de su difunto padre y estaba sentada tras el escritorio. Llevaba unas gafas de cristal grueso mientras leía con atención un libro enorme.

–Buenas tardes, señorita –dijo el mago mientras escudriñaba la habitación discretamente.

Se dio cuenta de que el charco de sangre había sido cubierto por una discreta alfombra de angora.

–Señor Spector –dijo ella sin apenas apartar la vista del libro–. Por favor, siéntese.

El hombre se acomodó en el sofá y dijo:

–Me gustaría pedirle su opinión profesional sobre algo, señorita Rees.

–Adelante.

–Me gustaría que me hablara sobre los estados de fuga.

Fuera lo que fuera que Lidia hubiera esperado, estaba claro que no había sido aquello. Se quedó pensando un momento.

–Un estado de fuga consiste en una fragmentación de la memoria, un distanciamiento entre uno mismo y la consciencia propia. Desde el punto de vista del individuo, puede haber perdido el conocimiento por completo y, sencillamente, haber vuelto en sí en el momento adecuado.

–¿Podría este individuo hipotético hacer cosas en estado de fuga que no haría consciente?

–Sin duda. Podría ir a cualquier parte y hacer cualquier cosa.

–¿Podría cometer un crimen?

–Con toda facilidad. Podría hacer cualquier cosa. Lo que sea.

–¿Qué más sabe sobre la enfermedad?

–Bueno, sigue siendo más o menos un misterio. De normal, tiene su origen en los mecanismos de afrontamiento de la niñez. Un niño afligido ideará una manera de distanciarse de los acontecimientos en cuestión y de convencerse a sí mismo de que tales acontecimientos le están ocurriendo a otra persona. Con el tiempo, eso se convertirá en la verdad. Su personalidad, su mismísimo ser, se fusionará y entrará en este estado casi de trance. Durante ese tiempo, no tendrá conocimiento de ninguna de sus acciones.

–Entonces, si a su padre lo hubiera asesinado un hombre en estado de fuga, ¿quiere decir que no podría hacérsele responsable?

–No, porque, verá, a duras penas habría sido él mismo. Habría sido otra persona, un fantasma desconocido que habita dentro de su propio cráneo.

Spector lo meditó.

–Es una idea aterradora.

–Ajá. Pero imagine lo aterrador que es para el hombre que lo sufre. Saber que están pasando todas esas cosas y que eres el responsable pero que no tienes voluntad propia para controlarlas…

–Entonces, ¿sería posible que un hombre cometiera un asesinato en uno de esos estados de fuga?

Ella lo miró con detenimiento, como si acabara de verlo realmente por primera vez.

–Un hombre podría hacer cualquier cosa –dijo.

–¿Y qué puede decirme sobre los sueños?

–¿Se refiere a los de Floyd Stenhouse? Supongo que ha estado leyendo las notas de mi padre…

–Por supuesto. Su padre señala que un sueño es como un poema: inventa y reinventa su propio lenguaje, es lírico y ambiguo y, lo que es más importante, nunca va directo al grano. Así que un sueño es la búsqueda de la claridad, una revelación de imágenes y símbolos. Con eso en mente, ¿qué opina de los sueños de Floyd Stenhouse?

–Mi padre desarrolló criterios para descodificar sueños. En primer lugar, planteaba una capa superficial y fílmica a la que denominaba «continente tangencial». Aquí encontramos aspectos con correlaciones exactas en el mundo de la vigilia. Por ejemplo: un estudiante a punto de presentarse a un examen tendrá de antemano sueños sobre dicho examen. Sin embargo, debajo de esa primera capa se encuentra una segunda a la que llamó «corpúsculo jugoso». Se trata del reino de los símbolos. Cuando el comportamiento y la vida del individuo durante la vigilia se separan de forma significativa del inconsciente instintivo, el corpúsculo jugoso se vuelve más pronunciado y los sueños asumen un aspecto alegórico y figurado. Este es el caso del señor Stenhouse.

–¿Y qué me dice de sus sueños específicamente? ¿Cómo los interpreta?

–Solo hay una manera de hacerlo: de forma simbólica. Por ejemplo, una lámpara representa la iluminación, el descubrimiento de un secreto. Los dientes son la violencia. El agua es el envejecimiento y los estragos del tiempo. Por lo tanto, que un hombre, el padre de Stenhouse, emerja de un lago tranquilo sujetando una lámpara parece representar el resurgir de una figura del pasado. Un secreto que se revela. Y las mandíbulas..., violencia y enfermedad.

–¿Y qué le dice eso del propio Stenhouse?

Lidia estaba muy seria cuando se quitó las gafas.

–Señor Spector, Stenhouse no es mi paciente. Yo no he tenido nada que ver en su diagnóstico. Creo que el único hombre que podría haber contestado a sus preguntas era mi padre.

El mago meditó aquello y, tras un instante de silencio, dijo:

–¿Y qué hay de sus sueños, doctora Rees?

–Yo no tengo sueños.

–¿Ninguno? Pero tiene usted una mente tan activa...

Ella entrelazó los dedos, pensativa.

–Digamos que... soy incapaz de soñar.

Se produjo otra pausa prolongada mientras Lidia y Spector se miraban fijamente el uno al otro como si fueran duelistas.

–Perdone la impertinencia –dijo el mago–, pero ¿quería usted a su padre?

–Eso es como preguntarle a la Tierra si quiere al sol.

–¿Ah, sí?

Ella lo miró por encima de las gafas.

–Anselm Rees me creó a su imagen y semejanza.

–Parece usted amargada.

–Soy tan incapaz de sentir amargura como soy incapaz de soñar.

Su rostro estaba desprovisto de toda emoción.

Cuando llevaba dos días investigando, el inspector George Flint tuvo su primer y único golpe de suerte. Se había resignado a una larga y tortuosa campaña de investigación para identificar al Hombre Serpiente. Sin embargo, cuando regresó a Scotland Yard, fue recibido por un sargento Hook inusualmente alegre.

–Reconozco esa sonrisita, Hook. Parece que ha encontrado algo.

–Y tanto que sí, señor –contestó el sargento.

La cuestión era que, cuando Anselm Rees había emigrado desde Viena hasta Londres, había pedido que se enviaran con él los archivos de sus trabajos académicos. Aquel catálogo meticulosamente cuidado de registros escritos a mano se encontraba en aquel momento en la Universidad de Oxford a la espera de ser integrado en la inmensa colección de libros de psiquiatría de la Biblioteca Bodleiana.

–Estaba un poco preocupado, señor –dijo Hook–, pues temía que nuestra única fuente fueran los registros de los pacientes de la clínica del valle del Wachau. Habría sido difícil encontrarlos en buenas condiciones, pero resulta que la mayoría quedaron destruidos hace unos años por un incendio. Ahora bien, el doctor

Rees también mantenía su propia copia de los registros. Así que, al final, solo he necesitado cruzar algunas referencias. Acabo de recibir un telegrama de Viena confirmando los registros de defunción.

–¿Y?

–El nombre real del Hombre Serpiente era «Bruno Tanzer».

–«Bruno Tanzer»… –Flint le dio vueltas al nombre en la lengua–. ¿Y qué hemos descubierto de Tanzer?

–Tan solo lo que me han contado las autoridades vienesas. Tanzer tenía una esposa, pero murió de una epidemia de gripe. Aunque sí que le dio una hija, que nació en 1900. Eso significa que ahora tendría…

–Treinta y seis años –acabó el inspector–. En este caso tan solo hay una mujer que podría encajar con el papel de la hija del Hombre Serpiente, y esa es Della Cookson. –Le dedicó una sonrisa al sargento–. Hook, se ha superado una vez más. Siga trabajando, a ver qué más puede averiguar. Yo me marcho al Teatro Pomegranate.

Cuando llegó al Pomegranate, Joseph Spector se encontró a Benjamin Teasel, que estaba solo en el bar. El productor estaba contemplando con tristeza un vaso de ginebra rosa. Desde que había perdido el cuadro, parecía haber envejecido varias décadas, pero, al ver al mago, se puso en pie de un salto.

–¡Joseph! ¿Tienes alguna noticia, viejo?

–¿Alguna noticia?

–¡Sí, noticias! ¡*El nacimiento*! ¿De qué pensabas que estaba hablando? Necesito que obres tu magia para mí, Joseph.

–Sabes que haré lo que pueda por ti, Benjamin, pero tienes que recordar que ha muerto un hombre. Y, además, un hombre famoso. Semejantes acontecimientos tienden a avivar la imaginación colectiva más que el robo de un cuadro.

–Por eso te lo estoy pidiendo a ti en concreto –continuó Teasel con un humor juguetón forzado y edulcorado. Le pasó un brazo por los hombros cubiertos por la capa–. Sé que tú, más que nadie, eres capaz de resolver ambos casos de un solo plumazo. Además,

¿de verdad crees que hay alguna posibilidad de que Della robara el cuadro y no matara también a su médico?

–Eso es... interesante –dijo Spector–. ¿Tienes alguna base para esa afirmación?

–Spector, no tengo nada. Lo único que sé es que cometí el error idiota, necio y claramente estúpido de mostrarle a esa malvada mujer mi última adquisición. Ella es la única que sabía que estaba allí y también es la única que podría haberme robado las llaves del cuello.

–Bueno, Benjamin –le regañó el mago–, ninguna de esas afirmaciones es cierta. Yo ya había asistido a alguna de tus fiestas y sé lo espesa que puede resultar la neblina del alcohol. Cuesta distinguir dónde acaba un invitado y empieza el otro. Cualquier otra persona podría haberse hecho con las llaves con facilidad.

–Bueno –replicó el productor con un tono de decisión en la voz–, tendrás que descubrirlo, ¿no?

Poco después, el inspector Flint irrumpió en el vestíbulo y se acercó al bar, donde estaban ellos.

–Spector, necesito hablar con usted.

El mago se excusó y siguió a Flint. Con discreción, ambos se abrieron paso entre bambalinas mientras el inspector detallaba el descubrimiento de la verdadera identidad del Hombre Serpiente.

–Entonces, tiene una hija –dijo Spector mientras se encendía un cigarrillo–. ¿De verdad cree que es Della?

Flint sacó su cuaderno de notas y lo examinó.

–Della Cookson –leyó–. Nombre de pila: Mabel Norman. No existen registros de nacimiento, pero sabemos por fuentes fidedignas que antes residía en el Hogar del Roble para Niños No Deseados. En otras palabras: es huérfana. Cuando cumplió la mayoría de edad, empezó a trabajar como criada en el Hotel Plaza. De ahí, pasó al coro de los Belmont Follies. El resto, como se suele decir, es historia.

–Entonces, ¿es posible que sea la hija del Hombre Serpiente?

–Es una posibilidad. También es lo más cerca que hemos estado de tener una pista en cuanto al móvil.

–¿Haciendo investigaciones, señor Spector?

La que había hablado era Lucy Levy. Tenía la espalda apoyada contra el muro de ladrillo, estirada como un gato. El mago se giró hacia ella.

–Pues resulta que sí. ¿Por qué? ¿Hay algo que quiera contarme?

Ella se rio. Se trataba de una risa practicada, propia de una escuela de teatro.

–En este teatro hay muchos misterios, ¿no es así? El pobre y viejo Benjamin pierde su cuadro. De entre todas las personas posibles, es Della Cookson la que consigue el papel de protagonista de esta horrible obra. Y luego, por supuesto, está Edgar Simmons.

–¿Edgar Simmons? –A Spector le sonaba el nombre. Ya lo había oído antes, pero ¿dónde?–. ¿Quién es Edgar Simmons? Tendrá que iluminarme, Lucy.

–Otro misterio que va a tener que resolver –dijo ella mientras se escabullía.

Tal vez quería que la siguiera, pero el mago no estaba de humor, así que se quedó de pie observando cómo se marchaba.

Cuando llegaron al camerino de la estrella, Della Cookson ya estaba vestida de pies a cabeza. Se miraba a sí misma en el espejo y apenas dio muestras de haberse percatado de su llegada.

–Caballeros –dijo de forma gélida–, ¿qué puedo hacer por ustedes?

–Solo hemos venido a desearte suerte, Della. Y a hacerte una o dos preguntas.

Flint dio un paso al frente.

–Señorita Cookson, por favor, dígame si alguna vez ha oído el nombre «Hombre Serpiente».

Ella los miró, pestañeando.

–Ese nombre no me suena de nada –contestó.

–Tómese un momento para pensarlo. «Hombre Serpiente» era el pseudónimo que se le dio a un paciente psiquiátrico alemán que se llamaba Bruno Tanzer. –La actriz sacudió la cabeza–. Tanzer murió por su propia mano. Se suicidó durante el otoño de 1921. Piénselo detenidamente. ¿Está segura de que no conoce a ningún Bruno Tanzer?

–Caballeros, no tengo ni idea de qué están hablando

–Muy bien –replicó Spector con resolución–. Supongo que era una esperanza vana. ¿Cómo te sientes con respecto a la actuación de esta noche?

–Bien. Muchas gracias, Joseph. Ya me conoces: cuando estoy sobre el escenario, todo va bien.

Tomando el relevo de Spector, el inspector intervino.

–Debe de costarle mucho.

Della suspiró.

–Actuar… es una existencia transitoria en el mejor de los casos… Como Edgar Simmons, ¿lo recuerdas, Joseph? Justo la semana pasada estuvimos hablando en el Ivy y me contó que las cosas empezaban a irle bien al fin, que había conseguido un trabajo bonito y cómodo, algo regular, pero lo siguiente que descubro es que se ha largado, que se ha marchado a algún lugar del extranjero. Además, tengo entendido que con bastante prisa…

–¿Simmons? Lucy Levy nos lo acaba de mencionar. ¿Quién es?

–¿Edgar? Oh, no es más que un actor de mediana edad. Se parecen mucho los unos a los otros, ¿verdad?

–Pero ¿ha desaparecido?

Ella dejó la pregunta pendiendo del aire, tentadora.

–«Desaparecer» es una palabra tan melodramática…

–¿Prefieres «esfumarse»? La cuestión es que se ha marchado, ¿es eso lo que intentas decirnos?

Ella lo miró con gesto de paciencia divina. En ese momento, le hubiera pegado interpretar a una monja.

–Sí, Joseph. Eso es precisamente lo que intento decir.

–¿Y cuándo lo viste por última vez?

–Oh, puede que hace una semana. Es una de esas personas que ves por aquí y por allá pero que, de pronto, ya no está.

Spector sonrió.

–Se dio prisa, ¿no? Una de sus muñequitas debía de tener marido.

–Puede ser. Pero, en realidad, solo estoy diciendo que nosotros, la gente del teatro, no tenemos nada de lo que podamos depender de verdad, nada tangible. Puedes estar en la cresta de la ola cuando bajas del escenario y, al día siguiente, encontrarte hundido en la miseria. Puede pasar así de rápido.

–¿Hay algo de lo que quieras hablarnos, Della?

–No. –Soltó una carcajada–. Es solo que me estoy poniendo sensiblera. Es curioso cómo los asesinatos tienden a afectarme de ese modo.

–Tienes por delante una carrera fenomenal con muchos años sobre los escenarios. No tienes nada que temer.

Della lo miró sonriendo, pero no dijo nada.

En el tocador, Flint vio un libro con las esquinas dobladas. Las letras del lomo decían EL RITO DE SANGRE DE CLAUDE WEAVER.

–¿Conoce usted a Claude Weaver? –le preguntó mientras se abalanzaba sobre el libro.

–¿Eh? No, no. Tan solo soy una admiradora. ¿Por qué?

Entonces, se produjo un silencio incómodo antes de que Spector dijera:

–Claude Weaver era uno de los otros dos pacientes del doctor Rees.

–Vaya –contestó Della sin inmutarse–, ¡menuda sorpresa! Pero no, nunca lo he conocido.

–¿Y qué me dice de Floyd Stenhouse? –preguntó el inspector.

La actriz los miró de golpe.

–¿Floyd? ¿Qué pasa con Floyd?

Flint frunció el ceño.

–Entonces, ¿lo conoce?

–Nos conocemos desde hace mucho, aunque no diría que le conozco exactamente...

–Pero sí que lo has visto en alguna ocasión –dijo Spector con tono tranquilizador.

–No últimamente...

–¿Cuándo? –insistió el mago.

–Cuando éramos jóvenes.

–Entonces, ¿erais amigos de la infancia? ¿Cómo era de joven?

–No podría decirte, no estábamos muy unidos...

Como sintió que había agotado aquella línea de investigación, Spector dio un paso hacia ella.

–Ahora, voy a enseñarte un pequeño truco de magia –le dijo con una sonrisa–. Si me permites... –Della lo miró pestañeando–. Veamos... –continuó el anciano.

Agarró y bajó de un armario de pared tres tazas blancas con un diseño idéntico. Las colocó sobre la mesa las unas junto a las otras dibujando una línea. Del bolsillo se sacó una pequeña pelota de goma. La lanzó al otro lado de la habitación, en dirección a Della, que la atrapó con unas manos con una manicura muy elegante.

–Coloca la pelota debajo de una de las tazas –le indicó él. Ella levantó la taza del centro y colocó la pelota debajo–. Ahora –continuó el hombre mientras les daba la espalda–, quiero que me engañes.

Durante unos veinte segundos, la actriz estuvo moviendo y cambiando de sitio las tazas. Spector, que estaba girado y tenía los ojos cerrados, podía oír el rozar de la porcelana sobre la superficie de madera de caoba. Flint observó todo aquello sin mediar palabra.

–Ya está –dijo Della.

Spector se dio la vuelta para mirarla a la cara, pero no sonrió. Mientras hablaba, apenas movió el rostro.

–¿Estás satisfecha? ¿Crees que no hay manera de que pueda saber bajo qué taza se encuentra la pelota? ¿Seguro que es imposible que lo haya visto? –La mujer asintió–. Entonces, prepárate para quedar fascinada –replicó él mientras se adelantaba y levantaba la taza de la izquierda para mostrar la pelota de goma–. Pensarás que, tal vez, haya sido suerte. Muy bien, vamos a repetir el experimento, ¿quieres?

Volvieron a repetirlo dos veces más, en las que el hombre se giró hacia la pared mientras Della movía las tazas. Cada una de las veces, el mago encontró la pelota.

–Como ocurre con todos los trucos de leer la mente –explicó él–, no se trata más que de un fraude viejísimo. Cuando he tomado las tazas, me he dado cuenta de que, aunque todas tienen exactamente la misma forma y el mismo diseño, cada una de ellas posee algo que la distingue de las otras. Esta de aquí tiene una mella diminuta en el borde. Esta otra tiene una rajita en el asa. Y la parte de debajo de esta está un poco descolorida, como si la hubieran dejado bocabajo al sol durante demasiado tiempo. Son cosas que apenas son visibles al ojo, especialmente con la luz tenue de un camerino, pero, si estás entrenado, puedes fijarte en este tipo de cosas con bastante facilidad. Y si no hubieran sido esos detalles concretos, habría sido cualquier otro.

»De todos modos, las he colocado de tal manera que no hubiera muchas posibilidades de que notaras cada imperfección. Me he situado de tal modo que mi sombra cayera sobre la taza descolorida para que, aunque lo hubieras notado, tu ojo hubiera convencido a tu cerebro de que era cosa de la sombra. Cuando te he pedido que colocaras la pelota debajo de una de las tazas, el deseo psicológico innato de buscar la simetría dictaba que la colocarías en la de en medio. Aunque, si no lo hubieras hecho, tampoco habría importado. He sabido con exactitud dónde se encontraba en todo momento. Por supuesto, no podía descartar la idea de que pudieras fijarte en alguno de los minúsculos desperfectos cuando estuvieras moviendo las tazas. Pero soy un artista: estaba dispuesto a arriesgarme.

»Y eso es todo. ¿Satisfecha?

–No mucho –contestó Della–. Es una solución muy sosa. Esperaba algo un poco más emocionante.

–Pero es que en eso consiste la magia, querida, en tomar lo mundano y convertirlo en algo extraordinario. Aun así, el truco nos enseña algo sobre la percepción, y es que, sin importar lo engañosa que creyeras estar siendo, la imagen que yo he tenido ha sido en todo momento más clara que la tuya. Tal vez hayas pensado que me estabas engañando, pero, por supuesto, era yo el que te estaba engañando a ti desde el principio.

Ella le dedicó una sonrisa, pero, en cierto sentido, fue dura y sin ganas, no le llegó a los ojos.

Mientras salían del Pomegranate, Flint se detuvo para murmurar al oído de Spector.

–¿Por qué tanto jaleo con Edgar Simmons? Nunca antes había oído su nombre.

–Siempre soy precavido con los nombres que aparecen varias veces en diferentes contextos...

–No se distraiga, Spector –le advirtió el inspector–. Su preocupación principal tiene que ser Anselm Rees. No lo olvide. No quiero que se lance a un callejón sin salida con respecto a ese actor desaparecido. ¿Acaso no desaparecen los actores continuamente?

–Oh, sin duda –asintió el mago rápidamente–. Pero, en general, cuando lo hacen, nadie los recuerda.

Dieron un pequeño rodeo por el escenario. Lucy Levy estaba ensayando algunas líneas. No eran las suyas, sino las de Della. Era evidente que deseaba de todo corazón arrebatarle el papel principal.

–Señorita Levy, perdóneme por interrumpirla, pero tengo que hacerle una pregunta. Parece muy decidida a que me interese por Edgar Simmons. ¿Hay algo que quiera contarme?

Ella lo miró con los ojos muy abiertos, como si quisiera decir: «¿Quién, yo?».

–He oído que le gustan los misterios. Eso es todo.

–Me ha dicho usted que ha desaparecido. Della Cookson me ha dicho lo mismo. ¿Cuándo ocurrió?

–Oh, no lo sé. Estaba aquí un día y al día siguiente... ya no estaba.

Spector se giró hacia Flint.

–¿Cree que podría encontrar la dirección de Edgar Simmons? –El inspector lo fulminó con la mirada–. Ya lo sé, ya lo sé. «No se distraiga». Pero hay ciertos sujetos muy deseosos de que me interese por el señor Simmons. Eso no puede ser coincidencia, ¿no?

Flint abrió la boca para decirle al viejo mago que, sin duda, podía ser coincidencia y que, de hecho, seguro que lo era, pero se detuvo. No tenía sentido discutir. En su lugar, se mostró de acuerdo y anotó en su libreta el nombre del actor desaparecido.

Cuando regresaron a Scotland Yard, Flint sirvió en su oficina dos vasos de *whisky* escocés para que ambos pudieran acomodarse y diseccionar después los descubrimientos del día.

–Creo que tal vez nos estemos centrando demasiado en la idea de que Della está involucrada –comenzó Spector–. No tengo dudas de que nos está mintiendo en algo. Pero, bueno, de momento no tenemos pruebas de que sea la hija del Hombre Serpiente.

–Tiene razón –rumió Flint entre sorbos de *whisky*–. He aquí una idea. Y tenga paciencia conmigo, porque tal vez le parezca un poco extraña. ¿Y si el Hombre Serpiente no se suicidó y lo mataron?

–Bueno, es cierto que los informes con respecto a su muerte son sospechosos. Sería bastante fácil disfrazar un asesinato como un suicidio provocado por la histeria. Pero eso limita el número de sospechosos, ¿no? Quiero decir..., si suponemos que Della no es la hija de Tanzer, no hay manera de que ninguno de los pacientes actuales del doctor hubiesen estado involucrados.

–No, pero... sí hay una manera de que Lidia hubiera podido estarlo.

–¡Era muy joven! Apenas tenía diez años cuando murió *Der Schlangenmann*, ¿no?

–Algunos niños nacen malos –dijo Flint con aire de sabiduría.

–Deje que me aclare. ¿Me está diciendo que, con diez años, Lidia Rees se coló en el sanatorio de su padre y le cortó el cuello a uno de sus pacientes? ¿A un hombre adulto?

Hay que decir que el razonamiento del inspector era lógico.

–Un hombre adulto que estaba sedado hasta el punto de perder la cabeza. Se sabe de niños que han cometido crímenes mucho más estrafalarios que ese.

–Pero, si lo que dice es cierto, ¿por qué nos habría llamado Lidia la atención sobre este crimen suyo tan atroz? ¿Por qué iba a mencionárnoslo?

–Usted mismo lo ha dicho, Spector. Nos estamos enfrentando a una psicología que no es la habitual.

–Pero tiene coartada.

–Bowman no es más que un bufón. Le cuesta saber en qué día vive. Diría lo que ella le pidiera que dijera.

–Eso es muy cierto, pero también tenemos que lidiar con los testimonios de los trabajadores del Savoy. Además de los de los pocos transeúntes del Palmyra.

–Mire –dijo el inspector, que empezaba a impacientarse–, no sé cómo lo hizo, pero todo este asunto apesta a una asesina que se cree muy lista y que no tiene miedo a ponernos la verdad delante de las narices porque cree que nunca seremos lo bastante inteligentes como para darnos cuenta.

El mago se recostó en su asiento.

–No es que esté en desacuerdo con usted, Flint. Estamos hablando de un asesino descarado que no teme que le pillen, alguien que ya no valora su propia vida. Y las personas así son siempre las más peligrosas. –Miró al inspector a los ojos–. Tenga cuidado, Flint. Vaya con cuidado.

Se terminaron las bebidas y Spector le deseó al policía las buenas noches. Fuera ya había oscurecido, pero, a través de la ventana, Flint observó cómo el viejo paraba un taxi y desaparecía en medio de la noche que estaba cayendo. Fue en ese momento cuando el inspector se dio cuenta de que detrás de él, en el umbral de la puerta de su oficina, había alguien merodeando con timidez.

–¿Qué quiere, Hook?

–Malas noticias, señor.

Le costaba mirarle a los ojos.

–¿De qué se trata?

–De la hija de Bruno Tanzer, señor. He escuchado parte de su conversación sin querer y me temo que no es posible. Murió en 1929 en Berlín.

Flint soltó el aire, pensativo.

–¿Cómo murió?

–Suicidio. Me temo que se rajó la garganta.

El inspector cerró los ojos y se frotó la frente de forma agresiva con las palmas de las manos.

–Así que el rastro se acaba ahí.

–Lo siento, pero eso es lo que parece.

–Tanzer no tenía ningún otro pariente ni ninguna otra relación que podamos rastrear.

–Lamento no poder darle mejores noticias, señor. Sé que tenían esperanzas en este asunto.

Tras un segundo, Flint dijo:

–No es culpa suya, Hook. Me marcho a casa. Necesito descansar bien para poner mis pensamientos en orden. Le recomendaría que hiciera lo mismo. Pero, antes, hágame un favor, ¿de acuerdo? De camino a casa, pare en la de Joseph Spector y dele la mala noticia.

Jerome Hook era el quinto de su familia en trabajar para defender la ley y el orden. Era lo único que conocía y, probablemente, lo único que conocería jamás. Cuando, si Dios quería, tuviera un hijo, le pasaría esos mismos conocimientos al pequeño. Comía, dormía y respiraba edictos y preceptos. Sin embargo, en sus veinticinco años de vida, jamás había conocido a un hombre como Joseph Spector. Y, ya que estamos, tampoco había visitado ningún lugar como la casa de Jubilee Court.

Clotilde, la criada, era una joven angulosa de unos veinte años con la piel blanca como la porcelana y el pelo castaño rojizo, rizado y recogido. Mientras lo contemplaba frente a la puerta, su rostro se mostró impasible.

–Estoy buscando al señor Spector –dijo mientras pasaba los pies por el empedrado sin saber muy bien qué hacer con las manos.

Ella no dijo nada, solo asintió con suavidad con la cabeza y se hizo a un lado para dejarle entrar en la casa.

Así que aquel era el aspecto que tenía el hogar de un mago… El pasillo era bastante anodino (tenía paneles de roble y estaba débilmente iluminado por unas lámparas de gas cubiertas de polvo) y no se diferenciaba demasiado del de la casa de los Rees. Sin embargo, cuando la joven lo condujo al estudio, fue como entrar en otro mundo.

–¡Ah! –exclamó Spector con lo que parecía un deleite sincero por la presencia de Hook–. Bienvenido a mi sanctasanctórum.

La estancia era increíble. Las paredes estaban cubiertas por pósteres viejos de espectáculos de variedades, muchos de los cuales incluían en algún lugar las palabras EL ESPECTACULAR SEÑOR SPECTOR. Era un torrente de color, como entrar dentro del cerebro extraño del viejo. Por supuesto, las estanterías estaban repletas de libros, pero, al parecer, aquel estudio también era un museo o una sala de trofeos y estaba lleno de disparates extraños y maravillosos. Una sirena de Fiji conservada dentro de un tarro alto de cristal en un fluido amarillento, una fila de cabezas reducidas y unidas las unas a las otras por las orejas hasta formar un macabro cordón, diversos artilugios de relojería, un armario de espiritismo con cortinas de terciopelo mullido, cartas del tarot y otros artículos desconcertantes de ocultismo. Curiosamente, también había un par de quemadores de incienso que otorgaban a la sala una pátina de niebla mohosa y, en cierto sentido, amenazadora. Era como si estuviera a punto de llevarse a cabo algún tipo de ritual oscuro.

–Cuidado con los huesos de Pulgarcito –dijo Spector.

Hook, desconcertado, estuvo a punto de tropezarse con un esqueleto pequeño que colgaba de un marco de alambre junto a la puerta como si fuera un limpiabotas.

Los dos hombres se sentaron junto a la chimenea. De algún modo, el mago parecía más extraño bajo la luz del fuego, ceroso, irreal. Debía de ser consciente de que esa imagen le pegaba.

–¿Té, sargento? ¿O puedo tentarle con un brebaje más atrevido?

–Un té está bien –contestó Hook.

Le costaba mantener alejados de su voz los gallos de adolescente insípido.

–Clotilde –dijo Spector mientras miraba a la criada silenciosa. Ella volvió a asentir y salió de la habitación–. ¿Y bien? ¿Qué puedo hacer por usted? –le preguntó al joven–. Si el inspector le ha enviado hasta aquí a buscarme, debe de ser una emergencia.

–Son malas noticias, señor. Della Cookson no es la hija del Hombre Serpiente.

–¿Cómo lo sabe?

–Porque la hija del Hombre Serpiente se suicidó en 1929.

Spector meditó sobre aquello.

–Ya veo. Bueno, supongo que tiene sentido. Imagino que el inspector estará bastante desanimado. Yo, por el contrario, no lo estoy. Verá, este es un caso con muchas facetas. Demasiadas. Por ejemplo, piense en esto. –Giró sobre su asiento y encendió el gramófono que tenía al lado. De él surgió el sonido de un violín solitario, coqueto y esperanzador, que flotaba como una paloma sobre escenas de miedo y carnicería–. Floyd Stenhouse –dijo el anciano–. ¿No es maravilloso?

–Tiene mucho talento –replicó Hook con una tos avergonzada.

–Por supuesto, ya sabemos que la genialidad y la locura van de la mano. Es lo que nos dice la historia. Y, por las notas de Rees, deduzco que el señor Stenhouse es un hombre movido por los tormentos del subconsciente. Tiene sueños... espantosos. Sueños monstruosos que rivalizan con las invenciones más oscuras de Edgar Allan Poe. Escuche esto. –Estiró el brazo y levantó la aguja del gramófono. No hubo un *diminuendo*, sino que la música se quedó en silencio con un chirrido abrupto. Entonces, centró toda su atención en el cuaderno–. Aquí hay una entrada fechada hace dos semanas: «En el sueño, el Paciente A está en la cama como siempre, removiéndose con fiebre. El sudor emana de su cuerpo y tiene convulsiones a causa de un retortijón en las entrañas. Poco a poco, comienza a darse cuenta de que no está solo. Recortada contra la luz de la luna al otro lado de la ventana de su habitación, ve una figura vestida de negro. Sabe que dicha figura, sea quien sea, es la causa de su agonía. Su instinto le lleva a arremeter y a golpear a la persona responsable de tanto dolor. Agarra algo de la mesa que tiene junto a la cama y se lo lanza a la figura. De inmediato, dicha figura se desvanece en una cascada de cristales rotos y el Paciente A se da cuenta de que no es más que un espejo resquebrajado».

–Todo esto no significa nada para mí, señor.

–¿No? ¿Quiere decir que no le parece interesante? ¿Ni siquiera un poco?

–Siento como si fuera voyerismo. Los sueños de un hombre son asunto suyo.

–Estoy seguro de que tiene razón en eso y, aun así, el señor Stenhouse parece demasiado dispuesto a compartir los suyos. Tan dispuesto, de hecho, que llamó por teléfono al doctor Rees en medio de la noche para describirle su última pesadilla mientras todavía la tenía fresca en la mente. Como es evidente, el propio doctor sentía mucho interés por los terrores nocturnos del músico atormentado. Tal vez preveía otro éxito de ventas en ciernes.

–¿Dónde quiere llegar, señor?

–Respóndame a una pregunta, Hook: ¿cuál fue la reacción inmediata del doctor Rees cuando Stenhouse empezó a recitarle el contenido de su sueño?

–Empezó a tomar nota. Olive Turner oyó la pluma rasgando el papel.

–¡Correcto! Comenzó a tomar nota de inmediato. Ahora, respóndame a esto: ¿qué ocurrió con esas notas?

Hook se quedó sin palabras. Después dijo:

–Las últimas notas fueron las que estaba tomando antes de que Olive le llevara el tentempié. No encontramos nada posterior a eso.

–¿Y eso qué quiere decir? ¿Que tal vez el asesino arrancara del cuaderno la página en cuestión? ¿Que tal vez hubiese en aquella página algo más que no quería que viéramos?

–Pero ¿por qué?

Spector sonrió.

–Creo que es posible que al fin estemos haciendo la pregunta correcta.

Cuando llegó a casa, el inspector George Flint se encontraba algo distraído. Su esposa le puso delante un cuenco de estofado de ternera que devoró entre gruñidos monosilábicos. Julia Flint era una mujer paciente y sabía que no podía esperar demasiado de su marido cuando se encontraba tan sumido en un caso. Sin embargo, incluso ella se sintió un poco perpleja ante su mirada vacía y vidriosa mientras permanecía sentado junto al fuego en el salón tenuemente iluminado.

No pasó mucho tiempo antes de que se quedara dormido en su sillón con los dedos entrelazados sobre la barriga. Julia volvió a entrar en la habitación con una cafetera, pero, cuando lo vio dormido, chasqueó la lengua una vez y se marchó sola a la cama.

Flint, desplomado sobre su asiento como un eco inconsciente de la pose en la que había muerto Anselm Rees, comenzó a roncar. Sin embargo, su sueño, que en apariencia era tranquilo, estaba siendo turbulento.

Se descubrió en una habitación sin puerta y sin ventanas. No había ninguna manera posible de entrar o salir. El lugar le resultaba familiar y, aun así, le daba miedo, pues desprendía una extraña sensación de amenaza. Recorrió las paredes en busca de algún panel falso o algún compartimento oculto. En el rincón más alejado de la estancia vio un baúl de madera del tamaño de un hombre. Con una punzada de miedo, se aferró a los brazos de su sillón y se puso en pie.

–Doctor –dijo una voz. Era la voz de una mujer, sonaba muy bajita y mecánica, como si procediera de un gramófono invisible–. ¿Doctor?

«¿Qué ocurre?», intentó decir. Sin embargo, su garganta no produjo ningún sonido.

–Doctor… –Se acercó al baúl con lentitud–. Doctor, tiene una visita.

Tenía la mano suspendida sobre el cerrojo del baúl. Para su sorpresa, cuando se disponía a abrirlo, se abrió por sí solo con un chasquido. Con un crujido, la tapa se elevó y de dentro empezó a surgir una figura.

Con un grito ahogado, Flint dio un paso atrás. La figura, que era una aglomeración de sombras sin forma, siguió elevándose hasta que quedó por encima de él. No conseguía terminar de centrar la mirada, pero distinguió a un hombre con un abrigo y un sombrero.

«¿Quién es usted?», intentó decir.

–Doctor –repitió la voz incorpórea de mujer–, tiene una visita.

Flint sintió un miedo familiar en el pecho. Con las manos enguantadas, la criatura hecha de sombras se inclinó hacia él y, al hacerlo, Flint empezó a distinguir poco a poco su rostro. No era un rostro humano. Tenía dos hileras idénticas de dientes afilados manchados de sangre y bilis. Tenía los ojos pequeños, redondos, brillantes y negros. Era el rostro de una serpiente con el tamaño de un hombre.

Con una sacudida priápica, Flint se despertó. El fuego se había extinguido y la luz del sol matutino se colaba a través de las cortinas del salón. Se incorporó jadeando y se angustió al comprobar que el sudor le había empapado la camisa. Se puso en pie poco a poco, como si fuera un anciano. Las rodillas le temblaron mientras se dirigía dando tumbos a la cocina para tomar un vaso de agua.

ACTO III

El cuento de la suplantación

(Del 15 al 17 de septiembre de 1936)

«–Es curioso, ¿no? –preguntó Bruce–. Muy curioso. Todo este tiempo en el que he estado intentando sonsacarte información, todo el mundo pensaba que tú estabas intentando sonsacarme información a mí.

–Tengo un don para hacer que las cosas salgan así –dijo Bewlay con absoluta seriedad».

Carter Dickson, *Mis mujeres muertas*

«No es que no puedan ver la solución. Es que no pueden ver el problema».

G. K. Chesterton, *La punta de un alfiler*

ENTREACTO II

El señor Weaver hace una compra

(Martes, 15 de septiembre de 1936)

La Ferretería de Morrison era un pequeño establecimiento en medio de una hilera de fachadas de Portobello Road. Su enorme escaparate rectangular estaba repleto de utensilios de hierro, escurridores, un tendedero, cañas de pescar, navajas suizas y otras cosas semejantes. El propietario, el señor Morrison, apenas había girado el cartel de la puerta que rezaba ABIERTO cuando Claude Weaver entró dando tumbos desde la calle. El escritor tenía un aspecto demacrado y desaliñado, pero, cuando se acercó al mostrador, sus modales y su forma de hablar fueron del todo calmados. Hablaba con claridad y autoridad.

–Quiero eso –dijo mientras señalaba un objeto que había en un expositor de cristal que se encontraba tras el mostrador.

–Buenos días para usted también, señor –contestó Morrison.

–Dese prisa –dijo Weaver mientras miraba su reloj de bolsillo.

Sin mediar palabra, el anciano propietario abrió el expositor y sacó el objeto. Henry Morrison no hizo caso a semejante descortesía y no le importó dedicar el tiempo necesario. Se tomó su tiempo abriendo el armario y, mientras lo hacía, aprovechó la oportunidad para mirar bien a aquel tipo bastante extraordinario que había irrumpido en su tienda al amanecer, procedente de la calle. Estaba pálido y calvo y la piel del cuello y la papada le colgaba con flacidez como si hubiese perdido algo de peso.

–¿Y para qué quiere el señor algo así?

–¿Para qué cree usted? ¡Protección! Lo necesito para protegerme.

El tendero se inclinó hacia delante, deleitándose con aquel melodrama.

–Así que tiene enemigos, ¿eh?

–¿Va a venderme el revólver o no? –espetó Weaver.

Pero el hombre ya estaba registrando la compra en la caja.

XII
La trampa del vampiro

El 16 de septiembre pasó en una bruma de diligencia sin orden. Todos estaban trabajando, incluido Spector (aunque es complicado saber qué es lo que hacía). De hecho, el anciano pasó una buena hora codeándose con actores en diferentes *pubs* y bares de la zona del Strand. Tenían mucho que contarle sobre Edgar Simmons, el actor desaparecido.

–Era un encanto –le dijo Mavis Le Fley mientras se tomaba su segunda ginebra rosa–, pero, en los últimos tiempos, estaba demasiado pagado de sí mismo.

–¿En qué sentido?

–Bueno, cuando llegamos a cierta edad, querido, puede resultar un poco difícil encontrar trabajo. Resulta bastante irritante cuando un tipo como Edgar viene a restregarte el éxito en la cara.

Todas las historias eran similares: Edgar Simmons, el actor envejecido, colmado de pronto de dinero y pagado de sí mismo. Sin embargo, nadie tenía nada más que añadir. Por suerte, Flint había conseguido dar con una dirección: la última casa de huéspedes en la que se había hospedado el actor. Cuando hubo agotado sus fuentes (y su hígado) en los diferentes bares para actores del West End, Spector se dirigió allí.

La casera tenía la melena pelirroja (de un rojo sangre muy llamativo) y el rostro asombrosamente blanco. A Spector le recordó a los relatos que había leído sobre la reina Isabel I, que había llevado más polvos y peluca que carne sobre sus viejos huesos. Tenía un acento musical procedente de las Hébridas que podría haberse quedado escuchando todo el día, pero era evidente que ella estaba ansiosa por ir al grano y sacar a aquel viejo decrépito de su encantadora casa.

–¿Simmons? –dijo ella–. ¡No pronuncie su nombre!

–Entonces, ¿no era un inquilino modélico?

–Como inquilino no daba ningún problema, señor Spector. Siempre fue tranquilo y limpio. Lo que sí me molestó fue cuando hizo las maletas y se marchó sin pagar el alquiler.

–¿Cuándo fue eso?

–El sábado. Desde entonces, ni lo he visto ni he sabido nada de él.

–¿Y nunca antes había hecho algo así?

–Nunca. Ni una sola vez. Ya ve, la gente acaba mostrándote su verdadera cara, ¿no es así?

En su mente, Spector vio la imagen de una figura ensombrecida frente a la puerta de Dollis Hill: un hombre con un abrigo largo, el ala del sombrero cubriéndole la frente y una bufanda tapándole la boca. El visitante del doctor, que tanto había perturbado a Olive Turner y cuya presencia en la periferia de la investigación suponía una frustración constante, ¿podría haber sido Edgar Simmons?

Flint detestaba los días como aquel. Mucho trabajo y ningún resultado que lo demostrara. Ni nueva información ni nuevas pistas.

Eso cambió casi a las siete de la tarde. El inspector estaba a punto de marcharse a casa y dar el día por terminado cuando empezó a sonar el teléfono de su escritorio.

Con recelo, descolgó el auricular.

–Flint al habla.

–Señor Flint, necesito su ayuda. –La voz pertenecía a Floyd Stenhouse y sonaba como si le ocurriera algo terriblemente malo–. ¿Puede venir de inmediato?

–¿Por qué? ¿Qué ha ocurrido?

–Hay alguien persiguiéndome.

–¿Quién?

–No lo sé. No lo había visto antes en toda mi vida, pero viene a por mí, eso se lo aseguro. Verá, estaba en el estudio y me ha seguido hasta aquí y ahora creo que está en el edificio.

El inspector chasqueó los dedos mientras señalaba la hoja de papel en blanco que tenía frente a él y uno de los sargentos de oficina que estaba de servicio le tendió un lapicero.

–¿Dónde se encuentra ahora mismo?

–Estoy en casa, en mi apartamento. Dufresne Court. Está en el edificio. Sé que está en el edificio, señor Flint. Venga lo antes posible.

–Quédese ahí, no vaya a ninguna parte. Voy para allá –contestó el policía antes de colgar el teléfono.

No encontró a Hook por ninguna parte. Un vistazo rápido a la sala de la brigada le permitió localizar a dos de los oficiales de uniforme de aspecto más robusto que la división podía ofrecer: los agentes Bream y Harrow. Eran hombres de buena reputación y, además, poseían una estatura física intimidante. Flint los reclutó para el viaje a Dufresne Court.

Fueron hasta allí en automóvil. Iban muy apretados, pero, aun así, el inspector encontró el hueco necesario para echar una pizca de tabaco en su pipa y encenderla.

Llegaron al inmenso edificio de estilo *art decó* en diez minutos. Flint encabezó la comitiva a través del recibidor de forma imperiosa. Royce, el portero, apartó la vista de su crucigrama.

–¿Puedo ayudarlos, caballeros?

–Hemos venido a ver a Floyd Stenhouse. Asuntos policiales.

Se dirigieron a grandes zancadas hasta el ascensor. Gracias a la fila de bombillas que había sobre la jaula de metal, Flint vio que se encontraba en el cuarto piso.

–No hay tiempo –dijo mientras se encaminaba hacia las escaleras–. Cuatro pisos. Ocho tramos de escaleras. Caballeros, espero que esta noche se sientan en forma.

Tras decir eso, empezó a subir los escalones de dos en dos. Cuando llegaron al cuarto piso (Flint apenas sudaba), el inspector los condujo hasta el hogar de Floyd Stenhouse. Llamó al timbre. Como no abrieron la puerta de inmediato, la golpeó con fuerza con el puño. Siguió sin haber respuesta. Miró de reojo a ambos agentes y estaba a punto de llamar de nuevo cuando de detrás de la puerta emergió un sonido suave, como si alguien estuviera tomando aire.

–¿Quién anda ahí? –preguntó una voz temblorosa.

–Soy Flint.

Al otro lado de la puerta se descorrieron varios cerrojos y cadenas. Se oyó el último chasquido de la llave al girar en la cerradura y, entonces, Floyd Stenhouse, sudoroso y demacrado, les dejó entrar en el apartamento. Cuando estuvieron dentro, el músico asomó la cabeza al pasillo para comprobar que hubieran llegado solos. Entonces, cerró la puerta de golpe y apoyó la espalda contra ella, como si se enfrentara a una fuerza invasora.

–¿Y bien? –preguntó Flint–. ¿De qué va todo esto?

–Sé lo que puede parecerle, pero no estoy paranoico, señor Flint. Créame, de verdad. Está aquí, por alguna parte. En el edificio. Quiere matarme.

El inspector dio una calada a su pipa y dijo:

–¿Por qué no vamos a sentarnos y me cuenta todo el asunto desde el principio?

Cuando todos estuvieron acomodados en sillones bajos y mullidos (los agentes, con las rodillas pegadas a las orejas, parecían muy incómodos), Floyd Stenhouse empezó a contarles su historia.

–Lo he visto cuando salía del estudio de Goode Street. Al principio, no le he dado importancia. –Se sirvió un brandi con mano temblorosa y derramó un poco del líquido dorado sobre la superficie de madera–. ¿Quieren algo de beber, caballeros?

–No. –El inspector respondió antes de que los policías de uniforme pudieran abrir la boca–. Continúe con su historia.

–No lo había visto en toda mi vida. Iba vestido con un abrigo largo y negro y un sombrero flexible con el ala doblada hacia abajo. Casi parecía como si, de algún modo, estuviera intentando ocultar el rostro, como si supiera que lo reconocería o lo recordaría. Llevaba una bufanda en torno al cuello que la tapaba incluso la boca.

–Entonces, ¿no ha podido distinguir sus rasgos faciales? ¿Y cómo puede estar seguro de que no lo había visto antes?

Stenhouse se humedeció los labios antes de dar otro trago al brandi.

–Sé que se tiene la idea de que soy un misántropo o algo así y tal vez lo sea. Conozco a muy pocas personas en Londres y a los que sí conozco son amigos cercanos, gente que nunca me haría una jugarreta así. De todos modos, al principio no le he dado importancia, pero entonces lo he visto en el ómnibus que me ha llevado a Charing Cross. Y, al final, cuando he llegado aquí, lo he visto cruzar la calle detrás de mí mientras entraba dentro.

–Harrow –Flint se giró hacia uno de los agentes de uniforme–, vuelva abajo y hable con el tipo del mostrador. Entérese de si ha visto a alguien merodeando por ahí. También tenemos que intentar encontrar al chico del ascensor.

–¿Pete? –preguntó Stenhouse–. ¿Qué pasa con él?

–No le hemos visto al llegar.

–No confío en ese chico –prosiguió el músico entre trago y trago de brandi.

–Ahora necesito que me responda a esta pregunta con mucho cuidado, señor Stenhouse. ¿Se le ocurre algún motivo por el que alguien querría seguirlo hasta aquí?

–Ha sido una amenaza, Señor Flint. Debe de pensar… No sé. Debe de pensar que sé algo.

–¿Sobre qué?

–¿Sobre qué iba a ser? Sobre el asesinato, por supuesto.

–A ver si lo he entendido bien –dijo el inspector mientras se asomaba por la ventana y miraba en dirección al patio empedrado que había más abajo–. Parece suponer que el hombre que le ha seguido a casa es el mismo que visitó Dollis Hill la noche que asesinaron a Rees.

–Bueno, ¿quién más podría ser?

–Se me ocurren muchas personas. Siendo realistas, podría ser cualquiera. ¿Qué ha visto en él que le haya convencido de que tenía algo que ver con el asesinato?

–Había algo en su mirada, señor Flint. Una mirada profunda en los ojos.

El inspector se giró hacia el otro policía.

–Bream, quiero que se quede aquí. No deje al señor Stenhouse solo ni un segundo, ¿entendido? Harrow y yo vamos a interrogar al portero y, después, registraremos el edificio de arriba abajo. A ver qué podemos encontrar.

El inspector salió al pasillo vacío y, después, se encaminó hacia el ascensor. Sus pasos resonaron de forma hueca sobre las baldosas. Muy a su pesar y pese a todo a lo que había tenido que enfrentarse a lo largo de los años que llevaba en Scotland Yard, sintió un cosquilleo de miedo recorriéndole la nuca, como una punzada en la base de la cabeza. Deseó llevar un revólver en la mano.

El ascensor estaba vacío. ¿Dónde estaba el chico? Aquel era el primer misterio. Flint y Harrow entraron dentro y fue el propio inspector el que pulsó el botón de bajar. Una vez en el recibidor, ambos volvieron a dirigirse al mostrador del portero.

–¿Ha visto entrar al edificio a alguien sospechoso?

Royce se sobresaltó.

–No, ¿por qué? Además de ustedes, no ha entrado nadie. El señor Stenhouse ha regresado hace una hora.

–¿Lo seguía alguien?

–Le aseguro que no lo sé.

Flint gruñó.

–¿Y qué hay de Pete Hobbs, el chico del ascensor?

–Lo más probable es que se esté tomando un descanso para fumar un cigarrillo, señor. Esos «descansos» son conocidos por durar más de una hora. Ya he informado a mis superiores.

–No estaba cuando hemos llegado.

–Como le digo, señor, su falta de atención es bien conocida. Tan solo puedo pedirle disculpas.

–Olvídese de las disculpas. ¿Dónde está? El ascensor estaba en el cuarto piso, pero no había nadie dentro.

Royce resultaba obstinado.

–No puedo más que pedirle disculpas. Tal vez esté en el patio que se encuentra detrás del edificio. Le acompañaría yo mismo, señor, pero me temo que a mí no se me permite abandonar mi puesto.

Flint y el otro agente se encaminaron hacia la puerta que les había indicado Royce, que comunicaba con las cocinas y la lavandería y, después, con el patio cuadrado y empedrado. El aire nocturno era frío y el inspector casi se estremeció cuando salió fuera. Pete Hobbs no estaba allí.

–Quédese aquí –le dijo al agente Harrow.

Entonces, atravesó el patio con cuidado. Le había llamado la atención un callejón estrecho que estaba justo enfrente y que, sin duda, conducía a la calle que se encontraba al otro lado. Mientras se acercaba al callejón, fue consciente del silencio, que lo envolvió como si fuera el capullo de un insecto. El aire estaba tranquilo. Las pocas luces que brillaban en las ventanas que quedaban a su espalda lanzaban unas sombras lánguidas sobre el patio. Sin embargo, el callejón estaba totalmente a oscuras.

–¡Pete! –exclamó Flint–. ¡Pete Hobbs! ¿Estás ahí? –Una sombra, una figura oscura y rápida, se cruzó en su campo de visión–. ¡Pete! ¿Eres tú? –La figura permaneció en pie, sin moverse. El inspector sintió la quemazón de unos ojos iracundos e invisibles posados sobre él–. ¿Quién es? ¿Quién anda ahí?

Por primera vez, se dio cuenta de lo vulnerable que se había vuelto. No podía ni ver ni identificar al hombre que estaba entre las sombras. No iba armado y ni siquiera llevaba una linterna.

El hombre (pues solo podía ser un hombre) seguía quieto frente a la entrada del callejón. No había ningún rasgo discernible, ni siquiera el abrigo o el sombrero. Flint se adentró hacia la oscuridad.

Entonces, llegó el disparo.

A menudo se habla de cómo resuenan las pistolas, pero en este caso hubiera resultado una obviedad. El sonido fue tan estremecedor y reverberó de manera tan terrible que pareció rebotar por todo el patio con un eco infernal. Flint se lanzó de bruces al suelo, pero la bala se desvió. Cuando el ruido del disparo aún estaba desvaneciéndose, se escuchó el sonido de unos pasos corriendo y alejándose por el callejón.

De pronto, Harrow estaba a su lado, ayudándole a ponerse en pie. El inspector jadeaba, incapaz de hacerse a la idea de lo cerca que había estado de la muerte.

–Se ha marchado por el callejón. Vaya tras él, Harrow. Pero, ¡por el amor de Dios!, tenga cuidado. ¡Va armado!

El agente salió disparado hacia el callejón tras el hombre sombra a la fuga.

Flint se acercó a la entrada cojeando. La farola que se encontraba en el extremo más alejado otorgaba a la calle un resplandor centelleante. Tan solo podía distinguir unos cubos de basura y unas cajas vacías. Sin embargo, mientras seguía hacia delante, rozó algo con el pie. Se arrodilló para examinarlo a la luz de una cerilla. Bajo el destello repentino de aquella pequeña llama naranja, vio que se trataba de un revólver. Una fina voluta de humo salía en espiral del cañón.

–¿Quién ha sido? –dijo una voz grave y ronca ahogada por el miedo. Flint se dio la vuelta y, gracias al brillo de la cerilla, pudo distinguir el rostro de Della Cookson–. ¿Quién ha disparado? –insistió ella con el ceño fruncido y la boca muy abierta.

Parecía totalmente estupefacta. Desde luego, aquella era una imagen que no querría que apareciera en la prensa sensacionalista.

–Señorita Cookson –dijo Flint en voz baja–, ¿qué la trae a usted por aquí?

Mientras Flint y Harrow comenzaban el registro de Dufresne Court, el agente Bream se quedó con Floyd Stenhouse en el apartamento 408. Su anfitrión le había ofrecido un cigarrillo que él había aceptado agradecido. Sin embargo, todavía no lo había encendido cuando sonó el timbre de la puerta. Stenhouse, que estaba intentando en vano encender una cerilla, dio una sacudida como si hubiera recibido una descarga eléctrica.

–¿Qué ocurre? ¿Quién es?

–Nada de lo que preocuparse, señor –dijo Bream mientras se quitaba el cigarrillo de los labios y se lo guardaba en el bolsillo para más tarde–. Será el inspector.

–Tenga cuidado, amigo. Solo digo eso.

El agente Bream se encaminó hacia la entrada.

Sin embargo, cuanto más se acercaba, más lento era su paso. Se dio cuenta de que la atmósfera extraña del lugar le estaba afectando y se preguntó quién estaría esperándole realmente al otro lado de la puerta. Dejó la mano suspendida sobre la manilla.

–¿Inspector? –preguntó.

Sin embargo, no hubo respuesta.

Tras tomar aire, abrió la puerta de golpe. Bream se encontró frente a un pasillo vacío. Salió del apartamento, miró a un lado y al otro y vio que el lugar estaba desierto.

–¿Quién es? –dijo Stenhouse con un tono de voz trémulo.

–Aquí no hay nadie –contestó él, perplejo.

–¿Qué?

El otro hombre apareció junto a él y también miró a un lado y a otro del pasillo. Fue entonces cuando oyeron el disparo.

–¿Qué ha sido eso? –gritó.

Todo aquel asunto era muy poco digno. Era obvio que el músico era un histérico.

–Un disparo, señor. Abajo, en algún lugar. Será mejor que vaya.

–Entonces, voy con usted.

–No se lo recomiendo, señor.

–Ah, ¿preferiría que me quedara aquí, solo? A saber cuántos son. Puede que ahí fuera haya todo un ejército.

–Bueno –dijo Bream mientras se encogía de hombros–. Será su funeral, señor Stenhouse.

Ambos hombres salieron al pasillo y el agente se dirigió hacia las escaleras.

–¿Dónde va? –preguntó Stenhouse.

–Voy a bajar andando.

–¿Por qué no en el ascensor?

–Créame, señor, en estas circunstancias, es mejor estar en lugares abiertos que enjaulados en una caja de metal.

Cuando llegaron al bajo, Bream abrió la marcha hasta el recibidor. Detrás de su mostrador, Royce parecía estar temblando.

–¿Qué ocurre? –aulló–. ¿Qué está pasando? Iría a echar un vistazo yo mismo, pero me temo que no se me permite…

–Nada de lo que preocuparse –mintió el agente con valentía–. Está todo bajo control.

Se dirigió hacia el patio con Floyd Stenhouse merodeando tras él. Sin embargo, a medio camino se encontró con un jadeante inspector Flint que, extrañamente, iba acompañado de Della Cookson.

–¿Qué demonios hacen ustedes dos aquí abajo? –preguntó el inspector–. ¿Por qué no están arriba? Les pedí que se quedaran en el apartamento.

–He pe-pensado que podría echarle una mano, señor –tartamudeó Bream.

–¿Y se ha traído a Stenhouse con usted? Por el amor de Dios, amigo mío, use el cerebro. De todos modos, no hay nada que pueda hacer. Había un hombre armado, pero se ha marchado. Harrow ha salido corriendo detrás de él, pero no ha podido alcanzarlo. El muy cabrón nos ha pillado totalmente desprevenidos.

–¿Dónde está Harrow?

–Sigue ahí fuera, hay que recoger las pruebas. Pero, venga, acompañemos al señor Stenhouse de nuevo arriba. También tengo un par de preguntas para usted, señorita Cookson.

Regresaron al vestíbulo. El portero seguía en estado de pánico.

–¿Qué ocurre? ¿Qué ha pasado? –exclamó.

–Solo ha sido una pequeña refriega en el patio. Puedo asegurarle que ya se ha acabado.

Se arremolinaron en torno al mostrador e intentaron desentrañar lo que acababa de ocurrir. ¿Quién había disparado? ¿A quién iba dirigido el disparo? El agente Harrow regresó enseguida, todavía sin aliento.

Flint volvió a centrar su atención en Della.

–Será mejor que nos diga qué está haciendo aquí, señorita Cookson. Y nada de mentiras, por favor.

Ella soltó un suspiro.

–No tengo forma de librarme esta vez, ¿verdad? Venía a visitarte a ti, Floyd.

–¿Al señor Stenhouse? ¿Y eso por qué?

La actriz dibujó una sonrisa taimada. Floyd pestañeó, avergonzado, y fue incapaz de mirar a nadie a los ojos.

–No sabía que existiese una ley que me lo prohibiera. Pero, como creo que ya sabe, somos viejos conocidos. Todavía nos escribimos cartas de vez en cuando. ¿No es así, Floyd?

–Es cierto, inspector –ofreció él–. Éramos amigos de la infancia.

Flint dio un golpecito a su cuaderno con la punta del lapicero. Después, miró a Della.

–Creo que no ha respondido a mi pregunta.

–He venido a pedirle a Floyd un favor. Un favor personal. No es nada que pueda ser importante para usted, así que no sé por qué debería contárselo.

–Creo que estará de acuerdo en que se encuentra en una situación complicada, señorita. Es la segunda vez que aparece en la escena de un crimen sin una explicación decente de por qué está ahí. Creo que se me perdonará por establecer una inquietante correlación entre ambos acontecimientos.

–Mire –espetó ella–, si ha de saberlo..., quiero decir..., si de verdad tiene que saberlo, he venido a ver a Floyd porque necesito que me preste algo de dinero.

Flint se quedó perplejo durante un instante. De pronto, se dio cuenta de la presencia de Royce, el portero, que estaba poniendo la oreja con discreción.

–¿Continuamos la conversación arriba? –preguntó.

Flint, Della, Stenhouse y los dos agentes, que aún seguían sin aliento, se dirigieron al ascensor. Podrían meterse a duras penas, estarían muy apretados, aunque eso era mejor que todo ese sinsentido de separarse. Las puertas automáticas se abrieron y Flint se quedó congelado.

A sus pies yacía lo que al principio le pareció un montón de arpilleras desparramadas por el suelo. Solo cuando se acercó un poco más se dio cuenta de que estaba contemplando la figura aovillada de Pete Hobbs.

–¡Atrás! –les dijo a los otros.

Él y los agentes se amontonaron para ver mejor. Della se cubrió la boca con la mano y dio la espalda a aquella imagen horrorosa. Flint se inclinó sobre el chico y le colocó la palma de la mano en el rostro, justo por debajo de los orificios nasales. De ellos no salía ningún aire.

–Está muerto –dijo el inspector–. Parece que lo han estrangulado.

Enroscado en torno a la garganta del desafortunado chico del ascensor había un trozo de cuerda. Se le había clavado con tanta fuerza en el cuello que le había sacado sangre. Aquello era obra de alguien con una fuerza casi sobrehumana.

–Lo que no entiendo es cómo ha llegado hasta aquí –continuó Flint, hablándole a nadie en particular. Se dirigió a Royce, que seguía negándose a abandonar el mostrador–. ¿Se ha movido el ascensor en algún momento desde que Harrow y yo hemos salido de él?

–No, señor.

–Bueno, entonces, ¿cómo ha llegado ahí el cadáver? ¿Ha visto a Pete Hobbs en algún momento? ¿Podría haberlo arrastrarlo alguien dentro mientras el ascensor estaba en este piso?

–No, señor. He estado vigilando las puertas del ascensor en todo momento. Si alguien se hubiera acercado siquiera, lo habría visto. Y le puedo prometer que nadie se ha acercado.

Flint alzó la vista hacia el techo del cubículo. Toda la anchura y la largura del mismo estaban ocupadas por una trampilla enorme de mantenimiento. Sin embargo, estaba cerrada por dentro con cerrojo.

–Así que nos encontramos ante otra imposibilidad –concluyó el inspector en voz baja.

Llamaron a la ambulancia, como es debido, así como al fotógrafo de escenas del crimen y a varios policías de uniforme para que patrullaran el perímetro y tomaran declaraciones. Sin embargo, Flint sabía que no encontrarían nada. Él había estado en la escena del crimen todo el tiempo, en el mismísimo momento en el que se había cometido el asesinato y, aun así, no había visto nada en absoluto.

El propio inspector supervisó el registro de arriba abajo de Dufresne Court, pero el quinto piso estaba deshabitado. Los apartamentos estaban vacíos y desnudos y no mostraban signos de que hubiese vivido alguien allí. A medida que descendían, fueron despertando e interrogando a los residentes, pero nadie había oído nada más que aquel molesto disparo que muchos habían confundido con el petardeo de algún vehículo. Todas las ventanas estaban bien cerradas y por ninguna parte había pruebas de allanamiento.

El patólogo que examinó a Pete Hobbs no les ofreció demasiada información.

–Puedo decirle que lo han matado en la última hora. Es muy reciente. Estrangulado. O, más bien, ejecutado con garrote.

–¿Puede decirnos algo de la cuerda?

–Sabré algo más cuando haya podido analizarla de forma aislada, pero, por ahora, diría que es poco probable. No es más que un trozo de cuerda corriente. Podría encontrarla en una fábrica, en un almacén, en un astillero o en cualquier lugar donde se aten cosas.

–Pero ¿está seguro del todo de que lo han matado en la última hora?

–Del todo.

–Entonces, eso deja fuera a Stenhouse –murmuró Flint–. Ha estado con nosotros todo el tiempo. A Della, no. Estaba en el patio cuando han disparado, pero podría haber matado al chico antes.

–Con todo el respeto –dijo el patólogo–, no creo que este crimen sea obra de una mujer.

Flint ignoró aquello.

–¿Tiene alguna idea de cómo podría haber entrado el asesino en el ascensor?

–Eso es cosa de su departamento, no del mío. Pero ¿está totalmente convencido de la sinceridad del portero?

–No necesito estarlo. Yo mismo he estado aquí abajo la mayor parte del tiempo. Y no sé cómo Hobbs podría haber entrado en el ascensor. No se ha movido del bajo desde el momento en el que yo mismo he salido con el agente Harrow y nadie ha entrado o salido mientras estaba en este piso.

El agente Bream asintió.

–Eso significaría que ha muerto mientras estaba ocurriendo todo el asunto del patio.

–Ya veo –continuó el inspector–. Ha sido todo una cortina de humo, una distracción. Quería que nos separáramos. Y ha funcionado. Aunque eso plantea una pregunta: ¿por qué tenía que morir el chico del ascensor?

–Debía de saber o haber visto algo.

–Pero el portero ha tenido una imagen clara de las puertas del ascensor en todo momento –comentó el agente–. Está convencido de que nadie ha entrado o salido del ascensor mientras ha estado en el bajo todos esos minutos.

–Y, desde el momento del disparo, nosotros hemos estado todos juntos.

–Entonces, tal vez debería pedirle ayuda a su amigo el mago –propuso el patólogo con demasiada ligereza–. Esto parece más su campo que el mío.

Flint se alejó sin decir nada más.

En las escaleras del edificio se había reunido un grupo de periodistas. Mientras el inspector salía, se dispararon los objetivos y estallaron las lámparas fotográficas. En medio del alboroto, distinguió fragmentos de algunas preguntas.

–¿Se trata de otro crimen imposible, señor?

–¿Siguen sin saber quién lo ha hecho?

–¿Ha sido el mismo hombre?

–¿Es cierto que ha ocurrido en un ascensor, inspector?

–¿Cuánto va a costar que atrapen al asesino fantasma, señor?

Flint no dijo nada. Se quedó de pie en lo alto de las escaleras mientras los reporteros se disputaban la primera fila y, en silencio, llenó su pipa. La encendió y aspiró una bocanada cálida del humo del tabaco. Después, con aire de decisión, se alejó. Los fotógrafos contemplaron cómo se marchaba. Casi había amanecido.

XIII

Espina, el loco

(Miércoles, 16 de septiembre de 1936)

Flint tuvo una sensación de *déjà vu* cuando atravesó el umbral de The Black Pig en Putney. Joseph Spector estaba en su habitual sillón en el cuartito y, en aquella ocasión, tenía extendida frente a él una baraja de tarot. Era ya la mañana del día 16, pero el polvo de la debacle de la noche anterior todavía no se había asentado.

–¿Quiere que le lea el futuro? –le preguntó el viejo.

–¿Se ha enterado?

–¿De lo del chico del ascensor? Me temo que sí. Las malas noticias vuelan.

–¿Y qué opina al respecto?

–Por el momento, no mucho. Aunque sí hay una cosa que sé.

–¿Cuál?

–¿Se acuerda de Royce, el portero?

–¿Que si me acuerdo de él? He estado interrogándolo las últimas ocho horas.

–Bueno, resulta que hacerle entrega de mi tarjeta de visita fue una inversión que ha merecido la pena. Me ha llamado por teléfono esta mañana. Para ser completamente sincero, parece que le da usted bastante miedo, inspector. Sin embargo, quería contarle a alguien lo que sabía.

–¿Y qué sabía?

–El nombre del hombre que huyó de usted en el callejón.

–¿Ah, sí? –Flint mostró un escepticismo evidente–. Bueno, dispare.

–Será mejor que se lo muestre –dijo Spector antes de llamar a alguien–. Bill, ¿podría entrar aquí, por favor?

En el cuartito entró un anciano. Aquel tipo era un mendigo pobre y disoluto, comido por las pulgas y cubierto de suciedad. Sin embargo, en sus ojos hundidos y enrojecidos había inteligencia y el dolor le marcaba las arrugas del rostro. Llevaba el brazo izquierdo en un cabestrillo.

–¿Quién es este? –preguntó Flint.

–Permítame que le presente a Bill Harper –dijo el mago.

Sin pestañear, con los ojos cansados y entrecerrados, el inspector insistió.

–¿Y quién es Bill Harper cuando está en su casa?

–¡Ajá! Esa es la cuestión. El pobre Bill ya no tiene casa. Por eso estaba anoche en aquel callejón. Puede que se haya percatado de que el pobre hombre ha sufrido un percance. Le disparó un hombre armado sin identificar. Pero tal vez preferiría contar la historia usted, Bill.

El anciano se sentó en un sillón e hizo una mueca cuando el cabestrillo que llevaba en el brazo rozó el borde de la mesa.

–Desde que me echaron de la fábrica, he estado durmiendo mal. Las noches se vuelven más frías y resulta difícil encontrar un sitio decente en el que apoyar la cabeza. Así que he estado merodeando por la parte trasera de los apartamentos.

Apoyándose en los codos, Flint se inclinó hacia delante. Había despertado su interés.

–¿En el callejón trasero de Dufresne Court?

–Eso es. Ese tipo, Royce, no está tan mal, ¿sabe? Me ha estado trayendo comida a escondidas de vez en cuando y cosas así. Pero bueno, la cuestión es que anoche estaba allí cuando comenzaron los disparos.

–¿Vio a alguien?

–Solo a usted, señor. Y a la dama. Estaba durmiendo cuando me despertaron sus gritos, así que me levanté para ver qué estaba pasando y fue entonces cuando ese capullo me disparó.

–La bala le rozó el brazo –le explicó Spector–. Y, como es natural en alguien a quien acaban de disparar, Bill se dio prisa en salir corriendo.

Flint gruñó.

–Entonces, ¿me está diciendo que era usted el hombre al que vi salir corriendo del callejón?

Bill asintió con aire sombrío.

–Los médicos me han dicho que no es demasiado serio, o que, al menos, podría haber sido peor.

–¿Y vio a la persona que disparó?

–No. Estaba acurrucado en el callejón cuando sentí un escozor, como si me hubiera picado una abeja. Entonces, un instante después, oí el disparo. Me asusté, señor, así que salí corriendo.

–¿Y dónde fue?

–Al hospital, señor. Estaba sangrando mucho.

La actitud del inspector se suavizó un poco.

–Espero que los médicos le trataran con amabilidad.

–Fueron sumamente amables, señor.

–Pero no tiene ni idea de quién apretó el gatillo, ¿no?

El mendigo sacudió la cabeza.

–En lo que respecta al señor Harper –intervino Spector–, las únicas personas en aquel patio eran usted y Della Cookson.

–Pero eso no me sirve. Alguien tuvo que disparar la pistola.

–Sin duda, pero, fuera quien fuera, desde luego no fue Bill, aquí presente. Ni nadie que cruzara por aquel callejón.

–Bueno, ¿y dónde nos deja eso?

Spector suspiró y se giró hacia el mendigo. Después, le tendió un billete de una libra.

–Vaya a comprarse algo de comer, viejo amigo –dijo.

El viejo se escabulló tan deprisa como había aparecido. Otro truco de magia de los de Spector. Entonces, el mago volvió a centrarse en Flint.

–Establecer una secuencia de unos acontecimientos como los que vivió usted anoche es una gran tarea. Todo es tan difuso y subjetivo... Depende de las interpretaciones de los individuos involucrados. Pero por usted, inspector Flint, lo intentaré.

Con una hoja de papel limpia y una pluma cargada de tinta, el anciano comenzó a esbozar una línea temporal de los acontecimientos.

Flint y su séquito habían llegado a Dufresne Court a las siete y media de la tarde anterior. Entre las ocho y las nueve, Pete Hobbs había sido asesinado y habían arrojado su cadáver al ascensor. Sin embargo, el ascensor no había parado en ninguna parte entre la planta baja y la cuarta ni había subido más allá de esta última. De todos modos, la planta quinta estaba desocupada. Con la escena establecida, el mago se centró en el incidente.

–¿Qué sabemos del hombre armado del patio?

–Nada.

–¿Sabemos a qué le estaba disparando?

–Todavía no, pero lo más probable es que fuese a mí.

–¿Por qué haría algo así? Sin duda, lo mejor habría sido huir sin más. Hacer ese disparo y no acertar fue un riesgo innecesario.

–¿Qué piensa usted entonces?

Spector no respondió a eso.

–¿Sabemos qué hacía allí Della Cookson?

–Afirma que iba a pedirle un préstamo a Stenhouse.

Spector arqueó una ceja.

–¿A Stenhouse? –Lo meditó un momento–. Tal vez sería buena idea que volviera a hablar con ella.

–Si quiere y cree que le va a servir de algo... Pero no pudo haber sido Della la que apretó el gatillo. Acuérdese de las huellas. Anoche, no llevaba guantes, por lo que, si hubiera sido ella la que disparó, sus huellas estarían por todo el revólver.

–A menos que hubiera algún tipo de truco –añadió el mago, pensativo–. Hay una manera en la que Della podría haber hecho ese disparo. Requeriría el uso de dos revólveres. Podría haberse puesto unos guantes y haber disparado el revólver un momento antes, utilizando algo para tapar el sonido. Como un almohadón, por ejemplo. Después, podría haber dejado el arma en el suelo a la espera de que la descubrieran. Entonces, podría haberse quitado los guantes, haber sacado otro revólver y haberlo disparado al aire para que sonara bien fuerte antes de volver a metérselo en el bolso. Entonces, cuando usted salió y encontró el revólver humeante, naturalmente supuso que era con ese con el que acababan de disparar. La ausencia de huellas parecería exonerar a Della.

–No espera que me trague todas esas tonterías, ¿verdad? Como es de esperar, revisé su bolso y no había un segundo revólver.

La sonrisa del mago era genuina.

–Entonces, podría haberse librado de él en cualquier otra parte. No, inspector, no espero que se trague todas estas tonterías. Al fin y al cabo, soy aficionado a explicar lo inexplicable.

–Que Dios me asista, pero, por más que lo intento, todavía no consigo precisar cómo encaja la señorita Della Cookson en todo este asunto.

–No es más que otro hilo en esta red especialmente enmarañada. Da la casualidad de que he estado leyendo sobre la cleptomanía –dijo Spector–. De verdad, es un tema muy interesante. De normal, más que una causa, es un síntoma, ¿sabe? Se dice que la verdadera raíz se encuentra en los llamados «traumas comórbidos». Lo que se encuentra en los cleptómanos no es el arquetípico deleite por el robo. Casi lo contrario. En su lugar, el ladrón se ve acosado por ansias que son casi como una compulsión física. Cuando se enfrenta a un objeto, simplemente tiene que hacerse con él, pero también se sentirá atormentado por la culpabilidad. A menudo recurrirá al consumo de drogas como apoyo. El paciente bien podría estar poseído por demonios. Es una compulsión que se escapa de su control, un aumento de presión en el cerebro. Y tan solo puede calmarlo robando.

»Algunas ideas equivocadas: el cleptómano no roba por beneficio propio, sino porque no puede no hacerlo; además, tampoco roba por enemistad o rencor. El robo apenas es un acto consciente y la única emoción que va asociada a él es una culpabilidad incapacitante. De normal, el objeto del robo será algún artilugio inútil. De hecho, es bastante raro que substraigan algo verdaderamente valioso. El valor monetario del objeto no se tiene en cuenta en absoluto.

Tras aquella pequeña lección, Spector observó a Flint como si estuviera intentando hacerse una idea de cuánto había comprendido el inspector de su argumento. Después, continuó:

–Durante mis viajes hace algunos años, visité por casualidad el Museo de Gante, en Bélgica. Allí tienen una secuencia notable de retratos de Théodore Géricault. Tienen más de cien años de antigüedad, pero siguen siendo muy esclarecedores, además de hermosos. La intención de Géricault era crear una secuencia que retratara modelos clínicos de una variedad de enfermedades mentales. Pintó a diez pacientes del psiquiátrico de Salpêtrière y, de algún modo, consiguió capturar la mismísima alma de cada desdichado individuo. Un logro considerable. Pero hay un cuadro en particular, *Retrato de un cleptómano*, que me ha estado obsesionando últimamente. Ese rostro rígido y obstinado, la tortuosa falta de brillo en los ojos... Está mirando a la nada y, aun así, muestra tanto tormento... Géricault fue uno de los primeros en retratar a los enfermos mentales como seres humanos como usted o como yo. Miró más allá de los rasgos de comportamiento y encontró la fragilidad y la delicadeza, la humanidad. Pienso mucho en ese retrato.

–¿Y ve esa misma «tortuosa falta de brillo» en los ojos de Della Cookson? –preguntó Flint.

Spector meditó la pregunta.

–Lo que veo cuando miro a los ojos a Della Cookson es algo totalmente diferente, algo más oscuro. Hace que me pregunte qué tormentos ha tenido que soportar a lo largo de su vida. ¿Podemos creer que se llevó *El nacimiento*? El instinto nos diría que no. La descripción que aparece en las notas del doctor Rees es la de una ladrona oportunista, una que roba porque puede y se lleva baratijas y objetos pequeños de poco valor. Lo importante es el propio objeto y sentir su peso en la mano, no el valor material ni nada tan ordinario. *El nacimiento* no es la clase de objeto que suele preferir nuestra actriz. Demasiado grande, voluminoso y engorroso. Además, tal como ya sabemos, su valor es de poca importancia para ella.

–No creo que pueda hacer unas afirmaciones tan generales sobre su carácter. Incluso a Rees le costaba determinar qué es lo que la motiva. ¿Se acuerda del reloj? Tuvo una oportunidad excelente de robar el reloj de Marcus Bowman, pero no lo hizo. No nos corresponde decidir si algo llamaría o no la atención de su desdichado cerebro.

–Entiendo lo que quiere decir –concedió el mago–, pero eso sigue dejándonos con la cuestión de la oportunidad. Hasta donde sabemos, todo lo que ha robado lo ha robado porque estaba ahí mismo. Sin embargo, *El nacimiento* no estaba «ahí» de ningún modo que pudiera ser significativo para ella: estaba cerrado bajo llave en un baúl que se encontraba debajo de la cama de Teasel, lejos de su alcance. Della no abre cajas fuertes ni fuerza cerraduras. Siempre ha sido más una carterista que una maestra del crimen.

»Piénselo detenidamente –añadió de pronto mientras se daba la vuelta hacia el inspector–. La respuesta está en las notas del doctor. Piense en aquel encuentro que tuvo con Marcus Bowman. Más allá del asunto del reloj, lo que a mí me interesa es el relato de Rees de lo que el propio Bowman dijo durante el encuentro. Según las notas, el joven reconoció a Della de inmediato. Sin embargo, cuando asistí al estreno de *La dama Muerte*, recuerdo con claridad haber oído a Bowman y a Lidia sumidos en una conversación incómoda en la que él fingió no saber quién era Della. Incluso se refirió a ella como «Hellen» Cookson, lo que no demuestra nada por sí solo, pero plantea algunas preguntas. ¿Por qué Marcus Bowman fingió no conocer a Della? ¿Y por qué justamente delante de Lidia?

Flint tamborileó los dedos sobre la mesa.

–Así que Bowman sí que conocía a la actriz y, a su manera torpe, intentaba impedir que Lidia lo descubriera.

Spector asintió.

–Sigamos esta línea de pensamiento un poco más. Bowman se esforzó por demostrar que conocía a Della en Dollis Hill, pero, después, en el Pomegranate, se esforzó por demostrar que no la conocía. Y Della no le quitó el reloj. El único motivo por el que no habría aprovechado esa oportunidad sería que ella también lo hubiera reconocido y se hubiera sentido sorprendida, incluso asustada. No había esperado verle allí y tampoco había querido hacerlo. ¿Por qué? No es demasiado aventurado concluir que estaban manteniendo algún tipo de relación clandestina. Una de las coincidencias vergonzosas de la vida: Della estaba teniendo una aventura con el futuro yerno de su psiquiatra. No es tan improbable como parece a simple vista. Bowman es especialmente hábil a la hora de conseguir invitaciones para los eventos de la alta sociedad. Y Della, al ser actriz, es siempre el centro de atención en tales eventos. En semejantes circunstancias, lo raro hubiera sido que no se hubieran visto antes.

»También hay algo más: a Benjamin Teasel le impresionó mucho la reacción de Della al cuadro cuando se lo mostró durante la fiesta. Al parecer, le dio la impresión de que había algo «inquietante» en la forma en la que lo miró. ¿Qué cree usted que quería decir con eso?

–Bueno –dijo Flint–, solo hay una manera de descubrirlo. Iremos a ver a Della otra vez. Llegaré al fondo de este asunto aunque muera en el intento. Pero, Spector, por favor, antes hágame un favor. Invíteme a una cerveza, ¿quiere?

Encontraron a Della sola en su camerino del Pomegranate. La mano le temblaba un poco mientras se maquillaba.

–¿Va a seguir adelante con la actuación? –preguntó el inspector.

–Sé que pensará que soy despiadada, pero no me importa. Tengo que ganarme la vida y, gracias a las aventuras de anoche, no conseguí hacerme con el préstamo de Floyd Stenhouse.

–Anoche no llegó a responder a mi pregunta, señorita Cookson. ¿Para qué quiere el dinero? ¿Es por algún chantaje?

–Si se tratara de eso –dijo ella mientras se recolocaba el corsé–, no sería asunto suyo.

–Señor Flint, si me permite... –intervino Spector–. Solo tengo una pregunta para ti, Della.

La actriz dio la espalda al espejo para mirarlo y en sus ojos había una ansiedad silenciosa.

–Puedes preguntar, Joseph.

–No es una pregunta sobre Floyd Stenhouse. O Pete Hobbs. Ni siquiera es sobre el doctor Rees. Es sobre *El nacimiento*.

–¿Qué ocurre?

–Hasta donde sabes, ¿le enseñó Benjamin Teasel el cuadro a alguien más la noche de la fiesta?

–No, no lo hizo. Y sé que es así porque me lo dijo él mismo. Me dijo que yo era la única a la que hacía «entrega de tal regalo».

–Y cuando te mostró el cuadro, ¿la habitación estaba a oscuras?

–Estaba iluminada por la luna. Solo podía ver gracias a la luz que entraba por aquella pequeña ventana. No encendió las lámparas porque decía que la obra se apreciaba mejor con luz natural, tal como estaba.

–Pero ¿estabais solos?

–Bastante solos. A menos que…

Se detuvo.

–¿Qué ocurre?

–Nada. Es probable que no sea nada.

Tal vez a Flint le hubiera gustado insistir más en el asunto, pero a Spector le pareció bien dejarlo atrás.

–¿Sabes algo sobre Manolito Espina?

–Solo que era pintor.

–Me parece que estás siendo modesta. Creo que sabes más cosas sobre él que eso. Pero tal vez no sepas que uno de los síntomas de su presunta locura era su convicción absoluta de que sus cuadros eran predicciones del futuro. La retorcida secuencia titulada *Paisajes del bajo infierno* resultó todavía más sorprendente cuando se desveló por primera vez porque Espina la acompañó con la advertencia de que era una representación de la vida. Tuvo suerte de que no lo quemaran en la hoguera.

El tono de voz de la actriz era plano.

–¿Qué quieres decir, Joseph?

–Solo que la verosimilitud en el arte puede tener un efecto extraño en la audiencia. No se puede negar que *El nacimiento* es una obra de genialidad deslumbrante, pero he estado intentando desentrañar por qué te afectó del modo en que lo hizo. –Siguió una breve pausa–. ¿Cuáles son los sujetos de la obra? –preguntó distraídamente.

–¿Acaso importa? –Spector pestañeó–. Una madre y su hijo –contestó la actriz con un suspiro.

–Esto son meras suposiciones –comenzó a decir el mago–. Y en un tribunal de justicia se considerarían difamación, pero no vas a denunciarme, ¿verdad, Della? Si unimos todos los pequeños detalles, y algunos no tan pequeños, se puede llegar a una clara conclusión: Marcus Bowman y tú habéis tenido una aventura. Esto ha debido de ser una fuente de considerable tormento emocional para ti. Sin embargo, ver una obra maestra del Renacimiento que representa a una madre con su hijo recién nacido te causó una reacción tan visceral que te hizo salir corriendo de la fiesta e ir directa a la otra punta de Londres para ver a tu psiquiatra.

La mujer sonrió sin alegría y habló con un tono de voz irritable.

–Creo que te estás andando con rodeos pero que lo has sabido desde el principio, ¿no es así? ¿No te preguntaste por qué me perdía tantos ensayos? Citas médicas. No solo con Rees; también tengo otro médico en Harley Street. Y, cuando empecé a notar ciertos... cambios, fui a verle para que me examinara.

–¿Y?

Ella resopló con arrogancia.

–No es que sea asunto tuyo, Joseph, y Dios no quiera que le digas una sola palabra a nadie, pero resulta que estoy embarazada de dos meses.

Spector asintió de forma respetuosa.

–¿Y el padre?

–¿Qué pasa con él?

–¿Lo sabe?

–No, no lo sabe. ¿De qué serviría?

–Es Marcus Bowman, ¿verdad?

–Sí, es Marcus. Por supuesto, no sabía que estaba prometido con la hija de Rees. Eso no es más que una infeliz coincidencia. Pero, con toda sinceridad, no podría decirte si haberlo sabido hubiera supuesto alguna diferencia.

El mago asintió, pensativo.

–¿Y qué vas a hacer?

–He intentado olvidarme del asunto, fingir que no está ocurriendo. Pero no hay forma de escapar de ello. Pronto resultará penosamente evidente para todo el mundo.

–Y has empezado a beber de nuevo.

–No sabía qué más hacer. –Estaba a punto de llorar–. No había nadie con quien pudiera hablar, nadie excepto el doctor Rees. Pero él se mostraba bastante reservado con todo el asunto. Se lo conté después del pase de la noche del estreno. Vino a mi camerino. Y no lo dijo con esas palabras, pero no pude evitar tener la sensación de que lo desaprobaba, así que intenté apartarlo de mi mente y centrarme en la obra. Eso solo empeoró las cosas. Y entonces, cuando Teasel me enseñó el cuadro...

Los ojos se le desbordaron y las lágrimas se le escurrieron por el rostro.

–Querida –dijo Spector mientras le daba una palmadita en el brazo–, puedo imaginármelo...

–Fue como... si me clavaran una estaca de hielo en el pecho. Sentí que podía morirme allí mismo de vergüenza y de miedo. ¡Menudo titular habría sido! –Soltó una carcajada ronca–. Salí de esa casa en cuanto pude. Me fui de la fiesta y me dirigí al único sitio al que se me ocurrió ir.

–La casa de Rees.

–Exacto. El taxi me llevó allí directamente. Pasaron tal vez unos quince minutos desde que me marché de la fiesta de Teasel hasta que llegué a Dollis Hill.

Todo aquel tiempo, el gesto de Spector había permanecido insondable.

–Benjamin está bastante convencido de que fuiste tú la que le robó el cuadro.

–Jamás haría algo así, Joseph. Tienes que creerme. Sé que conoces mi peculiar... aflicción. –Al decir aquello, fue incapaz de mirarlo a los ojos–. Pero jamás podría robar algo tan... hermoso, tan perfecto. Mirarlo hizo que me doliera el corazón.

–Aun así, tienes que admitir que es una coincidencia desafortunada.

–Sí, eso es lo peor. Maldita suerte la mía... De todos modos, tendré que dejar la producción en cuanto esto resulte demasiado engorroso de ocultar –dijo mientras bajaba la vista hacia su propio vientre–. Había mantenido la esperanza de no verme envuelta en un escándalo, pero ahora parece que será inevitable.

–No necesariamente. Después de todo, las criadas y prácticamente todos los presentes en la fiesta pueden confirmar que, cuando te marchaste, no llevabas un cuadro enorme con marco de madera. ¿Se te ocurre alguna otra persona que estuviera presente en la fiesta aquella noche que pudiera saber dónde guardaba Teasel *El nacimiento*?

Ella negó con la cabeza.

–Teasel y yo fuimos los únicos que estuvimos allí arriba. Bueno, no puedo demostrarlo, pero sé que éramos los únicos presentes en aquella habitación cuando abrió el baúl.

–Y el resto de invitados de la fiesta parecen poder confirmar la coartada de los demás. La única explicación sería que otra persona, alguien ajeno, hubiese entrado en la casa sin que nadie se diera cuenta. –Spector había empezado a hablar más rápido, como si estuviera a punto de hacer un gran descubrimiento–. Aunque las criadas que estaban de servicio nos dijeron que eso era imposible. Les hemos tomado la palabra porque estaban en posición de controlar las idas y venidas de los invitados.

–¿Dónde quiere llegar con eso, Spector? –le preguntó Flint.

–Una idea curiosa... ¿Recordáis la historia de Chesterton titulada *El hombre invisible*? En ella, un asesino aparentemente fantasma consigue escapar de la escena del crimen sin que lo atrapen. Nadie ha visto a ningún individuo entrar o salir de la casa en cuestión.

–¿Y bien? ¿Cómo se las había arreglado el tipo?

–En realidad, el problema es una cuestión de semántica y de lo que entendemos por «invisible». ¿Invisible en el sentido de «no puede ser visto por el ojo humano» o invisible en el sentido de «no percibido por el ojo humano»? A las criadas les dijeron que se había producido un robo, así que, como es natural, cuando les preguntamos si habían visto algo sospechoso, a alguna persona que no hubiera sido invitada o algo similar, se imaginaron a un ladrón prototípico, es decir: un hombre de complexión fuerte y aspecto huraño con un aire inquietante. Usaron su imaginación. Pero, como no se habían encontrado con nadie que encajara con esa descripción, se complacieron en confirmar que no había habido ningún invitado inesperado en absoluto.

–Ya veo –dijo Flint–. Así que cree que el ladrón era alguien que encajaba en el entorno, alguien que no tenía por qué ser un invitado necesariamente pero que tenía el aspecto de poder serlo.

–Exacto. Alguien vestido de forma elegante. Una mujer. A ojos de las criadas, alguien así no podría estar tramando algo. Así que, ya sea de forma consciente o no, la excluyeron del testimonio que le dieron a la policía.

–Pero, Joseph –intervino Della–, tienes que pensar que, quienquiera que se llevara el cuadro, tuvo que quitarle las llaves del cuello a Teasel. Por eso está tan obsesionado con que fui yo, porque estaba achispada y le di un beso antes de marcharme de la fiesta.

–Lo recuerdo, pero aquella fiesta fue una celebración bastante íntima. Estábamos todos bastante apiñados en aquella casa. Cualquiera podría habérselas quitado.

–¿Sin que se diera cuenta? Puede ser, pero sin duda se habría fijado si hubiese sido alguien a quien no había invitado, ¿no?

–No necesariamente. Después de todo, fue una ocasión en la que corrió bastante alcohol. Sin embargo, hay una cosa que creo que sí puedo asegurar: si lo hubiese hecho un hombre, Benjamin lo sabría. Pero creo que una mujer podría haberle pasado con facilidad los brazos por el cuello, tal vez mientras bailaban, y haberle robado las llaves sin que se diera cuenta.

–¿Crees que fue alguien con quien bailó? ¿Bailó con esa mujer pero no la reconoció? Eso significaría que habría ocurrido bastante tarde, cuando todo el mundo estaba demasiado borracho como para preocuparse de lo que estaba ocurriendo.

–Della, Benjamin está muy convencido de que tú eres la única que podría haberle quitado las llaves del cuello. Pero creo que ahora puedo ver por qué. Está tan desesperado por que seas tú porque quiere una excusa para echarte de la producción. Le viene muy bien que además seas una ladrona de arte.

–Pero ¡no lo soy! Tú me crees, ¿verdad, Joseph?

–Sí –contestó él mientras posaba una mano sobre la suya–. Creo de todo corazón que tú no robaste el cuadro. Y creo que puede que al fin estemos a punto de descubrir quién lo hizo.

–Entonces, ¿quién fue? ¿Tienes alguna idea?

–Bueno, vamos a sopesar nuestras opciones. Fue una mujer, porque una mujer habría sido capaz de rodear el cuello de Benjamin con los brazos de manera despreocupada para quitarle las llaves. Creemos que pasó en la última parte de la velada; es decir, después de que tú te hubieras marchado, ya que habría sido menos probable que Benjamin se diera cuenta tras haberse tomado unos cuantos tragos. Si hubiese sido alguien de la lista de invitados (algo que hemos desmentido, ya que todos fueron registrados y no se encontró nada), entonces podrían haberlo hecho en cualquier momento de la noche. Sin embargo, si nos guiamos por la suposición de que fue una persona ajena a la fiesta, entonces eso nos permite estrechar la franja de tiempo en la que podrían haber entrado en la casa.

»Tú te marchaste a las once. Digamos que la ladrona ya estaba en la casa a esas alturas aunque nadie se hubiera dado cuenta. Digamos que era alguien que podía mezclarse con el entorno a la perfección, alguien que podría haberse escabullido por las escaleras tras vosotros y haber estado escuchando en la puerta mientras Benjamin te enseñaba el cuadro.

El mago perdió el hilo, así que Flint intervino.

–¿Se le ha ocurrido algo?

–Sí. Gracias por tu tiempo, Della. Volveré a hablar contigo pronto.

–¿De qué iba eso? –le preguntó Flint mientras ambos se alejaban a grandes zancadas del Pomegranate–. ¿A qué ha venido ese numerito de hombre del misterio? Pensaba que al menos iba a mencionar el asesinato de anoche en Dufresne Court. ¿Y sabe quién se llevó el cuadro o no?

–Bueno, digamos que sé quién no se lo llevó. Della se quedó deslumbrada por *El nacimiento*. La representación de una madre con su hijo recién nacido es especialmente emotiva. Eso también explica por qué salió a toda prisa de la habitación antes de ir a visitar a su psiquiatra a la primera de cambio. La enormidad de su calvario empezaba a resultarle evidente y estaba empezando a darse cuenta de que no podía lidiar con ello. A partir de aquí, podemos reconstruir sus motivaciones. Se sintió conmocionada. Le causó una oleada repentina de emociones. Le generó una sensación de añoranza pero también de agonía interna porque en el rostro de aquella madre vio su propio rostro. Por eso se disculpó a toda prisa y se marchó de la fiesta de Teasel. Por eso atravesó Londres corriendo para ir a casa de Rees. Él era el único al que podía confiarle ese secreto suyo, el único hombre en el que podía apoyarse. Necesitaba ayuda, pero ¿qué se encontró al llegar a Dollis Hill? La escena del crimen de un asesinato. Era demasiado tarde, así que, como es natural, se sumió en el silencio.

»A partir de ahí, solo es cuestión de atar cabos. El préstamo que quería pedirle a Stenhouse era para pagar cierto procedimiento médico ilegal con el que podría hacerse cargo de su problema. Pero estoy seguro de que ni siquiera bajo pena de muerte conseguiríamos que lo admitiera.

–Si ese es el caso, entonces me está diciendo que no tuvo nada que ver ni con el robo ni con el asesinato del doctor Rees, ¿no es así?

–Así es.

–Entonces, ¿quién lo hizo?

–Ah, bueno, puede que también tenga unas cuantas ideas con respecto a eso. Pero este asunto ha de tratarse con tacto y con prudencia. Tengo que hablar con Marcus Bowman.

Encontraron a Bowman en Robinson's, el club de Regent Street del que era miembro. Estaba jugando al billar y bebiendo *whisky* escocés. Tras unas palabras del inspector, los acompañó al pasillo para que pudieran hablar con calma.

–¿Qué ocurre ahora? ¿Saben?, tengo trabajo que podría estar haciendo en este momento.

–Solo una preguntita para usted, señor Bowman –dijo Spector con una sonrisa educada–. Por favor, dígame por qué nos mintió sobre dónde se encontraba la noche del asesinato.

Fuera lo que fuese que Bowman había esperado, no había sido aquello.

–¿De qué demonios está hablando?

–Sabemos que Lidia y usted no estuvieron juntos toda la noche, tal como nos dijo al principio. Los informes de los testigos nos indican que crearon bastante alboroto en la pista de baile del Palmyra Club. Pero no estaban bailando, ¿verdad? Estaban discutiendo y fue una confrontación feroz, ¿me equivoco? Entonces ella se marchó y salió del club en un estado de agitación. Intentó seguirla, pero fue demasiado rápida para usted, ¿no es así? La perdió en medio de la noche londinense, así que tomó un taxi de vuelta a Dollis Hill. Pero estaba solo. Por favor, interrúmpame si algo de lo que estoy diciendo es incorrecto.

Bowman tragó saliva con fuerza.

–Le juro que solo fue una mentira piadosa. Yo no maté al viejo, pero ella tampoco.

–No, pero, tristemente, sí subestimó su inteligencia. Ella adivinó sus mentiras de inmediato. Tal vez incluso disfrutara jugando con usted. Claro que sabía lo de Della Cookson. Y sabemos que leyó las notas de su padre y las comentó con él en profundidad, así que comprendía la cleptomanía de Della.

»Muy bien, volvamos a la noche del asesinato. ¿Cómo comenzó la velada? Lidia y usted salieron a cenar. Hasta donde sabemos, aquella fue una situación civilizada, pero, después, se marcharon del Savoy y fueron al Palmyra. A partir de aquí, resulta más difícil seguirles la pista, pero sabemos que estuvieron bebiendo y que discutieron. Desde luego, no hay manera de confirmar que estuvieran en el club toda la noche.

Flint, que se sentía un poco al margen, añadió:

–No regresaron a la casa de los Rees.

Spector atacó el aire con un dedo.

–¡Exacto! No regresaron, pero podrían haber ido a casa de Benjamin Teasel con bastante facilidad. No está muy lejos del Soho.

–¿Y por qué harían eso?

Spector se giró hacia el inspector.

–¿Tan difícil es de imaginar que Lidia confrontaría a su prometido con respecto a la aventura que estaba manteniendo? Por supuesto, él lo negó. ¿No es así, señor Bowman? Pero ella lo sabía, así que se marchó hecha una furia. También sabía lo de la fiesta de Teasel porque habían invitado a su padre, así que debió de ir hasta allí a pie. La casa de la fiesta fue fácil de localizar en aquella calle crepuscular que, por lo demás, estaba tranquila. La música estaba alta y las luces resplandecían por todas partes.

»Así que se coló en la fiesta sin muchos problemas y pasó por delante de las criadas con su ropa fina y su característico aire de elegancia y privilegio. Una vez dentro, pudo observar a Della en la lejanía y seguirlos a ella y a Teasel por las escaleras. Tal vez pegara la oreja a la puerta o incluso mirara por el ojo de la cerradura mientras ellos contemplaban *El nacimiento*. El propio Teasel era incapaz de recordar con exactitud con quién había bailado aquella noche y quién podría haberle quitado las llaves. Pensaba que Della era la única que había estado con él mientras lo desvelaba. No contó con que hubiera una espectadora oculta. Pero a Lidia no le costaría demasiado quitarle las llaves, volver a escabullirse escaleras arriba y robar *El nacimiento* de su escondrijo.

–Pero, espere un momento –intervino Flint–. ¿Cómo lo sacó de la casa? Casi hemos dejado establecido que no hay manera de que hubiera podido sacarlo por delante de las criadas.

–Ah, sí. Me temo que eso es en parte culpa mía. Mire, estaba bastante obsesionado con la idea de que, cuando se llevaron el cuadro, todavía estaba dentro del marco.

–¿Quiere decir que se lo quitó?

–Exacto. No estoy seguro de qué usó exactamente, pero unas tijeras pequeñas o incluso una uña muy afilada podrían haberle servido. Es una idea horrible, pero creo que eso es lo que ocurrió.

–En tal caso, ¿no debería estar el marco todavía en la habitación?

–En principio, sí, pero, para complicar más las cosas, decidió robarlo también.

–¿Cómo?

–Bueno, Lidia no pensó que el marco tuviese ningún valor especial. Para ella, no era más que un estorbo. El cuadro era el auténtico objetivo de su plan, así que, una vez que quedó libre de su amarre dorado, creo que partió el marco en cuatro partes y las tiró por la ventana de una en una. Debieron de resonar sobre el asfalto de abajo, pero el *jazz* y el ruido general del jolgorio sin duda enmascararon el sonido. Entonces, se limitó a volver a cerrar la ventana y, con el cuadro enrollado y escondido en el interior de su vestido, salió de la fiesta con la misma velocidad con la que había llegado, haciendo una pausa para deshacerse de los fragmentos rotos del marco, por supuesto.

»Después, volvió a casa y, de camino, supongo que se deshizo del marco. Debió de sentirse muy complacida consigo misma.

Flint paseaba de un lado al otro del pasillo.

–Podría haber ocurrido así. Sí, supongo que sí. Teaseal creía que tan solo Della sabía que el cuadro estaba allí, así que, como es natural, centró su atención en ella. Y, dado que todos los asistentes que habían sido invitados fueron registrados por la policía, pareció un crimen imposible cuando, de hecho, no lo era en absoluto.

–¡Exacto! –replicó el mago con entusiasmo.

–Pero eso todavía nos deja con algunas preguntas. Por ejemplo, eso significaría que Lidia llevaba consigo el cuadro cuando llegó a Dollis Hill. ¿Qué hizo con él?

Tras girarse de nuevo hacia Bowman, el mago preguntó:

–Lidia robó *El nacimiento*, ¿verdad? Y usted la encubrió. Desde el club fue a casa de Teasel, ¿no es así? Tenía intención de enfrentarse a Della y sacar a la luz todo este asunto tan sórdido. Sin embargo, cuando se coló en la casa sin que se fijaran en ella y siguió al anfitrión y su invitada de honor escaleras arriba, se presentó ante ella un plan mejor. Teniendo en cuenta el historial del caso de Della, decidió lanzarse a por esa oportunidad de tenderle una trampa, si me perdona la forma de hablar. Así que se llevó el cuadro, lo escondió en alguna parte y sigue allí, ¿no es así?

Marcus palideció. Parecía a punto de desmayarse. Incluso el bigote se le había marchitado. Cuando habló, lo hizo con total claridad. Todos sus artificios lo habían abandonado.

–Tomé un taxi de vuelta a Dollis Hill, tal como ha señalado. Si se acuerda, yo había dejado allí mi automóvil para que Lidia y yo pudiéramos tomar un taxi. Me senté en el vehículo y esperé a que volviera a casa. Me daba demasiado miedo acercarme a la casa yo solo. No me apetecía hacerme el tonto con el viejo. No sabía dónde había ido ella o lo que había hecho, pero estaba seguro de que, al final, acabaría volviendo a casa, así que supuse que quedarme sentado a esperarla era una apuesta segura.

–Cuando se volvieron a encontrar, entraron juntos a la casa y fue como si no se hubieran separado el uno del otro en toda la noche.

Marcus asintió.

–Me di cuenta de que había pasado algo dudoso cuando aparecieron todos los coches de policía. Al principio, pensé que tal vez Lidia hubiera hecho alguna tontería. Me refiero a algo violento como atacar a Della con las uñas o algo así, pero, cuando entramos juntos en la casa y descubrí lo que le había pasado a su padre, no fue necesario decirnos nada el uno al otro. Ninguno de los dos podría o habría hecho algo así, pero, al mismo tiempo, ninguno de los dos tenía una coartada decente. Así que hicimos lo que cualquiera hubiera hecho en esa situación, la única cosa sensata que se podía hacer: mentir.

–Siendo sincero –dijo Spector tras una pausa–, no puedo decir que yo hubiera actuado de otro modo. Sin embargo, esto significa que usted estaba fuera de la casa de los Rees cuando ocurrió el asesinato.

Bowman se mantuvo callado durante un momento. Estaba pensando tanto que casi se podían oír los engranajes de su cerebro.

–Supongo que sí.

–Entonces es muy probable que viera al asesino marchándose de la casa.

–Las probabilidades parecen muy altas, ¿verdad?

–¿Y bien?

–Puede que lo haya visto, pero no sabría decirle quién era.

–Déjeme adivinar: ¿un hombre anodino con sombrero y abrigo?

–Un tipo salió por la puerta delantera sobre las once y cuarenta y cinco. El otro tipo apareció por el lateral como un minuto después. Ambos se marcharon en la misma dirección.

–Un momento –dijo Flint–. Sabemos lo del tipo que salió por la puerta delantera. Es el que visitó a Rees. Pero ¿quién era el que apareció por el lateral?

–No pude distinguirlo, pero, desde luego, hubo un hombre

que se escabulló por la verja lateral de la casa. Debía de venir del jardín trasero.

El inspector y el mago intercambiaron una mirada.

–Necesito que lo piense con calma antes de contestar, señor Bowman –dijo Flint–. ¿Quién era ese segundo hombre?

Bowman estaba sacudiendo la cabeza con suavidad.

–No lo sé, lo siento. Sé que les gustaría que pudiera decirles quién era, pero estaba lloviendo y llevaba el sombrero calado muy bajo.

–¿Está seguro de que procedía del jardín trasero de casa de los Rees?

–Sí, totalmente. Parecía ir siguiendo al tipo que salió por la puerta delantera.

Flint y Spector estaban pensando en lo mismo. Era fácil que aquel segundo hombre misterioso hubiese salido del jardín trasero. Después de todo, había huellas en aquella zona. Pero no era posible que hubiese abandonado el estudio a través de los ventanales. Estaba el asunto de la dichosa llave que los mantenía cerrados desde dentro. Y también estaba la cuestión de los parterres: un asaltante tendría que haberlos pisoteado para poder salir. Y, por supuesto, ninguna de las huellas se acercaban a la casa.

–¿Qué ocurrió entonces? –preguntó Spector.

–¿Después de que se marcharan los hombres? Seguí contemplando la casa un rato más. Supuse que uno de los tipos debía de ser el padre de Lidia. Pero, como es evidente, ahora ya sé que eso era imposible.

–¿Y?

–Entonces apareció Della. Vi cómo llamaba a la puerta y cómo el ama de llaves, cuyo nombre no recuerdo, la dejaba pasar.

–¿Y?

–Todo se quedó en calma durante un minuto o dos. Después, oí un grito fuerte, un grito de mujer procedente del interior. Así que salí del automóvil de un salto y fui corriendo por el camino hasta el lateral de la casa.

–Así que fue usted el que dejó el segundo rastro de huellas –sugirió Flint.

–Supongo que sí. Sin embargo, antes de haber recorrido cien

metros, una voz a mis espaldas me dijo: «¿Qué demonios crees que estás haciendo?». Como es de esperar, di un respingo tremendo, pero, cuando me di la vuelta, vi que se trataba de Lidia. Estaba junto a la verja. Acababa de salir del taxi. Corrí hasta ella, la besé y le supliqué que me perdonara. Le dije que deberíamos entrar dentro para resguardarnos de la lluvia, pero ella dijo que no, que todavía no podía ver a su padre.

–¿Y qué hicieron?

–Regresamos a mi automóvil. Nos quedamos sentados un rato. No hablamos mucho. No me di cuenta de que, después de todo, debía de haber pasado algo turbio en la casa hasta que llegó la policía. Así que nos dirigimos al interior y fingimos que llevábamos toda la noche juntos en el Palmyra, que acabábamos de bajarnos del taxi y que habíamos llegado juntos.

–¿Sin preguntas?

–Oh, hubo muchas preguntas, pero no hasta el día siguiente. Fue entonces cuando Lidia me dijo dónde había estado y que había robado el cuadro.

–¿Y qué le dijo usted?

–No podía decirle gran cosa. A la luz del día, con su padre muerto y todo eso, no parecía algo tan serio. Le dije que prefería olvidar todo lo ocurrido.

–Me temo, señor, que eso no va a ser posible –dijo Flint.

–Señor Bowman –intervino Spector–, por favor, dígame: ¿dónde está el cuadro?

–No lo sé. Les juro que no sé lo que hizo con él.

Inevitablemente, sus andadas los llevaron de vuelta a la casa de los Rees. Olive abrió la puerta con cansancio.

–¿Está Lidia en casa? –preguntó Flint.

La mujer asintió.

–Está en el estudio.

–Señora Turner –dijo Spector–, antes de que nos deje pasar, me gustaría que me hiciera un favor.

–¿De qué se trata?

–¿Podría echarle un vistazo a esta fotografía?

La imagen que le tendió mostraba a un hombre apuesto que no hacía mucho había dejado atrás el mejor momento de su vida. Había cierta arrogancia en su ceño y su llamado «pico de viuda» dibujaba un enorme arco salpicado de gris. El ama de llaves le prestó la debida atención.

–¿Conoce a este hombre? ¿Lo había visto antes?

Con lentitud, ella se inclinó para examinar la fotografía más de cerca.

–No –dijo al fin–. No lo había visto antes. ¿Por qué? ¿Quién es?

–¿Está segura? Por favor, piénselo con calma.

–Así lo estoy haciendo y puedo asegurarle que no lo había visto en toda mi vida.

Spector apartó la fotografía y se la volvió a meter en el bolsillo.

–Gracias.

El mago no se lo dijo, pero la imagen era una fotografía publicitaria de Edgar Simmons, el actor desaparecido. Sin mediar palabra, la mujer los condujo hasta el estudio.

–Doctora Rees.

Lidia estaba sentada en su escritorio y no apartó la vista de inmediato de los papeles que estaba consultando. Cuando lo hizo, Spector se dio cuenta de que tenía las mejillas un poco coloradas.

–Normalmente, cuando oía algo similar a «doctora Rees», se estaban dirigiendo a mi padre.

–Debe de costar acostumbrarse.

Ella ladeó la cabeza, pensativa.

–Me ha costado, sí, pero ya me he acostumbrado. Ahora, el estudio de mi padre es mío. Mañana me reuniré con mi primera paciente y me esforzaré al máximo para ayudarla.

–¿Della Cookson, por casualidad?

–No puedo decírselo. Eso rompería la confidencialidad entre médico y paciente, como seguro que ya sabe.

–Vaya, veo que se ha quitado el anillo de compromiso.

–Sí que está hecho usted un buen detective.

Con deferencia, Spector hizo una reverencia, como si todo el asunto le avergonzara.

–Lo siento, no es asunto mío, pero estos viejos ojos se fijan en cosas así.

–No me avergüenzo. Mi padre tenía razón con respecto a Marcus del mismo modo que tenía razón con todo lo demás. Y no importa cómo intente verlo: Marcus me traicionó. Supongo que ha mencionado a Della porque sabe que habían estado teniendo una aventura. Me trató como una idiota. Durante mucho tiempo, dirigí mi rabia hacia todo el mundo menos hacia él. Ahora, me estoy esforzando por remediarlo.

–Lo entiendo.

Ella le dedicó una leve sonrisa.

–No, no lo entiende. Cree que sí, pero no es lo mismo.

–Está intentando honrar a su padre.

–Tal vez. Sí... –dijo al fin–. Tal vez sea eso lo que estoy haciendo.

–Sin embargo, hay un aspecto de todo este embrollo que sigue sin resolverse –continuó el mago–. Me refiero al asuntillo de *El nacimiento*.

–¿Quiere decir que no lo ha encontrado todavía?

–No nos pongamos evasivos al respecto. Sé que fue usted la que se lo llevó de casa de Teasel. Sé que se coló en la fiesta tras abandonar a Marcus en el Palmyra Club. Cuando llegó de nuevo aquí, a Dollis Hill, debía de tener el cuadro encima. Así que... ¿qué hizo con él?

La joven doctora sonrió.

–Ya sabe todo lo demás. Me extraña que no sepa eso.

–Estoy de acuerdo, pero, en realidad, preferiría que me lo contara usted.

Ella miró a ambos hombres y esbozó una sonrisa parecida a la de una esfinge.

XIV

Cómo desaparecer por completo o la jaula de Proteo

–Podríamos arrestarla, ¿sabe? –dijo Flint mientras se alejaban en automóvil de Dollis Hill.

–Sí, podríamos, pero por robo, no por asesinato.

–Bueno, y después de todos estos tira y afloja, ¿quién cree que se esconde detrás de este asunto?

–Creo que… tal vez sea el momento de hacer otra visita a Claude Weaver.

Cuando llegaron a casa de Weaver, los recibió una criada. Claude estaba en el ático y, al parecer, sumido en la escritura de su nueva novela. Rosemary estaba en el salón, así que Flint y Spector se unieron a ella. Cuando le dijeron que tenía visitantes, el propio Weaver apareció enseguida. Flint prescindió de la conversación trivial.

–¿Dónde estuvo anoche? –le preguntó sin rodeos.

–¿Anoche? –El escritor apenas acababa de sentarse–. ¿No querrá decirme que han asesinado a otro desdichado?

–Por favor, responda a la pregunta, señor.

–Estuve aquí, en casa. Toda la noche.

–¿Alguien que pueda responder por usted?

–Mi esposa.

–Es cierto, inspector –dijo Rosemary–. Y no estoy muy segura de que me guste su tono de voz.

–Esto es un asunto muy serio. Me temo que ya no tengo ni el tiempo ni las fuerzas para andarme con cortesías. Señor Weaver, ¿hay alguien más que pueda dar fe de su paradero de anoche?

–No, nadie más.

Flint apretó la mandíbula.

–Ya veo. Ahora dígame, por favor, ¿alguna vez se ha encontrado con un joven llamado Pete Hobbs?

–¿Hobbs? No, el nombre no me suena de nada.

–Tal vez esta fotografía le refresque la memoria.

Flint sacó una fotografía del cadáver que mostraba el rostro muerto y delgado del pobre chico y los ojos cerrados por última vez.

–Santo cielo –dijo Weaver.

Rosemary no miró la imagen.

–Dígame, por favor, ¿alguna vez se encontró con Hobbs?

–¿Cómo...? ¿Cómo murió?

–Lo estrangularon hasta la muerte con un trozo de cuerda.

–Qué horror –comentó Rosemary, que tal vez estuviera hablando consigo misma.

–No, nunca lo he visto.

–¿Está seguro? Trabajaba como operario del ascensor en Dufresne Court.

–Nunca lo había visto y nunca he estado en ese edificio. No soy demasiado trotamundos.

–Es cierto –intervino su esposa–; no saldría de casa si no fuera necesario. Ha sido así desde que nos casamos.

–Sin embargo, mi imaginación ha sido mi salvación –dijo Weaver–, pues me ha llevado a sitios maravillosos e imposibles.

–¿Alguna vez ha escrito sobre asesinatos? –preguntó Flint mientras arqueaba una ceja con astucia.

–Escribo sobre poco más. Pero hable con cualquier novelista que ande buscando el éxito en el mundo literario londinense: la imaginación colectiva ansía sangre. Escribir de asesinatos significa dinero.

Spector estaba escudriñando las estanterías de Weaver. Los títulos resultaban tan escabrosos que bien podrían haberse desprendido de los lomos: *Escalada letal*, *El ídolo ensangrentado*, *Peligro en Mordlake*, *El enemigo invisible*... El mago sacó uno de forma aleatoria: *Los demonios de Denby*. La cubierta era un remolino estridente de colores en la que aparecía una joven de belleza cerosa que se encogía de miedo bajo la sombra de una especie de macabra gárgola viviente.

–Ese fue el primero que escribí –dijo Weaver mientras observaba la cubierta por encima del hombro del anciano–. Como ocurre con todas las obras de un principiante, le falta cierta sutileza, pero lo compensa con entusiasmo.

–Lo he leído –dijo Spector–. Me resultó muy atmosférico. Las localizaciones en concreto estaban muy bien descritas.

El escritor sonrió.

–Muy amable por su parte. Las saco de fotografías. Puedo mirar una imagen y sentir la esencia del lugar.

–Caballeros –los interrumpió Rosemary–, la cuestión es que, anoche, mi esposo estuvo aquí todo el tiempo. Si no me creen, pueden preguntar a los criados. Ellos se lo confirmarán con mucho gusto.

–Seguro que sí –dijo Flint antes de salir de la habitación.

–Esto empieza a ser ridículo –gruñó el inspector durante el viaje de vuelta–. Hay demasiados cabos y no puedo atarlos todos.

–Tiene razón –dijo Spector–. Nos enfrentamos a un puzle con demasiadas piezas. Puede que algunas de nuestras pistas conecten con otras, pero, teniendo en cuenta el conjunto como un todo, hay demasiadas inconsistencias. Es todo demasiado ornamentado y diáfano. –El viejo mago dibujó una sonrisa cansada–. Ay, Flint, usted sí que me encuentra buenos rompecabezas... En cierto sentido es maravilloso, pero en el otro...

Se frotó los ojos agotados.

Spector no quería volver a casa de inmediato, así que hizo que el inspector lo dejara en The Black Pig. Observó cómo el policía se alejaba hacia el crepúsculo con el automóvil. Después, regresó a su asiento habitual en el cuartito, se comió un pastel de guisantes y jamón (un ágape delicioso) y se bebió varias medias pintas de cerveza negra. El alcohol espeso y del color del alquitrán alimentó su cerebro tal como lo hace el carbón en una locomotora.

Bastante más alegre que cuando había llegado, Joseph Spector salió del *pub* a las ocho en punto. Había un corto paseo por calles frías, húmedas y estrechas hasta su casa en Jubilee Court.

Conforme se acercaba, se dio cuenta de que Clotilde había dejado la luz del porche encendida. Mientras subía los escalones de piedra hasta la puerta delantera, de pronto fue consciente del eco estruendoso de unos pasos que no eran los suyos y que lo perseguían. No se paró a mirar.

–¡Disculpe!

Siguió sin pararse.

–¡Disculpe!

Finalmente, sin haber metido todavía la llave en la cerradura, Spector se detuvo y se dio la vuelta. Subiendo los escalones detrás de él se encontraba Claude Weaver. Parecía alterado, nervioso y asustado.

–Señor Weaver, ¿qué hace aquí? ¿Ha estado siguiéndome?

–Señor Spector, por favor, entremos. Necesito hablar con usted. Es urgente.

El mago abrió la puerta para que ambos pudieran pasar al interior de la casa. Mientras atravesaban el salón, Weaver parecía inquieto y agitado.

–¿Ha cerrado con llave la puerta delantera? –le preguntó de pronto.

–Sí, por supuesto.

–¿De modo que nadie pueda entrar?

–Nadie. Bien, ¿va a decirme qué ocurre? –El escritor estaba jadeando y los hombros le subían y le bajaban–. Siéntese –le instó Spector de forma tranquilizadora. Weaver se dejó caer en un sillón sin dejar de jadear–. Déjeme que avise a Clotilde para que nos traiga té.

–Algo más fuerte, por favor.

El mago asintió y sacó del mueble bar un decantador de cristal tallado que resplandeció bajo la luz del fuego. Vertió un poco de *whisky* en un vaso y se lo tendió al hombre. El novelista se lo bebió de un solo trago y se recostó en el sillón. Al fin estaba empezando a recuperar el color en las mejillas.

–He ido a The Black Pig y allí me han dado su dirección. Señor Spector, necesito su ayuda. Hay alguien que me persigue.

–¿Qué le lleva a decir algo así?

–Lleva siguiéndome un tiempo. No sé quién es ni qué quiere. Tiene que comprender que... no podía contarles esto sin más delante de mi esposa. Tiene que ser secreto. Tiene que serlo. No sé qué haría si se descubriera...

–¿Ese hombre... está ahí fuera ahora mismo?

Weaver asintió.

–Pero, por favor, no vaya a mirar. No deje que sepa que yo lo sé.

–Descríbalo.

–No puedo verle el rostro. Lleva un abrigo largo negro y un sombrero de ala ancha.

–¿Y cuándo fue la primera vez que notó que le estaba siguiendo?

–Hace una semana más o menos.

–Ya veo. –Spector se quedó pensando un instante–. Espere aquí –añadió antes de dirigirse hacia la puerta.

–¿Qué está haciendo?

–Quédese donde está, por favor.

Mientras el novelista esperaba nervioso en el salón, Spector se arrastró de nuevo hasta el recibidor y echó un vistazo a través de la cortina. La calle estaba tranquila. Los faroleros estaban manos a la obra, atravesando la nebulosa luz crepuscular con sus linternas. Pero, en el lado más alejado de la calle, había una única figura sin iluminar. Era tal como Weaver la había descrito: una silueta ensombrecida con un abrigo largo y sombrero.

El anciano se apartó de la ventana y alcanzó el teléfono. Esperó en silencio mientras la operadora pasaba la llamada a Scotland Yard. Tardaron unos cuarenta segundos en establecer la conexión.

–Spector, ¿qué ocurre? –preguntó Flint.

Tenía la voz teñida de fatiga y tensión.

–Necesito que venga aquí ahora mismo –dijo el mago–. Y tráigase a algunos agentes de uniforme.

–¿Por qué? ¿Qué ocurre?

–Weaver está en mi casa y hay alguien con él. –Casi como si se le acabara de ocurrir, añadió–: Venga por la entrada sur. El tipo está vigilando la casa por la parte delantera.

–¿Quién es?

–No lo sabemos, pero encaja con la descripción que dio Olive de la noche del asesinato. También es posible que sea el que siguió a Stenhouse anoche.

El inspector no esperó a oír nada más. La conexión se cortó con un chasquido. Spector colgó el teléfono y regresó al salón. Sentado, Weaver lo miraba expectante.

–Flint está en camino.

–¿Qué?

El escritor se puso en pie de un salto.

–No se preocupe, llegaremos al fondo del asunto. Debería estar aquí en diez minutos. Tan solo tenemos que esperar.

–Spector, usted no lo entiende... No sé quién es ese hombre, pero creo que sí sé quién es, si entiende lo que quiero decir...

–Será mejor que me lo explique.

–¡No puedo! Por favor, no puedo contárselo a nadie. Nadie puede descubrirlo...

El novelista estaba rozando la histeria.

Hablaron en susurros, como si el hombre que estaba al otro lado de la calle pudiera oírlos. Cuando llamaron a la puerta de la cocina, ambos se sobresaltaron. Spector se dirigió a la parte trasera de la casa y, en silencio, dejó pasar al inspector Flint.

–Tengo hombres en la entrada de Jubilee Court. Están esperando a que les dé la señal.

–Bien –contestó el mago–. Venga por aquí.

Condujo a Flint por la casa, pasaron por delante de un Claude Weaver petrificado y salieron al recibidor. Spector le señaló la cortina.

–¿Lo ve?

Flint se inclinó hacia delante hasta que la nariz le rozó el cristal.

–Lo veo –dijo–. No queremos que este tipo vuelva a darnos esquinazo.

–¿Cree que es el que le disparó en Dufresne Court?

–Bueno, no puedo asegurarlo. Lléveme al piso de arriba, tengo que darles la señal a mis hombres.

Spector condujo a Flint por unas escaleras estrechas y chirriantes hasta la habitación de invitados, que estaba situada en la parte trasera del edificio. Allí, el inspector se sacó del bolsillo un mechero. Lo encendió con el pulgar regordete y calloso y la diminuta llama de luz naranja resplandeció brevemente.

–Vamos, hay que volver a la parte delantera.

Desde la ventana del rellano, el mago echó un vistazo a Jubilee Court. El hombre de negro seguía allí, esperando como una silueta siniestra. Sin embargo, no sabía que la oscuridad se cernía sobre él.

–Le aconsejo que agache la cabeza –le dijo el inspector mientras bajaba las escaleras–. La cosa podría ponerse fea.

Sin embargo, el anciano permaneció en el rellano. Observó cómo los agentes cercaban al hombre del abrigo largo y negro. Al fin, el gélido silencio se vio atravesado por el sonido estridente del silbato de Flint. Entonces, los policías se abalanzaron sobre su presa.

El hombre salió disparado, pero los agentes fueron demasiado rápidos para él. Lo derribaron al suelo y uno de ellos, Druitt, se arrodilló sobre su pecho. Cuando lo hubieron reducido por completo, Flint y Spector salieron de la casa. Claude Weaver, que temblaba y parecía a punto de derrumbarse, los siguió.

–¿De qué va esto? –rugió el hombre mientras le dejaban sin oxígeno.

El sombrero salió rodando y dejó a la vista un rostro joven. Tendría unos veinte años.

El inspector Flint se inclinó sobre él.

–Vaya, vaya. Llevamos un tiempo buscándole, jovencito. –Miró a los agentes–. Caballeros, pónganlo en pie, por favor.

Cada uno de los policías lo tomó de un brazo y, después, lo levantaron del suelo. Era un desconocido, alguien que ni Flint ni Spector habían visto antes. Iba bien afeitado y tenía un aspecto un poco sospechoso, pero, por lo demás, era del todo anodino.

–¿Quién es usted? ¿Qué está haciendo aquí?

–Estoy trabajando. Tengo un encargo.

–¿Tiene sus credenciales?

–Me llamo Walter Graves. Soy detective privado.

–¿Estuvo en casa del doctor Anselm Rees la noche del 12?

El joven abrió los ojos de par en par.

–¿Qué? ¿Cómo lo sabe?

–¿Ha estado siguiendo a Claude Weaver?

–Mire, no tiene derecho a hacer nada de esto.

–Cuéntenos la verdad. Alguien le ha contratado, ¿verdad? ¿Se trata de eso? Será mejor que nos lo diga.

–No tiene derecho a hacerme esas preguntas, sea policía o no. Conozco mis derechos. Todo este asunto es legal, tengo licencia.

Flint se dio la vuelta hacia Claude Weaver, que estaba al borde de sufrir un colapso.

–Supongo que este es el hombre que le ha estado siguiendo...

Boquiabierto, Weaver se limitó a asentir.

–Muy bien –añadió el inspector mientras se giraba de nuevo hacia el atribulado detective–. En tal caso, ¿quién le ha contratado?

–Ya se lo he dicho. Me llamo Walter Graves y trabajo para la agencia Wallace Enquiries.

Acercándose al hombre con un aire amenazador, Flint repitió:

–¿Y quién le ha contratado?

–No tiene derecho a preguntarme eso. No he incumplido ninguna ley. Solo soy un trabajador, como usted.

Uno de los agentes le agarró el brazo con más fuerza mientras se lo colocaba detrás de la espalda. Graves soltó un grito.

–¡Agente! –exclamó Flint–. No permito violencia bajo mi mando. El señor Graves está en lo cierto. Tenemos que conseguir una orden judicial. La documentación parece estar en orden –añadió mientras se la devolvía. Frunciendo el ceño, el tipo se la volvió a guardar en el abrigo–. Si no revela la identidad de su cliente de forma voluntaria, entonces la ley le obligará a hacerlo. Sin embargo, hay algo que sí puede decirnos: puede contarnos qué vio la noche que Rees murió.

–¿Una muerte? No sé nada de ese asunto. Mi trabajo era seguir a Claude Weaver y eso es lo que hice.

–¿Qué me dice de Floyd Stenhouse? ¿Fue a su domicilio en Dufresne Court anoche? ¿O preferiría hablarnos de ello en Scotland Yard?

–Mire, me contrataron para seguir a Claude Weaver y únicamente a Claude Weaver, ¿entendido?

–Voy a preguntárselo una vez más. ¿Qué es lo que le une a Anselm Rees? ¿Fue él el que le contrató?

–No, no fue el doctor el que me contrató.

–Se da cuenta de que esto le va a suponer un problema, ¿verdad?

El detective tenía los hombros hundidos en gesto de resignación.

–Lo único que ella quería era que lo siguiéramos; nada ilegal o indecoroso.

–¿De quién se trata? ¿Quién es la clienta?

–Eso no puedo decírselo –dijo el joven con tristeza.

Spector extendió la mano abierta. Después, la cerró con fuerza y, abriendo los dedos de nuevo, reveló un billete doblado de una libra.

–¿Quién es la clienta? –repitió con amabilidad.

El detective agarró el billete y se lo metió en el bolsillo interno del abrigo.

–En este caso, la policía está mirando en la dirección equivocada. Aquí no hay nada que ver. Su esposa quería que lo siguiéramos, eso es todo. Cree que está jugando a dos bandas.

El mago miró a Weaver y se dio cuenta de que aquella revelación era exactamente lo que el escritor había temido todo aquel tiempo.

–¿Lo ha contratado la señora Weaver?

–Es lo que acabo de decir, ¿no?

–¿Y lleva siguiéndolo dos semanas?

–Así es. Y puedo decirles que sea lo que sea que pase por la mente del señor Weaver, no es el asesinato.

–¿Cómo lo sabe?

–Porque lo he estado vigilando todo el tiempo.

–Entonces, ¿lo siguió cuando fue a casa de Rees?

–¿El día 12? Sí.

–¿Estuvo allí aquella noche?

–Es lo que he dicho, ¿no? Cuando se marchó del restaurante, fue el primer sitio al que se dirigió.

–Eh…

Weaver estaba empezando a sudar.

Spector y Flint le ignoraron y continuaron con su interrogatorio.

–¿Cuándo llegó?

–A las once y cuarto. Llamó a la puerta principal y lo vi entrar.

El inspector y el mago intercambiaron una mirada. Las once y cuarto. Ese había sido el momento en el que el visitante fantasma había aparecido en la puerta. Pero no era posible que hubiese sido Weaver, ya que la señora Turner lo habría reconocido. ¿No? Lo había visto en multitud de ocasiones, ¿no era así?

–¿Qué ocurrió entonces, señor Graves?

–Bueno, tenía que ver qué era lo que estaba ocurriendo en la casa, así que me arrastré hasta la parte trasera por la verja lateral.

–Espere un momento... Entonces, ¿usted estuvo en el jardín trasero de la casa de los Rees aquella noche?

–Sí, así es. Y, a través de los ventanales, podía ver el estudio.

Weaver parecía a punto de desmayarse.

–¿Cómo de cerca estuvo de la casa?

–No demasiado.

–¿Lo bastante cerca como para dejar huellas en los dos metros de parterres?

El detective sacudió la cabeza.

–Estuve bajo un árbol al fondo del jardín, resguardado de la lluvia. Pero la habitación estaba muy bien iluminada, así que podía verlo todo.

–¿Vio al doctor Rees?

–Claro que sí. Vi cómo dejaba entrar a Weaver. Después, se sentaron y estuvieron hablando varios minutos.

–¿Y qué pasó entonces?

–Weaver se marchó. No me quedé más; salté por encima del muro y volví a seguir el rastro de mi objetivo.

–Pero ¿Rees estaba vivo cuando usted se marchó?

–¡Claro que sí!

Spector pensó en aquello detenidamente.

–¿Pudo distinguir algo de lo que estuvieron hablando?

–No, pero, hasta donde sé, se mostraron amistosos. Estuvieron bebiendo.

–¿Bebiendo?

–Sí, la bebida la sirvió de una de esas cosas de cristal... ¿Cómo se llaman?

–Decantador. ¿Quién la sirvió?

–Rees. El doctor. Parecía *whisky*.

–¿Bebieron los dos?

El detective asintió. Fue entonces cuando Claude Weaver desfalleció. Sencillamente, se derrumbó hacia un lado sin previo aviso. Spector observó al autor caído sin emoción.

–Será mejor que lo lleven dentro –dijo Flint.

Dos de los agentes levantaron el cuerpo inconsciente, lo llevaron a casa del mago y se perdieron de vista.

–Bueno –dijo Spector–, esto cambia las cosas.

–¿Puede repetir eso? –replicó Flint–. Porque yo he pasado de no tener ni idea a estar totalmente confundido.

–¿De verdad? –El anciano estaba sonriendo–. Yo creía que esto dejaba las cosas mucho más claras.

Flint soltó un gemido de exasperación.

–Puede marcharse, señor Graves, pero mañana necesitaremos tomarle declaración.

Cuando toda la emoción se hubo calmado y Flint y Spector volvieron a estar solos en la sombría Jubilee Court, el inspector preguntó:

–¿Y qué cree que significa todo esto? Sin duda demuestra que el asesino tuvo que ser Claude Weaver.

–Yo creo que demuestra todo lo contrario.

El policía hizo una mueca.

–Por lo que nos ha contado Graves, Weaver era el visitante misterioso del que nos habló Olive Turner. Debió de equivocarse cuando dijo que no lo reconoció. Es obvio que no es la testigo infalible que creíamos que era. Estuvo en el estudio del doctor desde las once hasta las once y cuarenta y cinco. Pero ¿por qué no lo reconoció? ¿Iba disfrazado?

–Creo que la respuesta es mucho más sencilla que todo eso, inspector. Creo que nos dijo que no lo había visto nunca porque de verdad no lo había visto nunca.

–Pero Claude Weaver era un paciente habitual. Olive habrá visto a los tres pacientes en múltiples ocasiones.

–Sí. –Extasiado, el mago ensanchó su sonrisa–. ¿No es un truco maravilloso? Creo que, a pesar de todo su secretismo y todos sus embustes, Claude Weaver es un hombre bastante desafortunado. Se ha esforzado mucho por mantener un cierto tipo de vida que ha resultado ser insostenible. Ese, en todo caso, es su único delito. Fue un golpe de mala suerte lo que lo asaltó la noche en la que asesinaron a Rees. Olvídese de la afirmación del editor de que Weaver vio algo que lo dejó trastornado y le hizo salir del restaurante dando tumbos. Sabemos que no había nada que ver, pero ¿de qué estaban hablando?

Flint volvió hacia atrás en su cuaderno de notas.

–De libros de bolsillo o alguna tontería similar.

–Exacto. Y las palabras que el editor nos transmitió convenientemente fueron: «Los literatos siempre distinguirían un Claude Weaver auténtico de uno falso».

–¿Y eso fue lo que le hizo perderse en la noche dando tumbos?

–Para él, esas palabras fueron una epifanía.

–¿Qué?

Spector no contestó.

–Hay algo que todavía me preocupa sobre el sueño de Floyd Stenhouse. Si puedo lograr que encaje eso, entonces, encajará todo el asunto. Lo que quiero decir es que puede que haya algo más en esos sueños, algo que va más allá del simbolismo superficial. Respóndame a esto: cuando Floyd Stenhouse llamó a Anselm Rees la noche del 12, ¿qué hizo el doctor?

–Le regañó por llamarlo tan tarde.

–Sí. ¿Y qué más?

–Escuchó el sueño de todos modos.

–Bien. ¿Y?

–Y… –Flint reflexionó– tomó nota.

–¡Eso es! –El anciano chasqueó los dedos–. Olive Turner oyó cómo Rees rasgaba con la pluma el papel mientras tomaba nota del sueño de Stenhouse. Eso significa que…

–¿Qué ocurrió con esas notas?

–Exacto. Si el doctor escribió lo que Stenhouse le contó, ¿dónde están las notas? Es de suponer que el asesino se las llevó. Pero ¿por qué? Tal vez había algo en el sueño que, de algún modo, resultaba incriminatorio. Parece extraño o directamente imposible, pero

¿por qué otro motivo habrían desaparecido esas páginas? –Spector sonrió deslumbrante. Los engranajes estaban girando–. También desapareció algo más. Piense en lo que Olive Turner nos dijo sobre el estudio del doctor y lo que se encontró en el escritorio del difunto cuando la policía llegó al fin.

–Estoy pensando.

–Muy bien, le daré una pista. Walter Graves no podía ver mucho desde su posición entre los árboles, pero hay un detalle que sí pudo distinguir. ¿Cuál?

Aquel fue el turno de Flint de brillar al alcanzar la revelación.

–Las bebidas. Estaban bebiendo.

–Rees sirvió algo de beber para ambos del decantador de cristal. Sin embargo, cuando la policía llegó, solo había un vaso en el escritorio. Un único vaso en todo el estudio. Pero registraron por todas partes, ¿no? Entonces, ¿dónde está el segundo vaso?

Flint se miró los zapatos.

–¿Por qué se llevaría el asesino uno de los vasos?

–Tal vez por el mismo motivo por el que arrancó las páginas sobre el sueño de Stenhouse. Adivine el razonamiento que se esconde detrás de una de esas cosas y, con toda probabilidad, adivinará también el de la otra.

–Ya lo ha resuelto, ¿verdad, Spector? ¿Le importaría darme una pista?

–Todavía no. Pero pronto, Flint. Necesito organizar un par de cosas.

–¿Para qué?

Los ojos pálidos del mago resplandecieron bajo la luz de las lámparas.

–Para el gran final.

ENTREACTO III

Por el que se solicita respetuosamente la atención del lector

En el pasado, este sería el punto de la narrativa en el que se lanzaría un desafío al lector. «Tiene frente a usted todos los datos que va a necesitar para identificar al asesino del doctor Anselm Rees y Pete Hobbs, así como los medios por los que se llevaron a cabo dichos asesinatos», diría yo.

Sin embargo, a día de hoy, dichas prácticas resultan anticuadas y bastante demodé. Pero ¿quién soy yo para interponerme en la diversión de un lector? Es cierto que todas las pruebas están ahí y, además, a plena vista. Si entre ustedes hay algún aspirante a detective, ahora es el momento de darse a conocer. No hay premio, ya sea material o de otro tipo, más allá de la gloria silenciosa de haber triunfado en lo que un hombre sabio denominó «el juego más grandioso del mundo».

XV

Un último truco

(Jueves, 17 de septiembre de 1936)

Joseph Spector tenía una serie de instrucciones muy específicas. Para empezar, requerían que George Flint estuviese disponible a partir de las nueve de la mañana. Adormilado e irritable, el inspector llegó a la casa de los Rees en Dollis Hill cinco minutos pasada la hora. Jerome Hook iba con él y fue el propio Spector el que abrió la puerta.

–Ah, caballeros, me alegro de que hayan podido venir –dijo con sarcasmo.

–Spector, ¿de qué va esto? ¿Qué hacemos aquí?

–Pasen, pasen, rápido.

Entraron en el pasillo.

–¿Qué ocurre?

–Pronto llegarán unos invitados, pero, ahora mismo, tenemos el control de la casa. Lidia Rees ha pasado la noche en el Hotel Dorchester y Olive Turner ha consentido quedarse con su hermana. –Los condujo hasta la parte trasera de la casa y la cocina–. Si me hicieran el favor de esperar aquí... Si he calculado bien los tiempos, Floyd Stenhouse debería ser el primero en llegar.

Flint y Hook intercambiaron una mirada incómoda. A pesar de todo, el inspector no terminaba de fiarse de aquel anciano.

Efectivamente, Stenhouse fue el primero en llegar. Estaba tan nervioso como siempre y Spector lo acompañó hasta la salita. Allí, había algo extraño: sobre una mesita de madera se encontraba una pajarera de metal.

–Señor Spector, ¿qué significa todo esto? Me complace hacer

todo lo posible para ayudar a encontrar al asesino del doctor, pero...

–Este es Proteo –dijo el mago mientras señalaba la jaula–. Lo llamo así porque vive en una jaula de Proteo. Y porque, al igual que Proteo, es famoso por su maleabilidad, flexibilidad y adaptabilidad. –Levantó la jaula con la mano izquierda. A través de los estrechos barrotes se veía un precioso pajarito amarillo–. Tiene una compañera, por supuesto, ya que no puedo soportar la idea de que una criatura semejante esté encerrada para siempre en soledad, pero, para lo que nos ocupa, Proteo será suficiente.

Stenhouse se inclinó hacia delante y contempló al pájaro, que le devolvió una mirada imperiosa mientras ladeaba la cabeza.

–¿Flexibilidad? –repitió el violinista.

–Claro. Puede desaparecer a voluntad. ¿Lo ve?

Con un chasquido de los dedos del anciano, el pájaro desapareció.

El joven músico se incorporó de golpe con los ojos muy abiertos y vidriosos.

–¿Qué ha hecho con él?

–Nada de nada. Como le he dicho, el poder es solo suyo. Regresará cuando esté listo. –Tras aquello, Spector volvió a chasquear los dedos y el pájaro regresó–. Por favor, examine la jaula si así lo desea.

Stenhouse lo hizo y le lanzó una mirada desconcertada al pajarito.

–Pero ¿dónde ha ido?

Spector soltó una carcajada suave, deleitado por la perplejidad del joven.

–Un truquito encantador, ¿no es así? Y bastante desconcertante. Sin embargo, cuando lo enfrentas a algo que no sea el más básico de los escrutinios, resulta terriblemente sencillo. Todo depende de la jaula, por supuesto. El pájaro no se mueve nunca. Sin embargo, tanto en la parte superior como en la parte inferior de la pajarera hay unos espejos. Con una pequeña distracción básica como, por ejemplo, chasquear los dedos, el embaucador puede girar sin más la cornisa superior de la jaula para mover los espejos de modo que tapen al pájaro pero sigan reflejando una imagen perfecta de la cortina que hay detrás. –Se encogió de hombros y Stenhouse volvió a acomodarse en su asiento–. Creo que estará de acuerdo en que es bastante ordinario.

El músico soltó una risita avergonzada.

–Me ha engañado por completo.

–No estoy muy seguro de creerle –replicó el mago–. Creo que tan solo está siendo amable con un anciano. Después de todo, es una antigualla de truco. Se remonta más de mil años. Es cierto que este es un ejemplar especialmente bello de la especie...

–No sea modesto, Spector. Todos nosotros debemos aceptar tanto nuestras fortalezas como nuestras debilidades. Como músico, soy un genio. Como mago, señor, usted también lo es.

En ese momento, Spector se echó a reír.

–Bueno, he tenido reseñas peores –dijo–. Pero tenemos que señalar algo serio y es que acabo de mostrarle una de las muchas maneras en las que un cuerpo humano, ya sea vivo o muerto, puede desaparecer de una habitación cerrada.

Desde la puerta de la salita, Flint observó aquella conversación con aire distraído. No había descubierto nada nuevo.

Lidia Rees llegó a casa poco después de eso y con ella iba Olive Turner. Ambas mujeres habían quedado para tomarse el café de la mañana en el restaurante del Dorchester antes de volver a casa para la pequeña demostración de Joseph Spector. Ninguna de las dos parecía demasiado entusiasmada por la pajarera o por Floyd Stenhouse.

El siguiente vehículo en llegar fue el de Marcus Bowman. El zumbido del motor se pudo oír por todo Dollis Hill. Bowman fue recibido por el sargento Hook y atravesó el umbral con un silencio huraño. Cuando entró en la salita, Lidia lo miró una vez y apartó la vista. Él no dijo nada y se sentó en el rincón más alejado de la estancia.

–Gracias por venir, señor Bowman –dijo Spector, el venerable anfitrión–. No le haremos esperar demasiado. ¿Y quién sabe? Tal vez aprenda algo.

Flint permaneció en el pasillo. De su pipa salía una espiral de humo. Mientras el mago se acomodaba en su papel de anfitrión, el inspector estaba centrado en el asunto en cuestión. Además, estaba flanqueado por dos agentes que aseguraban la sala con discreción.

La siguiente en llegar fue Della Cookson. Se hicieron las presentaciones y el Paciente A y la Paciente B empezaron a ponerse al día. Su charla insustancial era forzada e incómoda, pero Joseph Spector estaba pendiente de cada palabra. Lidia estaba sentada y, bajo la luz fría del sol, parecía una estatua. Marcus Bowman se removía como si fuese un niño pequeño: se rascaba la rodilla, se pasaba la lengua por los labios o se apartaba el flequillo de la frente con un gesto suave de la cabeza. Sin embargo, tenía la mirada fija en el suelo y no se dio cuenta de la llegada de los nuevos invitados.

Spector se situó en la parte frontal de la estancia y se aclaró la garganta.

–Damas y caballeros, me alegro de que hayan tenido la oportunidad de conocer a mi buen amigo Proteo. Antes de que comencemos con el evento principal, me gustaría mostrarles una pequeña ilusión.

Les presentó una baraja esparcida con elegancia.

–Por favor, señorita Cookson, elija una carta. –Nerviosa, la actriz dio un paso al frente e hizo lo que le pedía–. Ahora, muéstresela a los demás.

Así lo hizo. Flint estiró el cuello para verla: el tres de bastos.

–Bien –prosiguió el mago.

Después le arrebató el naipe y lo sostuvo en el aire.

–Ahora, presten atención.

Todos contemplaron la carta que tenía entre los dedos. La sostuvo en alto durante un instante como si fuera un tótem pagano. Entonces, ¡chas!, se transformó delante de sus ojos. Los presentes ahogaron un grito. Después, durante un instante, se produjo un silencio de perplejidad. La carta se había transfigurado en una fotografía pequeña y cuadrada en un tono sepia. Era el retrato de una mujer joven de unos veinte años. Flint no la había visto nunca.

El mago, que todavía sostenía la fotografía sobre su cabeza, sonrió.

–¿Alguien reconoce a esta joven?

Silencio.

Poco a poco, la sonrisa desapareció de su rostro. Cuando volvió a hablar, su voz era fría como el hielo.

–Hay alguien que sí la conoce.

Le tendió la fotografía a Della y la fueron pasando entre todos los invitados, que intercambiaron miradas nerviosas y confundidas.

–Se llama Frieda Tanzer –dijo Spector– y es el motivo de que hoy estemos todos aquí reunidos.

–¿A quién más estamos esperando, Spector? –preguntó Flint desde el pasillo.

–Solo a los Weaver.

–En tal caso, creo que ya han llegado.

–Excelente.

Como si fuera una araña, el anciano se arrastró hasta la ventana y echó un vistazo a la calle. Efectivamente, un taxi había parado y la señora Weaver estaba saliendo de él. Spector se dirigió al recibidor.

Antes de que pudieran llamar al timbre, el mago abrió la puerta delantera. Claude Weaver estaba pálido y era evidente que todavía seguía padeciendo las secuelas de las aventuras de la noche anterior. Su rostro era como una máscara.

Spector recibió a la pareja y el sargento Hook les mantuvo la puerta abierta. Aunque nadie más lo sabía, el anciano estaba más nervioso entonces de lo que había estado en cualquier otro momento de aquel caso. En lo que a él se refería, aquella era la culminación de todos sus esfuerzos.

El efecto que tuvo la llegada de la pareja fue como el de un trueno. Todas las miradas se volvieron hacia ellos y Claude Weaver se las devolvió de uno en uno. Sus ojos se posaron en uno de los invitados.

–¿Qué está pasando aquí? –exclamó–. ¿Es este otro de sus trucos, Spector?

–Me temo que no –contestó el mago–. Me temo que todo esto es muy real.

La persona a la que estaba mirando el escritor era Floyd Stenhouse.

El músico, que parecía pegado a su asiento, no dijo ni una sola palabra, pero se quedó mirando fijamente a Weaver. Parecía un depredador a punto de atacar.

–Señor Weaver, por favor, ¿podría identificar a este hombre? –preguntó Spector.

–Bueno...

El novelista se trabó con las palabras. Su esposa, Rosemary, que estaba a su lado, le tomó del brazo. Él se aclaró la garganta y, después, con un tono de voz claro y estridente, dijo:

–Es Anselm Rees.

Stenhouse hundió los hombros y, antes de que pudiera moverse, el sargento Hook se colocó en la puerta para bloquear cualquier salida. El músico resopló.

–No tienen de qué preocuparse, caballeros –dijo–. No voy a darles ningún problema.

Después, dejó que lo esposaran.

–Es un error comprensible –dijo Spector–, sobre todo si tenemos en cuenta el hecho de que solo se vieron en una ocasión: la noche que asesinaron a Rees. Sabíamos que usted, señor Weaver, era el visitante misterioso. Pero lo que no nos paramos a considerar fue el hecho de que la persona a la que vio aquella noche no era el doctor Rees, que, tal vez, el verdadero doctor yacía inconsciente en el infame baúl de teca y que el hombre que habló con usted era en realidad su asesino.

–Un momento –dijo Flint–, eso no tiene sentido.

–Lo tendrá –continuó Spector–. Si me lo permiten, me remontaré justo al principio de todo.

–Claude Weaver, como muchos hombres casados, tiene una aventura. Pero, a diferencia de muchos hombres casados, se encuentra en una posición única. A saber: una posición de anonimato. Es un ermitaño famoso, aunque los términos sean, tal vez, contradictorios. Muchas personas conocen su nombre, pero muy pocos conocen su rostro. Eso le ofreció cierta licencia. Por supuesto, su esposa comenzó a sospechar, así que él se inventó una enfermedad mental, unos «estados de fuga» en los que podía caer cada vez que era incapaz de dar cuenta de su paradero. Y, sin saberlo, la señora Weaver cayó en su juego. Lo confrontó al respecto y organizó todo para que fuera a ver a un psiquiatra.

–¡Esto es escandaloso! –exclamó Rosemary Weaver.

Sin embargo, Flint se dio cuenta de que había dejado de agarrar el brazo de su marido.

–Aquí me ha perdido, Spector. ¿Por qué cayó en su juego?

–Organizó una cita semanal en la que Claude estaría fuera de casa, alejado de su mirada crítica.

–Sí, pero, sin duda, Rees le habría informado si Claude no hubiera aparecido para las citas o incluso si hubiera llegado tarde unos minutos.

–Cierto, pero está olvidando que Weaver es un conspirador magistral. Manteniendo la falacia de que temía por su propia salud mental, aceptó conservar la cita y, entonces, puso la maquinaria en marcha. En realidad, la persona que apareció por la casa de Dollis Hill para aquella primera cita podría haber sido cualquiera. Y podría haber sido cualquiera que se presentara como el Paciente C. Y, lo crean o no, así fue. Lo que hizo Claude Weaver fue recurrir a la ayuda de un actor de teatro sin demasiado trabajo para que se hiciera pasar por él durante los encuentros con Anselm Rees, lo que le dejaba libertad para continuar con sus amoríos ilícitos sin que lo molestara la atención de su esposa.

–Un actor sin demasiado trabajo... –repitió Della Cookson–. ¿Estás hablando de Edgar Simmons?

–Del mismo. Y el tal Edgar Simmons ahora parece haberse esfumado con mucha prisa. Imagino que habrá salido del país. Casi como si le hubieran pagado para hacerlo, ¿no les parece?

–Un momento –dijo Flint–. Entonces, ¿cada vez que el doctor hablaba del «Paciente C» o de «Claude Weaver» estaba hablando en realidad de Edgar Simmons?

–Exacto. Para mantener la consistencia, el actor y Weaver mantenían reuniones regulares para asegurarse de que el escritor estaba al día de lo que habían hablado durante las sesiones. Parecía el plan perfecto. Y, en realidad, lo era. Después de todo, funcionó durante mucho tiempo. Pero, como era inevitable, las sospechas de la señora Weaver regresaron. Se dio cuenta de que la simple idea de que Claude estuviera recibiendo tratamiento con el mejor psiquiatra del mundo no era suficiente para aplacar sus preocupaciones, así que decidió tomar medidas adicionales. Se dirigió a la agencia Wallace y les contrató para que un detective llamado Walter Graves siguiera a su marido.

»Claude Weaver no fue consciente de que Graves le estaba siguiendo el rastro hasta la semana del asesinato. Eso aumentó su paranoia y lo lanzó a un estado cercano a la psicosis, porque, ya ven, no tenía ni idea de qué haría si se revelaba su secreto.

»Todo esto también significa que había un paciente del doctor Rees que se presentaba como Claude Weaver y al que los habitantes de la casa llegaron a identificar como tal. Sin embargo, no era Claude Weaver.

»El verdadero Weaver sabía que el detective acabaría por interrogar al doctor Rees y que pronto se acabaría el juego, así que se apresuró a pagar a Edgar Simmons para quitárselo de en medio. Sin embargo, se sentía atrapado, como si las paredes fuesen a aplastarlo. Fue en ese estado mental en el que acudió a cenar con su editor la noche del día 12.

–¿De qué me está acusando?

El rostro del escritor se había tornado beis.

–Tan solo de falsedad e infidelidad, señor Weaver. Creo que estará de acuerdo en que son crímenes menores en comparación con un asesinato.

»En aquel estado mental afligido, tan solo fue necesaria una conversación con su editor sobre «Weavers falsos» para que se volviera loco. Salió dando tumbos del restaurante en un estado de rabia absoluta. Decidió dirigirse a Dollis Hill en un último intento desesperado de intentar razonar con el doctor Rees. Quería explicarle su situación y pedirle clemencia. Tal vez, comprarlo a él también. Así que, aquella noche, llegó aquí sin haber visto nunca antes al doctor. O, en efecto, a Olive Turner, que se sintió muy perturbada por su secretismo. Sin embargo, lo que usted no sabía cuando entró en el estudio aquella noche es que estaba interrumpiendo un elaborado plan de asesinato que ya estaba en marcha. Porque su visita no estaba planeada en absoluto, ¿no es así? Rees no le estaba esperando a usted. De hecho, el visitante al que estaba esperando no era otro que el Paciente A, Floyd Stenhouse. Verán, cuando estuvo de gira por Austria con la Filarmónica hace algunos años, el señor Stenhouse conoció a la hija del Hombre Serpiente.

–Frieda Tanzer era el amor de mi vida –dijo el músico con dificultad–. Solo descubrí lo de su padre y el tratamiento imprudente del doctor Rees que la condujo a su propio suicidio después de que se hubiera quitado la vida. Pero ¿qué puedo decir? Hay rencores que no se desvanecen con los años.

Spector volvió a tomar las riendas del asunto.

–Así pues, nos encontramos con el primer problema. ¿Cómo entró en el estudio el asesino? Este es el aspecto más sencillo de todo el caso. Nadie entró por la puerta principal. Sabemos que la lluvia comenzó en torno a las once de la noche, por lo que supusimos que nadie había podido entrar por los ventanales porque no encontramos huellas en los parterres húmedos. Dado que el asesinato no ocurrió hasta las once y cuarenta y cinco, imaginamos que el asesino debía de haber entrado después de que empezara a llover. Pero ¿y si había estado allí todo ese tiempo? Rees estaba esperando a un visitante. Podemos dar por sentado que era Stenhouse, que había pedido una cita en condiciones de máximo secreto. Imagino que le dijo a Rees que conocía las circunstancias de la muerte de *Der Schlangenmann* y que pretendía utilizarlas para hacer caer en desgracia al buen doctor. Algo por el estilo, algo delicado. Por eso Rees le pidió a Olive Turner que no acompañara al visitante: no quería arriesgarse a que oyera alguna parte de la conversación.

»Sin embargo, el músico pilló desprevenido al doctor al llegar temprano y a través del jardín trasero en lugar de por la puerta principal. Eso fue antes de las once en punto, que es cuando comenzó a llover, así que no dejó rastro en el parterre. Rees dejó pasar al estudio a su asesino a través del ventanal.

»Entonces, sirvió el *whisky* con el decantador. Llenó dos vasos.

Para el asesino, añadir una poción del sueño a su propio vaso y, después, en un momento de distracción, cambiarlo por el otro, era un juego de manos bastante sencillo. Muy pronto, su víctima deseada dio un trago de *whisky* y cayó casi inconsciente. El doctor Rees tenía las extremidades paralizadas y, sin duda, se dio cuenta del destino que le esperaba. Pero, por supuesto, al asesino le deleitaba inmensamente ver al anciano sufrir.

»A esas alturas, imagino que la lluvia ya caía a cántaros. Tal vez fuesen cerca de las once y cuarenta y cinco. Puedo visualizar al asesino desplegando la navaja y preparándose para cometer su acto simbólico de venganza. Pero, entonces, imaginen el horror que sintió en el pecho cuando, de repente, oyó que llamaban a la puerta. Volvió a meterse la navaja en el bolsillo a toda velocidad y depositó al inconsciente Anselm Rees en el enorme baúl de madera. El visitante, por supuesto, era Claude Weaver. El auténtico Claude Weaver, que, como ya sabemos, nunca había visto en realidad al doctor; ni una sola vez. Así que es natural que el escritor asumiera que el hombre que estaba en el estudio era Anselm Rees.

»Imagino que la conversación fue algo así: «Usted no me conoce, doctor Rees, pero tengo que pedirle un favor». Casi al instante, el asesino se dio cuenta de dos cosas: en primer lugar, de que el visitante lo había confundido con Rees, y, en segundo lugar, de que el motivo de aquella visita era algo comprometedor. En otras palabras: aunque sabía que su plan se había visto en peligro, seguía teniendo la mano ganadora. Así pues, hizo pasar al estudio a su involuntaria marioneta y escuchó su historia de engaño e infidelidad. Entonces, en su mente ya se estaba formando un plan, la idea de que, tal vez, podría inculpar a aquel tipo por el asesinato que todavía no había cometido. Así que le sirvió una bebida (con el vaso que no llevaba la droga, por supuesto) y escuchó su confesión.

»Cuando terminaron la consulta (y no olvidemos que Weaver de verdad pensó que estaba hablando con Rees), Stenhouse dejó salir del estudio al pobre y engañado escritor, que, por su parte, salió de la casa por la puerta delantera (cosa que observó Olive Turner) y desapareció en medio de la noche. Así pues, el asesino volvía a estar encerrado en el estudio y a solas con su víctima. Sacó del baúl al doctor, que seguía inconsciente, y lo volvió a dejar en la silla. Nadie vio esto, ya que Walter Graves, que había estado observando desde fuera, había seguido a su objetivo a otra parte en medio de la oscuridad. En ese momento dejó de perder el tiempo, sacó la navaja y asesinó al inconsciente Anselm Rees tal como estaba sentado.

»Podría haber salido de la oficina en ese momento y todo habría salido bien, pero entonces se acordó de la parte del plan que había diseñado para establecer su propia coartada: la llamada de teléfono. En ese instante, sonó el aparato que estaba en el escritorio. Se trataba de Peter Hobbs, al que el músico había pagado para que le ayudara a escabullirse de Dufresne Court y para que llamara al teléfono acordado a la hora acordada para disponer de una coartada. Por supuesto, el muchacho no sabía que había un asesinato involucrado en el asunto. Así que Stenhouse contestó el teléfono del escritorio interpretando el papel de Rees e imitando su voz y mantuvo aquella parte de la conversación consigo mismo. Garabateó en el papel para añadirle verosimilitud, pero se dio cuenta demasiado tarde de que su letra no coincidiría con la de Rees. Así que, cuando hubo terminado la conversación y tras haber colgado, arrancó las páginas.

»Ahora sabía que tenía que actuar con rapidez. Suponiendo que pudiera confiar en que el chico del ascensor guardara silencio, había establecido una coartada para sí mismo, pero todavía tenía que salir de la habitación. Estaba a punto de marcharse por la puerta del pasillo cuando oyó cómo Olive dejaba pasar a Della Cookson y cómo se acercaban a la puerta. Estaba en un apuro: Rees estaba muerto, así que no podía seguir imitándolo. Aquellas dos mujeres estaban desesperadas por entrar en el estudio, así que se dirigió a los ventanales y, al abrirlos, se dio cuenta de que no podría salir por allí ya que sería inevitable dejar sus huellas en el parterre. Sin embargo, hay un estrecho peldaño de piedra al otro lado del ventanal, un rincón diminuto[1] en el que, si se pegaba a

[1] Vea el lector la página 19.

la esquina oscurecida, podría ocultarse. De ese modo, pudo salir de la casa sin necesidad de pisar el parterre.

–En tal caso, ¿cómo consiguió dejar los ventanales cerrados desde dentro?

–No lo hizo. Es un truco básico. La llave estaba en el interior, dentro de la cerradura, y las damas fueron incapaces de abrir el ventanal cuando movieron la manilla, así que supusieron que los ventanales debían de estar cerrados.[2] Pero, en realidad, no lo estaban. Sencillamente, Stenhouse usó algún tipo de cuerda o cordón, tal vez incluso su propia corbata, para pasarlo por las manillas gemelas del exterior y, al atarlas con fuerza, creó la ilusión de que estaban cerradas desde dentro. Una vez que hubieron probado a abrir con las manillas y quedaron satisfechas al comprobar que las ventanas estaban cerradas, las damas volvieron a centrar su atención en el interior, es decir, en la propia habitación. Así pues, el músico pudo mirar por el cristal para comprobar en qué momento se quedaba todo tranquilo. Tan solo tuvo que esperar unos pocos minutos antes de que Della y Olive se dirigieran a la cocina. Entonces, pudo entrar de nuevo en el estudio, cerró con llave las ventanas, salió de puntillas al pasillo y abandonó la casa por la puerta principal mientras las dos damas se inflaban a beber brandi. Cualquier sonido que hubiera podido hacer quedó cubierto de forma natural por el gran chaparrón que estaba cayendo.

–¡Que me aspen! –dijo Flint.

–Por desgracia, Floyd Stenhouse no se había salido con la suya con tanta facilidad como había pensado. Estaba Pete Hobbs, la única persona que podría sumar dos más dos y arruinar la coartada que con tanto cuidado había planificado. Creo que en todo momento supo que tendría que matar a Pete, ¿no es así?

El músico parecía muy complacido consigo mismo.

–Sí, creo que sí.

–Así que ahora llegamos al desastroso asunto de Dufresne Court. Para cuando Anselm Rees estuvo muerto, es probable que Sten-

[2] Vea el lector la página 44.

house ya estuviera planificando su segundo asesinato. ¿Cómo es esa cita de *Macbeth*? «Estoy tan adentro en un río de sangre que, si ahora me estanco, no será más fácil volver que cruzarlo».

»Pero, a diferencia del primer asesinato, Stenhouse tenía que preparar dos cosas para poder llevar a cabo el truco del ascensor. Una era el timbre de la puerta y la otra el propio ascensor. Empecemos por el timbre: nuestro diligente músico lo manipuló para que sonara de forma automática a una hora determinada.

–¡Ajá! –dijo Flint con aire triunfal–. Sabía que había algo cuestionable en lo que ocurrió con Bream. Sonó el timbre y él fue a ver quién era, pero allí no había nadie. Eso es porque fue Stenhouse el que hizo que sonara desde el interior del apartamento, ¿verdad?

–En cierto sentido. Déjenme que me explique: cuando yo mismo visité el apartamento, me fije en un reloj despertador aparentemente inofensivo que había junto a la ventana.[3] En realidad, es probable que Stenhouse ya estuviera usándolo para experimentar con su plan. Como tal vez puede que sepan, un reloj despertador mecánico común acumula energía gracias a un mecanismo consistente en un resorte helicoidal. Nuestro asesino fue capaz de manipular el timbre usando este mismo principio. Desconectó el timbre del cableado, le quitó la parte eléctrica del interior y la sustituyó por los engranajes compactos y los resortes del reloj despertador. Por suerte para él, ambos sistemas no son demasiado diferentes y, aunque, como es obvio, el timbre no tiene la esfera del reloj, tiene una espiga metálica que puede conectarse con el resorte principal. Una vez colocado el dispositivo, lo único que tenía que hacer era quitar el timbre, darle cuerda al mecanismo, recolocar el timbre y esperar. El tiempo que transcurriera hasta que sonara la campana dependía de la fuerza con la que tensara el muelle. Supongo que por eso tardó un poco en responder cuando llamaron a la puerta: estaba calculando cuánto tiempo necesitaría para llevar a cabo su plan para, después, darle cuerda al mecanismo en consecuencia. Se dio a sí mismo cinco minutos.

[3] Vea el lector la página 82.

»Entonces, mientras Flint y Harrow estaban fuera y el agente Bream estaba concentrado en el pasillo gracias al timbre, Stenhouse aprovechó la oportunidad para sacar el revólver que tenía escondido y cubierto por un pañuelo para evitar las huellas dactilares y lo lanzó desde la ventana del apartamento hasta el patio de abajo. El revólver tenía el gatillo sensible, así que, cuando golpeó el suelo, disparó una bala. Ese fue el disparo que, por desgracia, hirió a Bill Harper.

–¿Por qué hizo eso? –preguntó Della Cookson.

–Para que la policía entrara en estado de pánico. Quería que, cuando descubrieran el cadáver de Pete Hobbs, las condiciones fueran perfectas. Además, eso lo ayudaba a distanciarse del ataque. Después de todo, tenía la coartada perfecta, pues había estado resguardado en su apartamento y escoltado nada más y nada menos que por un agente de policía.

–Creo que lo mejor será que nos diga cómo mató a Pete Hobbs.

Spector asintió con solemnidad.

–He dicho que tuvo que preparar dos cosas y que el timbre era la primera. Bueno, la segunda era el ascensor. ¿Alguno de ustedes ha oído hablar alguna vez de la llamada «trampa del vampiro»?

–Yo sí –dijo Della.

–Imaginaba que sería así. Es el término que en el teatro se le da a un tipo muy específico de trampilla. Debe su nombre a que su primera aparición fue en la adaptación teatral de *El vampiro*, de Polidori. Es una trampilla que mantiene su posición gracias a unas láminas con resorte que se separan cuando se les aplica presión y que vuelven a cerrarse de inmediato. Ese es el efecto que él buscaba conseguir con la trampilla del techo del ascensor: que se abriera bajo el peso del cadáver y que, después, volviera a cerrarse sola.

»Para conseguirlo, tomó una lámina de caucho natural y la clavó cubriendo tanto la escotilla como la bisagra que le permitía abrirse. Eso no debió de costarle demasiado; podría haberlo hecho en cualquier momento mientras Pete estaba en uno de sus «descansos para fumar», que, según dijo el portero, podían durar hasta una hora. Lo único que tenía que hacer era pintar por encima para que no se notara. Las reparaciones recientes explicarían el olor a pintura. Estoy seguro de que no necesito recordarle, inspector, que tanto el caucho como la pintura estaban a la vista en el apartamento de Stenhouse cuando fuimos a visitarlo la primera vez.[4] Y ese era el único ardid que necesitaba para hacer que funcionara el truco del ascensor.

»Después, invitó a Hobbs a su apartamento. Durante esa reunión, que debió de ocurrir en torno a las seis y media, le dio alguna bebida con droga que le hizo perder el conocimiento. Sabemos que el quinto piso del edificio está deshabitado, así que lo único que tuvo que hacer fue esperar a que el pasillo entre su apartamento y el ascensor estuviera despejado. Entonces, solo era cuestión de cargar con el cuerpo del muchacho hasta el ascensor y subir al quinto piso. También tenía que asegurarse de que la trampilla no tuviera el cerrojo puesto. A continuación, envió el ascensor al cuarto piso mientras él y el chico inconsciente permanecían en el quinto. Después, abrió la jaula para tener acceso al techo del ascensor.

»Le resultó relativamente fácil rodear el cuello del pobre muchacho con una cuerda floja y atar el otro extremo a la jaula del ascensor. Entonces, bajó por las escaleras a su apartamento para llamar al inspector Flint con la historia inventada del desconocido misterioso. Como es evidente, estaba jugando con el relato que Olive Turner le había dado a la policía en Dollis Hill. Cuando llegara la policía, habría alguien allí en todo momento que podría confirmar el paradero de nuestro músico. En resumen: fue un asesinato ejecutado de forma remota. Cuando Flint tomó el ascensor para bajar de nuevo, la cuerda que había en torno al cuello del muchacho se tensó y acabó con él. Así pues, quedó colgando en el hueco del ascensor y creó la ilusión de que había sido asesinado en un momento en el que Stenhouse estaba acompañado por la policía. También había deshilachado la cuerda lo suficiente de antemano como para que el peso de Pete ti-

[4] Vea el lector la página 83.

rando de ella hiciera que al final acabara partiéndose y que él se precipitara sobre el techo del ascensor una vez más. Eso causó que el cuerpo cayera con los pies por delante a través de la enorme trampilla cuadrada y que aterrizara dentro del cubículo. De ese modo, daba la impresión de que Hobbs había sido asesinado en el bajo y de que, de algún modo, habían depositado su cadáver en el ascensor.

»La única anomalía en este caso es la trampilla del techo. Aunque es cierto que es lo bastante grande como para que un cuerpo pueda caer por ella, eso habría hecho que se quedara abierta. Sin duda, la policía se habría dado cuenta de eso. Por eso la amañó con el caucho y la convirtió de manera efectiva en una «trampa del vampiro». El caucho mantuvo la trampilla en su sitio y creó la ilusión de que estaba cerrada con el cerrojo, pero permitió que se abriera bajo el peso del cuerpo al caer. Cuando el cadáver estuvo a salvo en el interior del ascensor, el caucho rígido y robusto recuperó su forma original y empujó la fina trampilla de madera de nuevo a su sitio.

»Stenhouse se aseguró de estar presente en el momento en el que se descubrió el cadáver y, mientras los tres policías lo examinaban y Della se daba la vuelta horrorizada[5], aprovechó la oportunidad para cerrar con rapidez el cerrojo de la trampilla una vez más de modo que cualquier registro diera como resultado un ascensor aparentemente cerrado de forma hermética. Las únicas pruebas de este crimen eran la cuerda atada a la jaula del ascensor del quinto piso y la lámina de caucho. Estoy seguro de que, a estas alturas, ambas cosas han sido destruidas.

Nadie habló durante un momento. Al final, fue Marcus Bowman el que acabó por romper el silencio.

–Bueno, eso lo explica todo, ¿no?

–No del todo –dijo Flint–. Resuelve muy bien los dos asesinatos, pero no nos dice nada del paradero de *El nacimiento*, el cuadro robado.

[5] Vea el lector la página 155.

–¡Ah, eso! –dijo Spector–. En realidad, eso es lo más sencillo de todo este asunto...

Sin embargo, antes de que pudiera explicarse, ocurrió algo. Stenhouse, que había permanecido esposado todo el tiempo mientras desentrañaban sus elaborados crímenes, se llevó la mano a la chaqueta con disimulo y, con un golpe de muñeca, sacó una navaja de afeitar.

Fue un movimiento tan veloz que al resto de los presentes les costó un momento darse cuenta de lo que estaba ocurriendo exactamente y, para entonces, la hoja estaba apoyada en la yugular palpitante de Della Cookson.

–Inspector Flint –dijo el músico–, voy a necesitar que retire a sus agentes del pasillo. La señorita Cookson y yo vamos a dar un paseo en automóvil. He visto uno amarillo fuera, en la calle. ¿De quién es?

Bowman, que había estado contemplando aquel espectáculo de violencia repentina con la boca abierta, bajó la vista al suelo.

–De Marcus –dijo Lidia–. Mi exprometido.

–Deme las llaves, señor Bowman.

El joven se puso en pie para hacerlo y, mientras sacaba el llavero, Spector se dio cuenta de que le temblaba la mano. El músico tomó las llaves y obligó a Della a dirigirse hacia la puerta.

–No sea idiota –dijo Flint.

Spector observó desde la ventana de la salita cómo el esposado Floyd Stenhouse forzaba a la actriz a entrar en el cupé amarillo y cómo, después, se subía detrás de ella.

Mientras Della encendía el motor y alejaba el vehículo del bordillo, el músico les devolvió una mirada sombría. La cuchilla resplandeció bajo la luz del sol.

Cuando el automóvil empezó a tomar velocidad, Spector y los invitados salieron a la calle para ver cómo el asesino y su cautiva se alejaban con un estruendo. Sin embargo, antes de que pudieran llegar al final de Dollis Hill Road, un disparo surcó el aire tranquilo de aquel barrio de las afueras. El neumático trasero izquierdo explotó y el vehículo se desvió hacia un lado con un chirrido dejando en el asfalto un arcoíris humeante de goma quemada. Della salió disparada, pero Floyd Stenhouse no.

El vehículo chocó con una farola de hierro y, durante un instante, el único sonido que se oyó fue el eco moribundo del metal estrujado y los cristales rotos. Pero, entonces, el tanque del combustible debió de prender con una chispa y los invitados contemplaron cómo el cupé ardía en llamas.

En cuanto quedó claro que no se podía hacer nada por Floyd Stenhouse, la atención de todo el mundo se centró en la persona que había disparado. Claude Weaver, que todavía estaba temblando, entregó el revólver por voluntad propia.

–¿Qué ocurre, Spector? –preguntó Flint.

Los dos habían vuelto a la salita de la casa de los Rees. Olive Turner estaba sirviendo un montón de azúcar en una hilera de tazas para el té. Todos ellos tenían los nervios bastante alterados.

–He intentado contárselo, Flint. Cuando Stenhouse nos ha interrumpido, estaba a punto de explicárselo.

–¿Lo del cuadro?

–Exacto, lo de *El nacimiento*. El truco consistía en tener en cuenta las circunstancias de la noche en que murió el doctor Rees. ¿Qué tuvo de diferente aquella noche en comparación con todas las que han pasado desde entonces? Cuando lo pensé desde esa perspectiva, la solución me resultó obvia.

Una pausa.

–¿De verdad?

–Así es. Verá, sabemos que Lidia vino directamente desde casa de Teasel a Dollis Hill, así que debía de llevar el cuadro encima. Pero lo que era diferente aquella noche es que estaba lloviendo. Marcus Bowman se escabulló al lateral de la casa y dejó su automóvil desatendido.[6] El mismo automóvil que ahora está convertido en una carcasa ennegrecida. Sin embargo, supongo que, esa noche, había desplegado la suave capota aunque solo fuera para

[6] Vea el lector la página 178.

resguardar la tapicería de los asientos traseros del torrente de agua. Siempre que hemos visto el vehículo, tenía el techo abierto. Pero, esa noche, estaba cubierto. Así que lo único que tuvo que hacer Lidia fue meter el cuadro con cuidado en la funda de la capota. Así, ya tenía el escondite perfecto.

Tras un largo silencio, Flint habló:

–Ya veo –dijo.

Estaba contemplando por la ventana el cupé destrozado que, en aquel momento, se estaba llevando la grúa. Y también la genialidad de Manolito Espina, que ascendía en espiral y se alejaba de Dollis Hill en una espesa voluta de humo negra.

Epílogo
El cuento del mago

Un mes después de los acontecimientos de Dollis Hill y la desafortunada muerte de Floyd Stenhouse, el inspector Flint llevó a Joseph Spector a cenar. Sacar al mago del cómodo escondite que era The Black Pig era una hazaña considerable, pero el inspector era el hombre indicado para llevarla a cabo. Cenaron en Brown's, el lugar en el que habían cenado Claude Weaver y su editor, Tweedy, la noche del asesinato de Rees. Haciendo caso a la recomendación del editor, Flint se pidió la trucha.

–¿Cómo estableció que Stenhouse era el asesino? –preguntó el inspector–. En mi opinión, podría haber sido cualquiera de ellos.

–Bueno –contestó Spector en medio de un bocado de *brisket*–. Stenhouse mencionó que había viajado bastante con la Filarmónica.[7] Era el único de nuestros sospechosos que lo había hecho y, por lo tanto, era el que más probabilidades tenía de haberse encontrado con Rees en cualquier otra parte de Europa. Mencionó que había visitado Viena en una ocasión. Eso fue en 1927 o 1928. Y fue allí donde conoció y se enamoró de la hija de *Der Schlangenmann*. Ella era preciosa, pero la torturaba lo que le había ocurrido a su padre; era un trauma del que nunca se recuperaría. Así que, cuando se quitó la vida, Floyd Stenhouse supo a quién culpar: al hombre que consideraba el orquestador de todos sus pesares, el doctor Anselm Rees, el hombre que había empujado al padre de su amada al suicidio. Llevaba bastante tiempo preparando su venganza y, cuando el destino arrojó al desdichado doctor Rees a su regazo, no perdió tiempo en buscarlo y presentarse como un paciente con la necesidad urgente de recibir

[7] Vea el lector la página 82.

tratamiento psiquiátrico. Todo fue una cortina de humo para facilitar su venganza.

–Entonces, ¿qué hay de los sueños? ¿Significaban algo, después de todo?

–Estoy seguro de que sí. De hecho, diría que presentaban la clave de todo el rompecabezas si hubiésemos sabido cómo buscarla.

–¿No cree que se los inventaba como excusa para poder concertar las sesiones continuas con Rees?

–Ni mucho menos. En todo caso, creo que suavizó los sueños para que resultasen más fáciles de digerir. Pero sí que hizo una corrección significativa. O, más bien, una sustitución: el hombre de la lámpara. Le dijo al doctor que era su padre, pero yo supongo que la figura demoniaca de sus sueños era el mismísimo Anselm Rees.

Flint estaba asintiendo.

–Sí. Encaja. Teniendo en cuenta que el doctor era alguien a quien Stenhouse, en su imaginación, había elevado hasta proporciones casi bíblicas, verlo en carne y hueso por primera vez tuvo que causarle una reacción psicológica considerable.

Estaban disfrutando del café posterior a la cena cuando aquel destello pícaro tan familiar regresó a los ojos pálidos de Spector.

–Antes de que demos la noche por terminada, un último truco para usted, Flint. Contemple cómo le leo la mente al camarero.

El mago se sacó el pañuelo doblado que llevaba en el bolsillo del pecho y se lo tendió al camarero. Del mismo bolsillo sacó una pluma, que también le entregó al joven.

–Ahora, muchacho, llévese el pañuelo y la pluma a la barra, por favor. Necesito que piense en un número entre el uno y el cincuenta y que, después, lo escriba en el pañuelo. ¿Entendido?

El joven camarero, que tenía los ojos resplandecientes y abiertos como platos, asintió. Spector le dio la espalda mientras escribía el número y doblaba el pañuelo. Entonces, los dos hombres volvieron a mirarse.

El anciano miró al perplejo muchacho con los ojos entrecerrados.

–Su número es el treinta y siete.

El camarero pestañeó y desdobló el pañuelo. Allí, grabado en tinta azul, podía leerse: «37».

Spector sonrió y le entregó una moneda de plata.

–Gracias, joven.

–Ha sido extraordinario –dijo Flint–, pero ¿cómo se hace un truco semejante?

–Es lo que se llama «magia espontánea», ya que no requiere un escenario, una cortina o un sombrero de copa. Puede hacerse en cualquier parte.

–Pero ¿cómo se hace?

Inclinando la cabeza con gesto humilde, Spector dijo:

–Es todo pura patraña, por supuesto. Esa pluma ni siquiera tiene tinta. El pañuelo que le he entregado al camarero ya llevaba escrito el número treinta y siete. Cuando lo ha desdoblado, en su interior ha encontrado escondido un soberano de plata que, sin duda, está en su bolsillo mientras hablamos. Me imagino que el resto puede deducirlo usted mismo.

–Oh.

–Siento decepcionarle, pero soy mago, y los magos tenemos cierta tendencia que los meros mortales como usted no tienen.

–¿Y cuál es? –dijo Flint.

La sonrisa de Spector se ensanchó.

–Que hacemos trampas.

Agradecimientos

Esta parece la oportunidad ideal para resaltar la obra de aquellos autores de misterio que siguen entusiasmándome e inspirándome. Específicamente: John Dickson Carr, Ellery Queen, Edward D. Hoch, Helen McCloy, Hake Talbot, Clayton Rawson, Nicholas Blake y Christianna Brand, por nombrar a unos pocos. Además, maestros posteriores a la Edad Dorada como Paul Halter y Soji Shimada han demostrado a través de la innovación continua que el «crimen imposible» todavía tiene mucho que ofrecer.

Me gustaría agradecer a la *Ellery Queen's Magazine* y a la *Alfred Hitchcock's Mystery Magazine* por publicar algunas de las primeras historias de Joseph Spector. Gracias también a todos aquellos que leyeron dichas historias y dijeron cosas bonitas sobre ellas.

Gracias a Gabriel Crescenzi por sus comentarios editoriales constantes y su buen ojo para los detalles, así como a Rob Reef y Dan Napolitano por leer los primeros borradores del libro.

Gracias a Michael Dahl y Ana Teresa Pereira por su amistad, ánimo y entusiasmo continuo hacia las historias de Spector.

Gracias a Georgia Robinson, Milan Gurung y Michael Pritchard. Por último, gracias a Otto Penzler por razones obvias.

Índice